Cultural Diversity
in HEALTH & ILLNESS

FOURTH EDITION

Top Left: Onion and garlic may be used in many ways by people from many cultural backgrounds. For example, onions may used in a poultice to reduce a fever; garlic may be eaten to purify the body or to control blood pressure, worn on a necklace to protect health, or hung in one's home to protect the family from evil spirits.

Center: Scented oils, purchased in a *botanica,* may be used to bring good luck; or for protection from various feared evils, such as enemies.

Lower left: The Buddha symbolizes the spiritual health practices of many people.

Lower right: Thousand-year eggs purchased in a grocery store in Boston's Chinatown are wrapped uncooked in either straw or carbon and stored in vats for a long period of time. They are eaten daily with rice for health maintenance.

Source: Spector Collection. Photography by Stephen E. Vedder, Photographic Production Supervisor, Boston College Audiovisual Services, Boston College, Chestnut Hill, Massachusetts, 1993.

Cultural Diversity in HEALTH & ILLNESS

FOURTH EDITION

Rachel E. Spector, PhD, RN, CTN, FAAN

Associate Professor
Boston College School of Nursing
Chestnut Hill, Massachusetts

APPLETON & LANGE
Stamford, CT

Copyright 1996 by Appleton & Lange
A Simon & Schuster Company
Copyright © 1991 by Appleton & Lange
Copyright © 1985, 1979 by Appleton-Century-Crofts

96 97 98 99 00 / 10 9 8 7 6 5 4 3 2 1

Prentice Hall International (UK) Limited, *London*
Prentice Hall of Australia Pty. Limited, *Sydney*
Prentice Hall Canada, Inc., *Toronto*
Prentice Hall Hispanoamericana, S.A., *Mexico*
Prentice Hall of India Private Limited, *New Delhi*
Prentice Hall of Japan, Inc., *Tokyo*
Simon & Schuster Asia Pte. Ltd., *Singapore*
Editora Prentice Hall do Brasil Ltda., *Rio de Janeiro*
Prentice Hall, *Upper Saddle River, New Jersey*

Library of Congress Cataloging-in-Publication Data

Spector, Rachel E., 1940–
    Cultural diversity in health and illness / Rachel E. Spector. —
4th ed.
        p.   cm.
    Includes bibliographical references and index.
    ISBN 0-8385-1397-2 (pbk. : alk. paper)
    1. Transcultural medical care—United States.   2. Health
attitudes—United States.   3. Transcultural nursing—United States.
I. Title.
    [DNLM: 1. Socioeconomic Factors.   2. Delivery of Health Care—
United States.   3. Attitude to Health.   4. Attitude of Health
Personnel.   5. Ethnic Groups.   WA 30 S741c 1995]
RA418.5.T73S64   1995
362.1'0425—dc20
DNLM/DLC   95-25684
for Library of Congress   CIP

Editor-in-Chief: Sally J. Barhydt
Production Editor: Sondra Greenfield
Designer: Janice Barsevich Bielawa

PRINTED IN THE
UNITED STATES OF AMERICA

ISBN 0-8385-1397-2

9 780838 513972

I would like to dedicate this text to
 Manny; Sam, Hilary, and Julia; Becky;
 my mother, Freda Needleman; and mother-in-law, Margaret Spector.
 To the memory of my father, Joseph J. Needleman; father-in-law, Sam Spector;
 and the memory of my beloved mentor, Irving Kenneth Zola.
 And to nurses:
 The healers who care.

Contents

Preface

In 1977 I wrote and in 1983 and 1990 revised *Cultural Diversity in Health and Illness*. The purpose of each edition of the book was to increase the reader's awareness of the dimensions and complexities involved in caring for people from diverse cultural backgrounds. I wished to share my personal experiences and thoughts concerning the introduction of cultural concepts into the education of health-care professionals. The books represented my answers to the questions: "How does one effectively expose a student to cultural diversity?" and "How does one examine health-care issues and perceptions from a broad social viewpoint?" As I had done in the classroom, I attempted to bring the reader into direct contact with the interaction between providers of care within the North American health-care system and the consumers of health care.

When I prepared the manuscript for the first edition, I was acquainted with the issues of health-care delivery as they primarily affected consumers of health care who were people of color—Asians, blacks, Hispanics, and American Indians. Since that time, I have had the opportunity not only to continue to be concerned with the initial issues but also to delve into the religious and ethnic differences that impinge on all people who are consumers of health care. In this text's second, third, and fourth editions, I have taken the opportunity to begin to pry open the door and to examine the differences that lie within all people of North America with respect to beliefs and practices affecting health and illness. My work has become increasingly exciting, for the more I explore and question, the more I know that one can spend an entire lifetime researching these questions, and the answers will never be the same. It is the stream of life and never, ever the same.

It might be believed that today's health-care providers are, for the most part, white and of middle-class background. That assumption, however, is truly flawed for, if one looks at the large numbers of people who provide health-care services, one finds diverse people from all walks of life. How well do we know one another? What has been categorized as the beliefs of consumers might certainly also apply to the personal health and illness beliefs and practices of health-care providers. Quite often, we not only do not understand the world view of the consumer, we also do not understand the world views of the providers with whom we practice.

I am neither a sociologist nor an anthropologist. I am a *nurse* and a *nursing educator*, and I have been and am committed to finding a way to alert nurses and other health-care providers to the beliefs about health and illness of a given health-care consumer. This book is an attempt to open the door to the immense diversity that exists within our North American societies, to demonstrate various methods one can use to open the mind to the beliefs of others, to describe some of these beliefs, and to refer to some of the countless available resources. Given the enormous social, political, and demographic changes now occurring, it is imperative for nurses and all health-care providers to have this knowledge. To this end, an annotated bibliography has been provided at the conclusion of each chapter to encourage further exploration into the appropriate literature, illustrations have been added, and activities that are fun and creative have been suggested to help this material come alive for the reader.

Those who provide health care in the next century are faced with a rapidly changing system of health-care delivery. Not only has health care become far more technical and far less personal, it has become increasingly difficult for people with marginal incomes and no insurance to acquire. The mechanisms for funding health care have changed drastically in the past few years, and numerous services have been curtailed. More services are being delivered in peoples' homes, and in delivering home care it is even more important to understand the cultural background of the client and family. To ensure safe and effective service to the consumer, it has become necessary to provide the student and the health-care professional with both the technical knowledge and the cultural understanding to meet the consumer's needs.

Just as the society is changing, the milieu in which one practices health care is also changing. No longer is the consumer willing to simply receive care; rather, the client desires the opportunity to participate in care-related decisions. No longer can the provider dictate a regimen; efforts must be made to collaborate with the consumer in determining a treatment plan. Unless the provider has a sound understanding of the consumer's values and perceptions regarding health and illness, the consumer's needs cannot be met satisfactorily.

The essential argument of this book is that the provider of health care (nurse, physician, social worker, and so forth) has been socialized into a distinct provider culture. This provider culture instills in its members its own norms regarding health and illness. When a member of this culture interacts with a person from a culture with differing norms, there is often a conflict in their beliefs. For this reason, I explore issues of health and illness in three areas:

1. Provider self-awareness
2. Consumer-oriented issues surrounding delivery and acceptance of health care
3. Examples of traditional health beliefs and practices among selected populations

Unit I focuses on the provider's knowledge of his or her own perceptions, needs, and understanding of health and illness (Chapter 2). The readers are then asked to develop a family history to determine what methods were practiced in their own families to prevent and treat illness. The result of what students have learned by doing this history and what it means to them are described and discussed in Chapter 3.

The concept of culture and the role it plays in one's perception of health and illness are explored. This exploration is first outlined in general terms: What is culture? How is it transmitted? What is ethnicity? How does it affect a person? These and other issues are analyzed in Chapter 4. The concept of culture is then taken from its broad anthropological and sociological definitions and brought into concrete and specific terms.

Unit II focuses on the broad issues of health-care delivery, healing, and the background demographics of the populations served. Much of the idealism that has been associated with the delivery of health care is not justified. Providers are often naive in their knowledge and awareness of the harsh realities of health care. In Chapter 5 the reader is exposed to the multifaceted problems of health-care delivery and some of the more negative aspects of the system, as well as to the important issue of human rights. Selected barriers and alternatives to the health system are also described.

The concept of faith also is explored in the context of healing. It is an increasingly important issue, which is evolving to a point where the professional must have some understanding of this phenomenon. Faith plays a major role in treatment—in outcome and in success of cure. Today people of diverse backgrounds acknowledge using faith healers and other types of healing methods. Therefore, healing, from both a natural tradition (Chapter 6) and a magicoreligious tradition (Chapter 7) is explored in this book.

Chapter 8 presents a discussion of the demographic backgrounds of each of the U.S. Census Bureau's categories of the population. One reason for this format is to illustrate the existing disproportions between the dominant culture and the emerging majority populations.

Once the study of each of these components has been completed, Unit III moves on to explore various ethnic groups in more detail. Chapter 14 is a presentation of a case study that describes a situation in the Mexican border areas of Texas where both traditional and modern health care is practiced. It describes the ongoing use of the *partera*, a lay midwife within the Mexican culture. The practice of the *partera* and the issues surrounding this practice are discussed.

These pages cannot do full justice to the richness of any one health-belief system. By presenting some of the beliefs and practices and suggesting background reading, however, the book can begin to sensitize the reader to the needs of a given group of people.

The Epilogue is devoted to an overall analysis of the book's contents and how best to apply this knowledge in health planning, health education, and health-care delivery for both the consumer and the health-care professional.

There is so much to be learned. Countless books and articles have now appeared that address these problems and issues. It is not easy to alter attitudes and beliefs or stereotypes and prejudices. Some social psychologists state that it is almost impossible to lose all of one's prejudices, yet alterations can be made. I believe the health-care provider must develop a sensitivity to personal fundamental values regarding health and illness. With acceptance of one's own values comes the framework and courage to accept the existence of differing values. This process of realization and acceptance can enable the health-care provider to be instrumental in meeting the needs of the consumer in a collaborative, safe, and professional manner.

The first edition of this book was the outcome of a *promesa*, a promise, I once made. The promise was made to a group of black and Hispanic students I taught in a medical sociology course in 1973. In this course, the students wound up being the "teachers," and they taught me to see the world of health-care delivery through the eyes of the health-care consumer rather than through my own well-intentioned eyes. What I came to see, I did not always like. I did not realize how much I did not know; I believed I knew a lot. I have held on to the promise, and my experiences over the years have been incredible. I have met people and traveled. At all times I have held on to the idea and goal of attempting to help nurses and other providers be aware of and sensitive to the beliefs and needs of their patients. I *know* that looking inside closed doors carries with it a risk. I *know* that people prefer to think that our society is a melting pot and that old beliefs and practices have vanished with an expected assimilation into mainstream North American life. Many people, however, have continued to carry on their traditional customs and culture from their native lands, and health and illness beliefs are deeply entwined within the cultural and social beliefs that people have. To understand health and illness beliefs and practices, it is necessary to see each person in his or her unique sociocultural world.

This book is written primarily for the student in basic nursing education. I believe it will be helpful also for nurses in all areas of practice, especially community health, long-term oncology, chronic care settings, and hospice centers. I am attempting to write in a direct manner and to use language that is understandable by all. The material is sensitive, yet I believe that it is presented in a sensitive manner. At no point is my intent to create a vehicle for stereotyping. I know that one person will read this book and nod "Yes, this is how I see it," and someone else of the same background will say "No, this is not correct." This is the way it is meant to be. It is incomplete by intent. It is written in the spirit of open inquiry, so that an issue may be raised and so that clarification of any given point will be sought from the patient as health care is provided. The deeper I travel into this world of cultural diversity, the more I wonder at the variety. It is wonderfully exciting. By gaining insight into the traditional attitudes that people have toward health and health care, I find my own nursing practice is enhanced, and I am better able to understand the needs of patients and their families. It is thrilling to be able to meet, to know, and to provide care to people from all over the world. It is the excitement of nursing.

You don't need a masterpiece to get the idea.

———*Pablo Picasso*

Acknowledgments

I have had a 25-year adventure of studying the forces of culture, ethnicity, and religion and their influence on health and illness beliefs and practices. Many, many people have contributed generously to the knowledge I have acquired over time as I have tried to serve as a voice for these beliefs and for the struggle for the inclusion of this information not only in nursing education but in the educational content of all helping professions—including medicine, social work, and allied health sciences.

I particularly wish to thank the following people for their guidance and professional support: Elsie Basque, Julian Castillo, Leonel J. Castillo, Jenny Chan, Dr. P. K. Chan, Joe Colorado, Mary Crockett, Elizabeth J. Cucchiaro, Mary A. Dineen, Norine Dresser, Celeste Dye, Terry Fermino, Laverne Gallman, Omar Hendrix, Orlando Isaza, Henry and Pandora Law, Hawk Littlejohn, Alfred Lui, Harold Lui, Patricia McArdle, Father Richard E. McCabe, S. Dale McLemore, Cathy J. Malek, Josie Morales, Virginia Swift, Sister Mary Nicholas Vincelli, Nora C. Wang, David Warner, and the late Irving Zola.

I also wish to thank my friends and family who have tolerated my absence at numerous social functions and the many people who have provided the numerous support services necessary for the completion of a project such as this. They include, at Appleton & Lange, Sally Barhydt, Editor-in-Chief, Nursing, who has been extremely helpful and supportive through the long days of preparing the final manuscript; Sondra Greenfield, Production Editor; and Janice Bielawa, Design Supervisor.

Boston College undergraduate and nursing students have been very helpful in reviewing the content.

Credit for the photographs in Chapter 7 goes to Robert W. Schadt, and for the cover photographs goes to Stephen E. Vedder, Photographic Production Supervisor, Boston College Audio Visual Services, Boston College, Chestnut Hill, Massachusetts.

Most of all, I want to acknowledge the support and love of my husband and family. Thank you.

There is something that transcends all of this
I am I . . . You are you
Yet. I and you
Do connect
Somehow, sometime.

To understand the "cultural" needs
Samenesses and differences of people
Needs an open being
See—Hear—Feel
With no judgment or interpretation
Reach out
Maybe with that physical touch
Or eyes, or aura
You exhibit your openness and willingness to
Listen and learn
And, you tell and share
In so doing—you share humanness
It is acknowledged and shared
Something happens—
Mutual understanding

—Rachel E. Spector

About the Author

Dr. Rachel Spector has been a student of culturally diverse health and illness beliefs and practices for 25 years and has researched and taught courses on culture and health care for the same span of years. Dr. Spector has had the opportunity to work in many different communities, including the American Indian and Hispanic communities in Boston, Massachusetts. Her studies in these culturals have taken her to many places, including much of the United States, Canada, Mexico, Cuba, Europe, Pakistan, and Israel. She was fortunate enough to collect traditional amulets and remedies in many of these diverse cultures and also to meet practitioners of traditional health care in those countries. She was instrumental in the creation and presentation of the exhibit "Immigrant Health Traditions" at the Ellis Island Immigration Museum, May 1994 through January 1995. She has exhibited health-related objects in several other settings.

Provider Self-awareness

Unit 1 enables you to become aware of beliefs about health and illness. You are helped to

1. Understand health traditions and the cultural phenomena that affect them.

2. Reexamine and redefine the concepts of health and illness

3. Understand the multiple relationships between health and illness

4. Associate the concepts of good and evil and light and dark with health and illness

5. Trace your family's practices in

   a. The protection and maintenance of health

   b. The prevention of illness

   c. The diagnosis and treatment of illness

6. Understand the behavioral variations in health and illness

7. Understand the variety of influences that culture and ethnicity have on the interpretations of the concepts of health and illness

8. Understand the interrelationships of culture, religion, and ethnicity relative to health and illness beliefs and practices

Before you read Unit 1, please answer the following questions.

1. How do you define health?

2. How do you keep yourself healthy?

3. How do you define illness?

4. What would you define as a minor, or "nonserious," medical problem? Give examples.

5. How do you know when a given health problem does not need medical attention?

6. Do you diagnose your own health problems? Give examples.

7. Do you use over-the-counter medications? Which ones and when?

1 Chapter

Health Care 2000—Meeting the Needs of a Multicultural Society

All things are connected. Whatever befalls the earth befalls the children of the earth.

— Chief Seattle Suqwamish and Duwamish[1]

The historic events of the 1960s served to make our society aware of the gaps that divided the multitudes of people constituting the North American population. In the aftermath of the events that shook the United States—political assassinations, student uprisings, the civil rights movement, and riots in Watts, Detroit, and Washington, DC—the focus on inequality entered the arena of health and health-care delivery. Just as other people stated their needs, health-care consumers demanded participation in and understanding of their care.

The decades of the 1970s, 1980s, and 1990s were and are times of dynamic social change that have profoundly affected the health-care delivery system. In the 1970s the war in Vietnam ended, and thousands of refugees from Vietnam, Cambodia, and Laos fled to the United States. Along with their social and personal problems, caused by the turmoil of war and refugee migration, came a system of traditional health and illness beliefs and practices. At present, people are flocking to the United States from Mexico, Central and South America, and Eastern Europe (as a result of the breakdown in the former Soviet Union). They, too, share the problems and hopes and dreams of earlier immigrants and have their traditional health and illness beliefs and practices.

President Lyndon Johnson's War on Poverty brought a sense that *health care* for all—rich and poor, old and young—would be a reality. The policy changes of the Reagan and Bush administrations, as well as the recent push to balance the federal budget, have, however, swept away these hopes. In 1995, as we observed the 30th anniversary of the passage of Medicare and

3

Medicaid, we found a system of health-care delivery that was in more chaos than it was in 1965. In fact, there are those who now see it on the verge of collapse. The health-care gap is well on its way to destroying people and opportunity.

Many other factors have served to create the complex situation that we face today. One of them has been the AIDS epidemic. In 1977, the year I wrote the first edition of this book, the disease was unknown. In 1983, the time of the second edition, I recall hearing that something was amiss but that "it was not too big a problem." Today, we are all aware of the enormity of this problem and the effect it is having not only on the health-care system but also on the black and Hispanic communities in particular. Other phenomena that further complicate our social medical picture include the increased numbers of people with resistant tuberculosis and the issues of homelessness, the breakdown of the family, the increasing epidemic of illicit drug use, and social violence. In one way or another, all of these social problems impinge on health care.

We have had to find a way of caring for the client that matches that client's perception of the health problem and its treatment. In many situations, this is not difficult; in other situations, it seems impossible. With the passage of time, a pattern emerges: for the health-care provider, the needs most difficult to meet are those of people whose belief systems are most different from the "mainstream" health-care provider culture.

When there is conflict between the provider's and the client's belief systems, the provider typically is unable to understand the conflict and, hence, usually finds ways of minimizing it. Ordinarily, the provider knows too little about a client's self-perception or beliefs regarding health and illness. For the provider, all that is important is knowing the scientific "hows" and "whys." In the past, we knew little of how this attitude affected the recipient of health care. Today we realize that such ignorance of client beliefs negatively affects the course of treatment; thus, the issue is crucial.

The providers usually are aware of—but generally have difficulty relating to—the personal and social problems of these people. Even though problems of this sort may account in part for a client's inability to cope with or to follow any kind of medical regime, professionals have been taught little or nothing about these problems and how they affected the patient, or how the patient related to them.

The following questions are a starting point: How does the client view life? What are his or her beliefs, values, and norms? What is the cultural background and how does it influence behavior? How do such factors affect the *meanings* of "health" and "illness"? What does health mean in terms of survival? How does one person's socialization differ from that of another?

When one completes an educational program and dons the attire of the profession—for example, the traditional white dress of the nurse—little thought is given to one's fallibility. One is now sanctioned by society to enter the professional world and deliver practiced and learned skills. One does not choose to answer to the client who fails to follow the treatment regimen of a physician or nurse, or who does not keep appointments, or who does not seek preventive health care. Once licensed, the provider feels secure in the scientific knowledge that took so long to master: does he or she not "know it all"? The person who fails to comply with treatment, does not attend a clinic appointment, or delays in seeking health care is of little concern. Surely, it is not the provider's fault that these situations continue to occur. Surely, the fault must lie with the consumer. We continue to rationalize, to look for scapegoats, and we can even wind up by labeling the client "lazy" or "stupid." In the narrowly defined world of the health-care provider, there is only room for blaming the client—who, in this instance, is the *victim*.

According to health-care providers, there are no alternative forms of healing; there are no other healers. The North American health-care provider has been socialized to believe that modern medicine as taught and practiced in Western civilization is the answer to *all* of humankind's needs. Has not modern medicine transcended all other forms of healing in technological skills and scientific understanding? With these extraordinary skills and this scientific sophistication, to cite an example, the dead can be brought back to life. When a heart or kidney fails, it can be replaced—either by a machine or by a transplanted organ. In the eyes of some consumers, however, Western medicine is not omnipotent, and the provider—with social, political, and humanistic concern—may be puzzled. Some people do not follow prescribed regimens, fail to maintain appointments at a clinic (i.e., they "elope," the term used when a person fails to return to a treatment facility), or spurn medical services or seek them as a last resort, and then leave the health system as quickly as possible. WHY?

The answers are deep and complex. Sometimes people fail to seek care or to take medication because they cannot afford to. The question one might then ask is: why don't health-care seekers accept the care or medicine when it is given to them? I suggest that perhaps consumers believe that the care and medicine that are offered cannot help them. Perhaps the consumers believe that the offered care will make them sicker or that a given regimen is incompatible with their illness. Until recently, a student in the health-care professions was not taught that clients may believe that the regimen or the medication that health care provides is incompatible with their illness. Much of this "incompatibility" is rooted in the opposite views the client and provider may have of a health problem. If a problem is not perceived in an agreed-on way, the prescribed treatments may well not be complied with. One source of such perceptual incompatibility lies within one's culturally and ethnically determined perceptions of the health condition.

Those who deliver health care may ask the following questions: "Why, with today's knowledge and communication, doesn't everybody know about and believe in the germ-transmittal of disease?" "Doesn't everybody know about epidemiology?" "Who has never heard of depression and schizophrenia?" "Is there anyone who doesn't believe in penicillin and thorazine?"

"Shouldn't everybody believe in and practice prevention and public health?" "What is there to believe in if not the medical model of disease?"

I believe there is a fundamental difference between the health beliefs of health-care providers and some consumers. Many (if not all) of these beliefs are set in motion and determined by our sociocultural ethnic backgrounds. In the following pages, I intend to develop the following arguments, that:

1. Each person enters the health professions with culture-bound definitions of health and illness.
2. Health professionals bring with them distinct practices for the prevention and treatment of illness.
3. Professionals' ideas change as they are socialized into the "health-care provider culture."
4. A schism develops between the provider of health services and the recipient.
5. If the provider becomes more sensitive to the issues surrounding health care and the traditional health beliefs of the consumer, more comprehensive health care can be provided.

I have validated this theory in three ways: first with an analysis of the works of Rosenstock[2] and Becker and colleagues.[3,4] The second analysis focuses on a holistic concept of health and a ninefold analysis of client and family-community health traditions. The third method of validation is within the context of cultural phenomena. These beliefs are then dependent on the person's level of heritage consistency as discussed in Chapter 4.

THE HEALTH BELIEF MODEL

The health belief model (Fig. 1–1) illustrates the consumer's perceptions of health and illness. This model can be modified to reflect the viewpoint of health-care providers. When this is implemented from the provider's viewpoint (Fig. 1–2), the material provides a means of reinspecting the differences between professional and lay expectations. Forging a link between the two helps one better understand how people perceive themselves in relation to illness and what motivates them to seek medical help and then follow that advice.

Perceived Susceptibility

How susceptible to a certain condition do people consider themselves to be? For example, a woman whose family does not have a history of breast cancer is unlikely to consider herself susceptible to that disease. A woman whose mother and maternal aunt both died of breast cancer may well consider herself highly susceptible, however. In this case, the provider may concur with this perception of susceptibility on the basis of known risk factors.

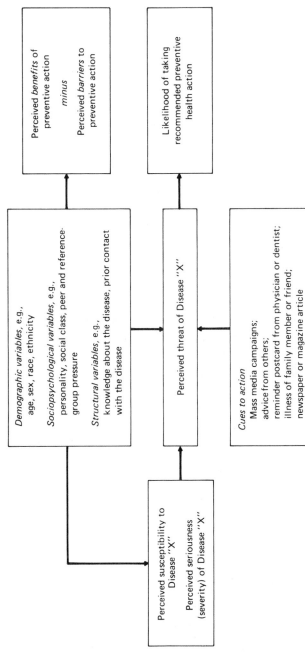

INDIVIDUAL PERCEPTIONS | MODIFYING FACTORS | LIKELIHOOD OF ACTION

Demographic variables, e.g., age, sex, race, ethnicity

Sociopsychological variables, e.g., personality, social class, peer and reference-group pressure

Structural variables, e.g., knowledge about the disease, prior contact with the disease

Perceived threat of Disease "X"

Cues to action
Mass media campaigns; advice from others; reminder postcard from physician or dentist; illness of family member or friend; newspaper or magazine article

Perceived susceptibility to Disease "X"

Perceived seriousness (severity) of Disease "X"

Perceived benefits of preventive action
minus
Perceived barriers to preventive action

Likelihood of taking recommended preventive health action

Figure 1–1. The health belief model as a predictor of preventive health behavior. (Reprinted with permission from Becker, M.H., Drachman, R.H., Kirscht, J.P., "A New Approach to Explaining Sick Role Behavior in Low-Income Populations," *American Journal of Public Health* 64(1974): 206.)

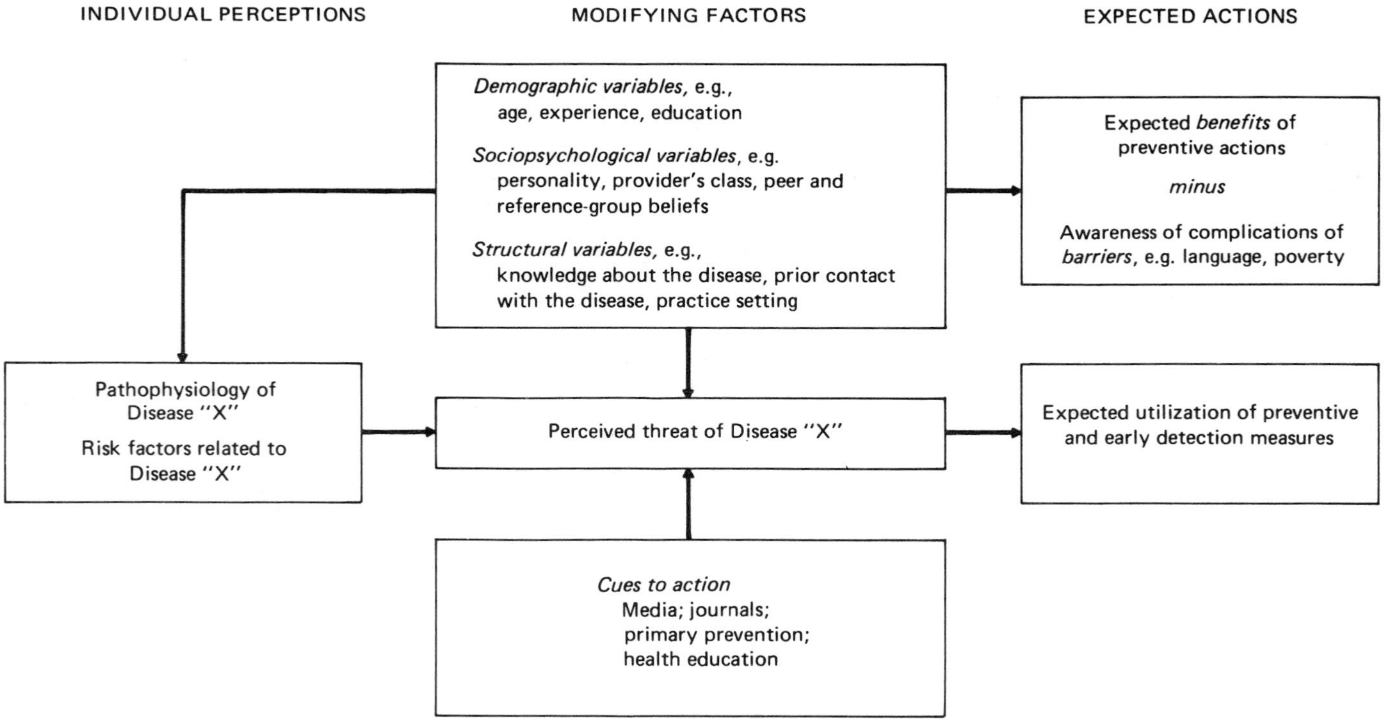

Figure 1–2. The health belief model from the provider's point of view.

Perceived Seriousness

The perception of the degree of a problem's seriousness varies from one person to another. It is in some measure related to the amount of difficulty the client believes the condition will cause. From a background in pathophysiology, the provider knows—within a certain range—how serious a problem is and may withhold information from the client. The provider may resort to euphemisms in explaining a problem. The patient may experience fear and dread by just hearing the name of a problem, such as in the case of cancer.

Perceived Benefits: Taking Action

What kinds of actions do people take when they feel susceptible, and what are the barriers that prevent them from taking action? If the condition is seen as serious, they may seek help from a doctor or some other significant person, or they may vacillate and delay seeking and using help. Many factors enter into the decision-making process. Several factors that may act as *barriers* to care are cost, availability, and the time that will be missed from work.

From the provider's viewpoint, there is a set definition of *who* should be consulted when a problem occurs, *when* during that problem's course help should be sought, and *what* therapy should be prescribed.

Modifying Factors

The *modifying factors* shown in Figures 1–1 and 1–2 indicate the areas of conflict between consumer and provider.

Demographic Variables: Race and Ethnicity. The variables of race and ethnicity are cited most often as problem areas when the provider is white and middle class and the consumer is a member of the emerging majority. In Chapter 2 I demonstrate the difficulty providers have in defining health and illness, and later chapters explore the meaning of heath and illness as perceived by both the nonwhite and white patient. Such perceptions vary not only among groups but also among individuals.

Sociopsychological Variables. Social class, peer group, and reference group pressures also vary between the provider and consumer and among different ethnic groups. For example, if the consumer's belief about the causes of illness is "traditional" and the provider's is "modern," an inevitable conflict arises between the two viewpoints. This is even more evident when the provider is unaware of the consumer's traditional beliefs. Quite often, class differences exist between the consumer and provider. The reference group of the provider is that of the "technological health system," whereas the reference group of the consumer may well be that of the "traditional system" of health care and health-care deliverers.

Structural Variables. Structural variables also differ when the provider sees the problem from one angle and the consumer sees it from a different angle.

Often, each is seeing the same thing but is using different terms (or jargon) to explain it. Consequently, neither is understood. Reference group problems also are manifested in this area, and the news and broadcast media are an important structural variable.

HEALTH TRADITIONS

A second way of analyzing health beliefs uses the concept of holistic health—including body, mind, and spirit—and explores what people do from a traditional perspective to maintain health, protect health or prevent illness,* and restore health.

Imagine *health* as a complex, interrelated, twofold phenomenon—the balance of all facets of the person—the body, mind, and spirit. The body includes all *physical* aspects, such as genetic inheritance, body chemistry, gender, age, nutrition, physical condition; the *mind* includes cognitive process, such as thoughts, memories, and knowledge of such emotional processes as feelings, defenses, and self-esteem. The *spiritual* facet includes both positive and negative learned spiritual practices and teachings, dreams, symbols, stories; gifts and intuition; grace and protecting forces; as well as positive and negative metaphysical or innate forces. These facets are in constant flux and change over time, yet each is completely related to the others and also related to the context of the person. The context includes the person's family, culture, work, community, history, and environment.[5]

The person must be in a state of balance with the family, community, and the forces of the natural world around him or her. This is what is perceived as health in a traditional sense and the way in which it is determined within most traditional cultures. *Illness*, on the other hand, is the opposite—the imbalance of one or all parts of the person (body, mind, and spirit); this person is in a state of imbalance with the family, community, or the forces of the natural world. The ways in which this balance, or harmony, is achieved, maintained, or restored often differ from the prevailing scientific health philosophy of our modern societies. Yet, many of the traditional health-related beliefs and practices exist today among people who know and live by the traditions of their own ethnoreligious cultural heritage.

Health, in this traditional context, has nine interrelated facets, represented by the

1. Traditional methods of maintaining health—physical, mental, and spiritual
2. Traditional methods of protecting health
3. Traditional methods of restoring health

---

*The phrase "protect health" is synonymous with "prevent illness."

	PHYSICAL	MENTAL	SPIRITUAL
MAINTAIN HEALTH	Proper clothing Proper diet Exercise/Rest	Concentration Social and Family support systems Hobbies	Religious worship Prayer Meditation
PROTECT HEALTH	Special foods and food combination Symbolic clothing	Avoid certain people who can cause illness Family Activities	Religious customs Superstitions Wearing amulets and other symbolic objects to prevent the "Evil Eye" or defray other sources of harm
RESTORE HEALTH	Homeopathic remedies lineaments Herbal teas Special foods Massage Acupuncture/ moxibustion	Relaxation Exorcism Curanderos and other traditional healers Nerve teas	Religious Rituals—special prayers Meditation Traditional healings Exorcism

Figure 1–3. The nine interrelated facets of health (physical, mental, and spiritual) and personal methods to maintain health, protect health, and restore health.

The traditional methods of health maintenance, protection of health, and restoration of health require the knowledge and understanding of health-related resources from within a given person's ethnoreligious cultural heritage. These methods may be used instead of or along with modern methods of health care. They are not alternative methods of health care in the sense that they are methods that are an integral part of a person's given heritage. Alternative medicine, on the other hand, is a system of health care persons may elect to use that is generic and not a part of their particular heritage. The burgeoning system of alternative medicine must not be confused with traditional health and illness beliefs and practices. In subsequent chapters of this book (Chapter 2 and 9 through 13) *traditional* health and illness beliefs and practices are discussed, following, in part, these models. (Figs. 1–3 and 1–4)

Traditional Health Maintenance
The traditional ways of maintaining health are the active, everyday ways people go about living and attempting to stay well, that is, ordinary

	PHYSICAL	MENTAL	SPIRITUAL
MAINTAIN HEALTH	Availability of Proper shelter, clothing, and food Safe air, water, soil	Availability of traditional sources of entertainment, concentration, and "rules" of the culture.	Availability and promulgation of rules of ritual and Religious worship Meditation
PROTECT HEALTH	Provision of the knowledge of necessary special foods and food combinations, the wearing of symbolic clothing, and avoidance of excessive heat or cold	Provision of the knowledge of what people and situations to avoid, family activities; Family activities	The teaching of: Religious customs Superstitions Wearing amulets and other symbolic objects to prevent the "Evil Eye" or how to defray other sources of harm
RESTORE HEALTH	Resources that provide Homeopathic remedies, lineaments, Herbal teas, Special foods, Massage, and other ways to restore the body's balance of hot and cold	Traditional healers with the knowledge to use such modalities as: relaxation exorcism, storytelling, and/or Nerve teas	The availability of healers who use magical and supernatural ways to restore health: including religious rituals, special prayers, meditation traditional, healings, and/or Exorcism

Figure 1–4. The nine interrelated facets of health (physical, mental, and spiritual) and communal methods to maintain health, protect health, and restore health.

functioning within society. These include such actions as wearing proper clothing—boots when it snows and sweaters when it is cold, long sleeves in the sun, and scarves to protect from drafts and dust. Many traditional ethnic groups or religions may also prescribe special clothing or head coverings.

The food that is eaten and the methods for preparing it contribute to people's health. Here, too, one's ethnoreligious heritage plays a strong role in the determination of how foods are cooked, what combinations they may be eaten in, and what foods may or may not be eaten. Foods are prepared in the homes and follow the recipes from the family's tradition. Traditional cooking methods do not use preservatives, and traditional cooks don't worry about vitamins. Most foods are fresh and well prepared. Traditional diets are followed, and food taboos and restrictions obeyed. Cleanliness of the self and the environment is vital.

Mental health in the traditional sense is maintained by concentrating and using the mind—reading and crafts are examples. There are countless games, books, music, art, and other expressions of identity that help in the maintenance of mental well-being. Hobbies also contribute to mental well-being.

The key to maintaining health is, however, the family and social support systems. Spiritual health is maintained in the home with family closeness— prayer and celebrations. Rights of passage and kindred occasions are also family and community events. The strong identity with and connections to the "home" community are a great part of traditional life and the life cycle, and factors that contribute to health and well-being.

Many "special objects," such as hats to protect the eyes and face, long skirts to keep the body clean, down comforters to keep warm, special shoes for work and comfort, glasses to improve vision, and canes to facilitate walking, are used to maintain health, and they can be found in many traditional homes.

Traditional Health Protection

The protection of health rests in the traditional beliefs that harm, illness, and misfortune can be prevented by the ways in which one looks after oneself, how circumstances and people known to be harmful can be avoided, and how harmful elements that cannot be seen and understood can be avoided. Illness is not easily explained, and often people see it as a punishment for bad behavior or a curse from a jealous neighbor or stranger.

The physical protection of health consists of following strictly prescribed diets or the wearing of special garments, such as fringes.

The mental aspects of protecting health consist of the avoidance of certain people who one suspects can bring harm to them or make them sick. It also involves a strong sense of identity with family and community.

The spiritual aspects of protecting health consists of the adherence to religious customs and rituals, the following of everyday superstitions, the wearing of amulets, and the use of talismans.

Traditional Restoration of Health

The restoration of health in the physical sense could be accomplished by the use of traditional remedies, such as herbal teas, lineaments, special foods and food combinations, massage, and other activities.

The restoration of health in the mental domain may be accomplished by the use of various techniques, such as exorcism, calling on traditional healers, using teas or massage, and seeking family and community support.

The restoration of health in the spiritual sense can be accomplished by healing rituals; religious healing rituals; or the use of symbols and prayer, meditation, special prayers, and exorcism.

These nine traditional facets of personal health are predicated on the person knowing the health traditions of his or her ethnocultural heritage, the family passing on and teaching these methods to following generations, and the ethnoreligious community having resources available to the person to meet his or her health needs.

This model forms the basis for the study of traditional health and illness beliefs and practices. These traditions are shaped and altered by cultural phenomena that also affect health.

CULTURAL PHENOMENA AFFECTING HEALTH

Giger and Davidhizar have identified six cultural phenomena that vary among cultural groups and affect health care.[6] These are environmental control, biological variations, social organization, communication, space, and time orientation.

Environmental Control

Environmental control is the ability of members of a particular cultural group to plan activities that control nature or direct environmental factors. Included in this concept are the complex systems of traditional health and illness beliefs, the practice of folk medicine, and the use of traditional healers. This particular cultural phenomenon plays an extremely important role in the way clients respond to health-related experiences, including the ways in which they define health and illness and seek and use health-care resources and social supports.[7]

Biological Variations

The several ways in which people from one cultural group differ biologically (i.e., physically and genetically) from members of other cultural groups constitute their biological variations. The following are significant examples:

1. Body build and structure, including specific bone and structural differences between groups, such as the smaller stature of Asians
2. Skin color, including variations in tone, texture, healing abilities, and hair follicles
3. Enzymatic and genetic variations, including differences in response to drug and dietary therapies
4. Susceptibility to disease, which can manifest itself as a higher morbidity rate to certain diseases within certain groups
5. Nutritional variations, countless examples of which include the "hot and cold" preferences found among Hispanic Americans, the *yin* and *yang* preferences found among Asian Americans, and the rules of the kosher diet found among Jewish and Islamic

Americans. A relatively common nutritional disorder, lactose intolerance, is found among Mexican, African, Asian, and Eastern European Jewish Americans[8]

Social Organization

The social environment in which people grow up and live plays an essential role in their cultural development and identification. Children learn their culture's responses to life events from the family and its ethnoreligious group. This *socialization* process is an inherent part of heritage—cultural, religious, and ethnic background. *Social organization* refers to the family unit (nuclear, single-parent, or extended family), and the social group organizations (religious or ethnic) with which clients and families may identify. Countless social barriers, such as unemployment, underemployment, homelessness, lack of health insurance, and poverty, can also prevent people from entering the health care system.[9]

Communication

Communication differences are presented in many ways, including language differences, verbal and nonverbal behaviors, and silence. Language differences are possibly the most important obstacle to providing multicultural health care because they affect all stages of the client–caregiver relationship. Clear and effective communication is important when dealing with any client, especially if language differences create a cultural barrier. When deprived of the most common medium of interaction with clients—the spoken word—health-care providers often become frustrated and ineffective. Accurate diagnosis and treatment is impossible if the health-care professional cannot understand the patient. When the provider is not understood, he or she often avoids verbal communication and does not realize the effect of nonverbal communication, which is all too often the painful isolation of clients who do not speak the dominant language and who are in an unfamiliar environment. Consequently, clients experience cultural shock and may react by withdrawing, becoming hostile or belligerent, or being uncooperative.

Language differences can be bridged, however, with the use of competent interpreters. If the client does not speak the dominant language, a skilled interpreter is mandatory.[10]

Space

Personal space refers to people's behaviors and attitudes toward the space around themselves. *Territoriality* is the term for the behavior and attitude people exhibit about an area they have claimed and defend or react emotionally about when others encroach on it. Both personal space and territoriality are influenced by culture, and thus different ethnocultural groups have varying norms related to the use of space. Space and related behaviors have different meanings in the zones listed on the following page:

1. *Intimate zone*—extends up to 1½ feet. Because this distance allows adults to have the most bodily contacts for perception of breath and odor, incursion into this zone is acceptable only in private places. Visual distortions also occur at this distance.
2. *Personal distance*—extends from 1½ to 4 feet. This is an extension of the self that is like having a "bubble" of space surrounding the body. At this distance the voice may be moderate, body odor may not be apparent, and visual distortion may have disappeared.
3. *Social distance*—extends from 4 to 12 feet. This is reserved for impersonal business transactions. Perceptual information is much less detailed.
4. *Public distance*—extends 12 feet or more. Individuals interact only impersonally. Communicators' voices must be projected, and subtle facial expressions may be lost.

It must be noted that these generalizations about the use of personal space are based on studies of the behavior of European North Americans. Use of personal space varies between individuals and ethnic groups. The extreme modesty practiced by members of some cultural groups may prevent members from seeking preventive health care.[11]

Time Orientation

The viewing of the time in the present, past, or future varies among different cultural groups. Certain cultures in the United States and Canada tend to be future-oriented. People who are future-oriented are concerned with long-range goals and with health-care measures in the present to prevent the occurrence of illness in the future. They prefer to plan ahead in making schedules, setting appointments, and organizing activities. Others are oriented more to the present than the future, and may be late for appointments, because they are less concerned about planning ahead to be on time. This difference in time orientation may become important in health-care measures, such as long-term planning and explanations of medications schedules.[12,13] Figure 1–5 illustrates how a given person, with his or her unique ethnic, religious, and cultural background is affected by cultural phenomena.

The discussions in Chapters 9 to 13 focus on these phenomena, and examples are presented within the text and in table form. When discussing this topic, great care must be taken to keep in mind that the text illustrates different health traditions and is not intended to be stereotypical. The examples used to illustrate cultural differences run the risk of stereotyping. With careful listening, observing, and questioning, the provider is able to sort out the traditions of a given person.

Each of the preceding factors—the health belief models, the health traditions concepts, the cultural phenomena influencing health, and heritage consistency (discussed in Chapter 4)—are interrelated and woven together as manifestations of what and how people believe and practice in their experiences of health and illness.

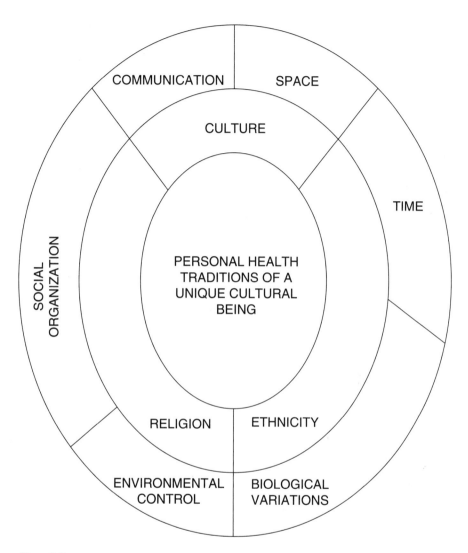

Figure 1–5.

REFERENCES

1. Nerburn, K. and Mengelkoch, L., eds. *Native American Wisdom.* (San Rafael, CA: New World Library, 1991), p. 1.
2. Rosenstock, I. M., "Why People Use Health Services." *Millbank Memorial Fund Quarterly* 44 (3) (July 1966): 97–127.
3. Becker, M. H., Drachman, R. H., Kirscht, J. P., "A New Approach to Explaining Sick Role Behavior in Low-Income Populations." *American Journal of Public Health* 64 (1974): 205–216.

4. Becker, M. H., Drachman, R.H., Kirscht, J. P., *The Health Belief Model and Personal Health Behavior.* (Thorofare, NJ: B. Slack, 1974).
5. Adapted from Spector, R. E., "Cultural Concepts of Women's Health and Health-Promoting Behavior." *Journal of Obstetric, Gynecologic, and Neonatal Nursing.* 24, 3 (1995): 241–245.
6. Giger, J. N. and Davidhizar, R. E. *Transcultural Nursing Assessment and Intervention* (2nd ed.) (St. Louis: Mosby Year Book, 1995), pp. 11–13.
7. Ibid., pp. 113–122.
8. Ibid., pp. 127–156.
9. Ibid., pp. 61–87
10. Ibid., pp. 19–38.
11. Ibid., pp. 43–59.
12. Ibid., pp. 89–109.
13. Adapted from Spector, R. E., "Culture, Ethnicity, and Nursing," in *Fundamentals of Nursing* (3rd ed.), eds. Potter, A. and Perry, A. (St. Louis: Mosby, 1992), pp. 99–103.

ANNOTATED BIBLIOGRAPHY

McCubbin, H. I., Thompson, E. A., Thompson, A. I., et al. *Sense of Coherence and Resiliency—Stress, Coping, and Health.* Madison, WI: The University of Wisconsin System, 1994.

This book develops the foundation of resiliency and the sense of coherence in family research relating to health and coping.

McCubbin, H. I., Thompson, E. A., Thompson, A. I., et al. *Resiliency in Ethnic Minority Families,* Vol. 1, *Native and Immigrant American Families.* Madison, WI: The University of Wisconsin System, 1994.

This book is the first volume in a two-volume series and it serves to address the issues facing racial and ethnic emerging majority families. The text focuses on the strengths and resiliency of the families, rather than on deficiency and deviance models. The authors and contributors pay attention to the role that culture and ethnicity play in the families' development of coping strategies and meaning given to stressful life events.

U.S. Department of Health and Human Services. *Healthy People 2000 National Health Promotion and Disease Prevention Objectives—Full Report with Commentary.* Boston: Jones and Bartlett, 1990.

The full report with commentary is an extremely useful text that addresses the health destinies of all of the people of this nation. It serves as a helpful resource for the development of strategies to address the health needs of the diverse populations and to meet these needs within the population.

2

Chapter

Health and Illness

Life is an adventure in a world where nothing is static; where unpredictable and ill-understood events constitute dangers that must be overcome, often blindly and at great cost; where man himself, like the sorcerer's apprentice, has set in motion forces that are potentially destructive and may someday escape his control. The very process of living is a continual interplay between the individual and his environment, often taking the form of a struggle resulting in injury or disease. Complete and lasting freedom from disease is but a dream remembered from imaginings of a Garden of Eden designed for the welfare of man.

—René Dubos, *Mirage of Health*

To begin our quest for a deeper understanding of the problems surrounding the delivery of adequate health care, we must ask two fundamental questions: "What is health?" and "What is illness?"

HEALTH

The answers to the first question are not as readily articulated as one would assume. One response may be a flawless recitation of the World Health Organization (WHO) definition of health as a "state of complete physical, mental, and social well being and not merely the absence of disease," given with great assurance—a challenge is neither expected nor welcomed but may evoke an intense dispute in which the assumed right answer is completely torn apart. Answers such as "homeostasis," "kinetic energy in balance," "optimal functioning," and "freedom from pain" are open to discussion. Experienced health-care providers may be unable to give a comprehensive, acceptable answer to such a seemingly simple question. It is difficult to give a definition that makes sense without the use of some form of medical jargon. It is also challenging to define "health" in terms that a lay person can understand. (We lack skill in understanding "health" from the lay person's perspective.)

One of the many definitions of health is in the *American Heritage Dictionary*.

> n. 1. The state of an organism with respect to functioning, disease, and abnormality at any given time. 2. The state of an organism functioning normally without disease or abnormality. 3. Optimal functioning with freedom from disease and abnormality. 4. Broadly, any state of optimal functioning, well being, or progress. 5. A wish for someone's good health, expressed as a toast.[1]

Murray and Zentner define health as "a purposeful, adaptive response, physically, mentally, emotionally and socially, to internal and external stimuli in order to maintain stability and comfort."[2]

These definitions—varying in scope and context—are essentially those that the student, practitioner, and educator within the health professions agree convey the meaning of "health." The most widely used and recognized definition is that of WHO. Within the socialization process of the health-care deliverer, the denotation of the word is that contained in the WHO definition. For other students, the meaning of the word "health" becomes clear through the educational experience.

In analyzing these definitions, one is able to discern subtle variations in denotation. If this occurs in the denotation of the word, what of the connotation? That is, are health-care providers as familiar with implicit meanings as with more explicit ones? If the following comment (made in a discussion of an article by Irwin M. Rosenstock) is accurate, the educational process is indeed deficient.

> Whereas health itself is in reality an elusive concept, in much of research, the stages involved in seeking medical care are conceived as completely distinct. The health professions are becoming increasingly aware of the *lack of clarity* in the definition of health.[3]

The framework of both education and research in the health professions continues to rely on the more abstract definitions of the word *health*. When taken in broader context, health can be regarded not only as the absence of disease but also as a reward for "good behavior." In fact, a state of health is regarded by many people as the reward one receives for "good" behavior and illness as punishment for "bad" behavior. You may have heard something like "She is so good; no wonder she is so healthy," or a mother admonishing her child, "If you don't do such and such, you'll get sick." Situations and experiences may be avoided for the purpose of protecting and maintaining one's health. On the other hand, some people seek out challenging, albeit dangerous, situations with the hope that they will experience the thrill of a challenge and still emerge in an intact state of health. One example of such behavior is driving at high speeds.

Health can also be viewed as the freedom from and the absence of evil. In this context, health is analogous to day, which equals good light. Conversely, illness is analogous to night, and evil, and dark. Illness, to some, is seen as a punishment for being bad or doing evil deeds; it is the work of vindictive evil spirits. In the modern education of health-care providers, these concepts of health and illness are rarely, if ever, discussed, yet if these concepts of health and illness are believed by some consumers of health-care services, understanding these varying ideas is important for the provider.

We each enter the health-care community with our own culturally based concept of health. During the educational and socialization process in our profession—nursing, medicine, or social work—we are expected to shed these beliefs and adopt the standard definitions. In addition to shedding these old beliefs, we learn, if only by unspoken example, to view as deviant those who do not accept the prevailing, institutional connotation of the word *health.*

The material that follows illustrates the complex process necessary to enable providers to return to and appreciate their former interpretations of health, to understand the vast number of meanings the word *health* has, and to be aware of the difficulties that exist with definitions such as that of the World Health Organization.

How Do You Define Health?

You have been requested to describe the term *health* in your own words. Many may initially respond by reciting the WHO definition. What does this definition really mean? The following is a representative sample of actual responses.

1. Being able to do what I want to do
2. Physical and psychological well-being, "physical" meaning that there are no abnormal functions with the body, all systems are without those abnormal functions that would cause a problem physically, and "psychological" meaning that one's mind is capable of a clear and logical thinking process and association
3. Being able to use all of your body parts in the way that you want to—to have energy and enthusiasm
4. Being able to perform your normal activities, such as working, without discomfort and at an optimal level
5. The state of wellness with no physical or mental illness
6. I would define health as an undefined term: it depends on the situations, individuals, and other things

In the initial step of the *unlocking* process,* it begins to become clear that no single definition fully conveys what health really is. We can all agree on the WHO definition, but when asked "What does that mean?" we are unable to clarify or to simplify that definition. As we begin to perceive a change in the connotation of the word, we may experience dismay, as that emotional response accompanies the breaking down of ideas. When this occurs, we begin to realize that as we were socialized into the provider culture by the educational process our understanding of *health* changed, and we moved a great distance from our older cultural understanding of the term. The following list includes the definitions of health given by students at various levels of education and experience. The students ranged in age from 19-year-old college juniors to adult nursing trainees and graduate students in both nursing and social work.

- *Junior students*
  A system involving all subsystems of one's body that constantly work on keeping one in physical and mental condition
- *Senior students*
  Ability to function in activities of daily living to optimal capacity without requiring medical attention
  Mental and physical wellness
  The state of physical, mental, and emotional well-being.
- *RN students*
  Ability to cope with stressors. Absence of pain—mental and physical
  State of optimal well-being, both physically and emotionally
- *Graduate students*
  State of well-being that is free from physical and mental distress. I can also include in this social well-being, even though this may be idealistic.
  Not only the absence of disease but a state of balance or equilibrium of physical, emotional, and spiritual states of well-being

It appears that the definition becomes more abstract and technical as the student advances in the educational program. The terms explaining health take on a more abstract and scientific character with each year of removal from the lay mode of thinking.

Can these layers of jargon be removed, and can we help ourselves once again to view health in a more tangible manner?

In probing this question, let us think back to the way we perceived health before our entrance into the educational program. I believe that the farther

---

*The *unlocking* process includes those steps taken to help break down and understand the definitions of both terms, *health* and *illness,* in a living context. It consists of persistent questioning: "What is health?" No matter what the response, the question "What does that mean?" is asked. Initially, this causes much confusion, but in classroom practice—as each term is written on the blackboard and analyzed—the air clears and the process begins to make sense.

back one can go in one's memory of earlier concepts of health the better. Again, the question "What is health?" is asked over and over. Initially, the responses continue to include such terms and phrases as "homeostasis," "freedom from disease," or "frame of mind." Slowly, and with considerable prodding, we are able to recall earlier perceptions of health. Once again, health becomes a *personal, experiential* concept, and the relation of *health* to *being* returns. The fragility and instability of this concept also are recognized as health gradually acquires meaning in relation to the term *being*.

This process of unlocking a perception of a concept takes a considerable amount of time and patience. It also engenders dismay that briefly turns to anger and resentment. One may question why the definitions acquired and mastered in the learning process are now being challenged and torn apart. The feeling may be that of taking a giant step backward in a quest for new terminology and new knowledge.

With this unlocking process, however, one is able to perceive the concept of health *in the way that a vast number of health-care consumers may perceive it*. The following illustrates the transition that the concept passed through in an unlocking process from the WHO definition to the realm of the health-care consumer.

- *Initial responses*
  Feeling of well-being, no illness
  Homeostasis
  Complete physical, mental, and social well-being
- *Secondary responses*
  Frame of mind
  Subjective state of psychosocial well-being
  Activities of daily living can be performed
- *Experiential responses*
  (Health becomes tangible; the description is illustrated by using qualities that can be seen, felt, or touched.)
  Shiny hair
  Warm, smooth, glossy skin
  Clear eyes
  Shiny teeth
  Being alert
  Being happy
  Freedom from pain
  Harmony between body and mind

Even this itemized description does not completely answer the question, "What is health?" The words are once again subjected to the question, "What does that mean?" and once again the terms are stripped down, and a paradox begins to emerge. For example, "shiny hair" may in fact be present in an ill person or in a person whose hair has not been washed for a long time, and a healthy person may not always have clean, well-groomed, lustrous hair.

It becomes clear that no matter how much one goes around in a circle in an attempt to define *health,* the terms and meanings attributed to the state can be challenged. As a result of this prolonged discussion, one never really comes to an acceptable definition of health, yet, by going through the intense unlocking process, one is able finally to understand the ambiguity that surrounds the word. We are, accordingly, less likely to view as deviant those people whose beliefs and practices concerning their own health and health care differ from ours.

How Do You Keep Yourself Healthy?

Preventive Care and Health Maintenance. Health can be seen from many viewpoints, and many areas of disagreement arise with respect to how this word can be defined. "Health is not merely an end in itself, but rather a means of attaining human well-being within the natural constraints in which man finds himself."[4] To state it another way

> . . . any aspect of health for an individual, or the determiners of what he does or does not do in relation to some aspect of health, is some combination of the effects of his physical body: what he knows about it, what he feels about it, and how significant others react to it.[5]

The preparation of health-care workers tends to organize their education from a perspective of illness. Rarely (or superficially) does it include a study of the concept of *health.* Today, however, the emphasis is shifting from acute care to preventive care. The need for the provider of health services to comprehend this concept is, therefore, crucial. As this movement for preventive health care takes hold, becomes firmly entrenched, and thrives, multiple issues must be resolved in answering the question, "What is health?" Unless the provider is able to understand health from the viewpoint of the consumer, a barrier of misunderstanding is perpetuated. It is difficult to reexamine complex definitions dutifully memorized at an earlier time, yet an understanding of health from a client's viewpoint is essential to the establishment of preventive health-care services because the perception of health is a complex psychological process. It is selective in that "man sees what he wants to see or expects to see."[6] There tends to be no established pattern in what individuals and families see as their health needs and how they go about practicing their own health care,[7] yet their perception of health is sanctioned and given meaning when it is brought to a level of awareness where it can be interpreted and used in planning.[8]

Health maintenance and the prevention of illness are by no means new concepts. As long as human beings have existed, they have used a multitude of methods—ranging from magic and witchcraft to present-day immuniza-

---

HEALTHFUL HINTS FROM LONG AGO

A sassafras root carried in the pocket guards against illness. (Superstition of Old Saint Simons)

Asefetida worn on a string around the neck protects a child from many diseases; and, a buckeye carried in the pocket protects against rheumatism. (Blue Ridge and Great Smoky Mountains)

A single, pierced nutmeg, worn around the neck on a string, will protect you from boils, croup, body lice, and various lung diseases. (New England)

A well-ventilated bedroom will prevent morning headaches and lassitude. (1914 Almanac)

---

tion—in an ongoing effort to maintain good health and prevent debilitating illness. Raquel Cohen sees prevention as "a plea for early intervention to help people deal more successfully with the difficulties arising from man's struggles to adapt to society."[9] Another current viewpoint regarding prevention is advanced by Richard Stark: "Health maintenance has become our national obsession. Logic suggests that in order to maintain health we must prevent disease, and that is best accomplished by eating balanced meals, exercising regularly, and seeing the doctor once a year for a checkup."[10] The annual ritual of visiting a physician has been extensively promoted by the medical establishment and is viewed as effective by numerous lay people. A doctor's statement often is required by a person seeking employment or life insurance.[11] Furthermore, the annual physical examination has been advertised as the key to good health. A "clean bill of health" is considered essential for social, emotional, and even economic success. This clean bill of health is bestowed only by the members of the medical profession. The general public has been conditioned to believe that health is guaranteed if a disease that may be developing is discovered early and treated with the ever-increasing varieties of modern medical technology.[12] For all those who believe in and practice the annual physical and screening for early detection of a disease, however, there are some—both within and outside the health-care professions—who do not subscribe to it.[13] Preventive medicine grew out of clinical practice associated either with welfare medicine or with industrial or occupational medical practice. The approach of preventive medicine and health maintenance is now developing as a new focus for health-care practice in the United States.[14]

In fact, it is possible to determine an image of the overall health beliefs and status of the American population. The classic study completed in 1985 by the National Center for Health Statistics included the topic of health promotion and disease prevention as part of the National Health Interview Survey questionnaire. This survey is a continuing, cross-sectional, nationwide survey conducted by household interview. The sample consisted of 36,399 eligible households. The provisional findings (1986) revealed the following health practices within the sample.

- *General health habits*
  Most adults eat breakfast every day (55%), get 7 to 8 hours of sleep each night (66%), and have a usual place for health care (78%).
- *Weight*
  One fourth of men and one half of women in the sample were attempting to lose weight.
- *Preventive examinations for women*
  About one half of women had a Pap smear test or a breast examination. It was found also that the majority of women (87%) know how to examine their breasts for lumps, but only one third do so.
- *Seat belts*
  Seat belt use is increasing rapidly.
- *Child safety*
  The majority of families with children under 10 years of age have heard of the Poison Control Centers and have a telephone number for the center in their area. Almost all of the adults with children under 5 years of age know about child safety seats.
- *Home safety*
  About two fifths of homes do not have a smoke detector.
- *High blood pressure*
  Three quarters of adults had their blood pressure taken by health professionals over a given year, and women and persons over 65 were more likely to do this than men and younger people.
- *Heart disease*
  A large majority of adults was aware of three of the four principal risk factors associated with heart disease.
- *Stress*
  One half of adults reported experiencing at least a moderate amount of stress, and many felt that stress had had an impact on their health.
- *Exercise*
  Less than one half (40%) of the adult population exercises on a regular basis.
- *Cigarette smoking*
  There has been a downward trend in smoking since 1964. However, 3 in 10 adults still smoke.
- *Alcohol use*
  With the exception of cirrhosis of the liver, the adult population appeared less knowledgeable about the effects of alcohol on health than the effects of smoking. Eight percent of adults were classified as heavier drinkers (two or more drinks per day), 19% as moderate drinkers, and 24% as lighter drinkers (three drinks or less per week).[15]

Health Status and Determinants

Health, United States, 1992 is the 17th report on the health status of the nation and presents national trends in public health statistics. The following selected examples are relevant:

1. Between 1980 and 1990 the *elderly population* grew more rapidly than other age groups.
2. The overall percentage of live-born *infants weighing less than 2,500 grams* has remained stable, but the proportion of *infants weighing less than 1,500 grams* (those at greatest risk of death and disability) increased 18% for infants of black mothers and 6% for infants of white mothers during this period. In 1990, the percentage of black infants weighing less than 1,500 grams was three times that for white infants.
3. Between 1980 and 1990 the age-adjusted death rate for *heart disease*, the leading cause of death, declined 25%. In 1990, the mortality rate was almost twice as great for white men as for white women and more than 60% greater for black men than for black women.
4. Between 1980 and 1990 the age-adjusted death rate for *stroke* declined 32%; however, in 1990 the age-adjusted death rate was twice as great for black men as for white men and almost 80% greater for black women as for white women.
5. In 1990, the age-adjusted death rate for *human immunodeficiency virus (HIV) infection* increased by 13%.
6. In 1991, the health status of black Americans continues to lag behind that of white Americans. The age-adjusted proportion reporting *fair or poor health* was 76% greater for black persons than for white persons.
7. Between 1985 and 1991 the prevalence of *smoking* declined by 25% for college graduates, but declined by only 7 to 9% for those with 12 or fewer years of education.[16]

Healthy People 2000

Healthy People 2000: National Health Promotion and Disease Prevention and Objectives is a statement of national opportunities. This prevention initiative presents a national strategy for significantly improving the health of the American people in the decade preceding the year 2000. This document recognizes that lifestyle and environment factors are major determinants in disease prevention and health promotion. It provides strategies for significantly reducing preventable death and disability, for enhancing quality of life, and for reducing disparities in health status between various population groups within our society.

Healthy People 2000 defines three broad goals:

1. To increase the span of healthy life for all Americans
2. To reduce health disparities among Americans
3. To achieve access to preventive services for all Americans

These goals are supported by 300 specific objectives. Subordinate objectives for the emerging majority and other special populations have also been established. The 22 priority areas, showing a sample of one objective from each, are as follows:

1. Physical activity and fitness
   Sample Objective: Increase community availability and accessibility of physical activity and fitness facilities.
2. Nutrition
   Sample Objective: Reduce overweight to a prevalence of no more than 20% among people aged 20 and older and no more than 15% among adolescents aged 12 to 15.
3. Tobacco
   Sample Objective: Reduce cigarette smoking to a prevalence of no more than 15% among people aged 20 and older.
4. Alcohol and other drugs
   Sample Objective: Reduce deaths caused by alcohol-related motor vehicle crashes to no more than 8.5 per 100,000 people.
5. Family Planning
   Sample Objective: Reduce pregnancies among girls aged 17 and younger to no more than 50 per 100,000.
6. Mental Health and Mental Disorder
   Sample Objective: Reduce suicides to no more than 15 per 100,000 people.
7. Violent and Abusive Behavior
   Sample Objective: Reduce homicides to no more than 7.2% per 100,000 people.
8. Educational and Community-Based Programs
   Sample Objective: Establish community health promotion programs that address at least three of the *Healthy People 2000* priorities and reach at least 40% of each state's population.
9. Unintentional Injuries
   Sample Objective: Reduce deaths caused by unintentional injuries to no more than 29.3 per 100,000 people.
10. Occupational Safety and Health
    Sample Objective: Reduce deaths from work-related injuries to no more than 21 per 100,000 full-time workers.
11. Environmental Health
    Sample Objective: Perform testing for lead-based paint in at least 50% of homes built before 1950.

12. Food and Drug Safety
    Sample Objective: Reduce outbreaks of infections due to *Salmonella enteritidis* to fewer than 25 outbreaks yearly.
13. Oral Health
    Sample Objective: Reduce dental caries so that the proportion of children with one or more caries is no more than 35% among children aged 6 to 8 and no more than 60% among adolescents aged 15.
14. Maternal and Infant Health
    Sample Objective: Reduce the infant mortality rate to no more than 7 per 1,000 live births.
15. Heart Disease and Stroke
    Sample Objective: Reduce coronary heart disease deaths to no more than 115 per 100,000 people.
16. Cancer
    Sample Objective: Reverse the rise in cancer deaths to achieve a rate of no more than 130 per 100,000 people.
17. Diabetes and Chronic Disabling Conditions
    Sample Objective: Reduce to no more than 8% the proportion of people who experience a limitation in major activity due to chronic conditions.
18. HIV Infection
    Sample Objective: Confine the prevalence of HIV infection to no more than 800 per 100,000 people.
19. Sexually Transmitted Diseases
    Sample Objective: Reduce gonorrhea to an incidence of no more than 225 cases per 100,000 people.
20. Immunization and Infectious Diseases
    Sample Objective: Reduce indigenous cases of vaccine-preventable diseases, such as Rubella to 0.
21. Clinical Preventive Services
    Sample Objective: Increase years of life to at least 65.[17]

Health Diaries. Keeping a 30-day health diary is recommended to increase awareness of one's own health status and health practices. If an illness occurs, record what is done for it, why it is done, and what type of health-care services were used.

Comments will be most revealing! We recognize that, in spite of the fact that we are learning proper methods of health maintenance, we have poor nutritional and sleeping habits and rarely, if ever, seek medical help for what some of us consider "serious" bodily complaints. At best, seeking care is delayed until we give up the idea that our symptoms will disappear. This diary has a very sobering effect. It also is used as an additional humanizing tool. The term *humanizing* is used here because just as we treat ourselves or delay in seeking help, we also ought not to judge people who, for various reasons, treat themselves or delay in seeking health care.

The following exercise is designed to help the reader tune in to his or her own daily health status.

Keep a daily record of your health—physical, mental, and spiritual—status and behavior for 30 days. Include in this record medications taken (prescription and nonprescription), eating, sleeping, exercise, recreational, and spiritual activities. When appropriate, note the reasons for your actions.

The daily record, or diary, enables you to see how you react to the various stresses and strains of daily life. It reveals the intricacies of your daily lifestyle—the things you take for granted. For example: Do you eat three balanced meals a day? Do you get enough rest? Do you exercise?

At the end of 30 days, reread this diary and analyze it in relation to recommended health practices.

Typical entries for such a record follow.

- *Monday*
  Overslept (went to bed 3:00 AM)
  Skipped breakfast
  Dozed in class
  Coke and cheese crackers for lunch
  2 aspirins (headache)
  Hamburger and french fries for supper
  Crashed at 8:00 PM
- *Tuesday*
  Up at 6:30 AM for clinical
  Milk and toast for breakfast
  Exercise—walk in hospital corridors
  Supper—lasagne, wine
  Headache—2 aspirins
  Bed 8:00 PM (couldn't study)
- *Wednesday*
  Up at 7:00 AM for 8:30 lecture
  Walked to hospital
  No breakfast (not hungry)
  Peanut butter & jelly for lunch
  PM snack—milk & candy bar
  Study until 2:00 AM
  2 aspirins (headache)
- *Thursday*
  Up at 6:30 AM for clinical
  Coffee and cheese sandwich for breakfast
  Walked to hospital (it rained)
  Almost slept on ward
  No lunch (out of funds—no time to cash check)
  Coke
  Walked in hospital corridors

In summary, this section has attempted to deal solely with the concept of *health*. The multiple denotations and connotations of the word have been explored. A method for helping you to tune in to your health has been included, as has the government's goals for creating healthy people by the year 2000.

ILLNESS

The world of illness is the one that is most familiar to the nurse and other providers of health care. It is in this world that the provider feels most comfortable and useful.

Many questions about illness need to be answered: What determines illness? How does someone know when he or she is ill? What provokes a person to seek help from the health-care system? At what point does self-treatment seem no longer possible? Where does a person go for help? And to whom?

We tend to regard illness as the absence of health, yet it has been demonstrated in the preceding discussion that *health* is at best an elusive term that defies a specific definition! Let us look at the present issue more closely. Is illness the opposite of health? Is it a permanent condition or a transient condition? How does one know he or she is ill?

The *American Heritage Dictionary* defines "illness" as "Sickness of body or mind. b. sickness. 2. *obsolete*. Evil; wickedness."[18]

As with *health,* the word *illness* can be subjected to extensive analysis. What is illness? A generalized response, such as "abnormal functioning of a body's system or systems," evolves into more specific assessments of what we observe and believe to be wrong. Illness is a "sore throat," a "headache," or a "fever"—the latter determined not necessarily by the measurement on a thermometer, but by the flushed face, the warm-to-hot feeling of the forehead, back, and abdomen, and the overall malaise. The diagnosis of "intestinal obstruction" is described as pain in the stomach (abdomen), a greater pain than that caused by "gas," accompanied by severely upset stomach, nausea, vomiting, and marked constipation.

Essentially, we are being pulled back in the popular direction and encouraged to reuse lay terms. We initially resist this because we want to employ professional jargon. (Why reuse lay terms when our knowledge is so much greater?) It is crucial that we be called to task for using jargon. We must learn to be constantly conscious of the way in which the laity perceives illness and health care.

Another factor emerges as the word *illness* is stripped down to its barest essentials. Many of the characteristics attributed to health occur in illness, too. You may receive a rude awakening when you realize that a person perceived as healthy by clinical assessment may then—by a given set of symptoms—define himself as ill (or vice versa). For example, in summertime, one may see a person with a red face and assume that she has a sunburn. The person may, in fact, have a fever. A person recently discharged from the hospital, pale and barely able to walk, may be judged ill. That individual may consider himself *well*, however, because he is much better than when he entered the hospital—now he is able to walk! Thus perceptions are relative, and, in this instance, the eyes of the beholder have been clouded by inadequate information. Unfortunately, at the provider's level of practice, we do not always ask the patient: "How do you view your state of health?" Rather, we determine the patient's state of health by objective and observational data.

As is the case with the concept of health, one learns in nursing or medical school how to determine what illness is and how people are expected to behave when they are ill. Once these terms are separated and examined, the models that health-care providers have created tend to carry little weight. There is little agreement as to what, specifically, illness is, but one nonetheless has a high level of expectation as to what behavior should be demonstrated by both the client and provider when illness occurs. One discovers that we have a vast amount of knowledge with respect to the acute illnesses and the services that ideally must be provided for the acutely ill person. When contradictions surface, however, it becomes apparent that our knowledge of the vast gray area is minimal, for example, whether someone is ill or becoming ill with what may later be an acute episode. Because of the ease with which we often identify cardinal symptoms, we find we are able to react to acute illness and may have negative attitudes toward those who do not seek help when the first symptom of an acute illness appears. The questions that then arise are: What is an acute illness, and how do we differentiate between it and some everyday indisposition that most people treat by themselves? When do we draw the line and admit that the disorder is out of the realm of adequate self-treatment?

These are certainly very difficult questions to answer, especially when careful analysis shows that even the symptoms of an acute illness tend to vary from one person to another. In many acute illnesses, the symptoms are so severe that the person experiencing them has little choice but to seek immediate medical care. Such is the case with a severe myocardial infarction, but what about the person who experiences mild discomfort in the epigastric region? Such a symptom could lead the person to conclude he or she has "indigestion," and to self-medicate with baking soda, an antacid, milk, or Alka-Seltzer. A person who experiences mild pain in the left arm may delay seeking care, believing the pain will disappear. Obviously, this person may be as ill as the person who seeks help during the onset of symptoms but will, like most people, minimize these small aches because of not wanting to assume the sick role.

The Sick Role

The work of Talcott Parsons helps explain the phenomenon of "the sick role." In our society, a person is expected to have the symptoms viewed as illness confirmed by a member of the health-care profession. In other words, the sick role must first be legitimately conferred on this person by the keepers of this privilege. One cannot legitimize one's own illness and have one's own diagnosis accepted by the society at large. "A legitimate procedure for the definition and sanctioning of the adoption of the sick role is fundamental for both the social system and the sick individual."[19]

Role is defined sociologically (1) as the set of expectations and behaviors associated with a specific position in a social system (social role) or (2) as the way a person tends to react to a social situation (individual role).[20] Illness "is not merely a 'condition' but also a social role."[21] There are four main components inherent in the sick role.

1. "The sick person is exempted from the performance of certain of his/her normal social obligations."[22] An example is a student nurse who has a severe sore throat and decides that she does not want to go to her clinical assignment. For her to be exempted from the day's activities, she must have this symptom validated by someone in the health services, either a physician or the nurse on duty. Her claim of illness must be legitimized or socially defined and validated by a sanctioned provider of health-care services.

2. "The sick person is also exempted from a certain type of responsibility for his/her own state."[23] For example, an ill person cannot be expected to control the situation or be spontaneously cured. The student with the sore throat is expected to seek help and then to follow the advice of the attending physician or nurse in promoting recovery. The student is not responsible for recovery except in a peripheral sense.

3. "The legitimization of the sick role is, however, only partial."[24] When one is sick, one is in an undesirable state and *should* recover and leave this state as rapidly as possible. The student's sore throat is acceptable only for a while. Beyond a reasonable amount of time—as determined by the physician, peers, and the faculty— legitimate absence from the clinical classroom setting can no longer be claimed.

4. "Being sick, except in the mildest of cases, is being in need of help."[25] Bone fide help, as defined by the majority of American society and other Western countries, is the exclusive realm of the physician. In seeking the help of the physician, the person now not only bears the sick role but in addition takes on the role of patient. Patienthood carries with it a certain prescribed set of responsibilities, some of which include compliance with a medical regimen, cooperation with the health-care provider, and following orders without asking too many questions. All of this leads to the illness experience.

The Illness Experience

The experience of an illness is determined by what illness means to the sick person. Furthermore, illness refers to a specific status and role within a given society. Not only must illness be sanctioned by a physician for the sick person to assume the sick role, but it must also be sanctioned by the community or society structure of which the person is a member. This experience can be divided into four stages that are sufficiently general to apply to any society or culture.

Onset. Onset is the time when the person experiences the first symptoms of a given problem.[26] This event can be slow and insidious or rapid and acute. When the onset is insidious, the patient may not be conscious of symptoms or may think that, by waiting, the discomfort will go away. If, on the other hand, the onset is acute, the person is positive illness has occurred and immediate help must be sought. "This stage is seen as the prelude to legitimization of illness."[27]

Diagnosis. In the diagnostic stage of the illness experience, the disease is identified or an effort is made to identify it.[28] The person's role is now sanctioned, and at this point, the illness is socially recognized and identified. At this point, the health-care providers make decisions pertaining to appropriate therapy. During the period of diagnosis, the person experiences another phenomenon: dealing with the unknown, which includes fearing what the diagnosis will be.

For many people, going through a medical work-up is an unfamiliar experience. This is made doubly difficult because they are asked and expected to relate to strange people who are doing unfamiliar and often painful things to their bodies and minds. To the lay person, the environment of the hospital or the physician's office is both strange and unfamiliar, and it is natural to fear these qualities. Quite often, the ailing individual is faced with an unfamiliar diagnosis. Nonetheless, the person is expected to follow closely a prescribed treatment plan that usually is detailed by the health-care providers but that, in all likelihood, may not accommodate a particular lifestyle. The situation is that of a horizontal–vertical relationship, the patient being figuratively and literally in the former position, the professional in the latter.

Patient Status. During the period of being a patient, the person adjusts to the social aspects of being ill and gives in to the demands of his or her physical condition.[29] The sick role becomes that of patienthood, and the person is expected to shift into this role as society determines it should be enacted. The person must make any necessary lifestyle alterations, become dependent on others in some circumstances for the basic needs of daily life, and adapt to the demands of the physical condition as well as to treatment limitations and expectations. The environment of the patient is highly structured. The boundaries of the patient's world are determined by the providers of the health-care services, not by the patient. Herein lies the conflict.

Much has been written describing the environment of the hospital and the roles that people in such an institution play. As previously stated, the hospital is typically unfamiliar to the patient, who, nevertheless, is expected to conform to a predetermined set of rules and behaviors, many of which are unwritten and undefined for the patient—let alone *by* the patient.

Recovery. The final stage—recovery—is "generally characterized by the relinquishing of patient status and the assumption of pre-patient roles and activities."[30] There is often a change in the roles a person is able to play and the activities performed once recovery takes place. Often recovery is not complete. The person may be left with an undesirable or unexpected change in body image or in the ability to perform expected or routine everyday activities. One example might be that of a woman who enters the hospital with a small lump in her breast and who, after surgery, returns home with only one breast. Another example is that of a man who is a laborer entering the hospital with a backache and returning home after a laminectomy. When he returns to work, he cannot reassume his job as a loader. Obviously, an entire lifestyle must be altered to accommodate such newly imposed changes.

From the viewpoint of the provider, this person has recovered. Her or his body no longer has the symptoms of the acute illness that made surgical treatment necessary. In the eyes of the former patient, illness persists because of the inability to perform as in the past. So many changes have been wrought that it should come as no surprise if the person seems perplexed and uncooperative. Here, too, there is certainly conflict between society's expectations and the person's expectation. Society releases the person from the sick role at a time when, subjectively, the person may not be ready to relinquish it.

Table 2–1 is a tool designed for the assessment of the patient during the four stages of illness. Originally designed as a sociological measuring tool, the material has been altered here to meet the needs of the health-care provider in achieving a better understanding of patient behavior and expectations. If the provider is able to obtain answers from the patient to all of the questions raised in Table 2–1, understanding the patient's behavior and perspective and subsequent attempts to provide safe, effective care become easier.[31]

Another method of dividing the illness experience into stages was developed by the late Dr. Edward A. Suchman. He described the five components that follow.

The Symptom Experience Stage. The person is physically and cognitively aware that something is wrong and responds emotionally.[32]

The Assumption of the Sick Role Stage. The person seeks help and shares the problem with family and friends. After moving through the lay referral sys-

TABLE 2-1. A TOOL FOR THE ASSESSMENT OF THE PATIENT DURING THE FOUR STAGES OF ILLNESS

Onset	Diagnosis	Patient Status	Recovery
		A. The Meaning of the Illness	
1. What symptoms does this patient complain of?	1. Does he or she understand the diagnosis?	1. Has his or her perception of the illness changed?	1. What are signs of recovery?
2. How does he or she judge the extent and kind of disease?	2. How does he or she interpret the illness?	2. What are the changes in his or her life as a consequence of it?	2. Can he or she reassume prepatient role and functions?
3. How does this illness fit with his or her image of health? Himself, Herself?	3. How can he or she adapt to the illness?	3. What is his or her goal in recovery—the same level of health as before the illness, attainment of a maximal level of wellness, or perfect health?	3. Has his or her self-image been changed?
4. How does the disease threaten him or her?	4. How does he or she think others feel about it?	4. How does he or she relate to medical professionals?	4. How does he or she see present state of health—as more vulnerable or resistant?
5. Why does he or she seek medical help?		5. What are his or her social pressures leading to recovery?	
		6. What is motivating him or her to recover?	
		B. Behavior in Response to Illness	
1. How does he or she control anxiety?	1. What treatment agents were used?	1. How does he or she handle the patient role?	1. Are there any permanent aftereffects from this illness?
2. How are affective responses to concerns expressed?		2. How does he or she relate to the medical personnel?	2. How does he or she reassume old role?
3. Did he or she seek some form of health care before he or she sought medical care?			

From: Aiksen, L., Wellin, E., Suchman, E., et al. *A Conceptual Framework for the Analysis of Cultural Variations on the Behavior of the Ill.* Unpublished report. (New York City Department of Health, no date). Reprinted with permission.

tem, seeking advice, reassurance, and validation, the person is temporarily excused from such responsibilities as work, school, and other activities of daily living as the condition dictates.[33]

The Medical Care Contact Stage. The person then seeks out the "scientific" rather than the "lay" diagnosis, wanting to know: "Am I really sick?" "What is wrong with me?" "What does it mean?" At this point, the sick person needs some knowledge of the health-care system, what the system offers, and how it functions. This knowledge assists in selecting resources and in interpreting the information received.[34]

The Dependent-Patient Role Stage. The patient is now under the control of the physician and is expected to accept and comply with the prescribed treatments. The person may be quite ambivalent about this role, and certain factors (physical, administrative, social, or psychological) may create barriers that eventually will interfere with treatment and the willingness to comply.[35]

The Recovery or Rehabilitation Stage. The role of patient is given up at the recovery stage, and the person resumes—as much as possible—his or her former roles.[36]

The Illness Trajectory

Yet another way of explaining illness is to follow the trajectory of a given illness that a given person may experience. The term *trajectory* is applied to the following phases as they summarize the social science approaches that have been discussed to answer our second fundamental question: "What is illness?" and begin to shift our focus to the responses and experiences people have to and with illness. The focus now begins to move to the active role the patient plays in shaping and experiencing the course of a given illness.[37] For example, the person with an illness may experience the following trajectory: acute illness, comeback or recovery, stable status, unstable status, deterioration, and death. The acute phase most often is treated in the acute care hospital, and the early phases of comeback and rehabilitation occur in this setting. The management of the chronic phase, except for acute episodes, is performed at home or in an institution that is either a rehabilitation facility or a long-term care institution (Fig. 2–1). The illness profoundly affects the lives of the ill and their families—financially, emotionally, and spiritually. Further consideration of this phenomenon is found in Chapter 5.

Morbidity and Mortality

There are countless indicators of the prevalence of diseases in the general population. As one example, the data presented in Table 2–2 illustrates the changes in age-adjusted death rates from 1970 to 1990 per 100,000 resident population.

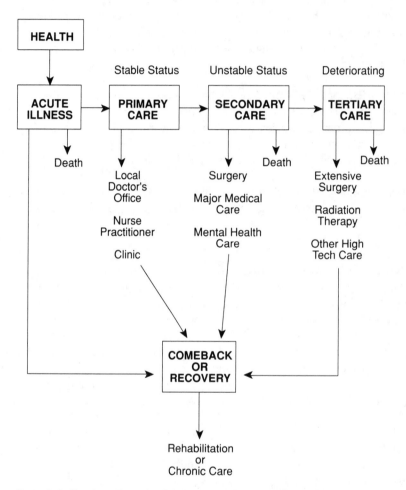

Figure 2–1. The Illness Trajectory. This figure depicts the illness trajectory described in the text and the sources of health care for the various health problems.

TABLE 2–2. AGE-ADJUSTED DEATHS FROM SELECTED CAUSES OF DEATH: UNITED STATES, 1970–1990 PER 100,000 RESIDENT POPULATION

Cause of death	1970	1980	1990
All causes	714.3	585.8	520.2
1. Diseases of the heart	253.6	202.0	152.0
2. Malignant neoplasms	129.8	132.8	135.0
3. Cerebrovascular diseases	66.3	40.8	27.7
4. Chronic obstructive pulmonary diseases	123.3	15.9	19.7
5. Motor vehicle accidents	27.4	22.9	18.5
6. Pneumonia and influenza	22.1	12.9	14.0
7. Diabetes mellitus	14.1	10.1	11.7
8. Human immunodeficiency virus infection	—	—	9.8
9. Suicide	11.8	11.4	11.5
10. Homicide	9.1	10.8	10.2

From: National Center for Health Statistics. *Health United States, 1992* and *Healthy People 2000 Review.* DHHS Pub. No. (PHS)93–1232 Hyattsville, MD: Public Health Service, (1993), p. 45. Reprinted with permission.

In summary, this section has introduced the reader to the concept of illness, as explored from the pure act of definition and then broadened through the sociological aspects of roles and behaviors. The writings of a number of sociologists have been examined in terms of applicability to nursing practice, observation, and experience. Material related to mortality has been included to further illustrate the phenomenon of illness.

REFERENCES

1. *American Heritage Dictionary of the English Language,* s.v. "health."
2. Murray, R. and Zentner, J. *Nursing Concepts for Health Promotion* (Englewood Cliffs, NJ: Prentice-Hall, 1975), p. 6.
3. Discussion of article by Rosenstock, I. M. "Why People Use Health Services." *Millbank Memorial Fund Quarterly* 44(3) (July 1966): 94–127.
4. Hilleboe, H. E. "Preventing Future Shock: Health Developments in the 1960's and Imperative for the 1970's; The Eleventh Brontman Lecture." *American Journal of Public Health* (Feb 1972): 139.

5. Russell, R. D. "Teaching for Meaning in Health Education: The Concept Approach." *Journal of School Health* 71 (Jan 1966): 13–14.
6. Harmon, F. L. *Principles of Psychology* (Milwaukee: Bruce Publishing Co., 1938), p. 14; Dember, W.N. *The Psychology of Perception* (New York: Holt, 1960), pp. 3–4.
7. Schneiders, A. A. *Introductory Psychology* (New York: Rinehart, 1960), p. 185.
8. Knutson, A. *The Individual, Society, and Health Behavior* (New York: Russell Sage Foundation, 1965), p. 159.
9. Cohen, R. "Principles of Preventive Mental Health Programs for Ethnic Minority Populations." *American Journal of Psychiatry* 128(12) (June 1972): 79–83.
10. Stark, R. "The Case Against Regular Physicals." *New York Times Magazine* (25 July 1976), p. 10.
11. Yohalen, S. B. *New York Times Magazine* (15 August 1976), p. 58.
12. Spector, M., and Spector, R. "Is Prevention Myth or Reality?" *Health Education* 8(4) (July-Aug 1977): 23–25.
13. Ibid.
14. Freymann, J. G. "Medicine's Great Schism: Prevention vs. Cure." *Medical Care* 13(7) (July 1975): 533.
15. National Center for Health Statistics, Thornberry, O. T., Wilson, R. W., and Golden, P. M. "Health Promotion Data for the 1990s: Objectives, Estimates from the National Health Interview Survey of Health Promotion and Disease Prevention, United States, 1985." *Advanced Data from Vital and Health Statistics.* No. 126. DHHS Pub. No. (PHS)86–1250. (Hyattsville, MD: Public Health Service, Sept 19, 1986) p. 2.
16. National Center for Health Statistics (1993) *Health United States, 1992* and *Healthy People 2000 Review.* DHHS Pub. No. (PHS) 93–1232 (Hyattsville, MD: Public Health Service), p. 45.
17. Ibid., pp. 249–362.
18. *American Heritage Dictionary of the English Language,* s.v. "illness."
19. Mechanic, D. *Medical Sociology* (New York: Free Press of Glencoe, 1968), p. 80.
20. Popenoe, D. *Sociology* (New York: Appleton, 1974), p. 681.
21. Parsons, T. "Illness and the Role of the Physician: A Sociological Perspective," in *Medical Care: Readings in the Sociology of Medical Institutions,* eds. Scott, W. R. and Volkart, E. H. (New York: Wiley, 1966), p. 275.
22. Ibid.
23. Ibid.
24. Ibid.
25. Ibid., p. 276.
26. Alksen, L., et al. *A Conceptual Framework for the Analysis of Cultural Variations in the Behavior of the Ill* (unpublished report) (New York City Department of Health; no date), p. 2.
27. Ibid., p. 3.
28. Ibid.
29. Ibid.
30. Ibid.
31. Ibid.
32. Suchman, E. A. "Stages of Illness and Medical Care." *Journal of Health and Human Behavior.* 6(3) (Fall 1965): 114.
33. Ibid., p. 115.

34. Ibid.
35. Ibid.
36. Ibid., p. 116.
37. Strauss, A. and Corbin, J. M. *Shaping of a New Health Care System* (San Francisco: Josey-Bass; 1988), pp. 5–6.

ANNOTATED BIBLIOGRAPHY

Apple, D., ed. *Sociological Studies of Health and Sickness: A Source Book for the Health Professions.* New York: McGraw-Hill, 1960.
   This anthology covers such areas as the recognition of the need for health care, the patient's viewpoint, psychosocial process in illness, and the organization of hospitals. The essays address such broad questions as "Should I have a checkup?" "What occurs when patient and physician misunderstand each other?" "What are the psychosocial determinants of illness?" and "What is the social organization of hospitals?"

Bakan, D. *Disease, Pain and Sacrifice: Toward a Psychology of Suffering.* Chicago: University of Chicago Press, 1968.
   Bakan explores the conviction that amelioration of suffering through understanding is the superior option. He describes the aspects of suffering from biological, psychological, and existential standpoints. Very highly recommended.

Becker, M. H. *The Health Belief Model and Personal Health Behavior.* Thorofare, NJ: B. Slack, 1974.
   This monograph traces the history of the health belief model and its various uses in explaining and understanding health behavior in both health and illness.

Dubos, R. J. *Man Adapting.* New Haven, CT: Yale University Press, 1965.

Dubos, R. J. *Man, Medicine and Environment.* New York: Praeger, 1968.

Dubos, R. J. *Mirage of Health.* Garden City, NY: Doubleday, Anchor Books, 1961.
   In these three books, Dubos analyzes various aspects of human beings and their relationship to the environment. He does not explore wonder drugs but rather the wonders of life.

Freeman, H., Levine, S., and Reeder, L. G., eds. *Handbook of Medical Sociology,* 2nd ed. Englewood Cliffs, NJ: Prentice-Hall, 1972.
   This handbook helps to bridge the knowledge gap that exists between the biological and social sciences. It explores such areas as the sociology of illness, practitioners, patients, and medical settings, the sociology of medical care, and the strategy, method, and status of medical sociology.

Herzlich, C. *Health and Illness: A Social Psychological Analysis.* Translated by D. Graham. New York. Academic Press, 1973.
   Herzlich reports findings based on a study conducted in France in the 1960s: an exploration of people's attitudes toward health and illness. It investigates topics such as the individual, the way of life, and the genesis of illness, nature, constraint, and society, mechanisms and dosage, health and illness, the dimensions and limits of illness, the sick and the healthy, and health and illness behavior.

Jackson, R. C., and Morton, J. *Family Health Care: Health Promotion and Illness Care.* Based on the proceedings of the 1975 Annual Institute for Public Health Social Workers, University of California, Berkeley.

In this work, attention is given to the broad topics of perspectives of health services to the family, strategies for the promotion of health and family functioning, and family-focused care for the ill.

Jaco, E. G., ed. *Patients, Physicians, and Illness: Sourcebook in Behavioral Science and Medicine*. Glencoe, IL: Free Press, 1958.

This anthology is a sourcebook in behavioral science and medicine. It covers a wide range of topics, including social and personal components of illness and health, community and sociocultural aspects of medical care and treatment, and the patient. Authors include L. Saunders, T. Parsons, and M. Zborowski.

Kiev, A., ed. *Magic, Faith and Healing: Studies in Primitive Psychiatry Today*. New York: Free Press of Glencoe, 1964.

Another anthology, Kiev's book explores the wide number of abnormal states of mood, thought, and behavior and the multitude of folkways that are employed throughout the world to treat disorders.

Knutson, A. L. *The Individual, Society and Health Behavior*. New York: Russell Sage Foundation, 1965.

Herein human beings are dealt with as members of society; emphasis is placed on those aspects of their behavior that are of concern to public health. The study covers a broad range of topics, including the general characteristics of humankind, men and women in their social environment, values, attitudes, and beliefs, and the communication process.

Leff, S., and Leff, V. *From Witchcraft to World Health*. New York: Macmillan, 1957.

Leff and Leff report on a battle that is fought to save lives. The book relates the history of public health from the medicine man to WHO. It covers such topics as primitive humans and Egyptian, Greek, and Roman medicine and follows the development of public health through the first half of the twentieth century.

Lynch, L. R., ed. *The Cross-Cultural Approach to Health Behavior*. Rutherford, NJ: Fairleigh Dickenson University Press, 1969.

This book explores the interrelationships between sociocultural background and health behavior. The articles that are included investigate the values and beliefs about health of many people through the United States and the world.

Mechanic, D. *Medical Sociology: A Selective View*. New York: Free Press of Glencoe, 1968.

Three major sections comprise this book. The first section substantively develops a view of illness as part of the larger social interest and deviant behavior. The second explores such issues as the factors that affect mortality and morbidity. The third analyzes the various organizational contexts of practitioner-patient interactions.

Opler, M. K., ed. *Culture and Mental Health*. New York: Macmillan, 1959.

This anthology on social psychiatry demonstrates ways in which cultural patterns affect mental health in a worldwide perspective. Opler includes papers from every continent where work has been done.

Paul, B., ed. *Health, Culture, and Community: Case Studies of Public Reactions to Health Programs*. New York: Russell Sage Foundation, 1955.

Numerous case studies of public reactions to health programs are reported in this anthology. The cases demonstrate to health workers the kind of working relationship that ought to exist between the providers of health care and social scientists.

Pearsall, M. *Medical Behavioral Science: A Selected Bibliography of Cultural Anthropology, Social Psychology, and Sociology in Medicine*. Louisville: University of Kentucky Press, 1963.

An outstanding bibliography of books published through 1962 that relate to health-care practices by means of cultural anthropology, social psychology, and sociology.

Popenoe, C. *Wellness.* Washington, DC: YES! Inc., 1977.

This book is an annotated bibliography that contains numerous books relevant to health. A sample of topics that are presented includes anatomy and physiology, body work, cooking, healing, and use of herbs. Good reference.

FURTHER SUGGESTED READINGS

Articles

Becker, M. H., et al. "A New Approach to Explaining Sick Role Behavior in Low-Income Populations." *American Journal of Public Health* 64 (1974): 205–216.

Boyce, T., and Michael, M. "Nine Assumptions of Western Medicine." *Man and Medicine* 1 (Summer 1976): 311–335.

Brody, H. "The Systems View of Man: Implications for Medicine, Science and Ethics." *Perspectives in Biology and Medicine* 17 (1973): 71–92.

Cass, R. "Holistic Health: Sorting the Good from the Bad." *Journal of Christian Nursing* 3(3)(Summer 1986): 3.

Cohen, R. "Principles of Preventive Mental Health Programs for Ethnic Minority Populations." *American Journal of Psychiatry* 128 (12) (June 1972): 79–83.

Dubos, R. "The Diseases of Civilization: Achievements and Illusions." in *Mainstreams of Medicine: Essays on the Social and Intellectual Context of Medical Practice,* ed. King, L. Austin: University of Texas Press, 1971.

Engel, G. L. "The Need for a New Medical Model: A Challenge for Biomedicine." *Science* 196 (8 April 1977): 129–136.

Freyman, J. G. "Medicine's Great Schism: Prevention vs. Cure." *Medical Care* 12(7)(July 1975): 533.

Glazier, W. H. "The Task of Medicine." *Scientific American* 228 (April 1973): 13–17.

Hartog, J., and Hartog, E. A. "Cultural Aspects of Health and Illness Behavior in Hospitals." *Western Journal of Medicine.* 139(6) (December 1983): 910–916.

Hayes-Bautista, D., and Harveston, D. S. "Holistic Health Care." *Social Policy* 7 (March/April 1977): 7–13.

Hilleboe, H. E. "Preventing Future Shock: Health Developments in the 1960's and Imperative for the 1970's; The Eleventh Brontman Lecture" *American Journal of Public Health* (February 1972): 139.

Mategaonkar, D. W. "Health for All by AD 2000. Our Role—Wholistic Approach." *Christian Nurse* (313) (April 1984): 4–10.

Mull, C. S., Cox, C. L., and Sullivan, J. S. "Religion's Role in the Health and Well-being of Elders." *Public Health Nursing* 4(3) (Sept 1987): 151–159.

Murphy, E. K. "Court Actions Regarding Refusal of Blood Products." *AORN Journal* 49(3) (March 1989): 874, 876, 878–879.

National Center for Health Statistics, Thornberry, O. T., Wilson, R. W., and Golden, P. M. Health promotion data for the 1990 objectives, estimates from the National Health Interview Survey of Health Promotion and Disease Prevention, United States, 1985. *Advance Data from Vital and Health Statistics.* No. 126. DHHS Pub. No. (PHS)86–1250. Hyattsville, MD: Public Health Service, September 19, 1986.

Parsons, T. "Illness and the Role of the Physician: A Sociological Perspective," in *Medical Care: Readings in the Sociology of Medical Institutions,* ed. Scott, W. R. and Volkort, E. H. New York: Wiley, 1966.

Redker, N. S. "Health Beliefs, Health Locus of Control, and the Frequency of Practice of Breast Self-Examination in Women." *Journal of Obstetric, Gynecologic, and Neonatal Nursing* 18(1) (January-February 1989): 45–51.

Rosenstock, I. M. "Why People Use Health Services." *Millbank Memorial Fund Quarterly* 44(3)(July 1966): 94–127.

Russell, R. D. "Teaching for Meaning in Health Education: The Concept Approach." *Journal of School Health* 71 (January 1966): 13–14.

Sheldon, A. "Toward a General Theory of Disease and Medical Care." in *Systems and Medical Care,* eds. Sheldon, A., Baker, F. and McLaughlin, C. P. Cambridge, MA: MIT Press, 1970.

Spart, R. "The Case Against Regular Physicals." *New York Times Magazine* (25 July 1976): 10, 11, 38–41.

Spector, M., and Spector, R. E. "Is Prevention Myth or Reality?" *Health Education* 8 (4)(July-August 1977): 23–25.

Suchman, E. A. "Stages of Illness and Medical Care." *Journal of Health and Human Behavior* 6 (Fall 1965): 114–28.

Wiggins, L. R. "Health and Illness Beliefs and Practices among the Old Order Amish." *Health Values: Achieving High Level Wellness* 7(6) (November-December 1983): 24–29.

Wilson, M. C., Redican, K. J., and Gaines, J. "Cults: Potential Dangers to High Level Wellness." *Health Values: Achieving High Level Wellness* 7(6) (November-December 1983): 4–9.

Chapter

Familial Folk Remedies

As modern medicine becomes more impersonal, people are recalling with some wistfulness old country cures administered by parents and grandparents over the generations.[1]

　　　　　　—F. Kennet, Folk Medicine—Fact and Fiction

Given the difficulty of defining health and illness, it can be assumed that you may have little or no working knowledge of personally practiced "folk medicine" within your own family. In addition to exploring the already described questions regarding the definitions of health and illness, it is beneficial to your understanding to describe how you treat minor illnesses and how you protect your health or prevent illness. A common form of self-medication and treatment is the use of aspirin for headaches and colds or occasional diet supplements with vitamins. Initially, one may admit to using tea, honey, and lemon and hot or cold compresses for headaches and minor aches and pains. For the most part, however, we tend to look to the health-care system for the treatment of minor illness.

Folk medicine is related to other types of medicine that are practiced in our society. It has coexisted, with increasing tensions, along side modern medicine and was derived from academic medicine of earlier generations. There is ample evidence that the folk practices of ancient times have only in part been abandoned by modern health-care belief systems, for many of these beliefs and practices continue to be observed today. Today's popular medicine is, in a sense, commercial folk medicine. There are two varieties of folk medicine.

1. Natural folk medicine—or rational folk medicine—represents one of a human's earliest uses of the natural environment and

uses herbs, plants, minerals, and animal substances to prevent and treat illnesses.
2. Magicoreligious folk medicine—or occult folk medicine—represents the use of charms, holy words, and holy actions to prevent and cure illnesses.[2]

NATURAL FOLK MEDICINE

This form of folk medicine has been and is widely practiced in the United States and throughout the world. In general, this form of prevention and treatment is found in old-fashioned remedies and household medicines. These remedies have been passed down for generations, and many are in common use today. Much folk medicine is herbal in nature, and the customs and rituals related to the use of these herbs varies among ethnic groups. Specific knowledge and usages are addressed throughout this text. Commonly, across cultures these herbs are found in nature and are used by humans as a source of therapy. How these medicines are gathered and specific modes of use may vary from group to group and place to place. In general, folk medical traditions prescribed the time of year in which the herb was to be picked; how it was to be dried; how it was to be prepared; the method, amount, and frequency of taking, and so forth.[3] Chapter 6 explores this system in more detail.

Magicoreligious Folk Medicine

This form of folk medicine, too, has existed for as long as humans have sought to protect and restore their health. It has now come to be labeled by some as "superstition," yet for believers, it may take the form of religious practices related to health protection and healing. Chapter 7 addresses this belief system in more detail. One example of this is a form of unofficial religious healing that is not connected to churches, known as "powwowing," "charming," or "conjuring." In these practices, charms, amulets, and physical manipulations are used in the attempt to cure an illness.[4]

Were you ever ill? What did your mother or grandmother do to take care of you? Who did they seek advice from first? Did they consult someone in your own ethnic or religious community to find out what was wrong? What remedies did they use? Do you know the health and illness beliefs and practices that were or are a part of your heritage? In an attempt to bring to your consciousness the overall history and health belief-related folklore* knowledge of your family, the following procedure is useful.

Since the folk history of each family is unique, you may want to discover more than health beliefs and practices with this interview. Ask questions

---

Folklore: the body of skills and knowledge passed on from one person to another for specific reasons.

about your family surname, traditional first names, family stories, the history of family "characters" or notorious family members, how historical events affected your family in past generations, and so forth. Then, in interviewing your maternal[†] grandmother or greataunt and your mother, obtain answers to the following questions.

1. What is the family's ethnic background?
   Country of origin?
   Religion?
2. What did *they* do to maintain health?
   What did *their mothers* do?
3. What did *they* do to protect health?
   What did *their mothers* do?
4. What home remedies did *they* use to restore health?
   What did *their mothers* use?

There are two reasons for exploring your familial past. First, it draws your attention to your ethnic heritage and belief system. Many of your daily habits relate to early socialization practices that are passed on by parents or additional significant others. Many behaviors are both unconscious and habitual, and much of what you believe and practice is passed on in this manner. By digging into the past, remote and recent, you can recall some of the rituals you observed either your parents or grandparents perform. You are then better able to realize their origin and significance. There are many beliefs and practices that are ethnically similar. Socialization patterns also tend to be similar among ethnic groups. Religion also plays a role in the perception of, interpretation of, and behavior in health and illness.

The maternal side is selected for the interview because in today's society of interethnic and interreligious marriages, it is assumed that the ethnic beliefs and practices related to health and illness of the family are more in tune with the mother's family than with the father's. By and large, nurturance has been the domain of women in most cultures and societies. The mother tends to be the person within a family who cares for family members when illness occurs. She also tends to be the prime mover in preventing illness and seeking health care. It is the mother who tells the child what and how much to eat and drink, when to go to bed, and how to dress in inclement weather. She shares her knowledge and experience with her offspring, but usually the daughter is singled out for such experiential sharing.

A second reason for this examination of familial health practices is to sensitize you to the role your ethnic heritage has played. You must reanalyze the concepts of health and illness and, once again, view your own definitions from another perspective. If the familial background is presented in a class setting, the peer group is able to see these people in a different light. A group observes similarities and differences among its members. You discover

---

[†]An explanation for this choice follows in the text.

peer beliefs and practices that you originally had no idea existed. You may then be able to identify the "why" behind many daily health habits, practices, and beliefs.

Quite often, you may be amazed to discover the origins of these health practices. Reflecting on their origin may help to explain the "mysterious" behavior of a roommate or friend. It is interesting to discover cross-ethnic practices within one's own group. Some people have believed that a given practice was an "original," practiced only by their family. Many religious customs, such as the blessing of the throat, are now conceptualized in terms of health and illness behavior. Table 3-1 lists a sample of responses to the questions that students obtained from members of the maternal side of their families.

CONSCIOUSNESS RAISING

Recognizing Similarities

In my experience, as the group discussion continues, people realize that many personal beliefs and practices do in fact differ from what they are being taught in nursing or medical education to accept as the right way of doing things. Participants begin to admit that they do not seek medical care when the first symptoms of illness appear. On the contrary, they usually delay seeking care and often elect to self-treat at home. They also recognize that there are many preventive and health-maintenance acts learned in school they choose not to comply with. Sometimes they discover they are following an entire self-imposed regiment for health-related problems and are not seeking any outside intervention.

Another facet of a group discussion is the participants' exposure to the similarities that exist among them in terms of protection and health maintenance. To their surprise and delight, they find that many of their daily acts, routines that are taken for granted, directly relate to methods of maintaining and protecting health.

As is common in most large groups, students seem to be shy at the beginning of this exploration. As more and more members of the group are willing to share their experiences, however, other students feel more comfortable and share more readily. A classroom tactic I have used to break the ice is to reveal an experience I had on the birth of my first child. My mother-in-law, an immigrant from Eastern Europe, drew a circle around the child's crib with her fingers and spat on the baby three times to prevent the evil spirits from harming him. Once such an anecdote is shared, other participants have less difficulty in remembering similar events that may have taken place in their own homes.

Students have a variety of feelings about the self-care practices of their families. One feeling discussed by many students is *shame*. A number of students express conflict in their attitudes: they cannot decide whether to believe these old ways or to drop them and adopt the more modern ones they are learning in school. (This is an example of cognitive dissonance.) Many admit that this is the first time they have disclosed these beliefs and practices in public, and they are relieved and amazed to discover similarities with other students. The acts may have different names or be performed in a slightly different manner, but the uniting thread among them is to prevent evil (illness) and to maintain good (health).

Transference to Clients

The effects of such a verbal catharsis are long remembered and often quoted or referred to throughout the remainder of a course. The awareness we gain helps us to understand the behavior and beliefs of our patients better. Given this understanding, we are comfortable enough to ask patients how they interpret a symptom and how they think it ought to be treated. We begin to be more sensitive to people who delay in seeking health care or fail to comply with preventive measures and treatment regimens. We come to recognize that we do the same thing. I believe that the increased familiarity with home health practices and remedies helps us to project this awareness—and understanding—to the clients who are served.

Analyzed from a "scientific" perspective, the majority of these practices do have a sound basis. In the area of health maintenance (see Table 3–1), one notes an almost universal adherence to activities that include rest, balanced diet, and exercise.

In the area of protection various differences arise, ranging from visiting a physician to wearing a clove of garlic around the neck. Although the purpose of wearing garlic around the neck is "to keep the evil spirit away," the act also forces people to stay away: what better way to cut down exposure to wintertime colds than to avoid close contact with people?

One person remembered that during her childhood her mother forced her to wear garlic around her neck. Like most children, she did not like to be different from the rest of her schoolmates. As time went on, she began to have frequent colds, and her mother could not understand why this was happening. The mother followed her child to school some weeks later and discovered that she removed the garlic on her way to school—hiding it under a rock and then replacing it on the way home. There was quite a battle between the mother and daughter! The youngster did not like this method of protection because her peers mocked her.

A discussion of home remedies is of further interest when each of the methods presented is analyzed for its possible "medical" analogy and also for its prevalence among ethnic groups. Many of these practices and remedies, to the surprise and relief of students, tend to run throughout ethnic groups but have different names or contain different ingredients.

In this day of computers and sophisticated medicine, including transplants and intricate surgery, the most prevalent need expressed by people who practice folk medicine is to remove the "evil" that may be the cause of

TABLE 3–1. FAMILY HEALTH HISTORIES OBTAINED FROM STUDENTS OF VARIOUS ETHNIC BACKGROUNDS AND RELIGIONS

Austrian (United States), Jewish

Health Maintenance
Eat wholesome foods, homegrown fruits and vegetables
Bake own bread

Health Protection
Camphor around the neck (in the winter) in a small cloth bag to prevent measles and scarlet fever

Health Restoration
Sore throat: Go to the village store, find a salted herring, wrap it in a towel, put it around the neck, and let it stay there overnight; gargle with salt water
Boils: Fry chopped onions, make a compress, and apply to the infections

Black and Native American, Baptist

Health Maintenance
Eat balanced meals three times a day
Dress right for the weather

Health Protection
Keep everything clean and sterile
Stay away from people who are sick
Regular check-ups
Blackstrap molasses

Health Restoration
Bloody nose: Place keys on a chain around neck to stop
Sore throat: Suck yolks out of eggshell; honey and lemon; baking soda, salt, warm water, onions around the neck; salt water to gargle

Black African (Ethiopia), Orthodox Christian

Health Maintenance
Keep the area clean
Pray every morning when getting up from bed

Health Protection
Eat hot food, such as pepper, fresh garlic, lemon

Health Restoration
Eat hot and sour foods, such as lemons, fresh garlic, hot mustard, red pepper
Make a kind of medicine from leaves and roots of plants mixed together
Colds: Hot boiled milk with honey
Evil eye: They put some kind of plant root on fire and make the man who has the evil eye smile and the man talks about his illness

Canadian, Catholic

Health Maintenance
Cleanliness
Food: People should eat well (fat people used to be considered healthy)
Prayer: Health was always mentioned in prayer
Health Protection
Sleep
Lots of good food
Elixirs containing herbs and brewed, given as a vitamin tonic
Wear camphor around the neck to ward off any evil spirit; use Father John's medicine November to May

50

TABLE 3–1.—Continued

Canadian, Catholic—Continued

Health Restoration
Kidney problems: Herbal teas
Colds: Hot lemons
Infected wounds: Raw onions placed on wounds
Cough: Shot of whiskey
Sinuses: Camphor placed in a pouch and pinned to the shirt
Fever: Lots of blankets and heat make you sweat out a fever
Headache: Lie down and rest in complete darkness
Aches and pains: Hot Epsom salt baths
Eye infections: Potatoes are rubbed on them or a gold wedding ring is placed on them and the sign of the cross is made three times

Eastern Europe (United States), Jewish

Health Maintenance
Go to doctor when sick (mother)
Health care for others, not self (mother)
Reluctantly sought medical help (grandmother)
Health for self not a priority (grandmother)
Physician twice a year (mother)
Doctor only when pregnant (grandmother)

Health Protection
Observe precautions, such as dressing warmly, not going out with wet hair, getting enough rest, staying in bed if not feeling well (mother)
Not much to prevent illness—very ill today with chronic diseases (grandmother)
Vitamins and water pills

Heath Restoration
Colds: Fluids, aspirin, rest
Stomach upset: Eat light and bland foods
Muscle aches: Massage with alcohol
Sore throat: Gargle with salt water, tea with lemon and honey
Insomnia: Glass of wine
Chicken soup used by mother and grandmother

English, Baptist

Health Maintenance
Eat well; daily walks; read; keep warm

Health Restoration
Earache: Honey and tea, warm cod-liver oil in ear; stay in bed
Cold: Heat glass and put on back

English, Catholic

Health Maintenance
Lots of exercise; proper sleep; lots of walking; no drinking or smoking; hard work
Bedroom window open at night
Take baths
Never wear dirty clothing
Good housekeeping
Immediate clean-up after meals; wash pan before meals
Rest

TABLE 3–1.—Continued

English, Catholic—Continued

Health Protection
Maintain a good diet; fresh vegetables; vitamins; little meat; lots of fish; no fried foods; lots of sleep
Strict enforcement of lifestyle
Keep kitchen at 90°F in winter and house will be warm

Health Restoration
Cuts: Wet tobacco
Colds: Chicken soup; herb tea made from roots; alcohol concoctions; Vicks and hot towels on chest; lots of fluids, rest; Vicks, sulfur and molasses
Sore throat: Four onions and sugar steeped to heal and soothe the throat
Rashes: Burned linen and cornstarch

English, Episcopal

Health Maintenance
Thorough diet, vitamins
Enough sleep
Cod-liver oil

Health Restoration
Colds and sore throats: Camphor on chest and red scarves around chest

French (France), Catholic

Health Maintenance
Proper food; rest; proper clothing; cod-liver oil daily

Health Protection
Every spring give sulfur and molasses for 3 days as a laxative to get rid of worms

Health Restoration
Colds: Rub chest with Vicks; honey

French Canadian, Catholic

Health Maintenance
Wear rubbers in the rain and dress warmly; take part in sports; active body; lots of sleep

Health Protection
Sulfur and molasses in spring to clear the system
Cod-liver oil in orange juice
No "junk foods"; play outside; walk; daily use of Geritol; camphor on clothes; balanced meals

Health Restoration
Colds: Brandy with warm milk; honey and lemon juice; hot poultice on the chest; tea, whiskey, and lemon
Back pain: Mustard packs
Rashes: Oatmeal baths
Sore throat: Wrap raw potatoes in sack and tie around neck; soap and water enemas
Warts: Rub potato on wart, run outside and throw it over left shoulder

German (United States), Catholic

Health Maintenance
Wear rubbers; never go barefoot; long underwear and stockings
Wash before meals; change clothes often
Take shots
Take aspirin
Good diet

TABLE 3–1.—Continued

German (United States), Catholic—Continued

Health Protection
No sweets at meals
Drink glass of water at meals
Cod-liver oil
Plenty of milk
Exercise
Spring tonic; sulfured molasses

Health Restoration
Coughs: Honey and vinegar
Earache: Few drops of warm milk in the ear; laxatives when needed
Swollen glands or mumps: Put pepper on salt pork and tie around the neck
Constipation: Ivory soap suppositories
Sore throat: Saltwater gargle
Sore back: Hot mustard plaster
Stye: Cold tealeaf compress
Cramps: Ginger tea
Coughs: Honey and lemon; hot water and Vicks; boiled onion water, honey and lemon
Fever: Mix whiskey, water, and lemon juice and drink before bed; causes person to perspire and
    break fever
Headache: Boil a beef bone and break up toast in the broth and drink
Recovery diet: Boil milk and shredded wheat and add a dropped egg—first thing eaten after an illness

Iran (United States), Islam

Health Maintenance
Cleanliness
Diet

Health Protection
Dress properly for the season and weather; keep feet from getting wet in the rain
Inoculations
Health Restoration
Sore throat: Gargle with vinegar and water
Cough: Honey and lemon
Indigestion: Baking soda and water
Sore muscles: Alcohol and water
Rashes: Apply corn starch

Irish (United States), Catholic

Health Maintenance
Good food, balanced diet
Vitamins
Blessing of the throat
Wear holy medals, green scapular
Dress warmly
Plenty of rest
Avoid "fast foods"
Attitudes were important: "Good living habits and good thinking": "Eat breakfast—if late for school, eat a
    good breakfast and be a little later"; "Don't be afraid to spend on groceries—you won't spend on the
    doctor later."
Keep clean

TABLE 3–1.—Continued

Irish (United States), Catholic—Continued

Keep feet warm and dry
Outdoor exercise, enjoy fresh air and sunshine
Brush teeth; if out of toothpaste use table salt, or Ivory soap, or Dr. Lyon's Tooth Powder
Be clean, wear clean clothes
Early to bed ("Rest is the best medicine.")

Health Protection
Clean out bowels with senna for 8 days
Every spring, drink a mixture of sulfur and molasses to clean blood
Avoid sick people
Onions under the bed to keep nasal passages clear
During flu season, tie a bag of camphor around the neck
Never go to bed with wet hair
Eat lots of oily foods
Take Father John's Medicine every so often
Prevent evil spirits: Don't look in mirror at night and close closet doors
Drink senna tea at every vacation; cleans out the system
Maintain a strong family with lots of love
Be goal-oriented
Nurture a strong religious faith

Health Restoration
See doctor only in emergency
Fever: Spirits of niter on a dry sugar cube or mix with water; cold baths; alcohol rubdowns
Earache: Heat salt, put in stocking behind the ear
Colds: Tea and toast; chest rub; vaporizer; hot lemonade and a tablespoon of whiskey; mustard plasters; Vicks on chest; whiskey; Vicks in nostrils; hot milk with butter, soups, honey, hot toddies, lemon juice and egg whites; ipecac ("cruel but good medicine"); whiskey with hot water and sugar; soak feet in hot water and sip hot lemonade
Coughs: Cough syrup (available on stove all winter) made from honey and whiskey; Vicks on chest; mustard plaster on chest; onion-syrup cough medicine; steam treatment; swallow Vicks; linseed poultice on chest; flaxseed poultice on back, red flannel cloth soaked in hot water and placed on chest all night
Menstrual cramps: Hot milk sprinkled with ginger; shot of whiskey, glass of warm wine; warm teas; hot-water bottle on stomach
Splinters: Flaxseed poultice
Sunburn: Apply vinegar; put milk on cloth and apply to burn; a cold, wet tea bag on small areas such as eyelids
Nausea and other stomach ailments: Hot teas; caster oil; hot ginger ale; bay leaf; cup of hot boiled water; potato for upset stomach; baking soda; gruel
Sore throat: Paint throat with iodine, honey and lemon, Karo syrup; paint with kerosene oil internally with a rag and then tie a sock around the neck; paint with iodine or Mercurochrome and gargle with salt and water, honey, melted Vicks
Insect bites: Vaseline or boric acid
Boils: Oatmeal poultice
Cuts: Boric acid
Headaches: Hot poultice on forehead; hot facecloth; cold, damp cloth to forehead; in general, stay in bed, get plenty of rest and sleep, a glass of juice about once an hour, aspirin, and lots of food to get back strength
Stye: Hot tea bag to area

TABLE 3–1.—Continued

Italian (United States), Catholic

Health Maintenance

Hearty and varied nutritional intake; lots of fruit, pasta, wine (even for children), cheese, home-grown vegetables, and salads; exercise in form of physical labor; molasses on a piece of bread or oil and sugar on bread; hard bread (good for the teeth)

Pregnancy: Two weeks early: girl

Two weeks late: boy

Heartburn: baby with lots of hair

Eat (solved emotional and physical problems); fruit at end of meal cleans teeth; early to bed and early to rise

Health Protection

Garlic cloves strung on a piece of string around the neck of infants and children to prevent colds and "evil" stares from other people, which they believed could cause headaches and a pain or stiffness in the back or neck (a piece of red ribbon or cloth on an infant served the same purpose)

Keep warm in cold weather

Keep feet warm

Eat properly

Never wash hair or bathe during period

Never wash hair before going outdoors or at night

Stay out of drafts

To prevent "evil" in the newborn, a scissor was kept open under the mattress of the crib

To prevent bowlegs and keep ankles straight, up to the age of 6 to 8 months a bandage was wrapped around the baby from the waist to the feet

If infants got their nights and days mixed up, they were tied upside down and turned all the way around

Health Restoration

Chicken soup for everything from colds to having a baby

Boils: Cooked oatmeal wrapped in a cloth (steaming hot) applied to drain pus

Headache: Fill a soup bowl with cold water and put some olive oil in a large spoon; hold the spoon over the bowl in front of the person with the headache; while doing this, recite words in Italian and place index finger in the oil in the spoon; drop three drops of oil from the finger into the bowl; by the diameter of the circle the oil makes when it spreads in the water the severity of the headache can be determined (larger = more severe); after this is done three times the headache is gone

Kerchief with ice in it is wrapped around the head; mint tea

Upset stomach: Herb tea made with herbs sent from Italy

Sore throat: Honey; apply Vicks on throat at bedtime and wrap up the throat

Sprains: Beat eggs whites, apply to part, wrap part

Fever: Cover with blankets to sweat it out

Cramps: Creme de menthe

Poison ivy: Yellow soap suds

Colic: Warm oil on stomach

Acne: Apply baby's urine

Sucking thumb: Apply hot pepper to thumb

High blood pressure: In Italy for high blood pressure, colonies of blood suckers were kept in clay, where they were born; the person with high blood pressure would have a blood sucker put on his fanny, where it would suck blood; it was thought that this would lower his blood pressure; the blood suckers would then be thrown in ashes and would then throw up the blood they had sucked from the person. If the blood sucker died, it alerted the person to see a doctor because it sometimes meant that there was something wrong with the person's blood

Stomachache: Camilla and maloa (herbs) added to boiled water

Colds: Boiled wines; coffee with anisette

TABLE 3–1.—Continued

Pimples: To draw contents, apply hot flaxseed
Toothache: Whiskey applied topically
Backache: Apply hot oatmeal in a sock; place a silver dollar on the sore area, light a match to it, while the match is burning put a glass over the silver dollar and then slightly lift the glass, and this causes a suction, which is said to lift the pain out
To build up blood: Eggnog with brandy; marsala wine and milk
Muscle pain: Heat up carbon leaves (herb) and bundle in a hot cloth to make a pack (soothes any discomfort)

Norwegian (Norway), Lutheran

Health Maintenance
Cod-liver oil
Cleanliness
Rest
Health Protection
Immunizations
Health Restoration
Colds and sore throat: Hot peppermint drink and Vicks

Nova Scotian, Catholic

Health Maintenance
Sleep; proper foods
Health Protection
Cut up some onions and put them on back of stove to cook; feed them to all
Health Restoration
Colds: Boil carrots until jellied, add honey; as expectorant boil onions, add honey
Sore throat: Coat a tablespoon of molasses with black pepper
Earache: Put few drops of heated camphorated oil in ear; melt chicken fat and sugar, put in ear
Psoriasis: Hang a piece of lead around the neck
Earache with infection: To drain the infection, cut a piece of salt pork about 2 inches long and 3/4 inch thick and insert it into the infected ear and leave for a few days
Cold in the back: Alcohol was put in a small metal container, a piece of cotton on a stick was placed in the alcohol, ignited, and put in a *banky* (a type of glass resembling a whiskey glass); this was put on the back where the cold was and left for half an hour and a hickeylike rash would develop; it was believed that the rash would drain the cold
Skin ulcer and infection: A sharp blade was sterilized and used to make a small incision in the skin, and live blood suckers were placed in the opening, they would drain the infection out; when the blood sucker was full, it would fall to a piece of paper, be bled, placed in alcohol, and reused

Polish (United States), Catholic

Health Maintenance
Use of physician
Eating good, nutritious foods
Plenty of rest
Cod-liver oil
Health Protection
Exercise; good diet; eat fresh homegrown foods; work; good personal hygiene
Health Restoration
Headache: Take aspirin, hot liquids
Sore muscles: Heating pads and hot compresses
Colds: Drink hot liquids, chicken soup, honey

TABLE 3–1.—Continued

Swedish (United States), Protestant

Health Maintenance
Eat well-balanced meals
A lot of walking
Routine medical examinations
Cod-liver oil

Health Protection
Eat an apple a day
"I don't do a blooming thing"; eat well
Eat sorghum molasses for general all-round good health
Dress appropriately for weather
Blessing of the throat on St. Blaise Day

Health Restoration
Cough: Warm milk and butter
Rundown and tired: Eat a whole head of lettuce
Sick: Lots of juices and decarbonated ginger ale; lots of rest
Upset stomach: Baking soda
Sore throat: Gargle with salt and take honey in milk; herringbone wrapped in flannel around the neck
Anemia: Cod-liver oil
Bee stings: Poultice
Lumbago: Drink a yeast mixture
Black eye: Leeches
Earache: Warm oil
Congestion: Steamy bathroom
Fever: Blankets to sweat it out

the health problem. As students, we analyze and discuss a problem and its folk treatments and we begin to see how "evil" continues to be considered the cause of illness and how often the treatment is then designed to remove it.

Each person testifies to the efficacy of a given remedy. Many state that when their grandmothers and mothers shared these remedies with them, they experienced great feelings of nostalgia for the good old days when things seemed so simple. Some people may express a desire to return to these practices of yesteryear, whereas others openly confess that they continue to use such measures even now—sometimes in addition to what a health-care provider tells them to use or often without even bothering to consult a provider.

The goal of this kind of consciousness-raising session is to reawaken the participant to the types of health practices within her or his own family. The other purpose of the sharing is to make known the similarities and differences that exist as part of a cross-ethnic phenomenon. We are intrigued to discover the wide range of beliefs that exist among our peers' families. We had assumed that these people thought and believed as we did. For the first time, we individually and collectively realize that we *all* practice a certain amount of folk medicine, that we *all* have ethnically specific ways of treating illness, and that we, too, often delay in seeking professional health care. We learn that most people prefer to treat themselves at home and that they have their own ways of treating a particular set of symptoms—with or without a prescribed medical regimen. The previously held notion that "everybody does it this way" is shattered.

REFERENCES

1. Kennet, F. *Folk Medicine—Fact and Fiction: Age-Old Cures, Alternative Medicine, Natural Remedies* (New York: Crescent Books, 1976), p. 9.
2. Yoder, D. "Folk Medicine," in *Folklore and Folklife*, ed. R. H. Dorson (Chicago: University of Chicago Press, 1972), pp. 191–193.
3. Ibid, pp. 197–200.
4. Ibid, pp. 201–204.

ANNOTATED BIBLIOGRAPHY AND RESOURCE GUIDE

The following guide contains a sampling of the extensive references and resource materials available in the area of folk health traditions:

Readings

Britt, J., and Keen, L. *Feverfew*. London: Century, 1987.
   The authors describe the history and use of this common plant.
Deller, B., Hicks, D., and MacDonald, G., Coordinators. *Stone Boats and Lone Stars*. Hyde Park, Ontario: Middlesex Country Board of Education, 1979.
   The reminiscences of county residents fill the pages of this book, and it contains several pages of tried and true home remedies.
DeLys, C. *A Treasury of American Superstitions*. New York: Philosophical Library, 1948.
   This book contains a wealth of collected beliefs and practices that are inherent in many aspects of magicoreligious folk medicine.
Eichler, L. *The Customs of Mankind*. Garden City, NY: Doubleday, Page & Co., 1923.
   This book contains a wealth of background information related to many customs and practices in health-care-related aspects of human living.
Martin, L. C. *Wildflower Folklore*. Charlotte, NC: East Woods Press, 1984.
   This book is a collection of information on the most interesting and well-known wildflowers in the world; describes how they are used in treating illness and many of the superstitious beliefs about a given flower.
Shelton, F. *Pioneer Comforts and Kitchen Remedies—Oldtimey Highland Secrets from the Blue Ridge and Great Smoky Mountains*. High Point, NC: Hutcraft, 1965.
   This book contains several examples of the use of hundreds of well-known herbs and field plants.
Simmons, A. G. *A Witch's Brew*. Coventry, CT: Caprilands Herb Farm, undated.
   This is a collection of present and past popular beliefs concerning witches and contains many remedies and tall tales that are certainly a part of medical folk beliefs.
Zeitlin, S. J., Kotkin, A. J., and Baker, H. C. *A Celebration of American Family Folklore: Tales and Traditions from the Smithsonian Collection*. New York: Pantheon Books, 1977.

This information text contains a guide, Family Folklore Interviewing Guide and Questionnaire, that can be a helpful tool when investigating your background.

Other Readings of Interest

Delaney, J., Lupton, M. J., and Toth, E. *The Curse: A Cultural History of Menstruation.* Chicago: University of Chicago Press, 1988.

Jangl, A. M. and Jangl, J. F. *Ancient Legends of Healing Herbs.* Coeuor D'Alene, ID: Prisma Press, 1987.

Lawless, E. J. *God's Peculiar People.* Lexington, KY: University of Kentucky Press, 1988.

Martin, L. C. *Wildflower Folklore.* New York: The East Woods Press, 1984.

McClain, M. *A Feeling for Life: Cultural Identity, Community and the Arts.* Chicago: Urban Traditions, 1988.

Meyer, C. E. *American Folk Medicine.* Glenwood, IL: Meyerbooks, 1985.

Moldenke, H. N. and Moldenke, A. L. *Plants of the Bible.* NY: Dover Publications, 1952.

Rohde, E. S. *The Old English Herbs.* New York: Dover, 1971—original published in 1922.

Skelton, R. *Talismanic Magic.* York Beach, ME: Samuel Weiser, Inc., 1985.

Tierra, M. *The Way of Herbs.* NY: Pocket Books, 1990.

Weiss, G. and Weiss, S. *Growing and Using the Healing Herbs.* New York: Wings Books, 1985.

PUBLISHING HOUSES WITH LISTINGS RELATED TO FOLK MEDICINE

The following list is but a sample of the vast numbers of presses that publish materials related to folk life and medicine.

Illinois
University of Illinois Press
54 East Gregory Drive
Champaign, IL 61820

Kentucky
University Press of Kentucky
663 South Limestone Street
Lexington, KY 40506-0336

Michigan
Michigan State University Press
1405 South Harrison Road
Suite 25
Manly Miles Bldg.
East Lansing, MI 48823-5202

New Mexico
The University of New Mexico Press
Albuquerque, NM 87131

Pennsylvania
   University of Pennsylvania Press
   Blockley Hall, 13th floor
   Philadelphia, PA 19104-6261

North Carolina
   The University of North Carolina Press
   Post Office Box 2288
   Chapel Hill, NC 27515-2288

Tennessee
   AASLH Press
   172 Second Ave., North
   Nashville, TN 37201

   The University Of Tennessee Press
   293 Communications Building
   Knoxville, TN 37996-0325

FOLKLIFE CENTERS

The following is a listing of selected folklife centers in the United States. From these
centers, one may obtain films and literature related to folklife and medicine.

California
   Center for the Study of Comparative Folklore and Mythology
   University of California, Los Angeles
   Los Angeles, CA 90024

   California Folklore Society
   421 Baughman Ave.
   Claremont, CA 91711
   They Publish *Western Folklore*

Kentucky
   Appalshop
   P.O. Box 743A
   Whitesburg, KY 41858

Missouri
   Missouri Cultural Heritage Center
   Conley House
   Conley and Sanford Streets
   Columbia, MO 65211

Nevada
   Folk Arts Program
   Nevada State Council of the Arts
   329 Flint Street
   Reno, NV 89501

Tennessee
  Center for Southern Folklore
  1216 Peabody Avenue
  Memphis, TN 38104

Washington, DC
Within the federal government, resources for folklore and folklife endeavors in Washington, DC, are concentrated in four agencies.
  1. The Library of Congress
  2. The Smithsonian Institution
  3. The National Endowment for the Arts
  4. The National Endowment for the Humanities
  Although their programs are complementary, each operates under separate guidelines, supporting and coordinating activities that differ in purpose and scope.

American Folklife Center
The Library of Congress
Washington, DC 2054
(202) 287-6590
Folkline (202) 287-2000: A telephone information service
Folklife Sourcebook: A resource guide to relevant organizations
This center was created by Congress in 1976 to "preserve and present" American folklife. It is an educational and research program.

Archive of Folk Culture
The Library of Congress
Washington, DC 20540
(202) 287-5510
This is the public reference and archival arm of the American Folklife Center.

Office of Folklife Programs
Smithsonian Institution
955 L'Enfant Plaza, Suite 2600
Washington, DC 2056
(202) 287-3424
This office, created in 1977, is the coordinative office for folklife activities within the Smithsonian Institution.

National Council for the Traditional Arts
806 15th Street, NW, Suite 400
Washington, DC 20005
(202) 639-8370
This is a private, nonprofit organization that presents the National Folk Festival each year, organizes folk culture tours in this country and abroad, develops publications and radio programs, and offers consultant assistance.

The American Folklore Society
1703 New Hampshire Avenue, NW
Washington, DC 20009
Membership in this society, founded in 1888, is open to all persons interested in folklore. It serves as a forum for the preservation of folklore.

Ancestry
P.O. Box 476
Salt Lake City, UT 84110
This organization sells several publications that may be useful in developing your family history.

Chapter

Culture, Health, and Illness

Culture is a unified whole even unto psychosis and death.

—Jules Henry, *Culture Against Man*

In the fall of 1983, a young Hispanic man collapsed and died while playing football. The police, who took his mother to the hospital, did not tell her the seriousness of the injury, and she was informed of his death when she arrived at the hospital. The mother requested to see her son's body so that she could verify his death and perform certain religious rituals, such as washing him and anointing the body with oil. She was not allowed to see the body—the reason given was that it could not be touched because of the pending autopsy. Subsequently, the mother believed that the autopsy was the cause of her son's death. To add insult to injury, the mother was assisted to a Catholic Church that was not of her ethnocultural background and did not hold worship services in her language.[1]

Since the mid-1960s there has been a social explosion in the United States that has resulted in a surge of group consciousness. Blacks first, then Hispanics, Asian Americans, American Indians, and European American (white) ethnic groups began to assert their cultural group identity. The rejuvenation of ethnic identity eroded both the melting pot myth and the belief that an American culture would decrease group awareness.[2]

Today, yet another social explosion is occurring. This one is being caused by the profound forces of demographic change that are catapulting this nation into a universal nation. We are living in a pluralistic society, and it is becoming more and more evident that cultural differences are increasingly serving to isolate and alienate us one from another. J. D. Hunter has pointed out that merely educating people about the differences that underlie culturally determined beliefs is not enough; one must first confront competing ideals of truth. "The Differences must be confronted."[3]

Immigrants and their descendants constitute most of the population of the United States. Most Americans who are not themselves immigrants have

---

TEST YOUR ETHNIC KNOWLEDGE

1. What three nations provided the greatest numbers of immigrants to the U.S. from 1820 to 1975?
2. Immigrants from what nation are the *most* educated?
3. What ethnic groups has the best job status in America?
4. Who are the richest American Indians in the U.S.?
   Who are the poorest Indians in the U.S.?
5. What is the largest Indian tribe?
6. Who claimed to have invented the telephone?
7. Who were the original Siamese twins?
8. What do these names mean?
   a. Chattanooga
   b. Kalamazoo
   c. Milwaukee
   d. Poughkeepsie
   e. Yosemite
9. Who are (a) Belle Silverman, (b) Anna Maria Italiano, (c) Concetta Ignolia, and (d) Rocco Barbella?
10. How many different peoples in the world believe in the "evil eye"?
11. What are "leapers"?

Answers appear at end of chapter

---

ancestors who came from elsewhere (Table 4–1). The only people considered native are the American Indians, the Aleuts, and the Inuit (or Eskimos), for they migrated here thousands of years before the Europeans.[4]

Immigrants came to the United States seeking religious and political freedom and economic opportunities.[5] The life of the immigrant was fraught with difficulties—going from an "old" to a "new" way of life, learning a new language, and adapting to a new climate, new foods, and a new culture. Socialization of immigrants occurred in American public schools and Americanization became for some a process of "vast psychic repression."[6] In part, the concept of the melting pot was created in schools where children learned English, rejected family traditions, and attempted to take on the values of the dominant culture and "pass" as "Americans."[7] Furthermore, Greeley describes the immigrant ethnic group as a combination of European cultural backgrounds; American acculturation experiences; and common political, social, and economic interests. Greeley also argues that different origins produce cultural differences and that diverse experiences in America reinforced the old differences between ethnic groups and created new ones.[8] Jordan and Jordan describe the immigrant's life as very hard and lonely.[9]

Every immigrant group brought cultural attitudes toward health, health care, and illness, and within each of these groups widely varying health and illness beliefs and practices exist.[10]

TABLE 4–1. HIGHLIGHTS OF IMMIGRATION HISTORY 1798–1990

Year	Event
1798	Alien and Sedition Acts passed
1808	African slave trade prohibited
1819	First immigrant data collected
1824	Naturalization set at two years
1844	Nativist riots in Philadelphia
1846	Potato famine in Ireland results in massive Irish influx
1849	California gold rush; imported Chinese labor
1862	Homestead Act opens land to immigrants
1870	Naturalization extended to Africans
1882–1943	Chinese Exclusion Act
1886	Statue of Liberty opened
1892	Ellis Island Immigration Station opens
1898	Immigrants classified by "race"
1903	Political radicals banned from entering the United States
1907	1,004,756 people—a record—passed through Ellis Island
1908	"Gentleman's Agreement" restricts Japanese immigration
1910	Entrance barred to criminals, paupers, and diseased
1917	Literacy required for immigrants over 16
1924	Annual racial quotas established; border patrol begins
1942–1964	Bracero Program allows temporary workers
1975	Vietnam War ends; Indochinese refugee program
1980	Mariel boatlift from Cuba—125,000 people
1986	Amnesty for illegal aliens
1990	Ellis Island immigration museum opens

From: Lefcowitz, E. *The United States Immigration History Timeline* (New York: Terra Firma Press, 1990). Reprinted with permission.

ACCULTURATION AND HERITAGE CONSISTENCY

Health and illness can be interpreted and explained in terms of personal experience and expectations. We can define our own health or illness, and determine what these states mean to us in our daily lives. We learn from our own cultural and ethnic backgrounds *how* to be healthy, *how* to recognize illness, and *how* to be ill. Furthermore, the meanings attached to the notions of health and illness are related to the basic, culture-bound values by which we define a given experience and perception.[11]

To understand and appreciate differences in health and illness beliefs and practices that may be culturally determined, it is necessary to analyze theories relating to the Americanization of beliefs. This chapter presents two theories, the first type of which relates to socialization and acculturation and the quasi creation of a melting pot or some other common threads that are part of an American whole. The second, and opposite, theories analyze the degree to which people have maintained their traditional heritage. It then becomes possible to analyze health beliefs by determining a person's ties to the traditional heritage and culture rather than to signs of acculturation. The assumption is that there is a relationship in people between strong identities—either with one's heritage or the level at which one is acculturated into the American culture—and their health beliefs and practices. Support group needs and networks also may be related to the degree one is identified with the traditional heritage. The concept of heritage consistency is a new one in mainstream health-care provider circles. The following discussion focuses on both acculturation and heritage consistency.

Socialization

Socialization is the process of being raised within a culture and acquiring the characteristics of that group. Education—be it elementary school, high school, college, or nursing—is a form of socialization. For many people who have been socialized within the boundaries of a "traditional culture" or a non-Western culture, modern "American" culture becomes a second cultural identity. Those who immigrate here, legally or illegally, from non-Western or nonmodern countries, may find socialization into the American culture, whether in schools or in society, to be an extremely difficult and painful process. They may experience biculturalism, which is a dual pattern of identification and often of divided loyalty.[12]

Fundamental to understanding culturally determined health and illness beliefs and practices from different heritages requires moving away from linear models of process to more complex patterns of cultural beliefs and interrelationships. Several models exist to explain the phenomena of second-culture acquisition.

Acculturation

While becoming a competent participant in the dominant culture, a member of a minority culture is always identified as a member of that minority culture. The process of acculturation is involuntary in nature, and the member of the minority group is forced to learn the new culture to survive. Individuals experience second-culture acquisition when they must live within or between cultures.[13] Acculturation also refers to cultural or behavioral assimilation and may be defined as the changes of one's cultural patterns to those of the host society. In the United States, people assume that the usual course of acculturation takes three generations; hence, the adult grandchild of an immigrant is considered fully Americanized.

Assimilation

Acculturation also may be referred to as assimilation, the process by which an individual develops a new cultural identity. Assimilation is becoming in all ways like the members of the dominant culture. The process of assimilation encompasses various aspects, such as cultural or behavioral, marital, identification, and civic. The underlying assumption is that the person from a given cultural group loses this cultural identity to acquire the new one. In fact, this is not always possible, and the process may cause stress and anxiety.[14] Assimilation can be described as a collection of subprocesses: a process of inclusion through which a person gradually ceases to conform to any standard of life that differs from the dominant group standards and, at the same time, a process through which the person learns to conform to all the dominant group standards. The process of assimilation is considered complete when the foreigner is fully merged into the dominant cultural group.[15]

There are four forms of assimilation: cultural, marital, primary structural, and secondary structural. One example of cultural assimilation is the ability to speak excellent American English. It is interesting to note that in the United States 32 million people speak a language other than English as their primary language.[16] Marital assimilation occurs when members of one group intermarry with members of another group. The third and fourth forms of assimilation, those of structural assimilation, determine the extent to which social mingling and friendships occur between groups. In primary structural assimilation, the relationships between people are warm, personal interactions between group members in the home, the church, and social groups. In secondary structural assimilation there is nondiscriminatory sharing, often of a cold impersonal nature, between different groups in settings such as schools and workplaces.[17]

The concepts of socialization, assimilation, and acculturation are complex and sensitive. The dominant society expects that all immigrants are in the process of acculturation and assimilation and that the world view that we share as health-care practitioners is commonly shared by our clients. Because we live in a pluralistic society, however, many variations of health beliefs and practices exist.

When cultures clash, many misanthropic feelings, or "isms" (Table 4–2) can enter into a person's consciousness. Just as Hunter[18] proclaimed that the "differences" must be confronted, so too must stereotypes, prejudice, and discrimination be confronted. It is impossible to describe traditional beliefs without a temptation to stereotype. But each person is an individual; therefore, levels of heritage consistency differ within and between ethnic groups as do health beliefs. Another issue that rears its ugly head in this arena is that of prejudice. Prejudice occurs either because the person making the judgments doesn't understand the given person or his or her heritage or the person making the judgment generalizes an experience of one individual from a culture to all members of that group. An act of discrimination occurs when a person acts on prejudice and denies the other person's fundamental right.

The debate still rages between those who believe that America is a melting pot and that all groups of immigrants must be acculturated to an American norm and those who dispute theories of acculturation and believe that the various groups maintain their own identities within the American whole. The concept of "heritage consistency" is one way of exploring whether people are maintaining their traditional heritage and of determining the depth of a person's traditional cultural heritage.

TABLE 4–2. COMMON "ISMS" PLUS ONE NONISM

Belief	Definition
Racism	The belief that members of one race are superior to those of other races
Sexism	The belief that members of one gender are superior to the other gender
Heterosexism	The belief that everyone is or should be heterosexual and that heterosexuality is best, normal, and superior
Ageism	The belief that members of one age group are superior to those of other ages
Ethnocentrism	The belief that one's own cultural, ethnic, or professional group is superior to that of others. One judges others by their "yardstick," and is unable or unwilling to see what the other group is really about. "My group is best!"
Xenophobia	The morbid fear of strangers

From: Procedings of the Invitational Meeting, *Multicultural Issues in the Nursing Workforce and Workplace* (Washington, DC: American Nurses' Association, 1993).

Heritage Consistency

Heritage consistency is a concept developed by Estes and Zitzow to describe "the degree to which one's lifestyle reflects his or her respective tribal culture."[19] The theory has been expanded in an attempt to study the degree to which a person's lifestyle reflects his or her traditional culture, whether European, Asian, African, or Hispanic.[20] The values indicating heritage consistency exist on a continuum, and a person can possess value characteristics of both a consistent heritage (traditional) and an inconsistent heritage (acculturated). The concept of heritage consistency includes a determination of one's cultural, ethnic, and religious background (Fig. 4–1).

Culture. There is not a single definition of culture, and all too often definitions tend to omit salient aspects of culture or to be too general to have any real meaning. Of the countless ideas of the meaning of this term, some are of particular note. Fejos describes culture as "the sum total of socially inherited characteristics of a human group that comprises everything which one generation can tell, convey, or hand down to the next; in other words, the non-physically inherited traits we possess."[21] Another way of understanding the concept of culture is to picture it as the luggage that each of us carries around for our lifetime. It is the sum of beliefs, practices, habits, likes, dislikes, norms, customs, rituals, and so forth that we learned from our families during the years of socialization. In turn, we transmit cultural luggage to our children. A third way of defining culture, and one that is most relevant in areas of traditional health, is that culture is a "metacommunication system," wherein not only the spoken words have meaning, but everything else as well.[22]

All facets of human behavior can be interpreted through the lens of culture, and everything can be related to and from this context. Culture includes all of the following characteristics:

1. Culture is the medium of personhood and social relationships.
2. Only part of culture is conscious.

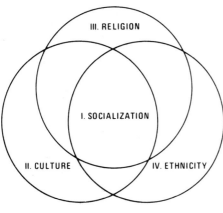

I. SOCIALIZATION	Extended family Place reared Visits home Raised with extended family Name
II. CULTURAL	Extended family Participation in folkways Language
III. RELIGION	Extended family Church membership and participation Historic beliefs
IV. ETHNICITY	Extended family Resides in ethnic community Participates in folkways Socializes with members of same ethnic group Identifies as ethnic-American

Figure 4–1. Model of heritage consistency.

3. Culture can be likened to a prosthetic device because it is an extension of biological capabilities.
4. Culture is an interlinked web of symbols.
5. Culture is a device for creating and limiting human choices.
6. Culture can be in two places at once—it is found in a person's mind and also exists in the environment in such form as the spoken word or an artifact.[23]

Culture is a complex whole, in which each part is related to every other part. It is learned and the capacity to learn culture is genetic, but the subject matter is not genetic and must be learned by each person in his or her family and social community. Culture also depends on an underlying social matrix, and included in this social matrix are knowledge, belief, art, law, morals, and custom.[24]

Culture is learned in that people learn the ways to see their environment—that is, they learn from the environment how to see and interpret what they see. People learn to speak, and they learn to learn. Culture, as the medium of our individuality, is the way in which we express our self. It is the medium of human social relationships in that it must be shared and creates social relationships. The symbols of culture—sound and acts—form the basis of all languages. Symbols are everywhere—in religion, politics, and gender— these are cultural symbols, the meaning of which varies between and within cultural groups.[25] The society in which we live and other forces—political, economic, and social—tend to alter the way in which some aspects of a particular culture are transmitted and maintained. Many of the essential components of a given culture, however, pass from one generation to the next unaltered. Consequently, much of what we believe, think, and do, both consciously and unconsciously, is determined by our cultural background. In this way, culture and ethnicity are handed down from one generation to another.

Ethnicity. Cultural background is a fundamental component of one's ethnic background. At this point, a definition of terms is called for so that we can proceed from the same point of reference.

> **Ethnic:** adj. 1. of or pertaining to a social group within a cultural and social system that claims or is accorded special status on the basis of complex, often variable traits including religious, linguistic, ancestral, or physical characteristics. 2. Broadly, characteristic of a religious, racial, national, or cultural group. 3. Pertaining to a people not Christian or Jewish; heathen; pagan: "These Are Ancient Ethnic Revels of a Faith Long Since Forsaken." (Longfellow)[26]

The term *ethnic* has for some time aroused strongly negative feelings and often is rejected by the general population. One can speculate that the upsurge in the use of the term stems from the recent interest of people in discovering their personal backgrounds, a fact used by some politicians who overtly court "the ethnics." Paradoxically, in a nation as large and comprising as many different peoples as the United States does—with the American Indians being the only true native population—we find ourselves still reluctant to speak of ethnicity and ethnic differences. This stance stems from the fact that most foreign groups that came to this land often shed the ways of the "old country" and quickly attempt to assimilate themselves into the mainstream, or the so-called melting pot.[27] We also need to clarify other terms.

> **Ethnicity:** n. 1. The condition of belonging to a particular ethnic group. 2. Ethnic pride.
>
> **Ethnocentrism:** n. 1. Belief in the superiority of one's own ethnic group. 2. Overriding concern with race.
>
> **Xenophobe:** n. A person unduly fearful or contemptuous of strangers or foreigners, especially as reflected in his political or cultural views.
>
> **Xenophobia:** A morbid fear of strangers.[28]

The behavioral manifestations of these phenomena occur in response to people's needs, especially when they are foreign-born and must find a way to function (1) before they are assimilated into the mainstream and (2) in order to accept themselves. These people cluster together against the majority, who in turn may be discriminating against them.

Indeed, the phenomenon of ethnicity is "complex, ambivalent, paradoxical, and elusive."[29] Ethnicity is indicative of the following characteristics a group may share in some combination.

1. Common geographic origin
2. Migratory status
3. Race
4. Language and dialect
5. Religious faith or faiths
6. Ties that transcend kinship, neighborhood, and community boundaries
7. Shared traditions, values, and symbols
8. Literature, folklore, and music
9. Food preferences
10. Settlement and employment patterns
11. Special interest with regard to politics in the homeland and in the United States
12. Institutions that specifically serve and maintain the group
13. An internal sense of distinctiveness
14. An external perception of distinctiveness[30]

There are at least 106 ethnic groups and more than 170 American Indian groups in the United States that meet many of these criteria.[31] People from every country in the world have immigrated to this country and now reside here. Some nations, such as Germany, England, Wales, and Ireland, are heavily represented; others, such as Japan, the Philippines, and Greece have smaller numbers of people living here. People continue to immigrate to the United States, the present influx coming from Viet Nam, Laos, Cambodia, Cuba, Haiti, Mexico, and South and Central American countries.

Table 4–3 shows the nations of family origins of the American population.

Religion.   The third major component of heritage consistency is religion. Religion, "the belief in a divine or superhuman power or powers to be obeyed and worshipped as the creator(s) and ruler(s) of the universe; and a system of beliefs, practices, and ethical values," is a major reason for the development of ethnicity.[32] The practice of religion is revealed in numerous cults, sects, denominations, and churches. Ethnicity and religion are clearly related, and one's religion quite often is the determinent of one's ethnic group. Religion gives the person a frame of reference and a perspective with which to organize information. Religious teachings—vis-á-vis health—help to present a meaningful philosophy and system of practices within a system of social con-

**TABLE 4–3. NATIONS OF FAMILY ORIGINS OF THE
AMERICAN POPULATION, 1994.**

Country of Origin	Percentage of Family Origins
German	20.3
England and Wales	13.4
Ireland	12.2
Africa	9.3
Italy	4.9
Scotland	3.9
American Indian	3.8
Poland	2.4
Mexico	3.1
Norway	1.8
Other	24.9

From: Smith, T. W. National Opinion Research Center, (Chicago,
IL: University of Chicago, 1994). Unpublished data.

trols having specific values, norms, and ethics. These are related to health in
that adherence to a religious code is conducive to spiritual harmony and
health. Illness is sometimes seen as the punishment for the violation of religious codes and morals.

The United States census has resisted asking questions about religion.
However, data of religious affiliations are available from the National Opinion Research Center's *General Social Surveys.* Table 4–4 lists religious affiliations in the United States in 1994.

Examples of Heritage Consistency
The factors that constitute heritage consistency are listed in Table 4–5. The following are examples of each factor.

1. **The person's childhood development occurred in the person's
   country of origin or in an immigrant neighborhood in the
   United States of like ethnic group.** For example, the person was
   raised in a specific ethnic neighborhood, such as an Italian,
   Black, Hispanic, or Jewish one, in a given part of a city and was
   exposed only to the culture, language, foods, and customs of
   that particular group.
2. **Extended family members encouraged participation in traditional religious and cultural activities.** For example, the parents sent the person to religious school, and most social
   activities were church-related.
3. **The individual engages in frequent visits to the country of origin or returns to the "old neighborhood" in the United States.**
   The desire to return to the old country or to the old neighborhood is prevalent in many people; however, many people, for
   various reasons, cannot return. The people who have come here

TABLE 4–4. RELIGIOUS AFFILIATION IN THE UNITED STATES, 1994

Religious Group	Percentage
Protestant	59.35
Baptist	20.8
Methodist	9.4
Lutheran	6.6
Presbyterian	4.75
Episcopal	2.2
No denomination given or nondenominational	15.6
Catholic	25.5
Jewish	2.0
None	9.2
Other—not Christian	3.9
Total	99.95

From: Smith, T. W. (1994). National Opinion Research Center (Chicago, IL: University of Chicago, 1994). Unpublished data.

to escape religious persecution or whose families were slaughtered during either World War or the holocaust may not want to return to European homelands. Other reasons why people may not return to their native country include political conditions in the homeland or no existing relatives or friends in that land.

4. **The individual's family home is within the ethnic community of which he or she is a member.** For example, as an adult the person has elected to live with family in an ethnic neighborhood.

TABLE 4–5. FACTORS INDICATING HERITAGE CONSISTENCY

1. Childhood development occurred in the person's country of origin or in an immigrant neighborhood in the United States of like ethnic group.
2. Extended family members encouraged participation in traditional religious or cultural activities.
3. Individual engages in frequent visits to country of origin or to the "old neighborhood" in the United States.
4. Family homes are within the ethnic community.
5. Individual participates in ethnic cultural events, such as religious festivals or national holidays, sometimes with singing, dancing, and costumes.
6. Individual was raised in an extended family setting.
7. Individual maintains regular contact with the extended family.
8. Individual's name has not been Americanized.
9. Individual was educated in a parochial (nonpublic) school with a religious or ethnic philosophy similar to the family's background.
10. Individual engages in social activities primarily with others of the same ethnic background.
11. Individual has knowledge of the culture and language of origin.
12. Individual possesses elements of personal pride about heritage.

5. The individual participates in ethnic cultural events, such as religious festivals or national holidays, sometimes with singing, dancing, and costumes.
6. **The individual was raised in an extended family setting.** For example, when the person was growing up, there may have been grandparents living in the same household, or aunts and uncles living in the same house or close by. The person's social frame of reference was the family.
7. **The individual maintains regular contact with the extended family.** For example, the person maintains close ties with members of the same generation, the surviving members of the older generation, and members of the younger generation.
8. **The individual's name has not been Americanized.** For example, the person has restored the family name to its European original if it had been changed by immigration authorities at the time the family immigrated or if the family changed the name at a later time in an attempt to assimilate more fully.
9. **The individual was educated in a parochial (nonpublic) school with a religious or ethnic philosophy similar to the family's background.** The person's education plays an enormous role in socialization, and the major purpose of education is to socialize a given person into the dominant culture. It is in the schools where children learn English and the customs and norms of American life. In the parochial schools, they not only learn English but also are socialized in the culture and norms of the particular religious or ethnic group that is sponsoring the school.
10. **The individual engages in social activities primarily with others of the same religious or ethnic background.** For example, the major portion of the person's personal time is spent with primary structural groups.
11. **The individual has knowledge of the culture and language of origin.** The person has been socialized in the traditional ways of the family and expresses this as a central theme of life.
12. **The individual expresses pride in his or her heritage.**[33] For example, the person may identify him or herself as ethnic American and be supportive of ethnic activities to a great extent.

It is not possible to isolate the aspects of culture, religion, and ethnicity that shape a person's world view. Each is part of the other, and all three are united within the person. When one writes of religion, one cannot eliminate culture or ethnicity, but descriptions and comparisons can be made. Referring to Figure 4–2 to assess heritage consistency can help determine ethnic group differences in health beliefs and practices. It can go a long way to enhancing the health-care provider's understanding of the needs of patients and their families and the support systems that people may have or need.

CULTURE AND HEALTH-CARE PROVIDERS

The United States was once considered a melting pot of diverse ethnic and cultural groups. One aspect of the American dream was that all of these diverse groups would blend into one common whole. This did not really occur, and today many groups cling to and identify more closely with their ethnic heritage. In fact, among third-, fourth-, or even subsequent-generation Americans, some desire to know where they come from (who they are). The phenomenon of seeking one's heritage is widespread in today's society.[34] A fine example of this is Alex Haley's classic book and the movie based on it, *Roots*, which documents his search for his family's roots.

Because the melting pot—which carried with it the dream of assimilation into a common culture—has proved to be a myth, it is now time to identify and both accept and appreciate the differences among people. It is suggested that this be done not to change people so that they are all alike but to better understand both one's own ethnic culture and the ethnic culture of other people living in this society. Within the health professions, this is mandatory. Because health-care providers learn from their culture the why and the how of being healthy or ill, it behooves them to treat each client with deference to his or her own cultural background.

Health-care professionals who have been socialized into a given culture and subsequently resocialized into what I define as the *provider culture* come into intimate contact with people who may choose to maintain their traditional perceptions and beliefs regarding health and illness. Here lies the paradox: one culture may believe, for example, that people should starve a cold and feed a fever; another may believe the opposite. Such differences in belief can result in elopements from clinics, broken appointments, and failures to follow prescribed regimens.

The Health-Care Provider's Culture

The providers of health care—physicians, nurses, social workers, dietitians, laboratory and departmental professionals—are socialized into the culture of their profession. Professional socialization teaches the student a set of beliefs, practices, habits, likes, dislikes, norms, and rituals (components already described as factors that comprise a given culture). This newly learned information regarding health and illness differs in varying degrees from that of the individual's background. As students become more and more knowledgeable, they usually move farther and farther from their past belief systems and, indeed, farther from the population at large in terms of its understanding and beliefs regarding health and illness. It is not uncommon to hear patients say

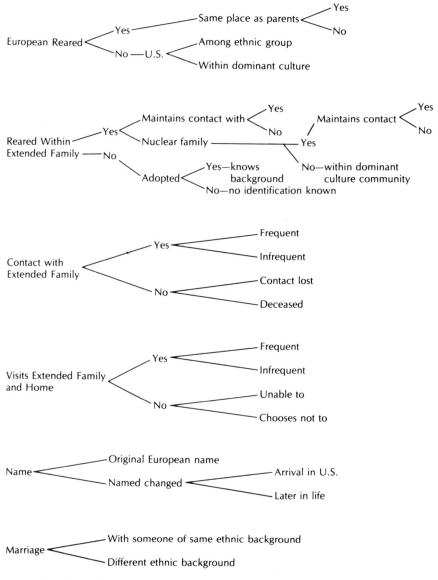

Figure 4–2a. Matrix of heritage consistency.

things like "I have no idea what the nurses and doctor are saying!" "They speak a foreign language!" "What they are doing is so strange to me."

In light of these ideas, health-care providers can be viewed as a foreign culture or ethnic group. They have a social and cultural system; they experience "ethnicity" in the way they perceive themselves in relation to the health-care consumer. Even if they deny the reality of the situation, health-care

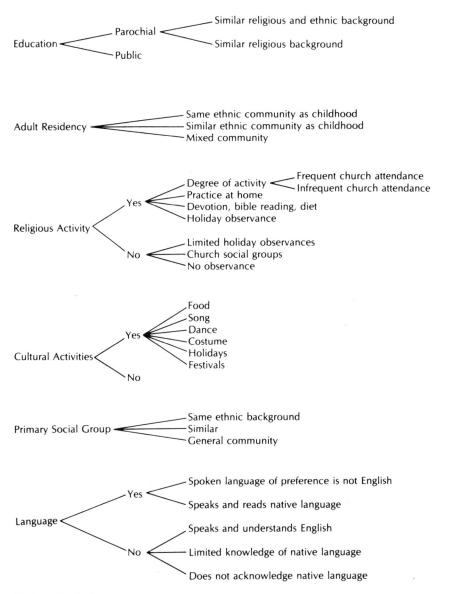

Figure 4–2b. Continued.

providers must understand that they are ethnocentric. Not only are they ethnocentric, but many of them are also xenophobic. To appreciate this critical issue, consider the following. A principal reason for the difficulty experienced between the health-care provider and the consumer is that health-care providers, with few exceptions, adhere rigidly to the Western system of health-care delivery. With few exceptions, they do not publicly sanction any methods of protection or healing other than scientifically proved ones. They ordinarily fail to recognize or use any sources of medication other than those that have been proved effective by scientific means. The only types of healers that are sanctioned are those that have been educated and certified according to the requirements of this culture.

What happens, then, when people of one belief system encounter people who have other beliefs regarding health and illness (either in protection or in treatment)? Is the provider able to meet the needs as perceived and defined by the patient? More often than not, a wall of misunderstanding arises between the two. At this point, a "breakdown in communications" occurs—and the *consumer* ends up on the short end of the situation.

Providers think that they comprehend all facets of health and illness. Granted that by training and education health-care providers are at a significant distance from the consumer-patient; I nevertheless suggest and *insist* that it is entirely appropriate for them to explore alternative ideas regarding health and illness and to adjust their approach to coincide with the needs of the specific client. In the past, health-care providers have tried to force Western medicine on one and all, regardless of result. It is time that health care coincided with the needs of the client instead of inducing additional conflict.

The following list outlines the more obvious aspects of the health-care provider's culture. In connection with later chapters, it can be referred to as a framework of comparison with various other ethnic and cultural beliefs and practices.

1. Beliefs
   a. Standardized definitions of health and illness
   b. The omnipotence of technology
2. Practices
   a. The maintenance of health and the protection of health or prevention of disease through such mechanisms as the avoidance of stress and the use of immunizations
   b. Annual physical examinations and diagnostic procedures, such as Pap smears
3. Habits
   a. Charting
   b. The constant use of jargon
   c. Use of a systematic approach and problem-solving methodology
4. Likes
   a. Promptness
   b. Neatness and organization
   c. Compliance
5. Dislikes
   a. Tardiness
   b. Disorderliness and disorganization

6. Customs
   a. Professional deference and adherence to the pecking order found in autocratic and bureaucratic systems
   b. Handwashing
   c. Employment of certain procedures attending birth and death
7. Rituals
   a. The physical examination
   b. The surgical procedure
   c. Limiting visitors and visiting hours

Culture and Epidemiology

Another area in which culture plays a broad role is in the interpretation of the causation of illness, or *epidemiology*. Science is inherent in the health-care educational process. In the study of epidemiology, the relationships among the host, agent, and environment are explored. The modern approach attributes the cause of disease (the agent) to bacteria, viruses, chemical carcinogens, pollutants, and so forth. The disorders have names, such as pneumonia, meningitis, influenza, polycystic kidney disease. Unless the student delves further into study of the field, he or she may well never become familiar with more traditional theories of epidemiology. For example, the concepts of "soul loss," "spirit possession," and "spells" are rarely, if ever, described and discussed during the educational process of health-care providers,[35] yet these ideas, too, contribute to people's perceptions of the cause of a given disease.

I have found many students who were not only familiar with such concepts as the "evil eye" but in some instances also took precautions to protect themselves against its effect. As discussed in Chapter 3, they often felt forced to take these precautions because of the beliefs of their mothers or grandmothers. After much thought, the acquisition of new facts, and further learning, many of the students chose to shed such beliefs and do not *consciously* practice what they had been taught by their families. Others, however, admitted to still holding such beliefs—but were constantly experiencing conflict. This groups of students can be viewed as a microcosm of the larger society. It is known that many people cling to familiar belief systems, a fact that lends comfort to them. (In what other way can some of the hardships of life be explained in a more satisfactory or acceptable manner?)

Another facet of epidemiology that one does not ordinarily encounter in academia is that of the causative agent's being another person and not a microbe. The idea of another person making someone ill by the use of witchcraft or voodoo (or some other form of magic) is an unusual subject within the constraints of a traditional medical curriculum. If the student is to study the cultural perceptions of health and illness, however, some knowledge of a belief in magic is important. The environment that fosters the use of these agents is one in which hate, envy, or jealousy may exist. The way of preventing illness involves not provoking the wrath of one's friends, neighbors, and enemies. A victim of disease may believe that his or her success provoked the envy of friends, that it attracted a witch's attention, or that someone was jealous of a new possession and put a hex on him or her. In the minds of people who still believe and practice traditional health beliefs, these contributing factors are as real as the bacteria and viruses of modern epidemiology are to health-care providers. Regardless of the provider's belief system, the provider needs to keep an open mind in order to provide *useful* care to consumers who retain traditional beliefs.

Culture and Response to Pain

- "Mr. Smith in room 222 is the ideal patient. He never has a single complaint of pain."
- "Mrs. Cohen in room 223 is a real complainer. She is constantly asking for pain medication and putting on her light."
- "Mrs. O'Mally in room 224 is an ideal patient. She never complains about pain. For that matter, she never complains."
- "Mr. Chen in room 225 says nothing. I often wonder what he is feeling."
- "Mrs. Petrini in room 226 dramatically cries every time I look at her and complains of pain at every opportunity."

These statements (however stereotypical) are descriptions of behaviors observed concerning patients' responses to the subjective feeling of pain. Social scientists, health-care researchers, and other professionals maintain that pain is a culture-bound phenomenon. How pain and discomfort—or, for that matter, most emotions—are presented varies among cultures. A person raised in one cultural background may be allowed the free and open expression of feelings, whereas a person from another culture may have been taught that (for a multitude of reasons) true feelings must never be revealed.

Let us say that the above statements were all made by the same nurse. Let us go one step further and say that each patient had the same operation on the same day. It would not be unusual, within the limits of general expectations, to see the different patients from differing cultures and ethnic groups exhibit the behaviors described. The fact that culture plays a role in behavior during illness was aptly demonstrated and strongly documented by Mark Zborowski in his study on pain.[36] Briefly, his findings were that Jewish and Italian patients generally responded to pain in an emotional fashion, and they tended to exaggerate the response, "old American Yankees" tended to be more stoic, and the Irish tended to ignore pain.[37] Presentation of this type of data often can lead to a major problem, *stereotyping*. I want to emphasize strongly that such descriptions are *general*; the results of one study are not necessarily applicable to a specific patient. Even within my own clinical experiences, however, I have observed events such as those described by the quotations. It is preferable to include and discuss such material rather than to ignore it—particularly inasmuch as numerous classical studies in anthropology, sociology, psychology, and social psychology support these data (see, for

ANSWERS (from "Test Your Ethnic Knowledge" on p. 64)

1. Germany 6,954,160
   Italy 5,269,992
   Great Britain 4,851,806
   (p 474)
2. Russian Americans between 25 and 34
   (p. 483)
3. White Anglo Saxon Protestants (p. 482)
4. a. The Aguas Callentes California of
      (p. 11)
   b. The Sesseton Sioux of South Dakota
      (p. 12)
5. Navaho—96,743 (p. 13)
6. Antonia Meucci (p. 27)
7. Chang and Eng (1811–1874), two
   Chinese men born in Siam (present-day
   Burma) (p. 164)

8. a. "rock rising to a point"
   b. "boiling pot"
   c. "gathering place by the river"
   d. "at the bottom of the water fall"
   e. "killer grizzly bear"
      (These are all American Indian
      names.) (p. 167)
9. a. Beverly Sills
   b. Anne Bancroft
   c. Connie Stevens
   d. Rocky Graziano
10. 67 different peoples—over 36% of the
    world's population (p. 244)
11. Mexican jumping beans (p. 50)

From: Bernardo, S. *The Ethnic Almanac*. (Garden City, NY: Doubleday, 1981). Reprinted with permission.

instance, findings reported by David Mechanic,[38] the late Edward Suchman,[39,40] and Irving Zola.)[41]

REFERENCES

1. Winerip, M. "Youth's Death: Sports System 'Broke Down.'" *New York Times*, 22 November 1983, pp. B1, B4.
2. Giordano, J. and Giordano, G. P. *The Ethno-Cultural Factor in Mental Health* (New York: Institute of Pluralism and Group Identity, 1977), p. 1.
3. Hunter, J. D. *Before the Shooting Begins—Searching for Democracy in America's Culture Wars.* (New York: The Free Press 1994), p. 236.
4. Thernstrom, S. ed. *Harvard Encyclopedia of American Ethnic Groups* (Cambridge, MA: Harvard University Press, 1980), p. vii.
5. McLemore, S. D. *Racial and Ethnic Relations in America* (Boston: Allyn and Bacon, 1980), p. 1.
6. Greeley, A. *Why Can't They Be Like Us? America's White Ethnic Groups* (New York: E. P. Dutton, 1975).
7. Novak, M. "How American Are You If Your Grandparents Came from Serbia in 1888?" in *The Rediscovery of Ethnicity: Its Implications for Culture and Politics in America*, ed. Te Selle, S. (New York: Harper and Row, 1973).
8. Greeley. *Why Can't They Be Like Us?*
9. Jordan, G. L. and Jordan, T. G. *Ernst and Li Sette Jordan: German Pioneers in Texas* (Austin: Von Blockman-Jones Co., 1971).

10. Castillo, L. J. "Keynote Address—'Communicating with Mexican-Americans—por su buena salud'" (Houston: Baylor College of Medicine, 1979).
11. Henry, J. *Culture Against Man* (New York: Random House, 1963), p. 323; and Bermann, E. *Scapegoat—The Impact of Death-fear on an American Family* (Ann Arbor: University of Michigan Press, 1973), pp. 2–4.
12. LaFrombose T., Coleman L. K., and Gerton, J. "Psychological Impact of Biculturalism: Evidence and Theory." *Psychological Bulletin* 114 (3, 1993): p. 395.
13. Ibid., p. 396.
14. Ibid.
15. McLemore. *Racial and Ethnic Relations*, p. 4.
16. U.S. Department of Commerce, Bureau of the Census. 1990 *Census of Population—Social and Economic Characteristics* (Washington, DC: Government Printing Office, 1993), p. 13.
17. McLemore. *Racial and Ethnic Relations*, p. 39.
18. Hunter, *Before the Shooting Begins*, p. 236.
19. Estes, G. and Zitzow, D. "Heritage Consistency as a Consideration in Counseling Native Americans" (Paper read at the National Indian Education Association Convention, Dallas, Texas, November 1980).
20. Spector, R. E. "A Description of the Impact of Medicare on Health-Illness Beliefs and Practices of White Ethnic Senior Citizens in Central Texas." Ph.D. diss., University of Texas at Austin School of Nursing, 1983; Ann Arbor, Mich.: University Microfilms International, 1983.
21. Fejos, P. "Man, Magic, and Medicine," in *Medicine and Anthropology*, ed. Goldston, I. (New York: International University Press, 1959), p. 43.
22. Matsumoto, M. *The Unspoken Way*. (Tokyo: Kodahsha International, 1989), p. 14.
23. Bohannan, P. *We, the Alien—An Introduction to Cultural Anthropology*. (Prospect Heights, IL: Waveland Press, 1992), p. 12.
24. Ibid., p. 13.
25. Ibid, pp. 11–14.
26. *American Heritage Dictionary of the English Language*, s.v. "ethnic."
27. Novak. "How American Are You?"
28. *American Heritage Dictionary*, s..v. "ethnicity," "ethnocentrism," "xenophobe."
29. Senior, C. *The Puerto Ricans: Strangers Then Neighbors* (Chicago: Quadrangle Books, 1965), p. 21.
30. Thernstrom. *American Ethnic Groups*, p. vii.
31. Ibid.
32. Abramson, H. J. "Religion," in *Harvard Encyclopedia of American Ethnic Groups*, ed. S. Thernstrom (Cambridge: Harvard University Press, 1980), pp. 869–875.
33. Spector. "Impact of Medicare," pp. 62–67.
34. Te Selle, S. ed. *Rediscovery of Ethnicity: Its Implications for Culture and Politics in America* (New York: Harper and Row, 1973).
35. Zola, I. K. "The Concept of Trouble and Sources of Medical Assistance: To Whom One Can Turn, with What and Why." *Social Science and Medicine* 6 (1972): 673–679.
36. Zborowski, M. "Cultural Components in Responses to Pain." *Journal of Social Issues* 8 (1952): 16–30.
37. Zborowski, M. *People in Pain* (San Francisco: Jossey-Bass, 1969).
38. Mechanic, D. "Religion, Religiosity, and Illness Behavior: The Special Case of the Jews." *Human Organization* 22 (1963): 202–208.

39. Suchman, E. A. "Sociomedical Variations Among Ethnic Groups." *American Journal of Sociology* 70 (1964): 319–331.
40. Suchman, E. A. "Social Patterns of Illness and Medical Care." *Journal of Health and Human Behavior* 6 (1965): 2–16.
41. Zola I. K. "Culture and Symptoms: An Analysis of Patients Presenting Complaints." *American Sociological Review* 31 (October 1966): 615–630.

ANNOTATED BIBLIOGRAPHY

Bermann, E. *Scapegoat*. Ann Arbor: University of Michigan Press, 1973.
    This book deals not only with the impact of fear of death on an American family but also with the role of culture in facing this event.
Boyle, J. S. and Andrews, M. M. *Transcultural Concepts in Nursing Care* (2nd ed.). Philadelphia: J. B. Lippincott, 1995.
    This book is a synthesis of the classic works of Leininger and other anthropologists who described cultural variations with respect to values, world views, and health. The authors are open in their descriptions of transcultural nursing principles and cultural variations in respect to health practices.
Dresser, N. *Our Own Stories—Cross-cultural Communication Practice*. White Plains, NY: Longman, 1993.
    This unique book helps the reader appreciate the difficulties new immigrants experience during the acculturation process. The text presents cultural issues through the eyes of people who experience these problems. It includes stories and examples of cultural norms, attitudes, behaviors, and expectations.
Galdston, I., ed. *Medicine and Anthropology*. New York: International Universities Press, 1959.
    Excellent background reading, this anthology explores the relation of anthropology to medicine in a number of outstanding articles.
Hunter, J. D. *Culture Wars—The Struggle to Define America*. New York: Basic Books, 1991.
    In this book, Hunter presents a riveting account of how the social and political forces of religious fundamentalists have joined forces in a battle against the progressive counterparts of American secular culture. It is applicable to the battles that are being fought against immigrants and the battles that are a part of the health-care delivery system, both the struggles within the system and those that exist between consumer and provider when the issue of traditional health practices emerges.
Hunter, J. D. *Before the Shooting Begins—Searching for Democracy in America's Culture War*. New York: Free Press, 1994.
    In this book Hunter further describes the emerging cultural conflicts in America today and the relevant political issues. He explores the issues that divide us as a nation and offers a voice of reason. His points on multiculturalism are vital reading for the serious student of cultural diversity in health and illness.
Kraut, A. M. *Silent Travelers: Germs, Genes, and the Immigrant Menace*. New York: Basic Books, 1994.
    Kraut presents compelling arguments about xenophobia, public health policy, the explanation of disease and how they interrelate with immigration policy. He traces

the history of cholera in the 1830s and HIV/AIDS in the 1990s and how each have shaped these policies. This book demonstrates how immigrants and minorities have played a role as scapegoats in American society.

Newman, K. D. *Ethnic American Short Stories.* New York: Pocket Books, 1975.

Numerous short stories that depict the literary perceptions and "laws" of various American ethnic groups are presented.

Rude, D., ed. *Alienation: Minority Groups.* New York: Wiley, 1972.

This book explores the values and goals of people who have sought to reshape American society. It examines the paradox in today's society that awards the expression of individuality but casts out those who by race, gender, politics, or mores are "different." It includes essays, poetry, and photography by those who are victims of oppression.

Ryan, W. *Blaming the Victim.* New York: Vintage Books, 1971.

Ryan demonstrates how the victims of poverty are blamed for their condition rather than the real villain—the inequality of American society.

Te Selle, S., ed. *The Rediscovery of Ethnicity: Its Implications for Culture and Politics in America.* New York: Harper and Row, 1973.

How "American" are we? This book attempts to answer this question with a number of outstanding contributions by such writers as Michael Novak, Arthur V. Shostack, and Rudolph J. Vecoli.

Zborowski, M. *People in Pain.* San Francisco: Jossey-Bass, 1969.

Zborowski examines the feeling of pain as a cultural experience for different peoples with unique histories.

FURTHER SUGGESTED READINGS

Articles

Ahoy, C. and Jung, M. "Community Health Nurses Working with Refugee Populations," in *Community Health Nursing* (3rd ed), eds. Archer, S. A. and Fleshman, R. P. Monterey, CA: Wadsworth Health Sciences, 1985, pp. 295–324.

Anderson, J. M. "The Cultural Context of Caring." *Canadian Critical Care Nursing Journal* 4(4) (December 1987): 7–13.

Anderson, J. and Chung, J. "Culture and Illness: Parents' Perceptions of Their Child's Long-term Illness." *Nursing Papers: Perspectives in Nursing* 14(4) (Winter 1982): 40–52.

Anderson, J. "An Acculturation Scale for Southeast Asians," *Social Psychiatry and Psychiatric Epidemiology* 28(3) (1993): 134–141.

Aroian, K. "Mental Health Risks and Problems Encountered by Illegal Immigrants, *Issues in Mental Health Nursing* 14(4) (1993): 379–397.

Baxter, C. "Culture Shock." *Nursing Times* 84(2) (January 13–19, 1988): 36–38.

Bebbington, P., Ghubash, R., and Hamdi, E. "The Dubai Community Psychiatric Survey: II. Development of the Socio-cultural Change Questionnaire." *Social Psychiatry and Psychiatric Epidemiology* 28(2) (1993): 60–65.

Bell, D. "For Whom the Bell Tolls," *PITT Magazine* 9(1) (1994): 12–15.

Bernal, H. and Froman, R. "The Confidence of Community Health Nurses in Caring Ethnically Diverse Populations." *Image: Journal of Nursing Scholarship* 19(4) (Winter 1987): 201–203.

Bilu, Y. and Witztum, E. "Working with Jewish Ultra-orthodox Patients: Guidelines for Culturally Sensitive Therapy." *Culture, Medicine, and Psychiatry* 17(2) (1993): 197–233.

Bush, M. T., Ullom, J. A., and Osborne, O. H. "The Meaning of Mental Health: A Report of Two Ethnoscientific Studies." *Nursing Research* 24(2) (March-April 1975): 130–138.

Clinton, J. "Sociocultural Issues Relevant to Health," in *Health Promotion Through the Life Span*, eds. Liem, C. and Mandle, C. St. Louis: C. V. Mosby, 1986.

Conway, F. J. and Carmona, P. E. "Cultural Complexity: The Hidden Stressors." *Journal of Advanced Medical Surgical Nursing.* 1(4) (September 1989): 65–72.

Cortes, C. E. "Limits to Pluribus, Limits to Unum—Unity, Diversity, and the Great Balancing Act," *National Forum—Multiculturalism and Diversity* 74(1) (1993): 6–9.

Davitz, L. J., Sameshima, Y., and Davitz, J. "Suffering as Viewed in Six Different Cultures." *American Journal of Nursing.* 76 (August 1976): 1296–1297.

Dobson, S. "Bringing Culture into Care." *Nursing Times* 76(6) (February 1983): 53, 56–57.

Dobson, S. M. "Conceptualizing for Transcultural Health Visiting: The Concept of Transcultural Reciprocity." *Journal of Advanced Nursing* 14(2) (February 1989): 97–102.

Fabrega, H. "A Cultural Analysis of Human Behavioral Breakdowns: An Approach to the Ontology and Epistemology of Psychiatric Phenomena," *Culture, Medicine, and Psychiatry* 17(1) (1993): 99–132.

Fielder, A. L. "Ambulatory Surgery: A Transcultural Approach." *Journal of Post Anesthesia Nursing* 3(3) (June 1988): 149–153.

Flaskerud, J. H. "A Proposed Protocol for Culturally Relevant Psychotherapy." *Clinical Nurse Specialist* 1(4) (Winter 1987): 150–157.

Friedman, M. L. and Musgrove J. A. "Perceptions of Inner City Substance Abusers about Their Families," *Archives of Psychiatric Nursing* 8(2) (1994): 115–123.

Furukawa, T. and Shibayama, T. "Predicting Maladjustment of Exchange Students in Different Cultures: A Prospective Study," *Social Psychiatry and Psychiatric Epidemiology* 28(3) (1993): 142–146.

Gaines, J. R., ed. "The New Face of America—How Immigrants are Shaping the World's First Multicultural Society," *Time* 142(21) (1993): 3–87.

Gale, B. J. "Psychosocial Needs of Older Women: Urban versus Rural Comparisons," *Archives of Psychiatric Nursing* 7(2) (1993):99–105.

Germain, C. P. "Cultural Concepts in Critical Care." *Critical Care Quarterly* 5(3) (December 1982): 61–78.

Hill, C. "Our Patients Have Culture—The Jewish Patient, Part I." *Clinical Management in Physical Therapy* 2(3) (Fall 1982): 5–6.

Hoeman, S. P. "Cultural Assessment in Rehabilitation Nursing Practice." *Nursing Clinics of North America* 24(1) (March 1989): 277–289.

Hogan, R. M. "Influences of Culture on Sexuality." *Nursing Clinics of North America* 17(3) (September 1982): 365–376.

Huttlinger, K. and Wiebe, P. "Transcultural Nursing Care: Achieving Understanding in a Practice Setting." *Journal of Transcultural Nursing* 1(1) (Summer 1989):17–32.

Jackson, L. E. "Understanding, Eliciting, and Negotiating Clients' Multicultural Health Beliefs," *Nurse Practitioner* 18(4) (1993): 30–43.

Johnston, J. B. "Giving Effective Emergency Care to Patients from Differing Cultures." *Emergency Nursing Reports* 2(6) (September 1987): 1–7.

Kellert, S. R. "A Sociocultural Concept of Health and Illness." *Journal of Medicine and Philosophy* 1(3) (March 1976): 222–228.

Kub, J. P. "Ethnicity—An Important Factor for Nurses to Consider in Caring for Hypertensive Individuals." *Western Journal of Nursing Research* 8(4) (November 1986): 445–456.

Lammers, P. K. "Dealing with Other Cultures and Religions Emphasized at Recent Ethics Conference." *Association of Operating Room Nurses Journal* 45(4) (May 1987): 1211–1212, 1214, 1216.

La Farque, J. P. "Role of Prejudice in Rejection of Health Care." *Nursing Research* 21(1) (January-February 1972): 53–58.

Leininger, M. "The Cultural Concept and Its Relevance to Nursing." *Journal of Nursing Education* 6 (April 1967): 27.

Leininger, M. "Cultural Care: An Essential Goal for Nursing and Health Care." *American Association of Nephrology Nurses and Technicians* 10(5) (August 1983): 11–17.

Leininger, M. "The Transcultural Nurse Specialist: Imperative in Today's World." *Nursing and Health Care* 10(5) (May 1989): 250–256.

Leininger, M. "Leininger's Theory of Nursing: Cultural Care Diversity and Universality." *Nursing Science Quarterly* 1(4) (November 1988): 152–160.

Leininger, M. "Transcultural Eating Patterns and Nutrition: Transcultural Nursing and Anthropological Perspectives." *Holistic Nursing Practice* 3(1) (November 1988): 16–25.

Leininger, M. "Transcultural Nurse Specialists and Generalists: New Practitioners in Nursing." *Journal of Transcultural Nursing* 1(1) (Summer 1989): 4–16.

Leininger, M. "Transcultural Nursing: Quo Vadis (Where Goeth the Field?)." *Journal of Transcultural Nursing* 1(1) (Summer 1989): 33–45.

Logan, B. L. and Semmes, C. E. "Culture and Ethnicity," in *Family Centered Nursing in the Community,* eds. Logan, B. B. and Dawkins, C. E., Menlo Park, CA: Addison-Wesley, 1986, pp. 97–130.

Long, R. "A Tale of Two Cultures." *Nursing Times* 4 (August 1977): 1215–1216.

Luna, L. "Transcultural Nursing Care of Arab Muslims. *Journal of Transcultural Nursing* 1(1) (Summer 1989): 22–26.

MacGregor, F. C. "Uncooperative Patients: Some Cultural Interpretations." *American Journal of Nursing* 67 (January 1967): 88–91.

Mandelbaum, J. K. "The Food Square: Helping People of Different Cultures Understand Balanced Diets." *Pediatric Nursing* 9(1) (January-February 1983): 13–16.

McDonald, R. "Community Issues: Cultural Exchange—Hindu, Sikh, and Moslem Religious Beliefs and Traditions, Part 2." *Nursing Mirror* 160(7) (February 13, 1985): 32–35.

McKenna, M. "Twice in Need of Nursing Care: A Transcultural Nursing Analysis of Elderly Mexican Americans." *Journal of Transcultural Nursing* 1(1) (Summer 1989): 46–52.

Muecke, M. A. "Overcoming the Language Barrier." *Nursing Outlook* (April 1970): 53–54.

Pasquali, E. A., Arnold, H. M., and DeBasio, N. "The Sociocultural Context of Behavior," in *Mental Health Nursing.* St. Louis: C. V. Mosby, 1989, pp. 89–119.

Patcher, L. M. "Culture and Clinical Care—Folk Illness Beliefs and Behaviors and Their Implications for Health Care Delivery," *Journal of the American Medical Association* 271(9) (1994): 690–694.

Post, S. G. "Psychiatry and Ethics: The Problematics of Respect for Religious Meanings, " *Culture, Medicine, and Psychiatry.* 17(1): 363–383.

Ragucci, A. T. "The Ethnographic Approach and Nursing Research." *Nursing Research* 21(6) (November-December 1972): 485–490.

Rosenbaum, J. N. "Depression: Viewed from a Transcultural Nursing Theoretical Perspective." *Journal of Advanced Nursing* 14(1) (January 1989): 7–12.

Sheebin, S. "Nursing Patients from Different Cultures." *Nursing 80* (June 1980): 78–81.

Spradley, B W. "Culture and Community," in *Community Health Nursing Concepts and Practice* (3rd ed). Glenview, IL: Scott, Foresman/Little, Brown Higher Education, 1990, pp. 131–161.

Stacy, S. "Nurses and Other People." *Australian Nursing Journal* 16(2) (August 1986): 54–57.

Sundquist, J. "Refugees, Labour Migrants and Psychological Distress. A Population-Based Study of 338 Latin-American Refugees, 161 South European and 396 Finnish Labour Migrants, and 996 Swedish Age-, Sex-, and Education-Matched Controls," *Social Psychiatry and Psychiatric Epidemiology* 29(1) (1994): 20–24.

"Symposium on Cultural and Biological Diversity and Health Care." *Nursing Clinics of North America* 12 (March 1977): 1.

Tripp-Reimer, T. "Cross-Cultural Perspectives on Patient Teaching." *Nursing Clinics of North America* 24(3) (September 1989): 613–619.

Valente, S. M. "Overcoming Cultural Barriers." *California Nurse* 85(8) (September 1989): 4–5.

Waldram, J. B. "Aboriginal Spirituality: Symbolic Healing in Canadian Prisons," *Culture, Medicine, and Psychiatry* 17(3) (1993): 345–362.

Walker, C. "Attitudes to Death and Bereavement among Cultural Minority Groups." *Nursing Times* 78(50) (December 1982): 2106–2109.

Williamson, K. M., Turner, J. G., and Chavigny, K. H. "Sociocultural Communities," in *Community Health Nursing an Epidemiologic Perspective Through the Nursing Process,* eds. Turner, J. G. and Chavigny, K. H., Philadelphia; J. B. Lippincott, 1988, pp. 133–154.

Wilson, H. S., and Kneisl, C. R. *Psychosocial Nursing Concepts: An Activity Book* (3rd ed.) Menlo Park, CA: Addison-Wesley, 1988.

Wing, D. M. "Community Participant-Observation: Issues in Assessing Diverse Cultures." *Journal of Community Health Nursing* 6(3) (1989): 125–133.

York, C R., and Stichler, J. F. "Cultural Grief Expressions Following Infant Death." *Dimensions of Critical Care Nursing* 4(2) (March-April 1985): 120–127.

Zola, I. K. "The Concept of Trouble and Sources of Medical Assistance: To Whom One Can Turn, With What and Why." *Social Science and Medicine* 6 (1972): 673–679.

Zola, I. K. "Culture and Symptoms: An Analysis of Patients Presenting Complaints." *American Sociological Review* 31 (October 1966): 615–630.

"Special Populations Claim RN Attention." *American Nurse* 19(8) (September 1987): 1, 8, 10.

RESOURCES

Transcultural Nursing Society

Official Journal: *Journal of Transcultural Nursing*
c/o Madonna University
College of Nursing and Health

36600 Schoolcraft Road
Livonia, MI 48150-1173
(313)591-8358

Transcultural nursing
certification information is available from
Dr. G. Roessler
8401 Munster Drive
Huntington Beach, CA 92646

Council on Nursing and Anthropology
c/o Dr. Millie Roberson
Nursing Department
Southeast Missouri State University
Cape Giardeau, MO 63701

Center for Multiculturalism and Health Care
Official Journal: *Journal of Multicultural Nursing*
Center for Multiculturalism and Health Care
P.O. Box 889
Chautauqua Institution
Chautauqua, NY 14722

2

Issues of Delivery and Acceptance of Health Care

Unit II covers the acquisition and use of health-care resources. The overall theme encompasses the problems that the client encounters.

Chapter 5 explores the experience of using the American health-care delivery system. It highlights a number of provocative issues, including barriers to health care and alternative health-care options. Enlarging on the earlier theme of folk health—illness beliefs and practices—Chapter 6 explores the natural traditions associated with healing, and Chapter 7 explores the magiocoreligious traditions and discusses healing, both ancient and modern. Chapter 8 presents the demographic backgrounds of the categories of population groups as defined by the U.S. Bureau of the Census. Each chapter provides a number of illustrative examples.

Unit II should enable the reader to

1. Understand the universal problems encountered in the use of the health-care system
2. Understand how the organized medical practice serves as an institution of social control

3. Understand how barriers (primarily poverty) serve to prevent people from accessing or fully using the health-care delivery system

4. Identify the alternative types of healing systems in contemporary society

5. Identify religious beliefs related to both the prevention and healing of illness

6. Identify demographic factors that influence health-care delivery

Before you begin to read this unit, please consider the following issues:

1. Who is the first person you turn to when you are ill?

2. Who do you go to, and where do you go from there?

3. You have just moved to a new location. You do not know a single person in this community. How do you find health-care resources?

4. Call the county medical society in your area and request the name of a surgeon. Now make an appointment with this doctor. (Assume you have a health problem that requires surgery.)

5. Visit an emergency room in a large city hospital. Visit an emergency room in a small community hospital. Spend several hours quietly observing what occurs in each setting.

   a. How long do patients wait to be seen?

   b. Are patients called by name?

   c. Are relatives or friends allowed into the treatment room with the patient?

6. Determine the cost of a day of hospitalization.

   a. How much does a room cost? How much is a day in the intensive care unit or coronary care unit? How much is time in the emergency room? How is a surgical procedure charged?

   b. How much is charged for diagnostic procedures, such as computed tomography (CT) scan or ultrasound? How much is charged for such equipment as a simple intravenous (IV) set-up?

   c. What are the pharmacy charges?

d. How many days, or hours, are women kept in the hospital after delivery of a child? Is the newborn baby sent home at the same time? If not, why not? What is the cost of a normal vaginal delivery and normal newborn care?

7. Visit a homeopathic pharmacy or a natural food store and examine the shelves that contain herbal remedies and information about alternative health care.

   a. What is the cost of a variety of herbal remedies used to maintain health or to prevent common ailments?

   b. What is the cost of a variety of herbal remedies used to treat common ailments?

   c. What is the range of costs for literature?

5

Chapter

Health-Care Delivery: Issues, Barriers, and Alternatives

American medicine, the pride of the nation for many years, stands on the brink of chaos. To be sure, our medical practitioners have their great moments of drama and triumph. But, much of U.S. medical care, particularly the everyday business of preventing and treating illness, is inferior in quality, wastefully dispensed, and inequitably financed. Medical manpower and facilities are so maldistributed that large segments of the population, especially the urban poor and those in rural areas, get virtually no care at all, even though their illnesses are most numerous and, in a medical sense, often easy to cure.[1]

—John Knowles, 1970

The health of the nation continues to be in crisis, and the observations of Dr. Knowles were indeed visionary in terms of the present circumstance. As we approach the year 2000, doctors in America administer the world's most expensive medical (illness) care system. The costs of American health care have soared from $4 billion in 1940 to the present $1 trillion a year enterprise that exceeds all the goods and services produced by half the states in the country. Health has become this country's biggest business, and it accounts for nearly one sixth of our economy. In fact, nearly $4,000 in 1994 was spent on health care for every man, woman, child, and fetus.[2] The health care system is both a source of national pride—for if one has the money, it certainly is possible to get the finest medical care in the world—and a source of

deep embarrassment, for those who are poor or uninsured may well be wanting of care.

Despite this high expenditure and the large numbers of hospital beds, we
were not healthier than people from other nations. In fact, 22 other nations
had lower infant mortality rates, and 26 had lower death rates from cardiovascular diseases. Furthermore, every developed nation except the United
States and South Africa had a form of national health insurance[3] (Fig. 5–1). In
1995, efforts to deal with this crisis and create national health-care reform
ground to a halt. The following examples serve to illustrate this situation:

1. In randomly selected hospitals in Massachusetts, the 1995 cost of
   a semiprivate room ranged from $385 to $975 per day, a bed in a
   pediatric intensive care unit was $1,700, an intensive care unit
   bed was $1,200, a coronary care unit bed was $1,760, and a surgical intensive care unit bed was $1,900; the cost of a myelogram
   was $250, a bone marrow transplant was $70,000, a CT scan was
   $784, and a cardiac catherization was $2,500.[4]
2. A patient admitted with a cardiac episode to a Boston area hospital for a 13-day stay had a hospital bill that came to $58,211.22—
   not including physician fees. The patient paid out of pocket $340;
   insurance covered the remainder. Just one item on this bill, a drug
   called alteplase recominant (a blood clot disolver) cost $8,892.92
   for one 10-milligram dose.* It is interesting to note that the patient's insurance covered these relatively expensive costs, yet the
   same insurance company and most other insurers demand that
   women and newborn infants be discharged from the hospital
   anywhere from 12 to 48 hours after a vaginal delivery and 72
   hours after a Cesarean section.[5] The daily cost for maternity and
   regular neonatal care is considerably less than the $4,478 paid for
   the cardiac patient, yet mother and child are forced to leave the
   hospital sooner than some think is medically advisable, precipitating significant problems for this population.
3. One consequence of New York City's public hospitals failing is
   that each year for the past 10 years, dozens of babies have died or
   been left to live with brain damage because of alleged mistakes
   and inexperience of doctors and poorly supervised midwives.
   The consequences of poor care in the delivery room have been
   devastating to all the users of the system—from women who
   never received any prenatal care to those who received impec-
   cable prenatal care.[6]
4. Charges of financial abuse are frequently noted, with examples of
   overbilling occasionally being published. One example is a hos-

---

*This medication is manufactured under the trade name Activase by a bioengineering firm,
Genentech, and is used for example, after a myocardial infarction to improve the ejection frac-
tion at rest and to reduce the prevalence of congestive heart failure.

HEALTH CARE

These industrialized nations have a national health program

Austrailia	Denmark	Ireland	Portugal
Austria	Finland	Italy	Romania
Belgium	France	Japan	Russia
Bulgaria	Germany	Netherlands	Spain
Canada	Great Britain	New Zealand	Sweden
Czechosiovakia	Greece	Norway	Switzerland
	Hungary	Poland	

These industrialized nations do not:

South Africa

United States

Figure 5–1. Adapted from a poster produced by the Rainbow Coalition of Vermont, the Progressive Coalition of Burlington, Vermont, and the Health Task Force of the National Committee for Independent Political Action in 1990.

pital in the Boston area that overbilled insurance companies over $900,000. The federal government estimates that 10% of the money spent on health care in the United States is lost to fraud, waste, and financial abuse. The home care infusion industry has been found to be riddled with abuses. Treatments that family members generally administer, such as total parenteral nutrition, cost from $200–900 per day. A 90-day treatment can range from

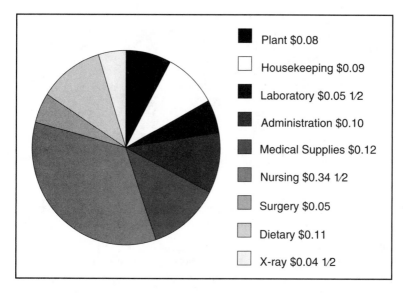

Legend:
- Plant $0.08
- Housekeeping $0.09
- Laboratory $0.05 1/2
- Administration $0.10
- Medical Supplies $0.12
- Nursing $0.34 1/2
- Surgery $0.05
- Dietary $0.11
- X-ray $0.04 1/2

Figure 5–2. Spending the Health Care Dollar—1956. *(Reprinted with permission from The Explanation for a Patient's Bill in 1956. Hospitalized for 10 days in a community hospital—total cost—$214.40.)*

$22,500 to $54,000. This cost covers a significant amount of equipment that is left over. Once something is taken to the home it cannot be brought back and reused.[7]

5. It has been found that the cost of drugs is higher in the United States than elsewhere in the world. For example, in 1992 prices for a 25-milligram tablet of the blood pressure medication captopril (Capoten) cost $0.48 in the United States and $0.43 in Canada; a 20-milligram capsule of the antiinflammatory, piroxicam (Feldine), cost $1.83 in the United States and $0.50 in the United Kingdom; and a 400-milligram tablet of the antibiotic, norfloxacin (Noroxin), cost $1.83 in the United States and $0.75 in the United Kingdom.[8]

How did we get to this critical situation? What factors converged to bring us to this dramatic breaking point? On the one hand, because of the unprecedented growth of biomedical technology, we have witnessed the tremendous advancement in medical science and in its ability to perform an astounding variety of life-saving procedures. On the other hand, not only can we no longer afford to finance these long dreamed-of miracles, but the dream has become a nightmare. Figures 5–2 and 5–3 illustrate the changing distribution of dollars spent for health care.

This chapter briefly traces the history of events and developments from 1850 to the present time that have led us to this destination. In addition, the common problems we all experience when we seek health care, the pathways we follow when we experience a health problem, the view of medicine as a

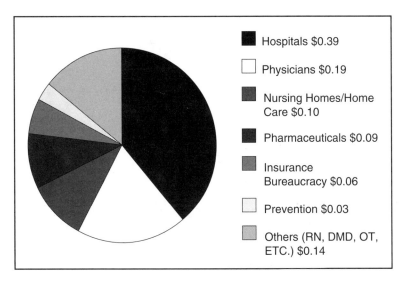

- ■ Hospitals $0.39
- □ Physicians $0.19
- ■ Nursing Homes/Home Care $0.10
- ■ Pharmaceuticals $0.09
- ■ Insurance Bureaucracy $0.06
- □ Prevention $0.03
- ■ Others (RN, DMD, OT, ETC.) $0.14

Figure 5–3. Spending the Health Care Dollar—1994. *(Reprinted from Califano, J. A., Jr. Radical Surgery— What's Next for America's Health Care? NY: Random House, 1994, pp. 21–47.)*

means of social control, the barriers to health care, and an introduction to health care alternatives are discussed. The reader is strongly encouraged to probe more deeply into each of these areas, and to that end, several timely and historical references conclude this chapter.

TRENDS IN DEVELOPMENT OF THE HEALTH-CARE SYSTEM

Our health-care system was once, during the days of the early colonists, a system of superstition and faith. It has evolved into a system predicated on a strong belief in science; the epidemiological model of disease; highly developed technology; and strong values of individuality, competition, and free enterprise. Two major forces—free enterprise and science—have greatly shaped the problems we now face. In Table 5–1, we readily observe how health problems have evolved from the epidemics of 1850 to the chronic diseases of today, notwithstanding the resurgence of tuberculosis and the AIDS epidemic. In 1850, health-care technology was virtually nonexistent, yet today it dominates the delivery of health care. We now take for granted such dramatic procedures as kidney, heart, and liver transplants. New technologies and biomedical milestones are materializing daily.[9]

Social organizations to control the use of technology did not exist in 1850, yet today they proliferate, with the federal government being expected to play a dominant role. The belief that health care is a *right* for all Americans is

TABLE 5–1. TRENDS IN THE DEVELOPMENT OF THE AMERICAN HEALTH-CARE DELIVERY SYSTEM, 1850–FUTURE

Date	Health Problems	Available Technology	Social Control of Technology
1850–1900	Epidemics and acute infections	Virtually none	None; individuals looked after themselves
1900–World War II	Acute health problems, trauma, individual infections	Beginning of the rapid growth of bio-medical sciences and technology	Beginning of so-cial and gov-ernment efforts to care for those who could not care for themselves
World War II–1990	Chronic diseases, such as heart disease, cancer, and stroke	Explosive growth of biomedical sciences and technology	"Health care as a right": government responsible to direct care for all
Future	Increase in chronic diseases and mental illness	Continued growth in biomedical tech-nology; some at-tempts to repersonalize care	Greater government control and efforts to control costs

Adapted with permission from: Torrens. "Historical Evolution and Overview of Health Services in the United States" in *Introduction to Health Services (3rd ed.)* eds. P. R. Williams, S. J. and Torrens, P. R. (Albany: Delmar Publishers Inc., 1988), p. 15.

still a predominant philosophy, yet the fulfillment of that right is still in question. The trends in the 1980s and early 1990s, such as the cutbacks in federal funding for health services and the attempt to turn the clock back on social programs, have led to a diminished and denigrated role for the government in people's health. There is growing and grave concern about the realization of this basic human right. Mounting social problems, such as toxic waste, homelessness, and 40 million people without health insurance, confound the situation.[10] These factors all affect the delivery of health care. The problems of acquiring and using the health-care system are ongoing.

HEALTH-CARE REFORM

In 1993 and 1994 both President and Mrs. Clinton made an extraordinary effort to study our complex health-care system and to reform it. That effort came to little, and the present political energy has shifted from health-care reform to welfare reform among other reforms in the House Republican's *Contract with America.*[11] Meanwhile, the costs of health care continue to soar, causing some hospitals to downsize their nursing staff in an effort to reduce costs. Throughout all President Clinton's campaign to control health-care costs, discussion focused on how to pay for care, but not really what to do to address the underlying high costs. The president sought health-care reform in the middle ground between competition and regulation and designed a plan to

1. Rely on market forces to hold down costs
2. Ensure a multitiered health-care system by encouraging all but the most wealthy to seek care in health maintenance organizations (HMOs)
3. Install new regulatory measures[12]

Ultimately, it was believed that the Clinton plan would create a few giant insurers and HMOs would dominate the market; most people would be forced into low-cost plans, doctors would be employed by the insurers or HMOs, hospitals would be controlled by insurers and HMOs, care would be multitiered, the bureaucracy would increase, costs would not be contained, and financing would be regressive.[13]

Although, as Small put it, "The goal of health care reform was to make access to comprehensive, affordable health care a right and not a privilege of all residents of the United States,"[14] at this writing, the plans for health-care reform are quietly simmering, and the costs continue to climb. Advances in and our use of technology is flourishing, and we continue to spend vast sums on the care of patients in the last year of life while delivering less and less preventive care. But as shown in Table 5–2, the United States does not rank first in the delivery of high-technology care such as transplants.[15]

During 1993 and 1994, many changes did occur in the health-care delivery system, and several milestones were reached, including

1. A majority of Americans who are privately insured were enrolled in managed care plans. These plans limit the choice of doctors

TABLE 5–2. TRANSPLANTS PERFORMED IN INDUSTRIALIZED NATIONS: 1989–1981

Nation	Total Number of Transplants	Transplants Per Million Per Year
France	1,708	13.4
Sweden	168	9.0
Canada	576	8.9
Australia	369	8.8
United Kingdom	1,000	8.2
United States	4,873	8.1
Denmark	90	7.8
New Zealand	59	7.4
Netherlands	232	6.6
Germany	757	5.6

From: Knox, R. A. and the U.S. General Accounting Office, "Studies Challenge view US as world leader in Medicare." March, 1994, *Boston Globe,* March 26, 1994, p. 3. Reprinted with permission.

and care plans. The workers in medium and large companies were presented with the option of managed care—65% enrolled.

2. The dominant force in managed care is the for-profit health maintenance organization.

3. Three fourths of all doctors signed contracts with managed programs to cover some of their patients and to accept oversight of their medical decisions.[16]

The for-profit HMOs compete to provide care for a preset fee, are run by larger insurance companies, and underprice established HMOs. Insurance companies and HMOs are presently dominating the system, and the private sector is creating large linkages. For example, one private hospital chain, Columbia/HCA Healthcare, has grown from a small regional facility to the owner of 311 hospitals—half of all the for-profit hospitals in the country. This chain includes not only private for-profit hospitals, but they are purchasing nonprofit hospitals as well.

The quality of care may or may not be better. Fees are paid on fixed amounts and the doctor is paid whether or not a given patient's symptoms are treated.[17]

COMMON PROBLEMS IN HEALTH-CARE DELIVERY

Many problems exist within today's health-care delivery system. Some of these problems affect all of us, and others are specific to the poor and to emerging majority populations. It has been suggested that the health-care delivery system fosters and maintains a childlike dependence and depersonalized condition for the consumer.[18] The following sections describe problems experienced by most consumers of health care.

"Finding Where the Appropriate Care is Offered at a Reasonable Price"

It may be difficult for even a knowledgeable consumer to receive adequate care. One summer, I was on vacation with my 11-year-old daughter. She complained of a sore throat for two days, and when she did not improve on the third day, I decided to take her to a pediatrician and have a throat culture taken. She was running a low-grade fever, and I suspected a strep infection. I phoned the emergency room of a local teaching hospital for the name of a pediatrician, but I was instructed to "bring her in." I questioned the practicality of using an emergency room, but the friendly voice on the other end of the line assured me: "If you have health insurance and the child has a sore throat, this is the best place to come." After a rather long wait, we were seen by an intern who was beginning his first day in pediatrics. To my dismay and chagrin, the young man appeared to have no idea of how to proceed. The resident entered and patiently demonstrated to the fledgling intern— using my daughter—how to go about doing a physical examination on a child. Since I had brought the child to the emergency room merely for a throat culture, I felt that what they were doing was unnecessary and said so. After much delay, the throat culture was taken; we were told we could leave and should call back in 48 hours for the report. As we left the cubicle, we had to pass another cubicle with an open curtain—where a woman was vomiting all over herself, the bed, and the equipment while another intern was attempting to insert a gastric tube. Needless to say, my daughter was distressed by the sight, which she could not help but witness. The reward for this trial was an inflated bill.

Two days later, I called back for the report. It could not be located. When it was finally "found," the result was negative. I took issue with this because it took 30 minutes for them to find the report. Perhaps this sounds a bit over-stated; however, I had the feeling that they told me it was negative just to get me off the phone.

I related this personal experience to bring out two major points. First, it is not easy to obtain what I, as a health-care provider, consider to be a rather minor procedure. Second—and perhaps more important—it was expensive!

The average health-care consumer in such a circumstance may very well have no idea of what is really going on. When health care is sought, one should have access to professionally performed examinations and treatment. When one is seeking the results of a laboratory test, the results should be available immediately at the agreed-on time and place instead of being lost in a jungle of bureaucracy.

"Finding One's Way Amidst the Many Available Types of Medical Care"

A friend's experience illustrates how hard it may be to find appropriate medical care. She had minor gastric problems from time to time and initially sought help from a family physician. He was unable to treat the problem adequately; therefore, she decided to go elsewhere. However, for many reasons—including anger, embarrassment, and fear of reprisal—she chose not to tell the family physician that she was dissatisfied with his care, nor did she request a referral. She was, for all intents and purposes, on her own in terms of securing an appointment with either a gastroenterologist or a surgeon. She very quickly discovered that no physician who was a specialist in gastroenterology would see her on a self-referral. In order to get an appointment, she had to ask her own general practitioner for a referral or else seek initial help from another general practitioner or internist. Since she had little money to spend on a variety of physicians, she decided to wait to see what would happen. In this instance, happily, she was fortunate and has had few further problems.

As a teaching and learning experience, I ask students to describe how they go about selecting a physician and where they go for health care. The younger students in the class generally seek the services of their families' physicians. The older or married students often have doctors other than those with whom they "grew up." These latter students generally are quite willing to share the trials and tribulations that they have experienced. When given the freedom to express their actions and reactions, most admit to having a great deal of difficulty in getting what they perceive to be *good* health care. A number of the older students state that they select a physician on the staff of the institution where they are employed. They have had an opportunity to see him at work and can judge, first hand, whether he is "good" or "bad." One mother stated that she worked in pediatrics during her pregnancy solely to discover who was the best pediatrician. A newly married student stated that she planned to work in the delivery room to see which obstetrician delivered a baby with the greatest amount of concern for both the mother and the child.

That is all well and good for members of the nursing profession, but what about the average lay person who does not have access to this resource? This question alerts the students to the specialness of their personal situations and exposes them to the immensity of the problem that the average person experiences. After individual experiences are shared, the class can move on to work through a case study such as the following.

Ms B. is a new resident in this city. She discovers a lump in her breast and does not know where to turn. How does she go about finding a doctor? Where does she go?

One initial course of action is to call the American Cancer Society for advice. From there, she is instructed to call the County Medical Society, since the American Cancer Society is not allowed to give out physicians' names. During a phone call to the County Medical Society, she is given the names of three physicians in her part of the city. From there she is on her own in attempting to get an appointment with one of them. It is not unknown for a stranger to call a physician's office and be told (1) "The doctor is no longer seeing any additional new patients," (2) "There is a six-month wait," or (3) "He sees no one without a proper referral."

The woman, of course, has another choice: she can go to an emergency room or a clinic, but then she discovers that the wait in the emergency room is intolerable for her. She may rationalize that because a "lump" is not really an "emergency," she should choose another route. She may then try to secure a clinic appointment, and once again she may experience a great deal of difficulty in getting an appointment at a convenient time. She may finally get one and then discover that the wait in the clinic is unduly long—which may cause her to miss a day of work.

"Figuring Out What the Physician is Doing"

It is not always easy for members of the health professions to understand what is happening to them when they are ill. Alas, what must it be like for the average person who has little or no knowledge of health-care routines and practices?

Pretend that you are a lay person who has just been relieved of all your clothes and given a paper dress to put on. You are lying on a table with strange eyes peering down at you. A sheet is thrown over you, and you are given terse directions—"breathe," "cough," "don't breathe," "turn," "lift your legs." You may feel without warning a cold disc on your chest or a cold hand on your back. As the physical examination process continues, you may feel a few taps on the ribs, see a bright light shining in your eye, feel a cold tube in your ear, and gag on a stick probing the inside of your mouth. What is going on? The jargon you hear is unfamiliar. You are being poked, pushed, prodded, peered at and into, jabbed, and you do not know why. If you are female and going for your first pelvic examination, you may have no idea what to expect. Perhaps you have heard only hushed whisperings, and your level of fear and discomfort is high. Insult is added to injury when you experience the penetration of a cold, unyielding speculum: "What is the doctor doing now and why?"

These hypothetical situations are typical of the usual physical examinations that you may encounter routinely in a clinic or private physician's office. Suppose you have a more complex problem, such as a neurological condition, for which the diagnostic procedures may indeed be painful and complicated. Have you ever had a CT scan? A magnetic resonance image (MRI)? An angioplasty? Quite often, those who deliver care have not experienced the vast number of procedures that are performed in diagnostic workups and in treatment. They have little awareness of what the patient is thinking, feeling, and experiencing. Similarly, because the names and the purposes of the procedures are familiar to health-care workers—don't forget, this is *their* culture—they may take their own understanding of the procedures for granted and have difficulty appreciating why the patient cannot understand what is happening.

"Finding Out What Went Wrong"

What did you do the last time a patient asked to read the chart? Traditionally, you uttered an authoritative "tsk," turned abruptly on white-heeled shoes, and walked briskly away. Who ever heard of such nerve? A patient asking to read a chart! In recent years, a "patient's bill of rights" has evolved. One of its mandates is that the patient has the right to read his or her own medical record. Experience, however, demonstrates that this right is still not always granted. Suppose one enters the hospital for what is deemed to be a simple medical or surgical problem. All well and good, if everything goes according to routine. However, what happens when complications develop? The more determined the patient is to discover what the problem is or why there are complications, the more the patient believes that the health-care providers are trying to hide something. The cycle perpetuates itself, and a tremendous schism develops between provider and consumer. Quite often, "the conspiracy of silence" tends to grow as more questions are asked. This unpleasant situation may continue until the patient is locked inside his or her subjective world. It is rare for a person truly to understand unforeseen complications. Nurses all too often enter into this collusion and play the role of a silent partner with the physician and the institution.

"Overcoming the Built-in Racism and Male Chauvinism of Doctors and Hospitals"

Students tend to have little difficulty in describing many incidents of racism and male chauvinism: that they are mostly women suffices, and that they are nurses adds meaning to the problem. Classroom discussion helps to identify subtle incidents of racism and to identify them as such. For example, students may realize that black patients may be the last to receive morning or evening care, meal trays, and so forth. If this is a normal occurrence on a floor, it is an indictment in itself. Racism may take another tack. Is it an accident that the black person is the last patient to receive routine care or has he consciously been made to wait? Does the fact that the black person may have to wait longest for water or a pill demonstrate racism on a conscious level, or is it subliminal?

Nurses recognize the subtle patronization of both themselves and of female patients. Once the situation is probed and spelled out, the students adopt a much more realistic attitude toward the insensitivity of those who choose a racist or chauvinistic style of giving care. Students have noted that when they are aware of what is happening, they are better able to take steps to block future occurrences. Some have written letters to me after they have begun or returned to the practice of nursing, stating that knowing the phenomenon is common helps them to project a stronger image in their determination to work for change.

PATHWAYS TO HEALTH SERVICES

When a health problem occurs, there is an established system whereby health-care services are obtained. The family is usually the first resource. It is in the domain of the family that the person seeks validation that what he or she is experiencing is indeed an illness. Once the belief is validated, health care outside of the home is sought. When one is dealing with the medical system in general, help is sought from a physician in the private office of a general practitioner, internist, or pediatrician or in a hospital emergency room or clinic.† This is known as the level of first contact, or the *entrance* into the health-care system.[19]

The second level of care, if needed, is found at the specialist's level: in clinics, private practice, or hospitals. Obstetricians, gynecologists, surgeons,

---

†It is not unusual for a family to be receiving care from many different physicians, with limited or no communication between the attending physicians. Problems and complications erupt when a physician is not aware that other physicians are caring for a patient. Let us not forget that in rural and remote areas, comprehensive health care is difficult to obtain. For patients who are forced to use the clinics of a hospital, there is certainly no continuity of care because intern and resident physicians come and go each year.

neurologists, and other specialists make up a large percentage of those who practice in medicine.[20]

The third level of care is delivered within hospitals that provide inpatient care and services. Care is determined by need, whether long-term (as in a psychiatric setting or rehabilitation institute) or short-term (as in the acute care setting and community hospitals).[21]

An in-depth discussion of the different kinds of hospitals—voluntary or profit-making and nonprofit institutions—is more appropriate to a book dealing solely with the delivery of health care (see the annotated bibliography at the end of this book). In our present context, the issue is: What does the patient know about such settings, and what kind of care can he or she expect to receive?

To many students, the problems of the ward are far removed from the scope of practice they know from nursing school and from what they ordinarily see in a work setting (unless they choose to work in a city or county hospital). Many students assume that the care they observe and deliver in a suburban or community hospital is the universal norm. This is a fundamental error in experience and understanding, which can be corrected if students are assigned to visit first the emergency room of a city hospital and then the emergency room of a suburban hospital in order to compare the two milieus. Unless students visit each setting, they fail to gain an appreciation of the major differences—how vastly such facilities differ in the scope of patients' treatment. Students typically report that in the suburban emergency room, the patients are called by name, their families wait with them, and every effort is made to hasten their visit. The contrast is astounding with people in urban emergency rooms who have waited for extended periods of time, are sometimes not addressed by name, and are not allowed to have family members come with them while they are examined. The noise and confusion are also factors that confront and dismay students when they are exposed to big-city emergency rooms.

MEDICINE AS AN INSTITUTION OF SOCIAL CONTROL

The people of today's death-denying, youth-oriented society have unusually high expectations of the healers of our time. We expect a cure (or if not a cure, then the prolongation of life) as the normal outcome of illness. The technology of modern health care dominates our expectations of treatment, and our primary focus is on the *curative* aspects of medicine, not on prevention.

As control over the behavior of a person has shifted from the family and church to a physician, "be good" has shifted to "take your medicine." The role that physicians play within society in terms of social control is ever-growing, so that conflict frequently arises between medicine and the law over definitions of accepted codes of behavior and the relative status of the two professions in governing American life.[22] The following examples serve to illustrate the "medicalization" of society.

"Through the Expansion of What in Life is Deemed Relevant to the Good Practice of Medicine"

This factor is exemplified by the change from a specific etiological model of disease to a multicausal one. The "partners" in this new model include greater acceptance of comprehensive medicine, the use of the computer, and the practice of preventive medicine. In preventive medicine, however, the medical person must get to the lay person before the disease occurs: clients must be sought out. Because of this, forms of social control emerge in an attempt to *prevent* disease: low-cholesterol diets, avoidance of stress, stopping smoking, getting proper and adequate exercise.

"Through the Retention of Absolute Control over Certain Technical Procedures"

This step is, in essence, the right to perform surgery and the right to prescribe drugs. In the life span of human beings, modern medicine can often determine life or death from the time of conception to old age through genetic counseling; abortion; surgery; and technological devices, such as computers, respirators, and life-support systems. Medicine has at its command drugs that can cure or kill—from antibiotics to the chemotherapeutic agents used to combat cancer. There are drugs to cause sleep or wakefulness, to increase or decrease the appetite, to increase or decrease levels of energy. There are drugs to relieve depression and stimulate interest. (In the United States, those mood-altering drugs are consumed at a rate higher than those medications prescribed and used to treat specific diseases). In addition, medicine can control what medications are available for legal consumption.

The controversy over amygdalin (Laetrile) is an example of how the medical establishment is thwarting the popular consumption of a drug. In spite of the scientific evidence that this drug is worthless, there is no evidence to date that it is harmful, and a significant number of people desire to use it in the hope of preventing or treating cancer. The ongoing battle between the proponents and opponents of Laetrile is a fascinating study in the power of modern medical social control and the factions that are attacking this power. Since 1977, the proponents have made headway in lobbying for legalization of the drug in a number of states, and a federal judicial ruling has permitted its use in individual cases.‡

"Through the Retention of Nearly Absolute Access to Certain Taboo Areas"

Medicine has almost exclusive license to examine and treat that most per-

---

‡In July of 1977, Laetrile was the focus of much attention. Since August 1977, more studies have been conducted seeking to prove its danger. On the other hand, Laetrile has been accepted by a number of additional states. This remains an ongoing issue.

sonal of individual possessions: the mechanics of mind and body. If it can be determined that some factor affects the body or the mind, that element can be interpreted as a medical problem, and it falls into the hands of practitioners of medicine for treatment. Such situations currently include the normal processes of pregnancy and aging, as well as the human behavior problems of drug addiction and alcoholism.

"Through the Expansion of What in Medicine Is Deemed Relevant to the Good Practice of Life"

This expansion is illustrated by the use of medical jargon to describe a state of being—such as the "health" of the nation or the "health" of the economy. Any political or economic proposal or objective that enhances the "health" of those concerned wins approval.

There are numerous areas in which medicine, religion, and law overlap. One example is how, in public health practice, law and medicine overlap in the creation of laws that establish quarantine and the need for immunization. As another example, a child is unable to enter school without proof of having received certain inoculations. Medicine and law also merge in areas of sanitation and rodent control, insect control. A legal–medical dispute can arise over the guilt or innocence of a criminal as determined by his "mental state" at the time of a crime.

Some diseases carry a social stigma: one must be screened for tuberculosis before employment, a history of typhoid fever permanently prevents a person from commercially handling food, venereal disease must be reported and treated, and even the ancient disease of leprosy continues to carry a stigma.

Abortion represents an area replete with conflict that involves politics, law, religion, and medicine. Those in favor of abortion rights believe that it is a woman's right to have an abortion and that the matter is confidential between the patient and her physician. Opponents argue on religious and moral grounds that abortion is murder. At the present time, the law sanctions abortion. In many states, however, Medicaid will no longer pay for an abortion unless the mother's life is in danger, a policy that makes it increasingly difficult for the poor to obtain these services.

Another highly charged area of conflict involves the practice of euthanasia. With the burgeoning of technological improvements, the definition of *death* has changed in recent years. It sometimes takes a major court battle to "pull the plug," such as in the Nancy Cruzan case.

Finally, one might ponder that although many daily practical activities are undertaken in the name of health—taking vitamins, practicing hygiene, using birth control, engaging in dietary or exercise programs— the "diseases of the rich" (cancer, heart disease, and stroke) tend to capture more public attention and funding than the diseases of the poor (malnutrition, high maternal and infant death rates, sickle cell anemia, and lead poisoning).

BARRIERS TO HEALTH CARE

Innumerable barriers restrict access to the health-care system, but the major such obstacle is poverty. Closely related to, but not necessarily occurring only among the poor, are the problems of access to all types of health-care facilities, transportation, and language barriers.

Poverty
There are countless ways to answer the question; "What is poverty?" One way of viewing poverty is to respond by listing the government programs or subsidies a person receives, such as public housing, government loans to attend college, Medicaid, Aid to Families with Dependent Children (AFDC), or food stamps. Another way of answering this question is the description used by the United States Bureau of Labor Statistics who counts the poor and describes the poor by age, education, location, race, family composition, and employment status. A third answer is the federal government definition of the "poverty threshold." This poverty threshold, developed in 1965, is based on pretax income only, excluding capital gains, and does not include the value of noncash benefits, such as employer-provided health insurance, food stamps, or Medicaid. The poverty threshold for an average family of four was $13,547 in 1992.[23] Table 5–3 presents selected facts about poverty.

Cycle of Poverty
Poverty is more than the absence of money. One way of analyzing the phenomenon is by observing the effects of the "cycle of poverty" as illustrated in Figure 5–4. In this cycle, the poor person lives in a situation that may create poor intellectual and physical development and poor economic production, and in which the birth rate is high; this living situation in turn causes poor production that creates insufficient salaries and a subsistence economy that forces the person to often reside in densely populated areas or remotely located rural areas where adequate shelter and potable water are scarce, and the person suffers from chronically poor nutrition. These phenomena all to often lead to high morbidity and accident rates, precipitating high health-care costs, which, in turn, prevent the person from seeking health-care services. This then leads to an increase in sickness and poor production, in a cycle that has yet to be broken. Other barriers that are interrelated to this cycle are the lack of access to health-care services, language issues, and transportation issues.[24]

One source of funding available to families in poverty is welfare. Today, welfare is under sharp scrutiny by politicians and members of society at large; efforts are underway to reform this system of funding the poor. A proposal costing $9.3 billion dollars is being considered to adopt a new way of dealing with poverty. The proposed Clinton Welfare Plan contains such ideas as the expansion of training and child care for families on welfare, the requirement that welfare recipients born after 1971 join a work program after they have re-

TABLE 5–3. SELECTED FACTS ABOUT POVERTY

1. Regardless of their own poverty status, 47.5% of students in high-poverty schools will have low achievement scores, compared with 11.9% in low-poverty schools.
2. One in four black high school graduates and almost one in eight white graduates are not likely to earn more than a poverty level income.
3. Whites make up only 17% of the urban poor but 55% of the rural poor. Among blacks, the proportion is 49% of the urban poor and 32% of the rural poor, and Hispanics make up 29% of the urban poor and 8% of the rural poor.
4. The inflation-adjusted value of Aid to Families with Dependent Children (AFDC) plus food stamps declined by 26% between 1972 and 1992.
5. In 1991, the number of white mothers (38.1%) on welfare was about equal to the number of African American mothers (38.8%).
6. The median single stay on welfare is 22 months.
7. On first receiving benefits, 70% of AFDC recipients are on welfare less than two years and only 7% stay on more than eight years.
8. Most Americans believe that the average family with a single mother and two children on AFDC receives $650 per month; the average is $376.
9. More American children lived in poverty in 1992 than in any year since 1965, although our Gross National Product grew 53.2% during the same period.
10. Every 30 seconds a child is born into poverty.
11. One in five American children—14.6 million—is poor.
12. As of 1990, the U.S. government spent about eight times more on the personal health of people 65 and over than on people under 19.
13. In 1990, 15 states had child poverty rates of 20% and above. In Mississippi and Louisiana, one in every three children were poor and in Arkansas the rate was one in four.
14. In 1991, an estimated 12 million children under the age of 18 (18.3% of all children) were hungry.
15. One out of 10 Americans makes use of food pantries, soup kitchens, and other food distribution programs.
16. A migrant farmworker child can be employed in agriculture even if younger than 10 years old. No other children of that age can be legally employed.
17. Migrant educational programs for kindergarten through grade 12 lose approximately half their original enrollment by the ninth grade. One in 10 completes 12th grade.
18. As of 1990, children under the age of 18 accounted for 40% of the poor and only 24% of the nonpoor.
19. Poverty cuts off phone access for 1 in 20 U.S. households. Almost one fifth (18.5%) of households nationwide living in poverty are without phone service.
20. Only 27% of the families with incomes below $14,000 have Medicaid; 35% have private insurance and 37% have no coverage at all.

From: Lavelle, R. *America's New War on Poverty—A Reader for Action.* (San Francisco: KQED BOOKS, 1995). Reprinted with permission.

ceived benefits for two years, provision of tough penalties for those who do not join work programs, a requirement that hospitals establish paternity, and removal of restrictions on payments to two-parent families.[25] The House of Representatives has passed a welfare reform bill at this writing. The issues of overcrowded housing, poor sanitation, and so forth that were illustrated in the cycle of poverty are not dealt with in any welfare reform plan.

Access

Several factors limit a given family's access to the health-care delivery system, including the availability and location of health-care facilities,

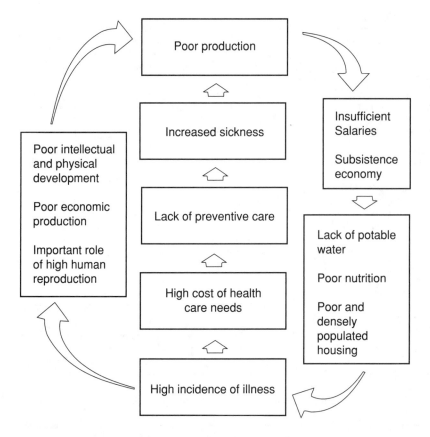

Figure 5–4. The Cycle of Poverty. *Reprinted with permission from Spector, M. "Poverty: The Barrier to Health Care," in Spector, R.* Cultural Diversity in Health and Illness. *New York: Appleton, Century, and Crofts, 1979, pp. 141–162.)*

transportation to these facilities, and any existence and type of health insurance. The lack of insurance, whether public (Medicaid) or private, is a rapidly increasing problem. A weakness of the current discussion on health-care reform is its lack of concern for coverage and benefits for the poor and minorities.

Transportation

The issue of transportation is never-ending and never-changing. All too frequently families are not able to get to health-care services because of geographic distance and therefore have to depend on other family members or friends for transportation. In many settings, the hospital responsible for providing free care is not in the same location as the families needing this care. Public transportation may be expensive and, in some locations, nonexistent.

Language

Many of the "new Americans," tend to retain their native language; as do many "old Americans" who may have immigrated here a generation ago. More and more immigrants arrive in the United States every year, thereby increasing the need for adequate interpreters. Yet, all too often, these services are not available. It goes without saying that communication is a major necessity in health-care delivery.

Alternative Therapies

Alternative, unconventional, or unorthodox therapies cover a broad spectrum of health beliefs and practices. Alternative, unconventional, or unorthodox therapies are medical practices that do not conform to the standards of the medical community, are not taught widely in the medical and nursing communities, and are not generally available in the allopathic health-care system, including the hospital settings. These include such therapies as acupuncture, massage therapy, and chiropractic medicine. *Alternative* therapies, in this text, refers to therapies that one may elect to use that are *not* a part of their cultural heritage; *traditional* therapies are those therapies that are a part of one's traditional cultural heritage. In other words, if a European American elects to use acupuncture as a method of treatment, he or she is seeking alternative treatment; a Chinese American using this treatment modality is using traditional medicine.

The use of alternative therapies is growing rapidly and are now frequently used by patients with cancer, arthritis, chronic back or other pain, stress-related problems, AIDS, gastrointestinal problems, and anxiety. In 1993, Eisenberg and colleagues reported the results of a national survey of 1,539 subjects. They found that about a third of all American adults use some form of unconventional medical treatment (Table 5–4). The most frequent

TABLE 5–4. NATIONAL PROJECTIONS OF EXPENDITURES FOR
UNCONVENTIONAL THERAPY IN THE UNITED STATES IN 1990.

Category of Expenditure	Estimated Billions of Dollars
Services of unconventional providers	11.7
Megavitamin supplements	0.8
Commercial diet supplements	1.2
Estimated total	13.7
Out-of-pocket expenditures	
Unconventional therapy	10.3
All hospitalizations	12.8
All physician services	23.5

From: Eisenberg, D. M., Kessler, R. C., Foster, C., et al. "Unconventional
Medicine in the United States: Prevalence, Costs, and Patterns of Use."
New England Journal of Medicine, 328 (1993): 251. Reprinted with
permission.

users are educated, upper-income white Americans in the 25–49 age group. They are most likely to live on the west coast. The total projected out-of-pocket expenditure for unconventional therapy was $10.3 billion in 1990.[26] The various types of alternative therapies include relaxation techniques; chiropractic; massage; imagery; spiritual healing; commercial weight loss programs; lifestyle diets, such as macrobiotics; herbal medicines; megavitamin therapy; self-help groups; energy healing; biofeedback; hypnosis; homeopathy; acupuncture; folk remedies; exercise; and prayer.[27]

The Institute of Noetic Sciences, founded in 1973, is a research foundation, an educational institution, and an organization that has over 40,000 members worldwide. It promotes philosophies of self-healing and research into this area.

The remainder of this book portrays these methods as they occur in both the dominant assimilated American culture and in the many traditional or immigrant cultures that now blend with the American whole.

GOALS OF HEALTH-CARE DELIVERY

In this chapter, we have explored, in a very limited way, many of the issues surrounding the American health-care delivery system by examining the trends that led to its character today, looking at the experiences a person may have in attempting to obtain care, and many of the issues related to care and the costs of the system. The struggles continue, and a balance between the high technology of the 1990s and the need for primary preventive care follows us into the new century.

REFERENCES

1. Knowles, J. "It's Time to Operate." *Fortune* (January 1970): 79.
2. Califano, J. *Radical Surgery—What's Next for America's Health Care?* (New York: Random House, 1994), p. 19.
3. Rooks, J. P. "Let's Admit We Ration Health Care—Then Set Priorities." *American Journal of Nursing* 96 (2) (June 1990): 39.
4. Boston College School of Nursing, Class of 1995. Random Survey of Hospital Costs in Massachusetts Hospitals, Unpublished data.
5. Ibid.
6. Baquet, D. and Fritsch, J. "New York's Public Hospitals Fail, and Babies Are the Victims." *New York Times.* (March 5, 1994): 1, 32, 33.
7. "Financial Abuse Creates Hemorrhage in US Health System." *Boston Sunday Globe.* (July 31, 1995): 1; and Golden, D. and Kurkjian, S. "Home-care Firm, Hospitals Are Allies in Profit." *Boston Globe.* (August 1, 1994): 1, 8.
8. Kong, D. "Study Finds Drugs' Prices Higher in US." *Boston Globe.* (March 6, 1995): 1, 7.

9. Torrens, P. R. "Historical Evolution and Overview of Health Services in the United States," in *Introduction to Health Services* (3rd ed.), eds. Williams, S. J. and Torrens, P. R. (New York: John Wiley & Sons, 1988), pp. 3–31.

10. McLaughlin, L. "Why Health Care Coverage Must Be Universal." *Boston Globe.* (July 25, 1994): 11.

11. Gingrich, N., Armey, D., and The House Republicans. *Contract with America—The Bold Plan.* (New York: Random House, 1994): pp. 9–12.

12. Eckholm, E. "While Congress Remains Silent, Health Care Transforms Itself". *New York Times.* (December 18, 1994): 1, 34.

13. Himmelstein, D. U. and Woolhandler, S. *The National Health Program Book—A Source for Advocates.* (Monroe, ME: Common Courage Press): 65, 76–77.

14. Small, N. R. "Long-Term Care—Can the Church Meet the Challenge of Reform?" *Journal of Christian Nursing.* (Summer, 1994, 11, 3): 15.

15. Knox, R. A. "Studies Challenge View of US as World Leader in Medicine." *Boston Globe.* (March 26, 1994): 3.

16. Eckholm, "Health Care Reforms Itself," p. 1.

17. Ibid.

18. Ehrenreich, B., and Ehrenreich, J. *The American Health Empire: Power, Profits, and Politics* (New York: Random House, Vintage Books, 1971), pp. 4–12. (The headings that follow this reference in the text are quoted from this book.)

19. Fry, J. *Medicine in Three Societies* (London: Aylesbury [Bucks], MTP, 1969), p. 22.

20. Ibid.

21. Ibid., p. 23.

22. Zola, I. K. "Medicine as an Institution of Social Control." *Sociological Review* 20 (4) (November 1972): 487–504. (The headings that follow this reference in the text are quoted from this article.)

23. Lavelle, R., ed. *America's New War on Poverty—A Reader for Action.* (San Francisco: KQED BOOKS, 1995): pp. 14–15.

24. Spector, M. "Poverty: The Barrier to Health Care." in Spector, R. *Cultural Diversity in Health and Illness,* (1st ed.) (New York: Appleton, Century, Croft, 1979): pp. 148–152.

25. "Reforming the Welfare System." *The Nation's Health.* (February 15, 1995): 1, 4.

26. Eisenberg, D. M., Kessler, R. C., Foster, C., et al. "Unconventional Medicine in the United States: Prevalence, Costs, and Patterns of Use." *New England Journal of Medicine.* (January 28, 1993): 246–252.

27. Ibid., p. 249.

ANNOTATED BIBLIOGRAPHY

Aday, L. A. *At Risk in America—The Health and Health Care Needs of Vulnerable Populations in the United States.* San Francisco: Jossey-Bass, 1993.

   The issue of vulnerable populations, programs needed to address the health needs of these populations, and payment for quality health-care programs are the major areas covered in this text.

Berwick, D. M., Godfrey, A. B., and Roessner, J. *Curing Health Care.* San Francisco: Josey-Bass, 1990.

This book presents a description of the methods that may be used to improve the quality of health care. Countless examples are included.

Califano, J. *Radical Surgery.* NY: Random House, 1994.

The former Secretary of Health and Human Services (1977–1979) paints a graphic picture of the tumultuous situation in the health-care delivery system.

Harrington, C. and Estes, C. L. *Health Policy and Nursing.* Boston: Jones and Bartlett, 1994.

This book provides the reader with an overview of current health-care problems that are of critical importance. Issues include health-care financing, personnel supply, and quality of health.

Kronenfeld, J. J. *Controversial Issues in Health Care Policy.* Newbury Park, CA: SAGE Publications, 1993.

This book presents the major controversial issues affecting health-care policy and delivery, including—disease patterns and AIDS, mental health, reproductive health, aging and long-term care, and the costs of health care.

Lavelle, R., ed. *America's New War on Poverty—A Reader for Action.* San Francisco: KQED Books, 1995.

As the title of this book implies, a "War on Poverty" is once again being waged in America, and the goal of this book is to help develop a discussion about poverty. Poverty faded as an issue and instead, issues of welfare reform and tax-cuts took over. This text graphically illustrates the reality that poverty still exists and that countless people are needy in this wealthy nation.

Lee, P. R. and Estes, C. L., eds. *The Nation's Health* (4th ed.). Boston: Jones and Bartlett, 1994.

Given that health-care reform is an important political topic, this text presents an in-depth analysis of many of the factors one must consider regarding this issue.

FURTHER SUGGESTED READINGS

Articles

Numerous articles are available on health-care delivery. The following are a sampling.

Abrams, F. R. "Withholding Treatment When Death Is Not Imminent." *Geriatrics* 42 (5) (1987): 77–84.

Aday, L. A. and Andersen, R. M. "The National Profile of Access to Medical Care: Where Do We Stand?" *American Journal of Public Health* 74 (12) (1974): 1331–1339.

Adler, H. M. and Hammett, V. "The Doctor-Patient Relationship Revisited: An Analysis of the Placebo Effect." *Annals of Internal Medicine* 78 (173): 595.

American Nurses Association. *Executive Summary—Nursing's Agenda for Health Care Reform.* Washington, DC: American Nurses Association, 1991.

Anderson, J. M. "Ethnicity and Illness Experience: Ideological Structures and the Health Care Delivery System." *Social Science Medicine* 22(11) (1986): 1277–1283.

Becker, P. H. "Advocacy in Nursing: Perils and Possibilities." *Holistic Nursing Practice* 1(1) (1986): 54–63.

Beyers, M. *Monograph: Arista 87—Nurses and the Delivery of Health Care Services Now and in the Future.* Indianapolis: Sigma Theta Tau, International, 1987.

Branch, L. G. "Health Practices and Incident Disability among the Elderly." *American Journal of Public Health* 75(12) (1985): 1436–1440.

Callahan, D. "The Limits of Medical Progress: A Principle of Symmetry." *The Center Report—The Center for Public Policy and Contemporary Issues* (New York: The Hastings Center) 2(1990): 2.

Cassell, E. J. "The Sorcerer's Broom—Medicine's Rampant Technology," *Hastings Center Report*, 23 (6) (1993): 32–39.

Chopoorian, T. and Craig, M. M. "Nursing and Health Care Delivery." *American Journal of Nursing* (December 1976): 1988–1991.

Daniels, N., Kamm, F. M., Rakowski, E., et al. Symposium: Meeting the Challenges of Justice & Rationing." *Hastings Center Report*, 24(4) (1994): 27–42.

DeParle, J. "Better Work Than Welfare but What if There's Neither? *New York Times Magazine*, pp. 40–59.

Fink, A., Siu, A. L., Brook, R. H., et al. Assuring the Quality of Health Care for Older Persons." *Journal of the American Medical Association* 258(14) (1987): 1905–1908.

Gibbs, N. "Sick and Tired." *Time* (July 31, 1989): 48–53.

Gibbs, N. "Love and Let Die." *Time* (March 19, 1990): 62–70.

Hoffman, F. and Wakefield, D. "Ambulatory Care Patient Classification." *Journal of Nursing Administration* 16(4) (1986): 23–30.

Hoopes, R. "When It's Time to Leave; Can Society Set an Age Limit for Health Care?" *Modern Maturity* (August-September, 1988): 38–43.

Hooyman, N. and Cohen, H. J. "Medical Problems Associated With Aging." *Clinical Obstetrics and Gynecology* 29(2) (1986): 353–373.

Inlander, C. B. "Can Nurses Cure a Sick System?" *Revolution: The Journal of Nurse Empowerment*, 2(2): 24–28.

Jencks, S. F. and Kay, T. "Do Frail, Disabled, Poor, and Very Old Medicare Beneficiaries Have Higher Hospital Charges?" *Journal of the American Medical Association* 257 (2) (1987): 198–202.

Kilner, J. F. "Selecting Patients When Resources are Limited: A Study of US Medical Directors of Kidney Transplantation Facilities." *American Journal of Public Health* 78 (2) (1988): 144–147.

Kitzhaber, J. "Rationing Health Care: The Oregon Model." *The Center Report—The Center for Public Policy and Contemporary Issues* (New York: The Hastings Center) 2 (1990): 3–4.

Knowles, J. "It's Time to Operate." *Fortune* (January 1970).

Lamm, R. D. "The Challenge of the American Health Care System." *The Center Report—The Center for Public Policy and Contemporary Issues* 2(1990): 1.

McDermott, W. "Medicine: The Public Good and One's Own." *Cornell University Medical College Alumni Quarterly* 4 (Winter 1977): 15–24.

Milio, N. "Values, Social Class, and Community Health Services." *Nursing Research* 16 (1) (1967): 26–31.

Orque, M. S. "Health Care and Minority Clients." *Nursing Outlook* 24(5) (1976): 313–316.

Perkins, Sr. M. R. "Does Availability of Health Services Ensure Their Use?" *Nursing Outlook* 22(8) (1984): 496–498.

Purtillo, R. B. "Justice in the Distribution of Health Care Resources." *Physical Therapy* 61(11) (November 1981): 1594–1600.

Regan, M. Editorial: Medicaid Reimbursement—Can We Save Money by Paying Doctors More? *The American Journal of Public Health.* 84(4) (1994): 548–559.

Roemer, M. I. "Health Care Financing and Delivery around the World." *American Journal of Nursing* (June 1971): 1158–1163.

Rosenbach, M. L. "The Impact of Medicaid on Physician Use by Low-income Children." *American Journal of Public Health* 79(1989): 1220–1226.

Schleffler, R. M., et al. "Severity of Illness and the Relationship between Intensive Care and Survival." *American Journal of Public Health* 72(5) (1982): 449–454.

Smith, D. R. "Porches, Politics, and Public Health," *American Journal of Public Health.* 84 (5) (1994): 725–730.

Snook, S. H. and Webster, B. S. "The Cost of Disability." *Clinical Orthopaedics and Related Research* 221 (August 1987): 77–84.

Somers, A. R. "The Changing Demand for Health Services: A Historical Perspective and Some Thoughts for the Future." *Inquiry* 23(Winter 1986): 395–402.

Townsend, P. "Toward Equality in Health Through Social Policy." *International Journal of Health Services* 11 (1) (1981): 63–75.

Ullman, D. "The Mainstreaming of Alternative Medicine," *Health Care Forum Journal,* (November/December, 1993): 24–30.

Wanzer, S. H., et al. "The Physicians Responsibility Toward Hopelessly Ill Patients." *New England Journal of Medicine* 320(1989): 844–849.

Waxman, H. A. "Kids and Medicaid: Progress but Continuing Problems." *American Journal of Public Health* 79(1989): 1217–1218.

White, K. L., Murnaghan, J. G., and Gaus, C. R. "Technology and Health Care." *New England Journal of Medicine* 287(24) (1972): 1223–1226.

Willwerth, J. "Do You Want to Die?" *Time* (May 28, 1990): 58–65.

Yankauer, A. "What Infant Mortality Tells Us." *American Journal of Public Health* 80 (1990): 653–654.

Zola, I. K. "Medicine as an Institution of Social Control." *Sociological Review* 20(4) (1972): 487–504.

Chapter 6

Healing: Natural Traditions

You can do nothing to bring the dead to life; but you can do
much to save the living from death.

—B. Frank School, 1924[1]

Health-care providers have the opportunity to observe the most incredible phenomenon of life: the recovery from illness. In today's society, the healer is the physician, and the other members of the health team all play a significant role in the prevention, detection, and treatment of disease. Yet human beings have existed, some sources suggest, for 2 million years. How, then, did the species *Homo sapiens* survive before the advent of modern technology? It is quite evident that numerous forms of healing existed long before the methodologies that we apply today.

In the natural course of any illness, the stricken individual can expect to experience the following set of events: he or she becomes ill; the illness may be acute, with concomitant symptoms or signs, such as pain, fever, nausea, bleeding. On the other hand, the illness may be insidious, with a gradual progression and worsening of symptoms, which might encompass slow deterioration of movement or a profound intensification of pain.

If the illness is mild, the person relies on self-treatment or, as is often the case, does nothing, and gradually the symptoms disappear. If the illness is more severe or is of longer duration, the person may consult expert help from a healer of one type or another, usually a physician.

The person recovers or expects to recover. As far back as historians and interested social scientists can trace in the history of humankind, this phenomenon of recovery has occurred. In fact, it made very little difference what mode of treatment was used; recovery was usual. It is this occurrence of natural recovery that has given rise to all forms of *healing* that attempt to explain a phenomenon that is natural. That is, one may choose to rationalize the success of a healing method by pointing to the patient's recovery. Over the generations, natural healing has been attributed to all sort of rituals, including trephining (puncturing the skull), cupping, magic, leeching, and bleeding. From medicine man to sorcerer,[2] the art of healing has passed through succeeding generations. People knew the ailments of their time and devised treatments for them. In spite of ravaging plagues, natural disasters, and pandemic and epidemic diseases, human beings as a species have survived!

In Chapter 5, the dominant health-care system in the United States is discussed: this system is called "allopathic." The word *allopathy* has two roots. One comes from Greek roots meaning "other than disease" because drugs are prescribed on a basis that has no consistent or logical relationship to the symptoms. The second definition for allopathy is derived from German roots and means "all therapies." Allopathy is a "system of medicine that embraces all methods of proven value in the treatment of diseases."[3] After 1855, the American Medical Association adopted the second definition of allopathy and has since that time exclusively determined who can practice medicine in the United States. For example, in the 1860s the American Medical Association refused to admit women doctors to medical societies, practiced segregation, and demanded the purging of homeopaths. Today, allopaths show little tolerance or respect for such other providers of health care as homeopaths, osteopaths, and chiropractors and for such traditional healers as lay midwives, herbalists, and medicine men.[4] Other forms of healing systems and healers in contemporary American society include homeopaths, chiropractors, osteopaths, Christian healers, and traditional healers.

HEALING

Heal, or *to heal*, is defined as the restoration to health, to get rid of sin, anxiety, or the like, to restore.[5] The philosophies of healing that people may express are woven through their personal philosophies, which are predicated on their heritage, as discussed in Chapter 4. Healing-related beliefs and practices vary among ethnoreligious groups, among nurses, and between nurses and patients. *Healing beliefs* are those beliefs that a person describes as creating or fostering the recovery from illness. *Modern beliefs*, or *allopathic beliefs*, are those that are recognized by contemporary health-care workers as established scientific healing beliefs, and *traditional beliefs*, or *homeopathic beliefs*, are those that generally are derived from one's heritage, for example, when a person believes that the "evil eye" or "envy" is the cause of illness, and the disease is best treated or healed by removing the "source of evil or envy."

Healing practices are the *actions* that one performs to treat or heal illness. *Modern healing practices* are those recognized by contemporary healthcare workers as established scientific ways of treating and curing illness using such methods as medications and surgery. This approach most often is dualistic—predicated on cartesian philosophy of dualistic humankind: mind and body. *Traditional healing practices* are, on the other hand, those derived from one's heritage, in which a person may use folk medicine or folk healers, often from a religious orientation, to treat their illness. These healers espouse and practice a deep spiritual commitment to healing. In these philosophies, humans are viewed as body, mind, and spirit—and greater than the sum of these part.

The tensions between allopathic and homeopathic philosophies certainly are not new but have been going on since the late 19th century. In this chapter, we explore the natural methods of healing, with an exploration of the health beliefs and practices of senior citizens and a brief overview of the alternative philosophical schools of health care that prevailed in the society in which they and their parents grew up. We present many examples of natural herbal remedies—popular then and now. Chapter 7 explores a number of healing methods, both ancient and modern. In addition, a historical overview is included on how such methods evolved, their purpose, and their practice. The relation of these healing practices to current religions is demonstrated by listing the types of beliefs and practices found in a number of religions in the United States. A description of various types of spiritual healers in today's society concludes the chapter. Each chapter on ethnic groups discusses healers indigenous to that community. Chapter 14 gives as a case study the role of lay midwives.

HEALTH TRADITIONS

An 82-year-old woman, who did not have diphtheria as a child, told me that she did not get the disease because she always wore *asafetida* around her neck, and a 93-year-old man remembers preventing lockjaw by washing all cuts with *turpentine* and ingesting turpentine with sugar when he had a cough.

The United States has a new and flourishing minority group, the aged. More and more people born between 1900 and 1920 are living into their seventh to tenth decades of life. In 1900, only 4% of the population was over 65. In 1976, this figure was 11% and, in 1990, 12.6%.[6] Figure 6–1 illustrates this phenomenon.

People over the age of 85 constitute the fastest growing segment of the population in this country. In the 1990 census, there were 3,080,000 persons counted at age 85 or older, and at least 210 Americans celebrate their 100th birthday every week[7] (Table 6–1). Furthermore, it has been predicted that the number of Americans over 85 may be nearly 24 million in the next 50 years and that, by the year 2040, the number of people 65 and older may be as high as 87 million.

This large minority population can be viewed in a context of strong survivors, when one realizes that those who are 80 and older were born in or before 1910 and those 65 and older were born in or before 1930. These people were born and grew up before the development and mandatory promulga-

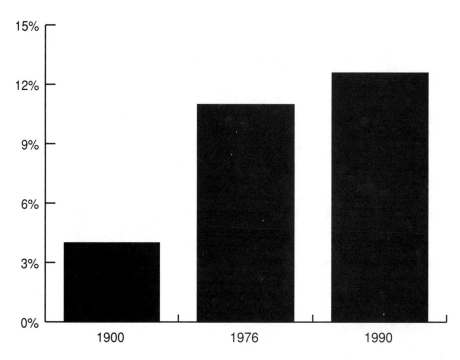

Figure 6–1. Percentage of Population 65 and Over, 1900, 1976, and 1990. *(Reprinted with permission from AARP Minority Affairs Initiative.) A Portrait of Older Minority Affairs.* Washington, DC. American Association of Retired Persons, 1987 (pamphlet); and U.S. Bureau of the Census, 1990 Census of the Population *General Population Characteristics United States,* Series 1990 CP-1-1 U.S. (Government Printing Office, Washington, D.C., 1992, p. 23.)

TABLE 6–1. ESTIMATED NUMBER OF PERSONS 65 YEARS OF AGE AND OVER BY SEX AND AGE: UNITED STATES, 1990[a]

Age (years)	All Persons	Sex	
		Male	Female
65 and older	31,242	12,565	18,677
65–74	18,107	7,941	10,165
65–69	10,112	4,532	5,579
70–74	7,995	3,409	4,586
75–84	10,005	3,766	6,290
75–79	6,121	2,400	3,722
80–84	3,934	1,366	2,568
85 and older	3,080	858	2,222

[a]Numbers in thousands.
From: U.S. Bureau of the Census, 1990 Census of the Population, *General Population Characteristics United States,* Series 1990 CP-1-1 U.S. (Washington, D.C.: Government Printing Office 1992), pp. 23, 24. Reprinted with permission.

tion of childhood immunizations for communicable diseases, such as

- *Smallpox*
  Immunization was not *mandatory* until 1915,[8] although it was recommended for use much earlier.
- *Diphtheria*
  Immunization was begun in 1933.
- *Pertusis*
  Immunization was begun in 1933.
- *Tetanus*
  Toxoids and antitoxin were not available until the mid-1940s.[9]

The more recent forms of immunization include those for poliomyelitis (Salk, 1955; Sabin, 1961) and trivalent measles, mumps, and rubella (1963).

The older cohort of this population survived the influenza epidemic of 1918–1919, and the entire population grew up through childhood and young adulthood without the availability of antibiotics, such as penicillin and erythromycin. Most of today's diagnostic and therapeutic procedures were nonexistent 50 years ago.

HEALTH BELIEFS AND PRACTICES

Health

As discussed in Chapter 2, the current connotation of *health* is predicated on the standard definition offered by the WHO, "a state of complete physical, mental, and social wellbeing and not merely the absence of disease." We may expand on that definition to define health as "the ability of a system to respond adaptively to a wide variety of environmental challenges."

In contrast, popular health education resources of the years 1920 to 1930 described health as

1. A general bodily expression of vigor as indicated by facial expression
2. No painful or unpleasant sensations being present
3. The bodily heat should be 98.4 degrees Fahrenheit
4. A pulse of 72 beats each minute, regular in force and time
5. A good appetite and digestion, with a daily bowel movement
6. The skin and kidneys should be acting normally
7. Well-balanced nervous system and a clear eye[10]

In 1924, School, a popular health educator, described "perfect health" in the following way.

Look attentively at the bright, open, manly countenance; there are no signs of mental decrepitude, physical bodily infirmities, nervous fear, and so forth. . . . as a sum total of the proper required performance of all functions, we have not only harmony and health, but happiness of mind, soul, and body as well.[11]

Illness is most often described as the opposite of health—the presence of disease. In contrast, literature from 1924 described illness as "any deviation from the above mentioned seven attributes of health, and as a condition that has been in existence for a long time or strong enough to make its presence inconvenient or troublesome to the patient."[12] The following are the attributes of illness:

1. The face of the patient, his position and actions show signs of suffering.
2. The temperature may vary widely from normal.
3. The pulse may be increased or decreased; may become harder or softer; may be irregular in force and rhythm.
4. The stomach and bowels may be disturbed, and this will be indicated by the condition of the tongue.
5. The urine and discharges from the bowels may be very much altered. The skin will be rough and harsh to the touch; and during fever, hot and dry.
6. The nervous system may present a great variety of symptoms. The eye will be dull and heavy except in special diseased conditions.[13]

Causes of Illness

The prevailing theories of illness causation include those of biological and stress-related phenomena. The agents attributed to be the causes of illness at the turn of the century were diverse. For example, tetanus generally was believed to be caused in children as a result of dentition and in adults as a result of a local source of irritation, such as a wound. A chief cause of rheumatism was believed to be the application of cold to the body when it was unusually heated, and land scurvy was believed to be caused by hard labor.[14]

Other possibilities for the cause of illness were

- Poor eating habits
- Improper food combinations
- Punishment from God

Illness Prevention or Health Protection

Popular forms of preventing illness or protecting health included

- The wearing of amulets, scapulars, and medals
- The practice of religion and going to church regularly
- The wearing of a shawl to protect oneself from drafts
- Not doing anything, such as smoking and drinking, in excess
- Maintaining a clean home

Remedies

Home remedies of both natural and patent medicine sources were used commonly to restore health (Fig. 6–2). The following are examples of patent remedies, several of which are still available and in popular use.

1. Swamp root was and is used as a diuretic because it "tends to promote the flow of urine thereby aiding the kidneys in their necessary work of eliminating waste matter" (from package description). It is 10.5% alcohol and contains buchu leaves, peppermint herb, cape aloes, oil of juniper, and balsam tolu incorporated in a syrup. It continues to be used, and one country drug store refused to sell its only bottle because they were saving it for a regular customer.

2. Turpentine was and is used to treat puncture wounds; a few drops on sugar was ingested to treat a cough.

Figure 6–2. An assortment of home remedies including those discussed in text. *(From Spector Collection).*

3. Syrup of black draught was, and currently is, used to treat constipation. It is made from casanthranol, senna, rhubarb, anise, methylsalicylate, cinnamon, clove, nutmeg, peppermint, spearmint, and menthol as flavorings. It is 5% alcohol.

4. Liniment, such as Sloan's liniment, which contains capsicum oleoresin, methylsalicylate, oil of camphor, turpentine oil, and oil of pine, although meant to be used externally for such ailments as rheumatism, arthritis, and minor sprains, often is taken by mouth to treat sore throats and coughs. It, too, can still be purchased.

5. Mustard plasters or other plasters, such as flaxseed, were placed on the chest and used to treat severe colds and coughs. The practice of cupping, that is, either slapping the back with cupped palms or taking a whiskey glass and heating the inside with a candle to create a vacuum, then applying it to the back to "draw out the phlegm," was reported.

6. Father John's Medicine, a wholesome family medicine that has been in use since 1855, is used to treat coughs and colds. It was originally compounded for Rev. Father John O'Brien of Lowell, Massachusetts, and he recommended it to his parishioners and friends for coughs. The active ingredients include cod liver oil, pure gum emulsifier, and glycerin, flavored with sugar, licorice, and flavoring oils. The preparation contains no alcohol or drugs.

Today's senior citizens are a "survival group," and the knowledge that they have regarding health and illness ought to be understood by all of us. They grew up in an era when a prevailing health belief was that the duty of every man and woman was to preserve health, not to attempt to combat diseases.

Alternative Systems

The decades of 1870 through 1930 were the time when the allopathic health-care model as we know it today was established.[15] During this time, however, not only were the roots of this system of health care becoming firmly established, but the ideas of the eclectic and other schools of medical thought were also prevalent. Other prevalent philosophies of health care included

Homeopathic Medicine. Homeopathic medicine was developed between 1790 and 1810 by Samuel C. Hahnemann in Germany. Homeopathy, or homoeopathy, comes from the Greek words *homoios* ("similar") and *pathos* ("suffering"). In the practice of homeopathy, the person, not the disease, is treated. The practitioner treats a given person by using minute doses of plant, mineral, or animal substances. The medicines are selected using the principle of the "law of similars." A substance that is used to treat a specific set of symptoms is the same substance that if given to a healthy person would cause the symptoms. The medicines are administered in extremely small doses. These medicines are said to provide a gentle but powerful stimulus to the person's own defense system and, in turn, to help the person heal.

Homeopathy was popular in 19th-century America and Europe because it was successful in treating the raging epidemics of those times. In 1900, 20% to 25% of physicians were homeopaths. Following the allopathic efforts to wipe out the homeopaths, the movement has greatly dissipated. A small group of homeopaths still exists in the United States, however, and there are larger practices in India, Great Britain, France, Greece, Germany, Brazil, Argentina, and Mexico.[16]

Osteopathic Medicine. Osteopathy, developed in 1874 by Dr. A. T. Still in Kirksville, Missouri, is the art of curing without the use of surgery or drugs. Osteopathy attempts to discover and correct all mechanical disorders in the human machine and to direct the recuperative power of nature that is within the body to cure the disease. It claims that if there is an unobstructed blood and nerve supply to all parts of the body, the effects of a given disease will disappear.

Osteopaths are fully qualified physicians who can practice in all areas of medicine and surgery. They, like the medical doctor, have completed four years of medical school, one year of internship, and generally a further residency in a specialty area. They take the same course work as do medical doctors, often use the same textbooks, and often take the same licensing examinations. There are 14 osteopathic medical schools in the United States and 214 hospitals. The lines of distinction between the medical doctor and the osteopath arise because the osteopath, in addition to using modern scientific forms of medical diagnosis and treatment, uses manipulation of the bones, muscles, and joints as therapy. Osteopaths also employ structural diagnosis and take into account the relationship between body structure and organic functioning when they determine a diagnosis. The osteopathic doctor has the same legal power to treat patients as a medical doctor.[17]

Chiropractic. Chiropractic is a controversial form of healing that has been in existence for well over 90 years. It, too, adheres to a disease theory and a method of therapy that differs from allopathy. It was developed as a form of healing in 1895 in Davenport, Iowa, by a storekeeper named Daniel David Palmer, also known as a "magnetic healer." Palmer's theory underlying the practice of chiropractic was that an interference with the normal transmission of "mental impulses" between the brain and body organs produced diseases. The interference is caused by misalignment or subluxation of the vertebrae of the spine, which decreases the flow of "vital energy" from the brain through the nerves and spinal cord to all parts of the body. The treatment consists of manipulation to eradicate the subluxation.

Chiropractic is practiced in two ways. One form is that of the "mixers," who use heat therapy, enemas ("colonic irrigation"), exercise programs, and other therapeutic practices. The other group, the "straight" chiropractors, who use only manipulation, disapprove of the practices of the "mixers." They believe that the other techniques are a form of allopathic medicine.[18]

Eclectic Medicine. The word *eclectic* means choosing, and it refers to choosing the means for treating disease. Methods and remedies from all other systems are selected from. This school of medicine believes that nature has curative powers, and practitioners seek to remove the causes of disease through the natural outlets of the body. They treat the cause of disease rather than the symptoms and do not use bleeding, antimony, and poisons to treat diseases.[19]

Hydrotherapy. A German farmer, Priessnitz, developed hydrotherapy in 1840. It includes the application of water, internally and externally, in any form at any temperature, with the belief that the water can have a most profound effect on the body.[20]

There were many popular theories of healing during this era that focused only on the mind, however, some examples of which follow.

Mesmerism. In the late 18th century, mesmerism was a popular form of healing by touch and was named for its founder, Friedrich Anton Mesmer. Mesmer believed that illness was a condition in which the body and mind of a person were influenced by a mysterious force emanating from another person. He further believed that the stars exerted an influence on people and that this force was the same as electricity and magnetism. Initially, he believed that stroking the body with magnets would bring about a cure for illness. He later modified this to the belief that touch alone could heal.[21]

Hypnotism. Hypnotism artificially creates a condition in which the person apparently is asleep and acts in obedience to the will of the operator as regards both motion and sensation. It was developed in 1841 by James Braid, an English surgeon.[22]

Mind Cure. Mind cure is the cure of disease by means of the mind alone, in which *faith* influences the cure of disease. Two prerequisites in faith healing are the desire to get well and faith in the treatment.[23]

Christian Science. The religious philosophy of scientism lies outside allopathic and most homeopathic philosophies and delivery systems, yet it is one of the forms of mind cure. It rejects allopathic practices and uses only spiritual means for healing. Christian Science was developed by Mary Baker Eddy in 1879 in Boston to "commemorate the word and works of our Master, which should reinstate primitive Christianity and its lost element of healing."[24] Furthermore, the doctrine teaches that those who really follow Jesus should follow Him in healing, which can be done through the mind. The definition of illness is that sickness is merely a false impression conveyed by an erring mortal mind. The fundamental propositions of Christian Science are

1. God is all.
2. God is good. Good is mind.
3. God, Spirit, being all, nothing is matter.
4. Life, God, omnipotent good, deny death, evil, sin, disease. Disease, sin, evil, death, deny good, omnipotent God, life.[25]

To the people who believe, Christian Science is a way based on the laws of God. It is devoted to lifting the burdens of sin and suffering from all humanity. It is an established church and deeply committed to the belief in the inspired teaching of Jesus and His disciples. Further consideration of this religious philosophy is found in Chapter 7.

Natural Remedies

The use of natural products—such as wild herbs and berries accessible to the healers—developed into today's science of pharmacology. Early humankind had a wealth of knowledge about the medicinal properties of the plants, trees, and fungi in their environment. They knew how to prepare concoctions from the bark and roots of trees and from berries and wild flowers. As an example, purple foxglove, which contains the cardiotonic digitalis, was used for centuries to slow the heart rate.

The current popularity of health foods has given rise to the popular use of various diets to protect health. In addition, health-food stores make available a number of medicinal teas and herbs. (A listing of commonly used herbs is presented in Table 6–2.) Almost 100 herbal teas are listed in a small paperback entitled *Herbal Tea Book*.[26] The herbs are listed alphabetically, and the source and use of each are given. An even larger listing is given in *Herbs: Medicine and Mysticism*[27] by Sybil Leek, who is known as one of the "world's foremost astrologers and witches." This book has a wide audience. Countless other sources are available.

As discussed in Chapter 5, Laetrile is considered by some to be a cure for cancer. Apart from numerous political ramifications within the health-care system, Laetrile creates another dilemma. If it has healing powers—even if limited to making people feel a little better until they die—one can appreciate its usefulness.[28] If Laetrile does not live up to the claim made of it, however, the public is falling prey to a pseudomedical hoax.

It is difficult to sort out which aspects of folk medicine have merit and which are a hoax. From the viewpoint of the consumer—if he or she has faith in the efficacy of an herb, a diet, a pill, or a healer—it is not a hoax. From the viewpoint of the medical establishment, jealous of its territorial claim, this same herb, diet, pill, or healer is indeed a hoax if it is *ineffective* and *prevents* the person from using the method of treatment the physician-healer believes is effective.

TABLE 6–2. COMMONLY USED HERBAL REMEDIES

Herb	Action	Use	Administration
Alfalfa (or Lucerne)	Stimulant, nutritive	Arthritis; weight gain; strength-giving	1 oz herb to 1 pint water; drink 1 cupful as tea
Anise (seed used)	Stimulant; aromatic; relaxant	Flatulence; dry coughs	2 tsp of seed to 1/2 pint water; dose: 1–3 tsp often
Bayberry (bark used)	Astringent; stimulant; emetic	Sore-throat gargle; cleanses stomach; douche; rinse for bleeding gums	1 oz powdered bark to 1 pint water; drink as tea
Blessed thistle	Diaphoretic; stimulant emetic	Reduces fevers; breaks up colds; digestive problems	1 oz herb to 1 pint water; small doses as desired
Bugleweed	Aromatic; sedative; tranquilizer; astringent	Coughs; relieves pulmonary bleeding, increases appetite	1 oz herb to 1 pint water; drink by glassful often
Catnip (leaves)	Diaphoretic; tonic; antispasmodic	Helpful in convulsions; produces perspiration	1 oz leaves to 1 pint water (measured by teaspoonful); tsp
Cayenne pepper (fruit and seed)	Stimulant	Purest and most positive stimulant in herbal medicine; healing of burns and other wounds; relieves toothaches	Powder in small doses; by mouth or topical
Chestnut, horse (bark and fruit)	Astringent; narcotic; tonic	Bark used for fevers; fruit to treat rheumatism	Bark: 1 oz to 1 pint water, tsp 4 times per day; fruit: tincture 10 drops twice per day
Chicory (root)	Diuretic; laxative	Liver enlargement; gout; rheumatic complaints	1 oz root to 1 pint water; take freely
Corn silk	Diuretic; mild stimulant	Irritated bladder; urinary stones; trouble with prostate gland	2 oz in 1 pint water; take freely
Dandelion (root)	Diuretic; tonic	Used in many patent medicines; general body stimulant; used chiefly with kidney and liver disorders	Roasted roots are ground and used like coffee; small cup once or twice per day
Ergot (fungus)	Uterine stimulant; sedative hemostatic	Menstrual disorders; stops hemorrhage	Liquid extract 10–20 minims by mouth
Eucalyptus	Antiseptic; antispasmodic, stimulant	Inhale for sore throat; apply to ulcers and other wounds	Local application or fluid extract in small doses by mouth

128

TABLE 6-2. Continued

Herb	Action	Use	Administration
Fennel (seeds)	Aromatic; carminative (expels air from bowels)	Gas; gout; colic in infants; increases milk in nursing mothers	Pour water (½ pint) on 1 tsp of seeds; take freely
Garlic (juice)	Diaphoretic; diuretic; stimulant; expectorant	Treats colds; diuretic; antiseptic	Juice, 10–30 drops
Goldenrod (leaves)	Aromatic; stimulant	Sore throat; general pain; colds; rheumatism	1 oz leaves to 1 pint water; small dose often
Hollyhock (flowers)	Diuretic	Chest complaints	1 oz flowers to 1 pint water; drink as much as needed
Ivy (leaves)	Cathartic; diaphoretic	Poultices on ulcers and abscesses	As a poultice
Ivy, poison (leaves)	Irritant; stimulant; narcotic	Rheumatism; sedative for the nervous system	Liquid extract 5–30 drops
Juniper berries	Diuretic; stimulant	Bladder and kidney problems; gargles; digestive aid	Oil of berries 1–5 drops
Licorice (root)	Demulcent	Coughs; prevents thirst	Powdered root
Lily of the valley (flower)	Cardiac stimulant; diuretic; stimulant	Headaches	½ oz of flowers to 1 pint water; tablespoon doses
Marigold (flowers and leaves)	Diaphoretic; stimulant	Flowers and leaves made into a salve for skin eruptions; relieves sore muscles, amenorrhea	1 oz herbs and petals to 1 pint water; 1 tbsp on mouth or topical application
Mistletoe (leaves)	Nervine; antispasmodic; tonic; narcotic	Epilepsy and hysteria; painful menstruation; induces sleep	2 to ½ pint water; 1 tbs often
Mustard (leaves)	Cooling; sedative	Hoarseness (excellent aid in recovering the voice)	Liquid extract; small doses
Nightshade, deadly (poison) (leaves and root)	Narcotic; diuretic; sedative; antispasmodic	Eye diseases; increases urine; stimulates circulation	Powdered leaves and root; small amounts
Papaya leaves	Digestive	Digestive disorders; fresh leaves; dry wounds	Papain; small doses

129

TABLE 6-2. Continued

Herb	Action	Use	Administration
Rosemary (leaves) (herb)	Astringent; diaphoretic; tonic; stimulant	Prevents baldness; cold; colic; nerves; strengthens eyes	1 oz herb to 1 pint water; small doses
Saffron (flower pistils)	Carminative; diaphoretic	Amenorrhea; dysmenorrhea; hysteria	1 dram flower pistils in 1 pint water; teacup doses
Thyme (dried herb)	Antiseptic; antispasmodic; tonic	Perspiration; colds; coughs; cramps	1 oz herb to 1 pint water; 1 tbs doses often

From: Leek S. *Herbs and Mysticism* (Chicago: Henry Regnery, 1975), pp. 73–235. Reprinted with permission.

REFERENCES

1. School, B. F., ed. *Library of Health Complete Guide to Prevention and Cure of Disease* (Philadelphia: Historical Publishing Co., 1924), book cover.
2. Leeson, J. "Paths to Medical Care in Lasaka, Zambia" (Master's thesis, University of Manchester, England; preliminary findings, 12 July 1967), p. 14.
3. Weil, A. *Health and Healing* (Boston: Houghton Mifflin, 1983), p. 17.
4. Ibid., pp. 22–25.
5. *American Heritage Dictionary of the English Language,* S.V. "heal."
6. U.S. Bureau of the Census, 1990 Census of the Population *General Population Characteristics United States,* Series 1990 CP.1-1 U.S. (Washington, D.C.: Government Printing Office, 1992), p. 23.
7. Lesnoff-Caravaglia, G. and Klys, M. "Life Style and Longevity," in *Realistic Expectations for Long Life,* ed. Lesnoff-Caravaglia, G. (New York: Human Sciences Press, 1987), p. 37.
8. Hanlon, J. J. and Pickett, G. E. *Public Health Administration and Practice* (7th ed.). (St. Louis: C. V. Mosby, 1979), p. 354.
9. Top, F. H. *Communicable and Infectious Diseases* (5th ed.). (St. Louis: C. V. Mosby, 1979), pp. 53–90.
10. Corish, J. L., ed. *Health Knowledge* (New York: Domestic Health Society, 1923).
11. School, B. F. *Guide,* pp. 35–44.
12. Ibid., p. 45.
13. Ibid., p. 48.
14. Ibid., p. 386.
15. Starr, P. *The Social Transformation of American Medicine* (New York: Basic Books, 1982), pp. 79, 145.
16. Homeopathic Educational Services, Berkeley, CA. Educational pamphlet. (Reprint. Harrisburg, PA: Pennsylvania Osteopathic Association, 1979.)
17. Denenberg, H. *Shopper's Guide to Osteopathic Physicians,* pamphlet.
18. Cobb, A. K. "Pluralistic Legitimation of an Alternative Therapy System: The Case of Chiropractic." *Medical Anthropology* 6(4) (Fall 1977): 1–23.
19. School, B. F. *Guide,* pp. 1545–1546.
20. Ibid., p. 1527.
21. Ibid., p. 1592.
22. Ibid., p. 1595.
23. Ibid., p. 1598.
24. Advertisement. "Why Is Prayer Being Prosecuted in Boston?" *Boston Globe,* April 11, 1990, pp. 24–25.
25. School, B. F. *Guide,* p. 1602.
26. Adrian, A. and Dennis, J. *Herbal Tea Book* (San Francisco: Health Publishing Co., 1976).
27. Leek, S. *Herbs: Medicine and Mysticism* (Chicago: Henry Regnery, 1975).
28. Richardson, J. A. and Griffin, P. *Laetrile Case Histories* (New York: Bantam, 1977).

7
Chapter

Healing: Magicoreligious Traditions

In the early summer of 1990, a Christian Scientist couple was convicted in Suffolk (Boston, MA) Superior Court of involuntary manslaughter in the death of their 2-year-old son. They had relied solely on prayers to heal their son of a bowel obstruction. The verdict was applauded by the prosecutor, for it set a precedent for children's rights. The Christian Scientists denounced it as an attack on their faith.

What is healing? What is the connotation of this word from a magicoreligious perspective? This chapter explores these questions by introducing a wide range of ideas and magicoreligious practices.

The professional history of nursing was born with Florence Nightingale's knowledge that "nature heals."[1] In more recent times, Blattner has written a text designed to help nurses assist patients to upgrade their lives in a holistic sense and to heal the person—body, mind, and spirit.[2] Krieger, in the *Therapeutic Touch*, has developed a method for teaching nurses how to use their hands to heal.[3] Wallace has described methods of helping nurses to diagnose and to deliver spiritual care. She points out that the word

> Spiritual is often used synonymously with religion, but that the terms are not the same. If they are used synonymously as a basis for assessment of nursing needs some of the patient's deepest needs may be glossed over. Spiritual care implies a much broader grasp of the search for meanings that goes on within every human life.[4]

In addition to answers to these questions from nursing, one is able to explore the concept from the viewpoints of anthropology, sociology, psychology, and religion.

From the fields of anthropology and sociology come texts that describe rituals, customs, beliefs, and practices that surround healing. Shaw contends that "for as long as man has practiced the art of magic, he has sought to find personal immortality through healing practices."[5] Burton describes traditional beliefs and indigenous healing rituals in Mandari and relates the source of these rituals as to how man views himself in relation to God and earth. In this culture, the healer experiences a religious calling to become a healer. Healing is linked to beliefs in evil and the removal of evil from the sick person.[6] Naegele describes healing in our society as a form of "professional practice."[7] He asserts, however, that "healing is not wholly a professional monopoly and that there are several forms of nonprofessional healing such as the 'specialized alternatives.'"[8] These include Christian Science and the marginally professional activities of varying legitimacy, such as chiropractic, folk medicine, and quackery.[9] He states: "To understand modern society is to understand the tension between traditional patterns and self-conscious rational calculations devoted to the mastery of everyday life."[10]

Literature from the field of psychology abounds with references to healing. Shames and Sterin describe the use of self-hypnosis to heal,[11] and Progoff, a depth-psychologist, describes *depth* as the "dimension of wholeness in man."[12] He has written extensively on how one's discovery of the inner self can be used for both healing and creation.

Krippner and Villaldo contend that there is a "basic conflict between healing and technology" and that "the reality of miracles, of healing, of any significant entity that could be called God is not thought to be compatible with the reality of science."[13] They further contend that healings are psychosomatic in origin and useful only in the sense of the placebo effect.[14]

The literature linking religion to healing is bountiful. The primary source is the Bible and prayers. Bishop discusses miracles and their relationship to healing. He states that the "miracles must be considered in relation to the time and place in which they occur."[15] He further describes faith and its relationship to healing and states that "*something* goes on in the process of faith healing."[16] He also points out that healing "is the exception rather than the rule."[17] Healing through faith generally is not accepted as a matter of plain fact, but it is an event to rejoice over.

Ford describes healing of the spirit and methods of spiritual healing for spiritual illness. He describes suffering in three dimensions: that of body, mind, and spirit.[18] He fully describes telotherapy—spiritual healing—which is both a means and an invitation. His argument is that full healing takes place only when there is agape love—divine love—and no estrangement from God.[19] Russell and Cramer assert that healing is the work of God alone. Russell asserts that "God's will normally expresses itself in health,"[20] and Cramer focuses on the unity of man with God and claims that permanent health is truth,[21] that healing is the gift of Jesus, and that it is a spiritual gift.[22]

RELIGION AND HEALING

Religion plays a vital role in one's perception of health and illness. Just as culture and ethnicity are strong determinants in an individual's interpretation of the environment and the events within the environment, so, too, is religion. In fact, it is often difficult to distinguish between those aspects of a person's belief system arising from a religious background and those that stem from an ethnic and cultural heritage. Some people may share a common ethnicity, yet be of different religions; a group of people can share the same religion, yet have a variety of ethnic and cultural backgrounds. It is never safe to assume that all individuals of a given ethnic group practice or believe in the same religion. The point was embarrassingly driven home when I once asked a Chicano woman if she would like me to call the priest for her while her young son was awaiting a critical operation. The woman became angry with me. I could not understand why until I learned that she was a Methodist and not a Catholic. I had made an assumption, and I was wrong. She later told me that not all Chicanos are Catholic. After many years of people making this assumption, she had learned to react with anger.

Religion strongly affects the way people interpret and respond to the signs and symptoms of illness. Today, just as it did in antiquity, religion also plays a role in the rites surrounding both birth and death. So pervasive is religion that the diets of many people are determined by their religious beliefs. Religion and the piety of a person determine not only the role that faith plays in the process of recovery but also in many instances the response to a given treatment and to the healing process. Each of these threads—religion, ethnicity, and culture—weave the fabric of each person's particular response to treatment and healing.

Ancient Rituals

Many of the rituals that we observe at the time of birth and death have their origins in the practices of ancient human beings. Close your eyes for a few moments and picture yourself living thousands and thousands of years ago. There is no electricity, no running water, no bathroom, no plumbing. The nights are dark and cold. The only signs of the passage of time are the changing seasons and the apparent movement of the various planets and stars through the heavens. You are prey to all the elements, as well as to animals and the unknown. How do you survive? What sort of rituals and practices assist you in maintaining your equilibrium within this often hostile environment? It is from this milieu that many of today's practices sprang.

Generally speaking, three critical moments occur in the life of almost every human being: birth, marriage, and death.[23] One needs to examine the events and rites that were attendant on birth and death in the past and to demonstrate how many of them not only are relevant to our lives today but also are still practiced.

In the minds of early human beings, the number of evil spirits far exceeded the number of good spirits, and a great deal of energy and time was devoted to thwarting these spirits. They could be defeated by the use of gifts or rituals, or, when the evil spirits had to be removed from a person's body, redemptive sacrifices were used. Once these evil spirits were expelled, they were prevented from returning by various magical ceremonies and rites. When a ceremony and incantation were found to be effective, they were passed on through the generations. It has been suggested and supported by scholars that from this primitive beginning, organized religion came into being. Today, many of the early rites have survived in altered forms, and we continue to practice them.[24]

The power of the evil spirits was believed to endure for a certain length of time. The third, seventh, and fortieth days were the crucial days in the early life of the child and new mother. Hence it was on these days, or on the eighth day, that most of the rituals were observed. It was believed that during this period, the newborn and the mother were at the greatest risk from the power of supernatural beings and thus in a taboo state. "The concept underlying taboo is that all things created by or emanating from a supernatural being are his, or are at least in his power."[25] The person was freed from this taboo by certain rituals, depending on the practices of a given community. When the various rites were completed and the 40 days were over, both the mother and child were believed to be redeemed from evil. The ceremonies that freed the person had a double character: they were partly magic and partly religious.

I have deliberately chosen to present the early practices of Semitic peoples because their beliefs and practices evolved into the Judaic, Christian, and Islamic religions of today. Because the newborn baby and mother were considered vulnerable to the threats of evil spirits, many rituals were developed to protect them. For example, in some communities, the mother and child were separated from the rest of the community for a certain length of time, usually 40 days. Various people performed precautionary measures, such as rubbing the baby with different oils or garlic, swaddling the baby, and lighting candles.[26] In other communities, the baby and mother were watched closely for a certain length of time, usually seven days. (During this time span, they were believed to be intensely susceptible to the effects of evil— hence, close guarding was in order.) Orthodox Jews still refer to the seventh night of life as the "watch night."[27]

The birth of a male child was considered more significant than that of a female, and many rites were practiced in observance of this event. One ritual sacrifice was cutting off a lock of the child's hair and then sprinkling his forehead with sheep's blood. This ritual was performed on the eighth day of life.[28] In other Semitic countries, when a child was named, a sheep was sacrificed and asked to give protection to the infant. Depending on regional or tribal differences, the mother might be given parts of the sheep. It was believed that if this sacrificial ritual was not performed on the seventh or eighth day of life, the child would die.[29] The sheep's skin was saved, dried, and placed in the child's bed for 3 or 4 years as protection from evil spirits.

Both the practice of cutting a lock of a child's hair and the sacrifice of an animal served as a ceremony of redemption. The child could also be redeemed from the taboo state by giving silver—the weight of which equaled the weight of the hair—to the poor.[30] Although not universally practiced, these rites are still observed in some form in some communities of the Arab world.[31]

Circumcision is closely related to the ceremony of cutting the child's hair and offering it as a sacrifice. Some authorities hold that the practice originated as a rite of puberty: a body mutilation performed to attract the opposite sex.[32] (Circumcision was practiced by many peoples throughout the ancient world. Alex Haley's *Roots* describes it as a part of initiating boys into manhood in Africa.) Other sources attribute circumcision to the concept of the sanctity of the male organ and claim that it was derived from the practice of ancestor worship. The Jews of ancient Israel, as today, practiced circumcision on the eighth day of life.[33] The Moslems of Palestine circumcise their sons on the seventh day in the tradition that Mohammed established. In other Moslem countries, the ritual is performed anywhere from the 10th day to the seventh year of life.[34] Again, this sacrifice redeemed the child from being taboo in his early stages of life. Once the sacrifice was made, the child entered the period of worldly existence. The rite of circumcision was accompanied by festivals of varying durations. Some cultures and kinship groups feasted for as long as a week.

The ceremony of baptism is also rooted in the past. It, too, symbolically expels the evil spirits, removes the taboo, and is redemptive. It is practiced mainly among members of the Christian faith, but the Yezidis and other non-Christian sects also perform the rite. Water was thought to possess magical powers and was used to cleanse the body from both physical and spiritual maladies, which included evil possession and other impurities. Usually, the child was baptized on the 40th day of life. In some communities, however, the child was baptized on the eighth day. The 40th (or eighth) day was chosen because the ancients believed that, given performance of the particular ritual, this day marked the end of the evil spirits' influence.[35]

Some rituals also involved the new mother. For example, not only was she (along with her infant) removed from her household and community for 40 days, but in many communities she had to practice ritual bathing before she could return to her husband, family, and community. Again, these practices were not universal, and they varied in scope and intensity from people to people.

As to death, it was believed that the work of evil spirits and the duration of their evil—whether it was 7 or 40 days—surrounded the person, family, and community at the time. Rites evolved to protect both the dying and dead person and the remaining family from the evil spirits. The dying person was cared for in specific ways (ritual washing), and the grave was prepared in set ways (storing food and water for the journey after death). Further rituals were performed to protect the deceased's survivors from the harm believed to be rendered by the deceased's ghost. It was believed that this ghost could return from the grave and, if not carefully appeased, gravely harm surviving relatives.[36]

Extensions of Rituals to Today's Practices

Early human beings, in their quest for survival, strove to appease and prevent the evil spirits from interfering with their lives. Their beliefs seem simple and naive, yet the rituals that began in those years have evolved into those that exist today. Attacks of the evil spirits were warded off with the use of amulets, charms, and the like. People recited prayers and incantations.[37] Because survival was predicated on people's ability to appease evil spirits, the prescribed rituals were performed with great care and respect. Undoubtedly, this accounts in part for the longevity of many of these practices through the ages. For example, circumcision and baptism still exist, even when the belief that they are being performed to release the child from a state of being taboo may not continue to be held. It is interesting also that adherence to a certain timetable is maintained. For example, as stated, the Jewish religion mandates that the ritual of circumcision be performed on the eighth day of life.

The practice, too, of closely guarding the new mother and baby through the initial hours after birth is certainly not foreign to us. The mother is closely watched for hemorrhage and signs of infection; the infant initially is watched for signs of choking or respiratory distress. This form of observation is very intense. Could factors such as these have been what our ancestors watched for? If early human beings believed that evil spirits caused the frequent complications that surrounded the birth of a baby, it stands to reason that they would seek to control or prevent these complications by adhering to astute observation, isolation, and rituals of redemption.

TRADITIONAL ETIOLOGY

The prevention and treatment of illness rests in the ability to understand the cause of a given illness or set of symptoms. Among those who hold traditional health and illness beliefs, some beliefs regarding the causation of illness differ from the modern model of etiology. Here illness is most often attributed to the "evil eye." The evil eye is primarily a belief that someone can project harm by gazing or staring at another's property or person.[38]

The belief in the evil eye is probably the oldest and most widespread of all superstitions, and it is found to exist in many parts of the world, such as Southern Europe, the Middle East, and North Africa.[39]

It is thought by some to be merely a superstition, but what is seen by one person as superstition may well be seen by another as religion. Various evil eye beliefs were carried to this country by immigrant populations. These beliefs have persisted and may be quite strong among newer immigrants and heritage consistent peoples.[40]

The common beliefs in the evil eye assert that

1. The power emanates from the eye (or mouth) and strikes the victim.
2. The injury, be it illness or other misfortune, is sudden.
3. The person that casts the evil eye may not be aware of having this power.
4. The afflicted person may or may not know the source of the evil eye.
5. The injury caused by the evil eye may be prevented or cured with rituals or symbols.
6. This belief helps to explain sickness and misfortune.[41]

The nature of the evil eye is defined differently by different populations. The variables include how it is cast, who can cast it, who receives it, and the degree of power that it has. In the Philippines, the evil is cast through the eye or mouth; in the Mediterranean, it is the avenging power of God; in Italy, it is a malevolent force like a plague and is prevented by wearing amulets.

In various parts of the world, various people cast it: in Mexico—strangers, in Iran—kinfolk, and in Greece—witches. Its power varies, and in some places, such as the Mediterranean, it is seen as the "devil." In the Near East, it is seen as a deity, and among Slovak Americans as a chronic but low-grade phenomenon.[42]

Among Germans the evil eye is known as *aberglobin* or *aberglaubisch,* and causes preventable problems, such as evil, harm, and illness. Among the Polish, the evil eye is known as *szatan.* Some "evil spirits" are equated with the devil and can be prevented by praying to a patron saint or guardian angel. *Szatan* also is prevented by prayer and repentance and the wearing of medals and scapulars. These serve as reminders of the "Blessed Mother and the Patrons in Heaven" and protect the wearer from harm. The evil eye is known in Yiddish as *kayn aynhoreh.* The expression *kineahora* is recited by Jews after a compliment or when a statement of luck is made to prevent the casting of an evil spell on another's health. Often the speaker spits three times after uttering the word.[43]

Agents of disease may also be "soul loss," "spirit possession," "spells," and "hexes." Here prevention becomes a ritual of protecting oneself and one's children from these agents. Treatment requires the removal of these agents from the afflicted person.[44]

Illness also can be attributed to people who have the ability to make others ill, for example, witches and practitioners of voodoo.[45] The ailing person attempts to avoid these people to prevent illness and to identify them as part of the treatment. Other "agents" to be avoided are "envy," "hate," and "jealousy." A person may practice prevention by avoiding situations that could provoke the envy, hate, or jealousy of a friend, acquaintance, or neighbor. The evil eye belief contributes to this avoidance.

Another source of evil can be of human origin and occurs when a person is temporarily controlled by souls not their own. In the Jewish culture, this controlling spirit is known as *dybbuk.* The word comes from the Hebrew word meaning "cleaving" or "holding fast." A dybbuk is portrayed as a "wandering, disembodied soul which enters another person's body and hold's fast."[46]

TRADITIONAL METHODS OF HEALTH PROTECTION

Among people who believe in traditional ways, illness is often attributed to the evil eye, *envidia,* and "witches."[47] In these instances, health may be protected by external controls, such as the avoidance of people who can bring it about by the "evil eye," the avoidance of *envidia,* that is, by not provoking the envy of others, and the avoidance of witches or others who can cast spells and other forms of evil.

Traditional practices used in the protection of health consist of

1. The use of protective objects—worn, carried, or hung in the home
2. The use of substances that are ingested in certain ways and amounts or eliminated and substances worn or hung in the home
3. The practices of religion, such as the burning of candles, the rituals of redemption, and prayer

Objects That Protect Health

Amulets are objects, such as charms, worn on a string or chain around the neck, wrist, or waist to protect the wearer from the evil eye or the evil spirits that could be transmitted from one person to another, or could have supernatural origins. For example, Figure 7-1 shows *malocchio* (1) worn by people of Italian origin to prevent the evil eye. The *mano milagroso* (2) is worn by many people of Mexican origin for luck and the prevention of evil. A *mano negro* (3) is placed on babies of Puerto Rican descent to prevent the evil eye. The *mano negro* is placed on the baby's wrist on a chain or pinned to the diaper or shirt and is worn throughout the early years of life. Both the Hand of God (4) (Israeli) and the Thunderbird (5) (Hopi Indian) are worn for protection and to bring good luck. The *Milagros* (6) are worn by some people of Mexican background to ward off evil. Amulets may also be written documents on parchment scrolls, and these are hung in the home. Figure 7-2 is an example of a written amulet acquired in Jerusalem. It is hung in the home to protect the family from the "evil eye," famine, storms, diseases, and countless other dangers. Table 7-1 describes several practices found among contemporary ethnic groups to prevent the "evil eye."

Bangles (7) (shown in Figure 7-3) are worn by people originating from the West Indies. The silver bracelets are open to "let out evil," yet closed to prevent evil from entering the body. They are worn from infancy, and as the

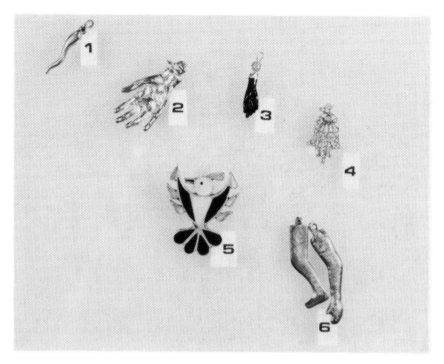

Figure 7–1. Objects that protect health. (1) *Malocchio.* (2) *Mano Milagroso.* (3) *Mano Negro.* (4) "Hand of God." (5) Thunderbird. (6) *Milagros.*

person grows they are replaced with larger bracelets. These bracelets tend to tarnish and leave a black ring on the skin when a person is becoming ill. When this occurs, the person knows it is important to rest, to improve the diet, and to take other needed precautions. Many people believe they are extremely vulnerable to evil, even to death, when these bracelets are removed. Some people wear numerous bangles. When they move an arm, the bracelets tinkle. It is believed that this sound frightens away the evil spirit. Nurses should realize that when these bracelets are removed, the person experiences a great deal of anxiety.

In addition to amulets, there are talismans (8) (Fig. 7-3). A talisman is believed to possess extraordinary powers and may be worn on a rope around the waist or carried in a pocket or purse. The talisman illustrated in Figure 7-3 is a marionette, and it protects the wearer from evil. It is recommended that people who wear amulets or carry a talisman *be allowed to do so in health-care institutions.*

Substances That Protect Health

The second practice uses diet to protect health and consists of many different observances. Figure 7-4 shows some food substances that can be ingested to

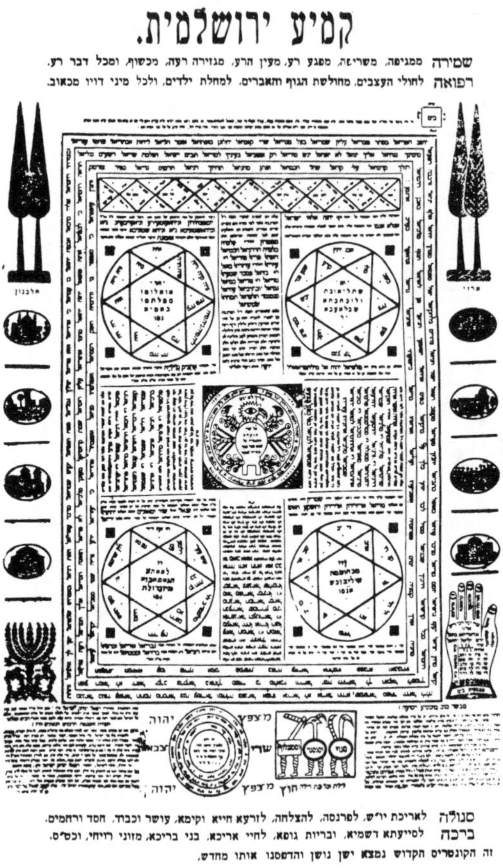

Figure 7–2. The Jerusalem amulet. This amulet serves as **protection** from pestilence, fire, bad wounds and infection, the evil eye, bad decrees and decisions, curses, witchcraft, and from everything bad; **heal** nervous illness, weakness of body organs, children's diseases, and all kinds of suffering from pain; as a **talisman** for livelihood for success, fertility, honesty and honor; and for charity, love, mercy, goodness, and grace. It also has the following admonition: "Know before whom you stand—The King of Kings The Holy One, Blessed be He." *(Translated by B. Koff, Jerusalem, Israel, 12/26/88. From the author's personal collection.)*

prevent illness. People from many ethnic backgrounds eat raw garlic or onions (9) in an effort to prevent illness. Garlic or onions also may be worn on the body or may be hung in the Italian, Greek, or Native American home. *Chachayotel* (10), a seed, may be tied around the waist by a Mexican person to prevent arthritic pain. Among traditional Chinese people, thousand-year-old eggs (11) are eaten with rice to keep the body healthy and to prevent illness. The ginseng root (12) is the most famous of Chinese medicines. It has universal medicinal applications and is used preventively to "build the blood," especially after childbirth. Tradition states that the more the root looks like a man, the more effective it is. Ginseng is also native to the United States and

TABLE 7–1. PRACTICES TO PREVENT THE "EVIL EYE"

Origin	Practices
Scotland	Red thread knotted into clothing
	Fragment of Bible worn on body
South Asia	Knotted hair or fragment of Koran worn on body
Eastern European Jews	Red ribbon woven into clothes or attached to crib
Sephardic Jews	Wearing a blue ribbon or blue bead
Italians	Wearing a red ribbon or the *corno*
Greek	Blue "eye" bead, crucifix, charms
	Phylact—a baptismal charm placed on baby
	Cloves of garlic pinned to shirt
Tunisia	Amulets pinned on clothing consisting of tiny figures or writings from the Koran
	Charms of the fish symbol—widely used to ward off evil
Iran	Cover child with amulets—agate, blue beads
	Children often may be left filthy and never washed to protect them from the "evil eye."
India/Pakistan	Hindus—copper plates with magic drawings rolled in them
	Muslims—slips of paper with verses from the Koran
	Black or red string around the baby's wrist
Guatemala	Small red bag containing herbs placed on baby or crib
Mexico	Amulet with red yarn
Philippines	Wearing of charms, amulets, medals
Puerto Rico	*Mano negro*

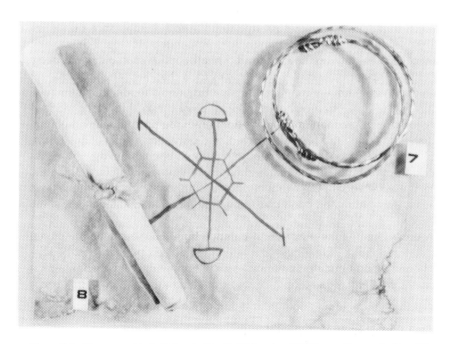

Figure 7–3. Shown are objects that protect health (7) Bangles. (8) Talisman *(From collection of the author, photographed by R. Schadt)*

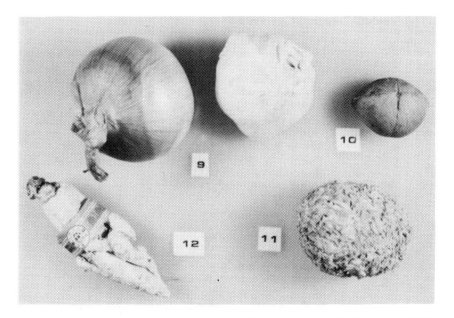

Figure 7–4. Substances that protect health are shown. (9) Garlic and onion. (10) Chachayotel. (11) Thousand-year-old egg. (12) Ginseng root. *(From collection of the author; photographed by R. Schadt)*

is used in this country as a restorative tonic. Another substance that is ingested is *Nervo Forza* (13), a vitamin tonic from Guatemala (Fig. 7-5).

Diet regimens also are used to protect health. It is believed that the body is kept in balance or harmony by the type of food that one eats.

Traditionalists have strong beliefs about diet and foods and their relationship to the protection of health. The rules of the kosher diet practiced among Jewish people mandate the elimination of pig products and shellfish. Only fish with scales and fins are allowed, and only certain cuts of meat from animals with a cleft hoof and that chew the cud can be consumed.[48] Examples of this kind of animal are cattle and sheep. Many of these dietary practices, such as the avoidance of pig products, are also adhered to by Muslims. Jews also believe that milk and meat must never be mixed and eaten at the same meal.[48]

In traditional Chinese homes, a balance must be maintained between foods that are *yin* or *yang*. These are eaten in specified proportions. In Hispanic homes, foods must be balanced as to "hot" and "cold." These foods too, must be eaten in the proper amounts, at certain times, and in certain combinations.

Religious Practices That Protect Health

A third traditional approach toward health protection centers on religion. Religion strongly affects the way people choose to prevent illness, and it

Figure 7–5. A tonic for health. *(From collection of the author)*

plays a strong role in the rituals associated with health protection. It dictates social, moral, and dietary practices that are designed to keep a person in balance and healthy. Many people believe that illness and evil are prevented by strict adherence to religious codes, morals, and religious practices. They view illness as a punishment for breaking a religious code. For example, I once interviewed a woman who believed she had cancer because God was punishing her for stealing money when she was a child. An example of a protective religious figure is the Virgin of Guadalupe (14), the patron saint of Mexico, who is pictured on medals that people wear or in pictures hung in the home (Fig. 7-6). She is believed to protect the person and home from evil and harm, and she serves as a figure of hope. Other religious practices include baptism as a ritual of cleansing that prevents evil from harming the person and circumcision as a redemptive practice, again to prevent illness and harm (Table 7-2).

Religion can, therefore, help to provide the believer with an ability to understand and interpret the events of the environment and life.

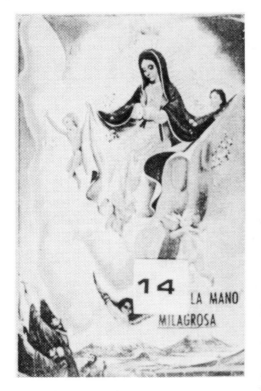

Figure 7–6. The Virgin of Guadalupe. *(From collection of the author; photographed by R. Schadt)*

BELIEFS THAT CAN AFFECT THERAPY

Ancient Forms of Healing

The crises of birth and death were certainly not the only ones to affect our ancestors. Illness also caused crises. Just as the people of ancient times developed ways of dealing with the events that surrounded birth and death, they evolved elaborate systems of healing. The cause of an illness, once again, was attributed to the forces of evil, which originated either within or outside the body. Early forms of healing dealt with the removal of evil. Once a method of treatment was found effective, it was passed down through the generations in slightly altered forms.

The people who healed often were those who received the gift of healing from a "divine" source. They frequently received this gift in a vision and were unable to explain to others how they knew what to do. Other healers learned their skills from their parents. Most of the healers with acquired skills were women, who subsequently passed their knowledge on to their daughters. People who used herbs and other preparations to remove the evil from the sick person's body were known as herbalists. Other healers included bone

TABLE 7–2. BIRTH-RELATED RELIGIOUS RITUALS

Religion	Practice	Time	Method
Baptist (27 bodies)	Baptism	Older child	Immersion
Church of Christ	Baptism	8 years	Immersion
Church of Jesus Christ of Latter Day Saints (Mormons)	Baptism	8 years or older	Immersion
Eastern Orthodox Churches	Baptism	Infants	Total immersion
Episcopalian	Baptism	Infant	
Friends (Quaker)	No baptism	Named	
Greek Orthodox	Baptism	40 days	Sprinkle or immersion
Islam	Circumcision	7th day	
Jewish	Circumcision	8th day	
Lutheran	Baptism	6–8 weeks	Pouring, sprinkling, immersion
Methodist	Baptism	Childhood	
Pentecostal	Baptism	Age of accountability	
Roman Catholic	Baptism	Infant	Pour water
Russian Orthodox	Baptism	Infant	Immerse three times
Unitarian	Baptism	Infant	

setters and midwives, and although early humankind did not separate ills of the body from those of the mind, some healers were more adept at solving problems by using early forms of "psychotherapy."

If the source of sickness-causing evil was within the body, treatment involved drawing the evil out of the body. This may have been accomplished through the use of purgatives that caused either vomiting or diarrhea, or by blood-letting: "bleeding" the patient or "sucking out" blood. (The barbers of medieval Europe did not originate this practice; bleeding was done in ancient times.) Leeching was another method used to remove corrupt humors from the body, and the reader may recall that in Chapter 3 leeching was mentioned by a student whose grandmother had treated illness by that method.

If the source of the evil was outside the body, there were a number of ways to deal with it. One source of "external" evil was witchcraft. In a community, there were often many people (or a single person) who were "different" from the other people. Quite often, when an unexplainable or untreatable illness occurred, it was these people (or person) who were seen as the causative agents. In such a belief system, successful treatment depended on the identification and punishment of the person believed responsible for the disease. (Certainly the practice of scapegoating is in part derived from this belief.) By removing or punishing the guilty person from the community, the disease would be cured. In some communities, the healers themselves were seen as witches and the possessors of evil skills. How easy it was for ancient humankind to turn things around and blame the person with the skills to treat the disease for causing the disease!

Various rituals were involved in the treatment of ill people. Often the sick person was isolated from the rest of the family and community. In addition, it was customary to chant special prayers and incantations on the invalid's behalf. Sacrifices and dances often were performed in an effort to cure the ills. Often the rituals of the healer involved reciting incantations in a language foreign to the ears of the general population ("speaking in tongues") and using practices that were strange to the observers. Small wonder, then, as superstition abounded, that at times the healers themselves were ostracized by the population.

Another cause of illness was believed to be the *envy* of people within the community. The best method, consequently, of preventing such an illness was to avoid provoking the envy of one's friends and neighbors. The treatment was to do away with whatever was provoking the envy—even though the act might have prevented a person from accomplishing a "mission in life," and the fear of being "responsible" may have been psychologically damaging.

Today we tend to view the healing methods of ancient people as primitive, yet to fully appreciate their efficacy, we need only make the simple observation that these methods in many forms exist today and have aided the survival of humankind!

Religious Beliefs and Healing

There are far too many religious beliefs and practices related to healing to include in this chapter. A discussion of religious healing beliefs from the Judeo-Christian background, however, is possible.

The Old Testament does not focus on healing to the extent the New Testament does. God is seen to have total power over life and death and is the healer of all human woes. God is the giver of all good things and of all misfortune, including sickness. Sickness represented a break between God and humans. In Exodus 15:26 God is proclaimed the supreme healer ("I will put none of the diseases upon you which I put upon the Egyptians; for I am the Lord, your healer.") and in another passage from Deuteronomy 32:39 it is stated "I kill, and I make alive. I have wounded and I heal." The traditionalist Jew believes that the "healing of illness comes from God through the mediation of His 'messenger,' the doctor." The Jew who is ill combines hope for a cure with faith in God and faith in the doctor.[49]

The healing practices of the Roman Catholic tradition include a variety of beliefs and numerous practices, both of a preventive and healing nature. For example, Saint Blaise, an Armenian bishop who died in AD 316 as a martyr, is revered as the preventor of sore throats. The blessing of the throats on his feast day (February 3) derives from the tradition that he miraculously saved the life of a boy by removing a fishbone that he swallowed.[50]

The saints concerned with other aspects of illness include the following:[51]

Saint	Problem
St. Anthony of Padua	Barrenness
St. Odilia	Blindness
Our Lady of Lourdes	Bodily ills
St. Peregrine	Cancer
St. Francis de Sales	Deafness
St. Joseph	Dying
St. Vitus	Epilepsy
St. Raymond Nonnatus	Pregnancy
St. Lucy	Eye disease
St. Teresa of Avila	Headache
St. John of God	Heart disease
St. Roch	Being bedridden
St. Dymphna	Mental illness
St. Bruno	Possession

Many more saints could be included. I refer you to other sources for information, and I also recommend that you ask patients for information.

In the United States people make pilgrimages to a number of shrines in search of special favors and petitions.

The oldest is the Shrine of Our Lady of La Leche, located in St. Augustine, Florida (Fig. 7-7A). This shrine was founded in 1620 by Spanish settlers as a sign of their love for the Mother of Christ. The shrine is visited by thousands of mothers to ask for the blessings of motherhood, a safe and happy delivery, a healthy baby, and holy children. Countless letters can be read at the shrine attesting to the powers of Our Lady of La Leche.[52]

Another shrine is that of Our Lady of San Juan (Fig. 7-7B) located in San Juan, Texas. This shrine houses a statue of the Virgin that was brought to Mexico by the Spanish missionaries in 1623. The statue was responsible for causing a miracle, and devotion to *La Virgen de San Juan* spread. The statue was brought to Texas in the 1940s after a woman claimed to have seen an image of the Virgin in the countryside around San Juan. The statue is housed at present in a beautiful new church, and pilgrims arrive daily to ask for healing and other favors. Again, countless letters are displayed attesting to the healing powers of this statue.[53]

A third shrine is that of St. Peregrine for Cancer Sufferers (Fig. 7-8), located in the Old Mission San Juan Capistrano in California. This statue is housed in a small grotto in the shrine. St. Peregrine was born in Italy in 1265 and died in 1345. He was believed to have miraculous powers against sickness and could cure cancer. This won for him the title "official patron for

Shrine
(Our Lady of La Leche)
MISSION
(Nombre De Dios)
On this site, September 8, 1565, Pedro Menendez de Aviles landed with a band of settlers to found St. Augustine, first permanent Christian settlement in the United States. Father Francisco Lopez de Mendoza Grajales, Spanish Diocesan Priest, offered here the First Mass in the nation's first Parish. The Spanish pioneers named this landing site Nombre De Dios — Name of God — and founded here the first Mission in the United States.

A

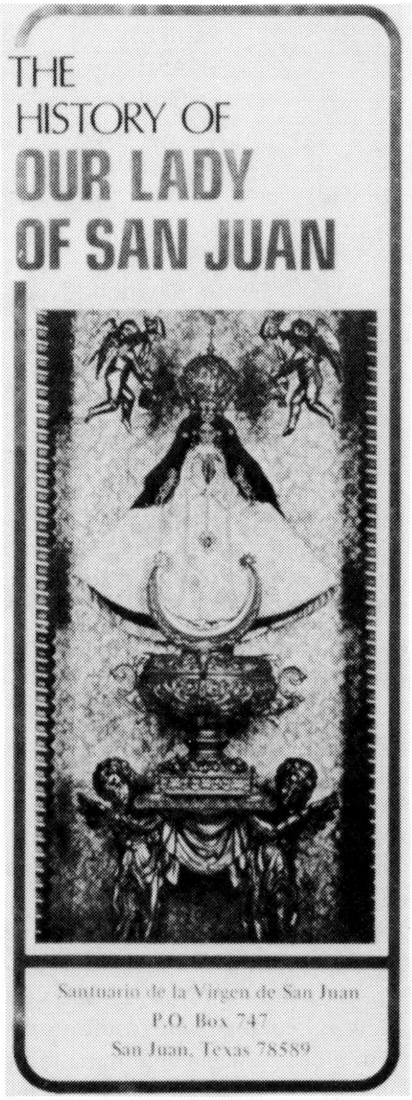
THE
HISTORY OF
OUR LADY
OF SAN JUAN
Santuario de la Virgen de San Juan
P.O. Box 747
San Juan, Texas 78589

B

Figure 7–7.A. Our Lady of La Leche Shrine and Mission. **B.** Our Lady of San Juan Shrine. *(From collection of the author)*

Saint Peregrine Shrine
for Cancer Sufferers

Statue of Saint Peregrine at
Old Mission San Juan Capistrano
Mission Founded November 1, 1776

Figure 7–8. Saint Peregrine Shrine. *(From collection of the author)*

cancer victims." Ten years ago a woman was afflicted with cancer and a lady gave her a prayer to St. Peregrine. The woman prayed for 6 months, and her cancer was arrested. In gratitude for this, the woman had a statue of the saint placed in the mission. Today, the belief in this saint has spread, and, again, countless documents attesting to his healing powers are on display in the mission.[54]

Table 7-3 summarizes the beliefs of people from several religious backgrounds with respect to health, healing, and several events related to healthcare delivery. Remember, this is a *summary*, and you are urged not to generalize from this guide when relating to an individual patient and family. It is important to show respect and sensitivity and an awareness and understanding of the different perspectives that may exist and to be able to convey to the patient and family your desire to understand their viewpoint on health care.

Healing and Today's Beliefs

It is not an accident or coincidence that today, more so than in recent years, we are not only curious but vitally concerned about the ways of healing that our ancestors employed. Some critics of today's health-care system choose to condemn it with more vociferous critics, such as Illich, citing its failure to create a utopia for humankind.[55] It is obvious to those who embrace a more moderate viewpoint that diseases continue to occur and that they outflank our ability to cure or prevent them. Once again, many people are seeking the services of people who are knowledgeable in the arts of healing and folk medicine. Many patients may elect, at some point in their lives, more specifically during an illness, to use modalities outside the medical establishment. It is important to understand these healers.

There are numerous healers in the general population, some of whom are legitimate and some of whom are not. They range from housewives and priests to gypsies and "witches." Many people seek their services. I have had occasion to meet with several of these folk healers. Without attempting to make a value judgment, I merely report on their skills and methods (Table 7-4).

One healer has an office in a community near where I live. He charges a nominal fee for consultation with either groups or individuals and then gives advice on how to solve a problem. He does not see physically ill people but prefers to help people who have moderate emotional and practical problems. His primary objective is to help people solve these problems. This man tends to be quite popular with young adults in the area, as he lends a "willing ear" and is "not too expensive." He does not keep his clients waiting long, and often the brief wait proves to be interesting because the waiting room is always the scene of an open discussion about his talents.

Another healer I knew was a young college student. He believed that he possessed certain spirits and skills that enabled him to heal. He had

TABLE 7–3. SELECTED RELIGION'S RESPONSES TO HEALTH EVENTS

Baha'i
"All healing comes from God."

Abortion	Forbidden
Artificial insemination	No specific rule
Autopsy	Acceptable with medical or legal need
Birth control	Can choose family planning method
Blood and blood products	No restrictions for use
Diet	Alcohol and drugs forbidden
Euthanasia	No destruction of life
Healing beliefs	Harmony between religion and science
Healing practices	Pray
Medications	Narcotics with prescription
	No restriction for vaccines
Organ donations	Permitted
Right to die issues	Life is unique and precious—do not destroy
Surgical procedures	No restrictions
Visitors	Community members assist and support

Buddhist Churches of America
"To keep the body in good health is a duty—
otherwise we shall not be able to keep our mind strong and clear."

Abortion	Patient's condition determines
Artificial insemination	Acceptable
Autopsy	Matter of individual practice
Birth control	Acceptable
Blood and blood products	No restrictions
Diet	Restricted food combinations
	Extremes must be avoided
Euthanasia	May permit
Healing beliefs	Do not believe in healing through faith
Healing practices	No restrictions
Medications	No restrictions
Organ donations	Considered act of mercy; if hope for
	recovery, all means may be taken
Right to die issues	With hope, all means encouraged
Surgical procedures	Permitted, with extremes avoided
Visitors	Family, community

Roman Catholics
"The prayer of faith shall heal the sick, and the Lord shall raise him up."

Abortion	Prohibited
Artificial insemination	Illicit, even between husband and wife
Autopsy	Permissible
Birth control	Natural means only
Blood and blood products	Permissible
Diet	Use foods in moderation
Euthanasia	Direct life-ending procedures forbidden
Healing beliefs	Many within religious belief system
Healing practices	Sacrament of sick, candles, laying-on of hands

TABLE 7–3. Continued

Roman Catholics—(Continued)	
Medications	May be taken if benefits outweigh risks
Organ donations	Justifiable
Right to die issues	Obligated to take ordinary, not extraordinary, means to prolong life
Surgical procedures	Most are permissible except abortion and sterilization
Visitors	Family, friends, priest
	Many outreach programs through Church to reach sick

Christian Science	
Abortion	Incompatible with faith
Artificial insemination	Unusual
Autopsy	Not usual; individual or family decide
Birth control	Individual judgment
Blood and blood products	Ordinarily not used by members
Diet	No restrictions
	Abstain from alcohol and tobacco, some from tea and coffee
Euthanasia	Contrary to teachings
Healing beliefs	Accepts physical and moral healing
Healing practices	Full-time healing ministers
	Spiritual healing practiced
Medications	None
	Immunizations/vaccines to comply with law
Organ donations	Individual decides
Right to die issues	Unlikely to seek medical help to prolong life
Surgical procedures	No medical ones practiced
Visitors	Family, friends, and members of the Christian Science community and Healers, Christian Science nurses

Church of Jesus Christ of Latter Day Saints	
Abortion	Forbidden
Artificial insemination	Acceptable between husband and wife
Autopsy	Permitted with consent of next of kin
Birth control	Contrary to Mormon belief
Blood and blood products	No restrictions
Diet	Alcohol, tea (except herbal teas), coffee, and tobacco are forbidden
	Fasting (24 hours without food and drink) is required once a month
Euthanasia	Humans must not interfere in God's plan
Healing beliefs	Power of God can bring healing
Healing practices	Anointing with oil, sealing, prayer, laying-on of hands
Medications	No restrictions; may use herbal folk remedies
Organ donations	Permitted

TABLE 7–3. Continued

Church of Jesus Christ of Latter Day Saints—(Continued)

Right to die issues	If death inevitable, promote a peaceful and dignified death
Surgical procedures	Matter of individual choice
Visitors	Church members (Elder and Sister) family and friends
	The Relief Society helps members

Hinduism
"Enricher, Healer of disease, be a good friend to us."

Abortion	No policy exists
Artificial insemination	No restrictions exist but not often practiced
Autopsy	Acceptable
Birth control	All types acceptable
Blood and blood products	Acceptable
Diet	Eating of meat is forbidden
Euthanasia	Not practiced
Healing beliefs	Some believe in faith healing
Healing practices	Traditional faith healing system
Medications	Acceptable
Organ donations	Acceptable
Right to die issues	No restrictions
	Death seen as "one more step to nirvana"
Surgical procedures	With an amputation, the loss of limb seen as due to "sins in a previous life"
Visitors	Members of family, community, and priest support

Islam
"The Lord of the world created me—and when I am sick, He healeth me."

Abortion	Accepted
Artificial insemination	Permitted between husband and wife
Autopsy	Permitted for medical and legal purposes
Birth control	Acceptable
Blood and blood products	No restrictions
Diet	Pork and alcohol prohibited
Euthanasia	Not acceptable
Healing beliefs	Faith healing generally not acceptable
Healing practices	Some use of herbal remedies and faith healing
Medications	No restrictions
Organ donations	Acceptable
Right to die issues	Attempts to shorten life prohibited
Surgical procedures	Most permitted
Visitors	Family and friends provide support

Jehovah's Witnesses

Abortion	Forbidden
Artificial insemination	Forbidden
Autopsy	Acceptable if required by law
Birth control	Sterilization forbidden
	Other methods individual choice

TABLE 7–3. Continued

Jehovah's Witnesses—(Continued)

Blood and blood products	Forbidden
Diet	Abstain from tobacco, moderate use of alcohol
Euthanasia	Forbidden
Healing beliefs	Faith healing forbidden
Healing practices	Reading scriptures can comfort the individual and lead to mental and spiritual healing
Medications	Accepted except if derived from blood products
Organ donations	Forbidden
Right to die issues	Use of extraordinary means an individual's choice
Surgical procedures	Not opposed, but administration of blood during surgery is strictly prohibited
Visitors	Members of congregation and elders pray for the sick person

Judaism
"O Lord, my God, I cried to Thee for help and Thou has healed me."

Abortion	Therapeutic permitted; some groups accept abortion on demand
Artificial insemination	Permitted
Autopsy	Permitted under certain circumstances All body parts must be buried together
Birth control	Permissible, except with orthodox Jews
Blood and blood products	Acceptable
Diet	Strict dietary laws followed by many Jews— milk and meat not mixed; predatory fowl, shellfish, and pork products forbidden; kosher products only may be requested
Euthanasia	Prohibited
Healing beliefs	Medical care expected
Healing practices	Prayers for the sick
Medications	No restrictions
Organ donations	Complex issue; some practiced
Right to die issues	Right to die with dignity If death is inevitable, no new procedures need to be undertaken, but those ongoing must continue
Surgical procedures	Most allowed
Visitors	Family, friends, rabbi, many community services

Mennonite

Abortion	Therapeutic acceptable
Artificial insemination	Individual conscience; husband to wife
Autopsy	Acceptable
Birth control	Acceptable
Blood and blood products	Acceptable
Diet	No specific restrictions
Euthanasia	Not condoned

TABLE 7–3. Continued

Mennonite—(Continued)

Healing beliefs	Part of God's work
Healing practices	Prayer and anointing with oil
Medications	No restrictions
Organ donations	Acceptable
Right to die issues	Do not believe life must be continued at all cost
Surgical procedures	No restrictions
Visitors	Family, community

Seventh-Day Adventists

Abortion	Therapeutic acceptable
Artificial insemination	Acceptable between husband and wife
Autopsy	Acceptable
Birth control	Individual choice
Blood and blood products	No restrictions
Diet	Encourage vegetarian diet
Euthanasia	Not practiced
Healing beliefs	Divine healing
Healing practices	Anointing with oil and prayer
Medications	No restrictions
	Vaccines acceptable
Organ donations	Acceptable
Right to die issues	Follow the ethic of prolonging life
Surgical procedures	No restrictions
	Oppose use of hypnotism
Visitors	Pastor and elders pray and anoint sick person
	Worldwide health system includes hospitals and clinics

Unitarian/Universalist Church

Abortion	Acceptable, therapeutic and on demand
Artificial insemination	Acceptable
Autopsy	Recommended
Birth control	All types acceptable
Blood and blood products	No restrictions
Diet	No restrictions
Euthanasia	Favor nonaction
	May withdraw therapies if death imminent
Healing beliefs	Faith healing: seen as "superstitious"
Healing practices	Use of science to facilitate healing
Medications	No restrictions
Organ donations	Acceptable
Right to die issues	Favor the right to die with dignity
Surgical procedures	No restrictions
Visitors	Family, friends, church members

Adapted with permission from: Andrews, M. M. and Hanson, P. A. "Religion, Culture, and Nursing" in *Transcultural Concepts in Nursing Care,* 2nd ed. (Boyle, J. S. and Andrews, M. M., eds.) (Philadelphia, J. B. Lippincott, 1995), pp. 371–406.

TABLE 7-4. COMPARISONS: TRADITIONAL HEALER VERSUS PHYSICIAN

Healer	Physician
1. Maintains informal, friendly, affective relationship with the entire family	1. Businesslike, formal relationship; deals only with the patient
2. Comes to the house day or night	2. Patient must go to the physician's office or clinic, and only during the day; may have to wait for hours to be seen; home visits are rarely, if ever, made
3. For diagnosis, consults with head of house, creates a mood of awe, talks to all family members, is not authoritarian, has social rapport, builds expectation of cure	3. Rest of the family usually is ignored; deals solely with the ill person and may deal only with the sick part of the person; authoritarian manner creates fear
4. Generally less expensive than the physician	4. More expensive than the healer
5. Has ties to the "world of the sacred"; has rapport with the symbolic, spiritual, creative, or holy force	5. Secular; pays little attention to the religious beliefs or meaning of a given illness
6. Shares the world view of the patient, i.e., speaks the same language, lives in the same neighborhood, or in some similar socioeconomic conditions, may know the same people, understands the lifestyle of the patient	6. Generally does not share the world view of the patient, i.e., may not speak the same language, live in the same neighborhood, or understand the socioeconomic conditions, may not understand the lifestyle of the patient

visions that interpreted for him the problems and ills of his clients. This young man maintained a special altar in his room, where he prayed to the "spirits." At that time, he did not charge for his services because he had just received the "message," and the art of healing was new to him. He admitted that he had formerly been a drug addict but was now enrolled in college and hoped to use his education and healing skills to make life better for the people of the streets.

The third healer I am personally acquainted with is a Catholic priest; he is extremely reluctant to call himself a "healer." He does claim, however, to have witnessed and participated in numerous healings. He conducts prayer meetings in his parish. He comes to my classes and lectures to the students on healing and the charismatic movement within the Catholic Church.[56] He defines healing as the "satisfactory response to crises by a group of people, individually or corporately." "Healing," as he explains it, "is applied in a broad, holistic approach; that is, body, mind, and spirit are not separated." His vision of reality is that of a person being full of the spirit of God. According to this priest, the healer has the ability to *heal* but not really to *cure*. He further explains that there are "three types of illness: spiritual, physical, and mental." In this context, faith is the underlying basis of healing, although he questions whether faith is the only component. Healing becomes a living process whereby that which is wounded or broken becomes whole.

A review of healing and spiritual literature reveals that there are four types of healing.

Spiritual Healing. When a person is experiencing an illness of the spirit, spiritual healing applies. The cause of suffering is personal sin. The treatment method is repentance, which is followed by a natural healing process.

Inner Healing. When a person is suffering from an emotional (mental) illness, inner healing is used. The root of the problem may lie in the person's conscious or unconscious mind. The treatment method is to heal the person's memory. The healing process is delicate and sensitive, and takes considerable time and effort.

Physical Healing. When a person is suffering from a disease or has been involved in an accident that resulted in some form of bodily damage, physical healing is appropriate. Laying on of hands and speaking in tongues usually accompany physical healing. The person is prayed over by both the leader and members of a prayer group (Fig. 7-9).

The priest referred to previously related an incident in which one of the members of the group was experiencing difficulty with ulcers and was not responding to conventional medical treatment. The man, who initially was embarrassed by the idea, allowed the prayer group and the priest to pray over him. In a short time, to his surprise, he recovered from his ulcers.

Deliverance, or Exorcism. When the body and mind are victims of evil from the outside, exorcism is used. In order to effect treatment, the person must be delivered, or exorcised, from the evil. The popularity of films such as *The Exorcist* gives testimony to the return of these beliefs. Incidentally, the priest who has lectured in my classes stated that he does not, as yet, lend credence to exorcisms; however, he was guarded enough not to discount it either.

Other Forms of Healing

Auric Healing. Another form of treatment is auric healing. John Richard Turner of Waltham, Massachusetts, considers himself to be an auric healer. He explains that "from the moment of birth until the last breath is taken, a person has a bioenergetic field surrounding his body," known as an "aura." If strong enough, it is believed to be transmittable and to have healing powers. By the use of touch, the person with the auric powers is able to effect cure for an ill person.[57] Mr. Turner, who is fairly well known in the Boston area, also claims to be quite popular in California. He states that he visits patients in the hospital along with the physician and that he has been successful in treating people in that setting.

church of saint ignatius of loyola

Liturgy of Anointing

THE CHURCH OF ST. IGNATIUS WILL PRAY FOR THE SICK AND ELDERLY IN THE PARISH ON THE FEAST OF CHRIST THE KING, NOVEMBER 20th AT THE LITURGY FOR ANOINTING AT 9:30 A.M.. AREA RESIDENTS, ESPECIALLY THOSE WHO ARE SICK, DISABLED OR ELDERLY, ARE WELCOME TO TAKE PART. EACH PERSON WHO DESIRES IT WILL BE BLESSED OR ANOINTED WITH HOLY OIL.

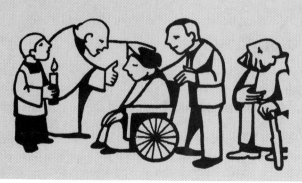

Figure 7–9. Sample of an announcement for a mass to be said for the sick. *(From collection of the author)*

Pilgrimages. The film, *We Believe in Niño Fidencio*, is a documentary on folk curing and penitent pilgrimages in northern Mexico. Shot in October 1971 in northern Mexico by Dr. and Mrs. John Olson (who were in Mexico doing research), the film is concerned with

> ... the belief system and ceremonies surrounding a folk curer, Fidencio Constantino, who practiced in Nuevo Leon from the early 1920's until his death in 1938, and who is presently the central figure in a widespread curing cult. Twice each year, upon the anniversaries of his birth and death, Espinazo (a town of about 300 population) is inundated by 10,000 to 15,000 people from Mexico and the United States who make pilgrimages in hopes of a cure and/or help from the Nino. It was during one of these celebrations that the film was made.
>
> Believers combine elements of traditional Catholicism, Indian dances, herbology, and laying-on-of-hands in effecting cures. It is believed that certain individuals receive the Niño's power to heal. They are called "Cajitas" or "Materias" (women), and "Cajones" (men)—"receptacles" of the Niño's power—and they cure in the name of Niño Fidencio and God. During the celebrations they roam Espinazo curing all who wish a cure-blessing. There are several "holy places" in Espinazo where curing is conducted: Fidencio's tomb, "temple," and death bed, two trees, a cemetery hill, the hill of the bell, and the "charco" or mudpond, where Fidencio conducted baptisms to cure his patients.
>
> The film includes references to other curing alternatives, and attempts to present some of the reasons why the believers continue to select this curing method in the face of modern medical alternatives in nearby towns and cities.
>
> As previously stated, Dr. Olson first learned about this cult in 1968–1969 while doing field research in Mina, a community in the same county as Espinazo. It was during this time that the Olsons met members of the cult (in Mina and Espinazo) including the local "materia," Cayetana, who appear in the film. The narration of the film is based on information and actual recorded interviews given by participants in the cult. Jon Olson is presently an Assistant Professor of Anthropology at California State University at Los Angeles.
>
> Extensive study of the Niño Fidencio complex has been done by Professor June Macklin (Connecticut College).[58]

Several healers in the South Texas area are known as *materias* and heal in the name of Niño Fidencio (Fig. 7-10).[59]

This chapter is no more than an *overview* of the topics introduced. The amount of relevant knowledge could fill many books. The issues raised here are those that, I think, have special meaning to the practice of nursing, medicine, and health-care delivery. We must be aware (1) of what people may be thinking that may differ from our own thoughts and (2) that sources of *help* exist outside the traditional medical community. As the beliefs of ethnic communities are explored in later chapters, I shall attempt to delineate who are

Figure 7–10. Assessment of a client performed by a *materia,* a healer who heals in the name of Niño Fidencio. *(Courtesy of Alma Martinez, Castroville, Texas. Photograph by R. Spector.)*

specifically recognized and used as healers by the members of the community, and I shall describe some of the forms of treatment employed by each community.

REFERENCES

1. Nightingale, F. *Notes on Nursing—What It Is, What It Is Not.* A fascimile of the first edition published in 1860 by D. Appleton and Co. (New York: Appleton-Century Co., 1946).
2. Blattner, B. *Holistic Nursing* (Englewood Cliffs, NJ: Prentice-Hall, Inc., 1981).
3. Krieger, D. *The Therapeutic Touch* (Englewood Cliffs, NJ: Prentice-Hall, Inc., 1979).
4. Wallace, G. "Spiritual Care—A Reality in Nursing Education and Practice." *The Nurses Lamp* 5(2) (November 1979): 1–4.
5. Shaw, W. *Aspects of Malaysian Magic* (Kuala Lampor, Malaysia: Nazibum Negara, 1975), p. 121.
6. Buxton, J. *Religion and Healing in Mandari* (Oxford: Clarendon Press, 1973).
7. Naegele, K. *Health and Healing* (San Francisco: Jossey-Bass, Inc., 1970), p. 18.
8. Ibid., p. 10.

9. Ibid., p. 107–108.
10. Ibid., p. 108.
11. Shames, R. and Sterin, C. *Healing with Mind Power* (Emmans, PA: Rodale Press, 1978).
12. Progoff, I. *Depth Psychology and Modern Man* (New York: McGraw-Hill, 1959).
13. Krippner, S. and Villaldo, A. *The Realms of Healing* (Millbrae, CA: Celestial Arts, 1976), p. viii.
14. Ibid., p. 37.
15. Bishop, G. *Faith Healing: God or Fraud?* (Los Angeles: Sherbourne Press, Inc., 1967), p. 45.
16. Ibid., p. 60.
17. Ibid., p. 119.
18. Ford, P. S. *The Healing Trinity: Prescriptions for Body, Mind, and Spirit* (New York: Harper and Row, 1971), p. 6.
19. Ibid., p. 67.
20. Russell, A. J. *Healing in His Wings* (London: Methuen and Co., Ltd., 1937), p. 221.
21. Cramer, E. *Divine Science and Healing* (Denver: The Colorado College of Divine Science, 1923), p. 11.
22. Ibid., p. 174.
23. Morgenstern, J. *Rites of Birth, Marriage, Death and Kindred Occasions Among the Semites* (Chicago: Quadrangle Books, 1966), p. 3.
24. Ibid., p. 5.
25. Ibid., p. 31.
26. Ibid., pp. 22–30.
27. Ibid.
28. Ibid., p. 36.
29. Ibid., p. 87.
30. Ibid., p. 46.
31. Ibid., p. 47.
32. Ibid., p. 48.
33. Ibid., p. 58.
34. Ibid., p. 53.
35. Ibid., p. 82.
36. Ibid., p. 117–60.
37. Ibid., p. 186.
38. Maloney, C., ed. *The Evil Eye* (New York: Columbia University Press, 1976), p. 14.
39. Ibid., p. vi.
40. Ibid., p. vii.
41. Ibid.
42. Ibid., p. xv.
43. Spector, R. E. "A Description of the Impact of Medicare on Health-Illness Beliefs and Practices of White Ethnic Senior Citizens in Central Texas." Ph.D. diss. University of Texas at Austin School of Nursing, 1983 (Ann Arbor, MI: University Microfilms International, 1983), pp. 126–127.
44. Zola, I. K. "The Concept of Trouble and Sources of Medical Assistance to Whom One Can Turn With What." *Social Science and Medicine* 6 (1972): 673–679.
45. Tallant, R. *Voodoo in New Orleans* (New York: Collier Books, 1946).
46. Winkler, G. *Dybbuk* (New York: Judaica Press, 1981), pp. 8–9.
47. Zola, "Concept of Trouble."

48. Steinberg, M. *Basic Judaism* (New York: Harcourt, Brace and World, 1947) pp. 125–126.
49. Ausubel, N. *The Book of Jewish Knowledge* (New York: Crown Publishers, 1964), pp. 192–195.
50. *Monthly Missalette* 15, no. 13 (February 1980): 38.
51. Foy, F. A., ed. *Catholic Almanac* (Huntington, IN: Our Sunday Visitor, 1980), pp. 305–313.
52. Information obtained during a visit to this shrine, July 1983.
53. Information obtained during a visit to this shrine, November 1981.
54. Information obtained during a visit to this shrine, March 1984.
55. Illich, I. *Medical Nemesis: The Expropriation of Health* (London: Marion Bogars, 1975).
56. MacNutt, F. *Healing* (Notre Dame, IN: Ave Maria Press, 1974); Kelsey, M. T. *Healing and Christianity* (New York: Harper and Row, 1973).
57. Turner, J. R., notes from a lecture delivered at a meeting of the World's Future Society held at Boston College, 16 March 1977.
58. Flyer on the film *We Believe in Niño Fidencio* (Jon and Natalie Olson, P.O. Box 14914, Long Beach, CA 90814).
59. Gardner, D. *Niño Fidencio. A Heart Thrown Open.* (Santa Fe: Museum of New Mexico Press, 1992).

ANNOTATED BIBLIOGRAPHY: CHAPTERS 6 AND 7

Belgium, D., ed. *Religion and Medicine.* Ames: Iowa State University Press, 1967.
   This book explores two dimensions of healing: religion and medicine. The essays it contains explore the nature of humankind and its problems in sickness and health.
Kelsey, M. T. *Healing and Christianity.* New York: Harper and Row, 1973.
   Kelsey presents a comprehensive history of the sacrament of healing in the Christian church from Biblical times to the present.
Leek, S. *Herbs: Medicine and Mysticism.* Chicago: Henry Regnery, 1975.
   Many herbs and their uses are described—both those in current use among the general population and those used among the Hopi Indian tribes.
MacNutt, F. *Healing.* Notre Dame, IN: Ave Maria Press, 1974.
   This book explores the charismatic movement in the Catholic Church. It describes in great detail the multiple forms of healing within the Church.
MacNutt, F. *The Power to Heal.* Notre Dame, IN: Ave Maria Press, 1977.
   In this book, Father MacNutt further describes his experiences within the healing ministry. He addresses such topics as "Healing through Touch," "Soaking Prayer," "Suffering and Death," and "When and When Not to Pray."
Montgomery, R. *Born to Heal.* New York: Coward, McCann and Geoghegan, 1973.
   This is the story of a dynamic man and his seemingly miraculous cures of tragic ailments, which run the gamut of human suffering. Mr. A. first devoted himself to healing in 1941 and experienced conflict with the traditional health system.
Morgenstern, J. *Rites of Birth, Marriage, Death, and Kindred Occasions among the Semites.* Chicago: Quadrangle Books, 1966.
   Morgenstern presents a fascinating history of the rites that preceded today's religions. It is hard to follow because the author tends to jump back and forth, but it is well worth the effort because its content is quite interesting.

Payer, L. *Medicine and Culture*. New York: Henry Holt & Co., 1988.

In this book, Payer supports the argument that there is a desperate need for the establishment of objective criteria for medical practices and procedures. She supports this by exploring cultural differences in health care and how medical practices are influenced by cultural norms and values.

Scott, W. R. and Volkhart, E. H. *Medical Care Readings in the Sociology of Medical Institutions*. New York: Wiley, 1966.

This anthology explores such topics as the varieties of healers, the relationships between healers and patients, and relationships between patients and hospitals.

Stoll, R. I., ed. *Concepts in Nursing—A Christian Perspective*. Madison, WI: Inter-Varsity Christian Fellowship of the USA, 1990.

This book presents a view of professional nursing practice from a Christian perspective. It covers such topics as values, relationships, communion, health, and stewardship.

FURTHER SUGGESTED READINGS

Articles

Allen, C. and Bennett, A. "Healing Memories—Reminiscence Therapy." *Nursing Mirror* 158(15) (April 11, 1984): vi–vii.

Althouse, L. W. "Healing and Health in the Judaic-Christian Experience: A Return to Holism." *Journal of Holistic Nursing* 3(1) (Spring 1985): 19–24.

Banonis, B. C. The Lived Experience of Recovering from Addiction: A Phenomenological Study." *Nursing Science Quarterly* 2(1) (Spring 1989): 37–43.

Barker, E. R. "Caregivers as Casualties—War Experiences and the Postwar Consequences for both Nightingale and Vietnam-era Nurses." *Western Journal of Nursing Research* 11(5) (October 1989): 628–631.

Bellert, J. L. "Humor: A Therapeutic Approach in Oncology Nursing." *Cancer Nursing* 12(2) (April 1989): 65–70.

Bibbings, J. "Honey, Lizard Dung, and Pigeon's Blood—Wound Dressing Through the Ages, Part 1." *Nursing Times* 80 (48) (November 28–December 4, 1984): 36–38.

Brand, P. and Yancey, P. "The Miracles of Everyday Healing: Expecting the Extraordinary Can Be Dangerous." *Journal of Christian Nursing* 2(2) (Spring 1985): 4–8.

Brittain, J. N. and Boozer, J. "Spiritual Care: Integration into a Collegiate Nursing Curriculum." *Journal of Nursing Education* 26(4) (April 1987): 155–160.

Bulbrook, M. J. T. "Health and Healing in the Future." *Canadian Nurse* 80(11) (December 1984): 26–29.

Burnard, P. "The Spiritual Needs of Atheists and Agnostics." *Professional Nurse* 4(3) (December 1988): 130, 132.

Carlson, G. E. "Minister of Health—The Parish Nurse." *American Journal of Maternal Child Nursing* 14(5) (September–October 1989): 305–306.

Clark, B. "The Healing Power of the Human Voice." *RN* 50(1) (January 1987): 19.

Cohen, L. "A Healing Game." 17(10) *Nursing* (October 1987): 152.

Connor, A. "More Than a Home: One Nurse's Vision of a Healing Community." *Journal of Christian Nursing* 5(4) (Fall 1988): 16–18.

Crawford, L. "Health, Healing, and the Placebo Response." *Physician Assistant* 11(8) (August 1987): 73–75, 78, 95–96.

Dopson, L. "Spiritual Healing—Hospital of St. John of God." *Nursing Times* 85(19) (1988–1989): 42–44.

Fanslow, C. A. "Therapeutic Touch: A Healing Modality Throughout Life." *Topics in Clinical Nursing* 5(2) (July 1983): 72–79.

Flanagan, K. "Faith and Other Medicines for 'Diseases of Spirit'." *Nevada RNformation* (May 1983): 10.

Flaskerud, J. H. and Rush, C. E. "AIDS and Traditional Health Beliefs and Practices of Black Women." *Nursing Research* 38(4) (July–August 1989): 210–215.

Geissler, E. M. "Nurturance: Old Friend, New Word." *Journal of Nursing History* 2(1) (November 1986): 61–65.

Goldstein, D. "A Traditional Navajo Medicine Woman—A Modern Nurse-Midwife— Healing in Harmony." *Frontier Nursing Service Quarterly Bulletin* 63(3) (Winter 1987): 6–13.

Gomez, G. E. "Folk Healing Among Hispanic Americans." *Public Health Nursing* 2(4) (December 1985): 245–249.

Grossman, R. "Healing in the Hollers." *Journal of Christian Nursing* 6(4) (Fall 1989): 14–17.

Gyulay, J. E. "Grief Responses." *Issues in Comprehensive Pediatric Nursing* 12(1) (January–February 1989): 1–31.

Holden-Lund, C. "The Effects of Relaxation with Guided Imagery on Surgical Stress and Wound Healing." *Research in Nursing and Health* 11(4) (August 1988): 235–244.

Hover-Kramer, D. "Creating a Context for Self-Healing: The Transpersonal Perspective." *Holistic Nursing Practice* 3(3) (May 1989): 27–34.

Hurwood, B. J. "Healing and Believing: A Special Report on Faith Healing in America." *Health* 16(6) (June 1984): 15–16, 21.

Jurgens, A. and Meehan, T. C. "Therapeutic Touch as a Nursing Intervention." *Holistic Nursing Practice* 2(1) (November 1987): 1–13.

Kiu, Y. C. "China: Traditional Healing and Contemporary Medicine." *International Nursing Review* 31(4/256) (July–August, 1984): 110–114.

Kutlenios, R. M. "Healing Mind and Body: A Holistic Perspective." *Journal of Gerontological Nursing* 13(12) (December 1987): 8–13.

Lamb, R. M. "Healing: Examining the Perspectives." *Journal of Holistic Nursing* 5(1) (Spring 1987): 23–27.

Lammers, P. K. "Dealing With Other Cultures and Religions Emphasized at Recent Ethics Conference." *Association of Operating Room Nurses Journal* 45(5) (May 1987): 1211–1212, 1214, 1216.

Lawless, J. P. "Visualizing the Healer." *Journal of Christian Nursing* 3(3) (Summer 1986): 12–14.

Leduc, E. "The Healing Touch." *American Journal of Maternal Child Nursing* 14(1) (January–February 1989): 41–43.

LePeau, P. "The Healing Effects of Forgiveness." *Journal of Christian Nursing* 4(2) (Spring 1987): 17–20.

Mancke, R. B., Maloney, S., and West, M. "Clowning: A Healing Process." *Health Education* 15(6) (October–November 1984): 16–18.

Martocchio, B. C. "Grief and Bereavement: Healing Through Hurt—Loss Through Death." *Nursing Clinics of North America* 20(20) (June 1985): 327–341.

McNall, M. C. C. and Benner, P. "Healing We Cannot Explain." *American Journal of Nursing* 89(9) (September 1989): 1162–1163.

Morrison, E. F. "The Assaulted Nurse: Strategies for Healing." *Perspectives in Psychiatric Care* 24(3/4) (1987–1988): 120–126.

Nelson, L. "How Can I Explain Why God Lets Patients Suffer?" *Journal of Christian Nursing* 4(3) (Summer 1987): 9.

Nelson, L. "The Nurse Responds: Focus on God's Character." *Journal of Christian Nursing* 4(3) (Summer 1987): 9.

Papantonia, C. T. "Holistic Approach to Healing, Part 2." *Home Health Care Nurse* 6(6) (November–December 1988): 31–35.

Pasquale, E. A. "The Evil Eye Phenomenon: Its Implications for Community Health Nursing." *Home Health Care Nurse* 2(30) (May–June 1984): 19–21.

Porter, R. and Watson, P. "Environment: The Healing Difference." *Nursing Management* 16(6) (June 1985): 19–24.

Reissler, P. C. "Body, Mind, and Soul: What are Holistic Healers Really After?" *Journal of Christian Nursing* 6(2) (Spring 1989): 8–14.

Rew, L. "Exercises for Spiritual Growth." *Journal of Holistic Nursing* 4(1) (Spring 1986): 20–22.

Rush, B. "Healing a Hidden Grief." *Journal of Christian Nursing* 3(3) (Summer 1986): 10–11.

Scandrett, S. L. "Relaxation and the Healing Process." *Journal of Holistic Nursing* 5(1) (Spring 1987): 28–31.

Schunior, C. "Nursing and the Comic Mask." *Holistic Nursing Practice* 3(3) (May 1989): 7–17.

Seamands, D. A. "Healing of Memories: What Is It? Is It Biblical?" *Journal of Christian Nursing* 3(3) (Summer 1986): 4–7, 9.

Schlemon, B. L. "Uncommon Miracles: Expecting the Extraordinary Can Be Healing." *Journal of Christian Nursing* 2(2) (Spring 1985): 9–11.

Sigamoni, M. "Healing and Wholeness." *Christian Nurse* (317) (December 1984): 17–18.

Sigamoni, M. "Healing and Wholeness." *Christian Nurse* (319) (April 1985): 17–20.

Stark, E. "Healing Hands: Therapists Tap into an Ailing Patient's Own Radiant Energy to Relieve Suffering." *Psychology Today* 23(7/8) (July–August 1989): 28, 30.

Stock, J. N. "A Pastor Responds: God Works Through Suffering." *Journal of Christian Nursing* 4(3) (Summer 1987): 6–7.

Strawn, J. M. "Foreword. Healing AIDS." *Holistic Nursing Practice* 3(4) (August 1989): vii–viii.

Stuart, E. M., Deckro, J. P., and Mandle, C. L. "Spirituality in Health and Healing: A Clinical Program." *Holistic Nursing Practice* 3(3) (May 1989): 35–46.

Swaby-Ellis, L. "A Pediatrician Responds: Give Comfort Before Answers." *Journal of Christian Nursing* 4(3) (Summer 1987): 7–9.

Swan, R. "The Law Should Protect All Children—Children in Faith Healing Sects." *Journal of Christian Nursing* 4(2) (Spring 1987): 40.

Tripp-Reimer, T. "Retention of Folk-Healing Practice (Matiasma) Among Four Generations of Urban Greek Immigrants." *Nursing Research* 32(2) (March–April 1983): 97–101.

Tubman, C. "Holistic Approach to Healing." *Home Healthcare Nurse* 6(5) (September–October 1988): 31–34.

Turner, I. M. "The Healing Power of Respect—A Personal Journey." *Occupational Therapy in Mental Health* 9(1) (1989): 17–32.

Turton, P. "Touch Me, Feel Me, Heal Me—Therapeutic Effects of Massage and the Laying On of Hands." *Nursing Times* 85(19) (May 10–16, 1989): 42–44.

Warner-Robbins, C. G. and Christiana, N. M. "The Spiritual Needs of the Person with AIDS." *Family and Community Health* 12(2) (August 1989): 43–51.

Westwood, C. "Aromatherapy—Oils for Healing." *Health Visitor* 59(8) (August 1986): 251.

White, F. J. "A Psychologist Responds: Listening Opens Doors." *Journal of Christian Nursing* 4(3) (Summer 1987): 5–6.

Williams, H. "Humor and Healing: Therapeutic Effects in Geriatrics." *Gerontion: A Canadian Review of Geriatric Care* 1(3) (May–June 1986): 14–17.

Wilson, E. D. "Spiritual Care: Helping a Guilt-Ridden Patient." *Journal of Christian Nursing* 5(2) (Spring 1988): 10–13.

Woods-Smith, D. "Therapeutic Touch—A Healing Experience." *Maine Nurse* 74(2) (February–March 1988): 3, 7.

Yates, A. "Sexual Healing." *Nursing Times* 83(32) (August 12–18, 1987): 28–30.

Yates, A. "Alternative Healing in the Classroom." *California Nurse* 80(10) (December 1984–January 1985): 10.

Yates, A. "God Uses Wounded Healers." *Journal of Christian Nursing* 5(11) (Winter 1988): 3.

Yates, A. "Does God Still Heal Miraculously?" *Journal of Christian Nursing* 2(2) (Spring 1985): 4–8.

Yates, A. "Interview with Jerome Frank, Ph.D., M.D.: Exploring Concepts of Influence, Persuasion, and Healing." *Journal of Psychosocial Nursing and Mental Health Services* 22(9) (September 1984): 32–34, 36–37.

Yates, A. "'Spiritual' Nursing Care: Liability Issue—Followers of Christian Science." *Regan Report on Nursing Law* 27(1) (June 1986): 4.

Chapter

The Influence of Demographics on Health Care

As we enter the 21st century, health-care workers are perched on the cutting edge of enormous demographic, social, and cultural change. Many of these changes will play a dramatic role in both the delivery of health care to patients, their families, and communities, and in the workforce and environment in which the provider practices. The emerging majority constituted 19.7% of the population in 1990[1] and is rapidly growing. The charts and comments in this chapter are designed to provide the reader with a brief overview of the demographic and economic backgrounds of the American population.

"Demography is destiny."[2] In order to understand the changes that are taking place in the health-care system, both in the delivery of services and in the profile of the people who are delivering services, we must look at the changes in the American population. The white majority is shrinking and aging; the black, Hispanic, Asian, and American Indian populations are young and growing. In California the demographic theme is that of a "minority majority" by 2005.[3] It is imperative for those of us who deliver health care to be understanding of and sensitive to cultural differences and to the effect of these differences on a given person's health and illness beliefs and practices.

If we look ahead to the year 2000 and beyond we may observe many interesting demographic shifts. The population of the United States will continue to grow, but more slowly. The young population, ages 0 to 17, will go from the 1990 number of 64.4 million to 67.4 million in 2000, and then will decline to 64.9 million in 2012. This trend is foreseeable because of the decline in the number of women moving into the child-bearing years. The decline will be in the number of white youth (Table 8–1).[4]

TABLE 8–1. PROJECTIONS OF THE U.S. POPULATION AGE 0–17: 1990–2010 (millions)

Youth	1990	2010	Change
Total Youth[a]	64.4	64.9	+0.5
White, non-Hispanic	45.2	41.4	−3.8
Hispanic (of any race)	7.2	9.8	+2.6
Black[b]	10.2	11.4	+1.2
Other Races[b]	2.2	2.8	+0.6

INCREASE IN TOTAL NONWHITE YOUTH +44 MILLION.
DECREASE IN TOTAL WHITE YOUTH −3.8 MILLION.

[a]Rounding.
[b]Includes small number of Hispanics; "other races" are Asian and American Indians.
From: Hodgkinson, H. L. *A Demographic Look at Tomorrow.* (Washington, D.C.: Institute for Educational Leadership, 1992), p. 5. Reprinted with permission.

TOTAL POPULATION CHARACTERISTICS

The 1990 census numbers (in thousands) are compared with the 1980 census in Table 8–2 and Figure 8–1. The 1980 census figure for the U.S. total population was 226,542,203, representing an increase of more than 24 million people since the 1970 census. The breakdown by percentage was 83.2% white; 11.7% black; 0.6% American Indian; 1.5% Asian/Pacific islander; 3.0% other;—that is, 16.8% of the population comprised people of color. It may also be noted that 6.4% of the population claimed Hispanic origin, but could be of any race.[5] In 1990, despite an estimated head count shortfall of 5.3 million people— many of whom were nonwhite or Hispanic city dwellers,[6] the overall population of the United States was counted as 248,709,873 people. This represents an increase of 22,167,670 people. The population broke down as 80.2% white; 12.2% black, 0.8% Native American; 2.9% Asian/Pacific islander; 3.9% Other;—that is, 19.8% of the population was comprised of people of color;

TABLE 8–2. COMPARISON: PERCENTAGE DISTRIBUTION OF THE POPULATION BY RACE AND HISPANIC ORIGIN: 1980 AND 1990[b]

United States	1980	Percentage	1990	Percentage
Total	226,542	100	248,710	100
White	188,341	83.2	199,686	80.2
Black	26,488	11.7	29,986	12.1
Other[a]	4,919	2.1	19,038	7.7
Hispanic Origin	14,608	6.4	22,354	9.0
Non-Hispanic	211,899	93.6	246,356	91

[a]These are aggregate data that combine Asian Americans, Pacific Islanders, and Native Americans.
From: U.S. Bureau of the Census, *1980 Census Population,* Press Release CB81-32 (February 23, 1981), and Supplementary Report, PC80-S1-1 (Washington, D.C.: U.S. Government Printing Office, May 1981).
[b]*1990 Census of the Population,* General Population Characteristics United States. (Washington, D.C.: U.S. Government Printing Office, U.S. Department of Commerce, Bureau of the Census, November 1992), p. 4. Reprinted with permission.

1980

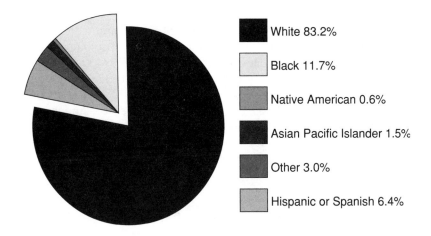

White 83.2%

Black 11.7%

Native American 0.6%

Asian Pacific Islander 1.5%

Other 3.0%

Hispanic or Spanish 6.4%

1990

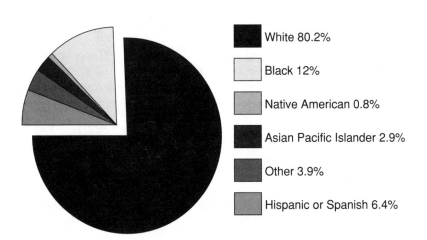

White 80.2%

Black 12%

Native American 0.8%

Asian Pacific Islander 2.9%

Other 3.9%

Hispanic or Spanish 6.4%

Figure 8–1. Percentage Distribution of the Population by Race and Spanish Origin: 1980. (Reprinted with permission from U.S. Department of Commerce, Bureau of the Census, *United States Summary: General Population Characteristics*, Washington, D.C.: Government Printing Office, 1980); and U.S. Bureau of the Census, 1990 Census of the Population *General Population Characteristics United States*, Series 1990 CP-1-1 Washington, D.C.: U.S. Government Printing Office, 1992, p. 4. Reprinted with permission).

and, it may also be noted that 9.0% of the population claimed Hispanic or Spanish origin, but could be of any race.[7] Note that the European American majority has shrunk by about 3% and there is an "emerging majority" of people of color.

Another way to view the census data from 1990 is to examine the breakdown of the non-Hispanic population. Separating out the Hispanic population reveals that the white, non-Hispanic population in 1990 was 187,137 (75.2%); the black population, including a small number of Hispanics, was 29,986 (12.1%); the Native American, Eskimo, and Aleut, including a small number of Hispanics, was 1,959 (0.8%); and the Asian/Pacific Islander population was 7,274 (2.9%). The Hispanic of any race represented 22,354 (9%).[8] In this analysis, it is evident that the white population is shrinking.

Several other noteworthy demographic changes are taking place for the total population, including

- The composition of households in the United States has changed. In 1990, 71% of all households were family households compared with 74% in 1980.[9] (Table 8–3).
- The young adult and the elderly populations have seen the greatest gains (Figs. 8–2, 3, 4A and B), with the 25 to 34 age group increasing from 39 million in 1980 to 43.2 million in 1990. This represents a growth rate of 10.8%, and this group now constitutes 16.3% of the total population. The 65-and-older population has increased from 25.5 million in 1980 to 31.2 million persons, or from 11.2% to 12.5% of the total population[10] (Table 8-4).
- The percentage of persons below the specified poverty level in 1991 in families with related children under 18 years of age was 12.7%. Families with related children under 18 years of age with a female head of household with no spouse present had a poverty level of 41.2% of the total families.[11]

TABLE 8–3. CHANGE IN U.S. HOUSEHOLD TYPE: 1980–1990

	1980-1990 Percentage Change	Number of Households (thousands) 1990
Total households	+15.5	93,347
Married couples, no children[a]	+15.0	27,780
Married couples with children[a]	−1.7	24,537
Single parent[a]—women	+21.2	6,599
Single parent[a]—men	+87.2	1,153
Singles living alone	+25.7	22,999
Singles living with nonrelatives	+45.3	4,258

[a]Children under age 18

From: Hodgkinson, H. L. A Demographic Look at Tomorrow. (Washington, DC: Institute for Educational Leadership, 1992), p. 5. Reprinted with permission.

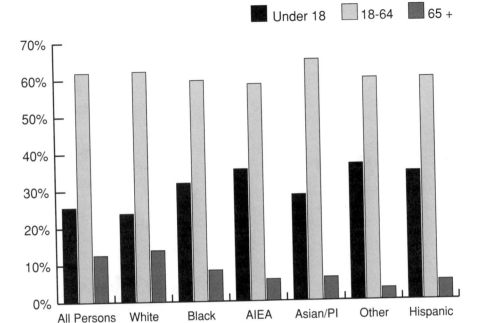

Figure 8–2. Percentage Distribution of Age by Race and Hispanic Origin: 1990. AIEA 5 American Indian, Eskimo, or Aleut; PI 5 Pacific Islander. (Reprinted with permission from the Bureau of the Census 1990 *Census of Population Social and Economic Characteristics United States*, Series 1990 CP-2-1. (Washington, D.C.: U.S. Government Printing Office, 1993), p. 24.)

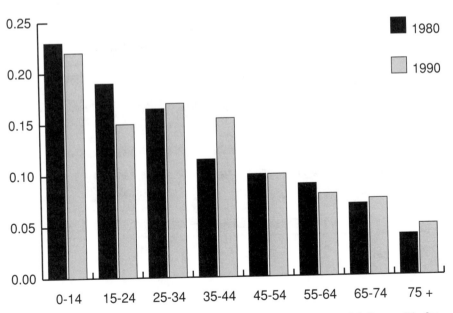

Figure 8–3. All Persons by Age: 1980 and 1990. (Reprinted with permission from U.S. Bureau of the Census. *1980 Census of the Population*, Supplementary Report, PC80-S1-1, (Washington, D.C.: U.S. Government Printing Office, May, 1981); and U.S. Bureau of the Census. *1990 Census of the Population*, General Population Characteristics, CP1-1, (Washington, D.C.: Government Printing Office, November, 1992), p. 23).

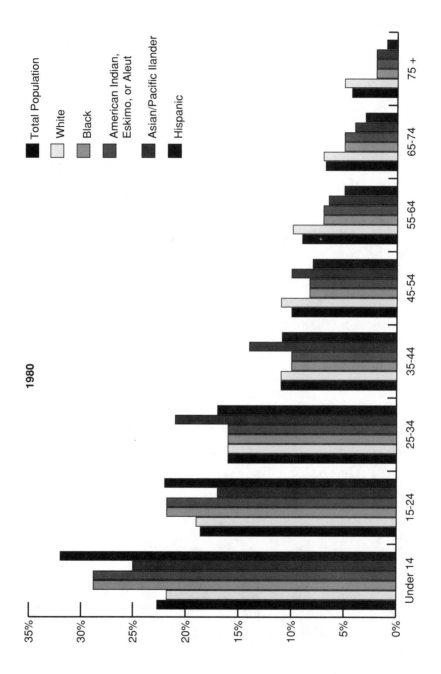

1980

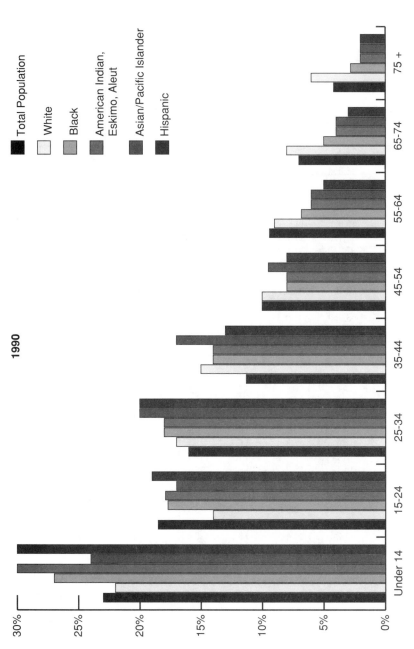

1990

Total Population
White
Black
American Indian, Eskimo, Aleut
Asian/Pacific Islander
Hispanic

Figure 8–4. Persons by Age, Race, and Hispanic Origin: 1990. (Reprinted with permission from U.S. Bureau of the Census. *1980 Census of the Population*, Supplementary Report, PC80-S1-1, (Washington, D.C.: Government Printing Office, May, 1981); and *1990 Census of the Population*, General Population Characteristics, CP1-1, (Washington, D.C.: Government Printing Office, November, 1992), p. 23.

TABLE 8-4. RACE AND HISPANIC ORIGIN, BY AGE AND SEX, FOR THE UNITED STATES: APRIL 1, 1990

Age (years)	Total	White	Black	American Indian, Eskimo, and Aleut	Asian/ Pacific Islander	Other	Hispanic Origin
			Race				
				Number (in thousands)			
All ages	248,710	199,686	29,986	1,959	7,274	9,805	22,354
Under 5	18,354	13,649	2,786	202	590	1,127	2,388
5–9	18,099	13,616	2,671	199	596	1,016	2,194
10–14	17,114	12,854	2,602	188	552	920	2,002
15–19	17,754	13,343	2,658	181	604	969	2,054
20–24	19,020	14,524	2,579	166	632	1,120	2,304
25–34	43,176	33,991	5,390	347	1,417	2,033	4,403
35–44	37,579	30,508	4,213	276	1,242	1,260	3,045
45–54	25,224	21,091	2,585	174	718	657	1,710
55–64	21,148	18,179	1,995	113	470	392	1,193
65–74	18,107	16,027	1,503	72	300	204	723
75–84	10,055	9,038	775	33	124	85	343
85+	3,080	2,788	230	9	30	23	95
Median age	32.9	34.4	28.1	26.2	29.8	23.9	25.5
Percentages							
All ages (years)	100	100	100	100	100	100	100
Under 5	7.4	6.8	9.3	10.3	8.1	11.4	10.6
5–9	7.3	6.8	8.9	10.1	8.2	10.3	9.8
10–14	6.9	6.4	8.7	9.6	7.6	9.4	9.8
15–19	7.1	6.7	8.9	9.2	8.3	9.9	9.2
20–24	7.6	7.2	8.6	8.5	8.7	11.4	10.3
25–34	17.4	17	18	17.7	19.5	20.7	19.7
35–44	15.1	15.2	14	14	17	12.8	13.6
45–54	10.1	10.5	8.6	8.9	9.9	6.7	7.6
55–64	8.5	9.1	6.7	5.8	6.4	3.9	5.3
65–74	7.2	8.0	5.0	3.7	4.1	2.0	3.2
75–84	4.0	4.5	2.6	1.7	1.7	0.8	1.5
85+	1.2	1.4	0.8	0.5	0.4	0.2	0.4
Sex							
Male	121,239	97,476	14,170	967	3,558	5,068	11,388
Female	127,470	102,210	15,816	992	3,716	4,737	10,966
Sex ratio (males per 100 females)	94.5	94.8	89.6	97.7	93.7	104.5	99.3

From: U.S. Bureau of the Census, *1990 Census of the Population,* General Population Characteristics United States, Series 1990 CP-1-1 (Washington, D.C.: 1992), U.S. Government Printing Office, p. 23. Reprinted with permission.

TABLE 8–5. MEAN EARNINGS IN 1989 BY RACE AND HISPANIC ORIGIN OF CIVILIAN PERSONS 18 YEARS AND OLDER WHO WORKED FULL TIME.

	Total	White	Black	American Indian, Eskimo, or Aleut	Asian or Pacific Islander	Hispanic Origin
Civilian Persons 18 and older	$30,219	$31,419	$22,525	$23,121	$31,979	$22,383
High school diploma	$23,549	$24,138	$19,720	$20,215	$22,105	$20,666
Bachelor's degree	$40,149	$41,276	$29,951	$31,740	$34,865	$33,155
Master's degree	$48,142	$49,242	$36,924	$38,498	$44,920	$41,129
Doctoral degree	$58,519	$59,305	$49,490	$69,290	$55,034	$52,649
Professional degree	$82,995	$84,472	$54,395	$50,906	$86,319	$63,320

From: U.S. Bureau of the Census, *1990 Census of the Population,* Education in the United States. Series 199CP-3-4 (Washington, D.C.: U.S. Government Printing Office, January, 1994), p. 474–476. Reprinted with permission.

- Mean earnings in 1989 for civilians over the age of 18 who worked full time was $30,219; for a person with a high school diploma, the mean earnings was $23,549; with a bachelor's degree, $40,149; master's degree, $48,142; doctorate $58,519; and a professional degree $82,995[12] (Table 8-5).

African American Population

The black population in the United States numbered 29,986,000 persons, or 12.1% of the total population in 1990. Black Americans have their origins in Africa, and their cultural heritage is a mixture of Caribbean cultures (including the West Indian), Native American, and northern European cultures. The greatest percentage (59.7%) of this population falls between the ages of 18 and 64, 32% is below 18 years of age, and 8.4% is 65 years old and older. The median age of this population is 28.1 years; 71.9% of the males and 77.9% of the females have a high school education.

The mean earnings in 1989 for black civilians over the age of 18 who worked year round full time were $22,525; earnings for a person with a high school diploma were $19,720; with a bachelor's degree, $29,951; master's degree, $36,924; doctorate, $49,490; and a professional degree, $54,395;[13] and, 25% of the people in this group were below the poverty level in 1990.[14]

American Indian, Aleut, and Eskimo Populations

The American Indian, Eskimo, and Aleut populations in the United States (Figs. 8-2, 8-4, and 8-6) numbered 1.9 million persons, or 0.8% of the total population. The greatest percentage (58.6%) of this population falls between the ages of 18 and 64, whereas 35.6% is below 18 years of age and 5.8% is 65 and older. The median age of this population is 26.2 years.

The mean annual earnings in 1989 for civilians in this group over the age of 18 who worked full time were $23,121; for a person with a high school diploma, the earnings were $20,215; with a bachelor's degree, $31,740; mas-

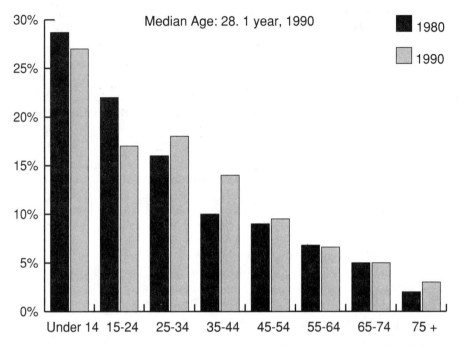

Figure 8–5. African (Black) Americans by Age: 1980 and 1990: (Reprinted with permission from U.S. Bureau of the Census, *1980 Census of the Population*, Supplementary Report, PC80-S1-1 (Washington, D.C. Government Printing Office, May, 1981); and *1990 Census of the Population*, General Population Characteristics, CP1-1, (Washington, D.C.: Government Printing Office, November, 1992), p. 23).

ter's degree, $38,498; doctorate, $69,290; and a professional degree, $50,906;[15] and 50.7% of the persons in this group were below the poverty level in 1990.[16]

Asian/Pacific Islander Population

Members of the Asian/Pacific Island communities in the United States have their origins in China, Hawaii, the Philippines, Korea, Japan, and Southeast Asia (Cambodia, Laos, and Viet Nam). With a 1990 population of 7,273,662, they constitute 3% of the population.

The greatest percentage of this population (65.1%) falls between the ages of 18 and 64, whereas 28.6% is below 18 years of age and 6.2% is 65 and older (see Figs. 8-2, 8-4, and 8-7). The median age of this group is 29.8 years. The percentage of this population 25 years and older that completed high school was 82%, and 39% has completed four or more years of college.

The mean annual earnings in 1989 for Asian/Pacific Islander civilians over the age of 18 who worked full time were $31,979; for a person with a high school diploma, $22,105; with a bachelor's degree, $34,865; master's degree, $44,920; doctorate, $53,034; and a professional degree, $86,319.[17] In this group, 13.1% was below the poverty level in 1990.[18]

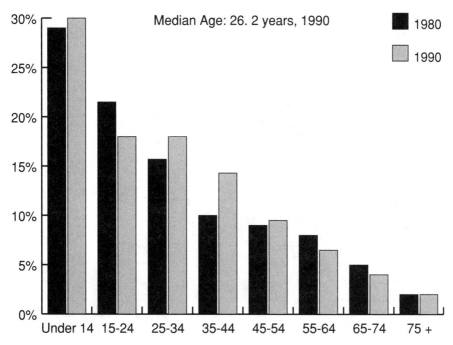

Figure 8–6. American Indian, Aleut, and Eskimo Persons by Age: 1980 and 1990. (Reprinted with permission from U.S. Bureau of the Census. *1980 Census of the Population*, Supplementary Report, PC80-S1-1. (Washington, D.C.: Government Printing Office, May, 1981) and *1990 Census of the Population*, General Population Characteristics, CP1-1, (Washington, D.C.: Government Printing Office, November, 1992), p. 23).

European American Population

In 1990, the white population in the United States numbered 199,686,070 persons, or 80.2% of the total population. This percentage decreased from 83.2% in 1980. The greatest percentage (62.2%) of this population falls between the ages of 18 and 64 years; the population under 18 is 23.9% (the lowest of all groups) and the population 65 and older is 13.9%, (the highest of all groups). The median age of this population is 34.4 years, the oldest of any group. (See Figs. 8–2, 8–4, and 8–8).

The mean annual earnings in 1989 for white civilians over the age of 18 who worked full time were $31,419; for a person with a high school diploma, the earnings were $24,138; with a bachelor's degree, $41,276; master's degree, $49,242; doctorate, $59,305; and a professional degree, $84,472.[19] In this group, 8.8% is below the poverty level.[20]

Hispanic American Population (of any race)

Hispanic Americans (of any race) originally came from Spain, Cuba, Central and South America, Mexico, Puerto Rico, and other Spanish-speaking countries. With a 1990 population of 22,354,059, or 9% of the total, they constitute

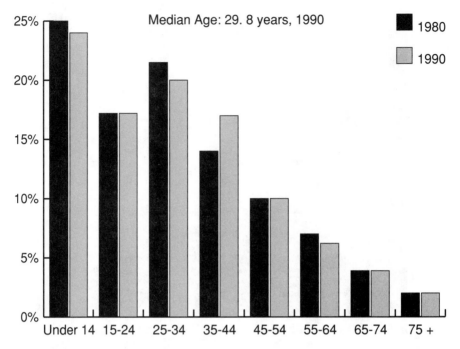

Figure 8–7. Asian/Pacific Islander Population by Age: 1980 and 1990. (Reprinted with permission from U.S. Bureau of the Census. *1980 Census of Population*, Supplementary Report, PC80-S1-1, (Washington, D.C.: Government Printing Office, May, 1981); and *1990 Census of the Population*, General Population Characteristics, CP1-1, (Washington, D.C.: Government Printing Office, November, 1992), p. 23).

the largest ethnic group in the American population. The greatest percentages of people come from the following countries (Fig. 8–9):[21]

Country	Percentage
Mexico	62.6
Central and South America	13.6
Puerto Rico	11.4
Cuba	4.9
Other	7.6

The greatest percentage (60.1%) of this population falls between the ages of 20 and 64, whereas 34.7% of the population is younger than 20 years, and 5.2% of the population is 65 and older; the median age of this population is 25.5 years (see Figs. 8–2, 8–3, 8–4, and 8–10). The mean earnings in 1989 for Hispanic American civilians over the age of 18 who worked full time were $22,383; for a person with a high school diploma, the earnings were $20,666; with a bachelor's degree, $33,155; master's degree, $41,129; doctorate, $52,649; and a professional degree, $63,320.[22]

In this group, 24.2% was below the poverty level.[23]

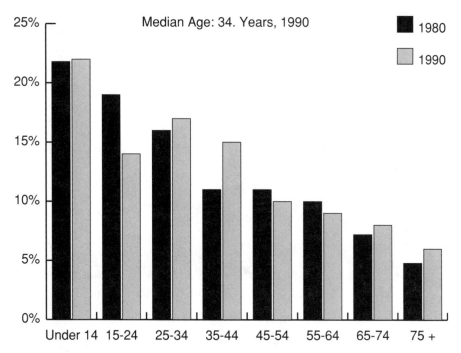

Figure 8–8. European (White) Americans by Age: 1980 and 1990. (Reprinted with permission from U.S. Bureau of the Census. *1980 Census of the Population,* Supplementary Report, PC80-S1-1 (Washington, D.C.: Government Printing Office, May, 1981); and *1990 Census of the Population,* General Population Characteristics, CP1-1, (Washington, D.C.: Government Printing Office, November, 1992), p. 23).

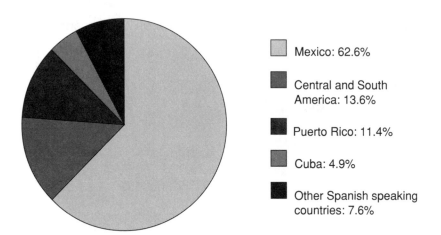

Figure 8–9. Hispanic American Origin of Persons Residing in Urbanized Areas of the United States: 1990. (Reprinted with permission from: U.S. Bureau of the Census. *1990 Census of the Population,* General Population Characteristics, CP1-1, (Washington, D.C.: Government Printing Office, November, 1992), p. 4).

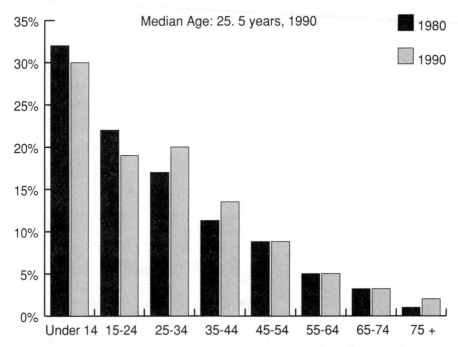

Figure 8–10. Hispanic Americans of Any Race by Age: 1980 and 1990. (Reprinted by permission from U.S. Bureau of the Census. *1980 Census of the Population*, Supplementary Report, PC80-S1-1, (Washington, D.C.: Government Printing Office, May, 1981); and *1990 Census of the Population*, General Population Characteristics, CP1-1, (Washington, D.C.: Government Printing Office, November, 1992), p. 23).

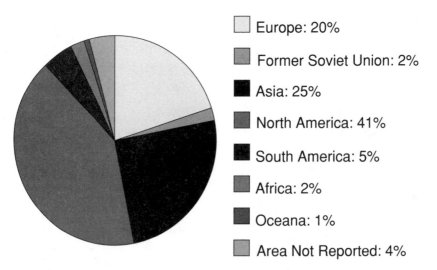

Figure 8–11. Place of Birth of Foreign-Born Persons: 1990. (Reprinted with permission from Bureau of the Census, *1990 Census of Population*, Social and Economic Characteristics United States, Series 1990 CP-2-1 (Washington, DC: U.S. Government Printing Office, 1993), p. 12.)

TABLE 8–6. TOP 10 COUNTRIES OF ORIGIN FOR IMMIGRANTS IN FISCAL YEAR 1994.

Country	Numbers
Mexico	6.2 million
Phillipines	1 million
Cuba	805,000
El Salvador	718,000
Canada	679,000
Germany	625,000
China	565,000
Dominican Republic	556,000
South Korea	533,000
Vietnam	496,000

From: United States Census Bureau Study, 8/28/1995; reported by the Associated Press, in *The Boston Globe*, v. 248, #60, August 29, 1995, p. 3.

New Immigrants

Since 1972 there has been an explosion in the numbers of people coming to this country—both with and without the necessary documentation. The people have come from all over the world, and the foreign-born population in 1990 totaled a record 19.8 million (8% of the total population), surpassing the previous highs of 14 million in 1930 and 1980 (Fig. 8–11). Foreign-born residents accounted for 8.7% of the population of the United States in 1994. Other factors relating to new immigrants include

- In 1940, 70% of the immigrants came from Europe. In 1992, 15% came from Europe, 37% from Asia, and 44% from Latin America and the Caribbean.[24]
- Altogether, the foreign born had a higher per capita income than the native born ($15,033 vs. $14,370) in 1989.[25]
- The median family income of foreign-born families was almost $4,000 less than that of the native born ($31,785 vs. $35,508).[26]
- The unemployment rate for the foreign born was 7.8% in 1990, compared with 6.2% for the native born.[27]
- The percentage of people in 1990 under 18 that were foreign-born in large American cities was as follows:

City	Percentage
Los Angeles	21
San Francisco	19
Dade County (Miami)	18
New York City	12
Houston	10[28]

• Cities where more than 50% of the residents are foreign born include

City	Percentage
Hialeah, Florida	70
Miami, Florida	60
Huntington Park, California	59
Monterey Park, California	52
Miami Beach, Florida and Santa Ana, California	51[29]

In 1990, 230,445,777 people were over the age of five in the United States. Of this population, more than 198 million (86%) speak only English at home. For the remaining 31,844,979 (14%), the spoken languages are: Spanish, 54%; French, 6%; German, 5%; Italian, 4%; other Indo-European, 13%; Chinese, 4%; other Asian, 8%; American Indian, 1%; and other languages, 5%. Of those who speak other languages, 1,845,243 (or 6%), speak no English at all[30] (Fig. 8–12).

The passage of Proposition 187 in California in November, 1994, and earlier laws relating to bilingual education in Texas, demonstrate the fact that many citizens are no longer willing to provide basic human services, such as

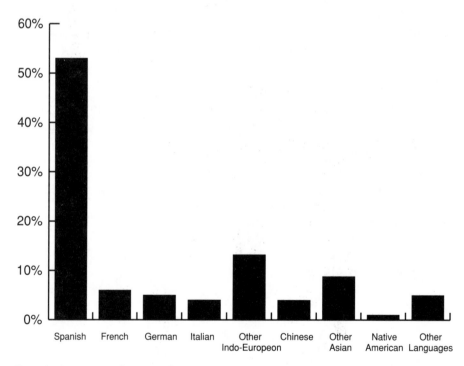

Figure 8–12. Languages Other Than English Spoken at Home by People over 5 Years of Age. (Reprinted with permission From Bureau of the Census, *1990 Census of Population* Social and Economic Characteristics United States, Series 1990 CP-2-1 (Washington, DC: U.S. Government Printing Office, 1993), p. 13).

health care and education to the new residents. Thus far, the implementation of these laws has been held up in the courts. Despite such efforts, however, it is evident that immigration to this country will continue. It is predicted that by the year 2020 immigration will be a major source of new people for the United States and will be responsible for whatever growth occurs in the United States after 2030. The United States will continue to attract about two thirds of the world's immigration and 85% of the immigrants will be from Central and South America.[31]

BACKGROUND INFORMATION: ETHNIC GROUP'S TRADITIONAL VIEWS ON HEALTH AND ILLNESS

In the discussion of the health and illness beliefs and practices of each ethnic group, the following information is included:

- Traditional definitions of health
- Traditional forms of epidemiological beliefs
- Traditional names and symptoms of a given disease
- Traditional sources of "medical" assistance
- Traditional remedies
- Problems the group encounters in dealing with the health-care system
- Current staffing levels of health-care providers

It must be kept in mind that this information is general; it is *not* specific to any one person. Nevertheless, a person's health care and behavior during illness may well have roots in that person's traditional belief system. Problems that arise when caring for a person from one of the ethnic or racial minority groups might be resolved with an understanding of that person's traditional beliefs. Understanding that these beliefs may well differ from our own can help us, as well as the consumer, to resolve the problems. In addition, the tendency to disrespect a person whose personal health-care practices differ from our own can be dissipated when we understand the underlying reasons for that individual's behavior.

All people agree that good health is essential for survival. If we are sick, we cannot work, we cannot provide food for ourselves, and we cannot survive and reproduce. Satisfactory health is mandatory for our existence. Yet the definition of health and the means of preserving it vary from people to people. Earlier in this book, we demonstrated that great disagreement exists among health workers as to what health is, yet we as professionals often expect other people to accept *our* "nondefinition."

As there are differences in the meaning of health, so are there differences in the meaning of illness. What does illness mean to others? Is it simply the symptoms of a disease, or is it more? What causes illness from a traditional viewpoint? Who are the native, traditional healers, and what methods do they use to treat and heal disorders? How do native healers differ from physicians? What resources are available to a person seeking traditional health care?

Research has been carried out by nurses, physicians, medical sociologists, anthropologists, and folklorists in the area of health and illness beliefs to discover and understand these folkways. There is currently much criticism among ethnic groups who have been studied. They question the meaning of these studies and the interpretations of the researchers. Despite these criticisms, however, the work of sociologists and anthropologists is helpful if used as a stepping-stone. In this unit, results of these studies are looked at from a specific standpoint. They are referred to and recommended for further examination in order to *help* health-care providers understand the behaviors and attitudes of the people for whom they care. In addition, bibliographic resources are included that have been recommended by the members of a given community.

It is important to note that much of the literature regarding the health and illness beliefs of any group of people is contradictory. One research report may indicate that a given group of people view health as a reward for good behavior. Another states that people of the same cultural background believe that health is a matter of chance—something that may be here today, but luck determines how long it remains. Yet another study indicates that some illnesses are believed to be caused by witchcraft and others by natural elements.

In no way, is it implied that any of these findings are universally accurate or that all health care should be based on them. What is important is to note that these studies give, in part, some understanding of *why* two (or more) conflicting viewpoints can exist between provider and consumer regarding a diagnosis and treatment regimen.

Statements about health practices of chosen ethnic communities are based not only on the existing literature, as noted, but also on the following:

1. Data collected from surveys of students, including ethnic students of color, over a 20-year period
2. Information shared by guest lecturers who are both health-care providers and members of the communities under discussion
3. Data collected from the author's interviews with health-care consumers and providers over a period of 20 years
4. Intense research in both community-based consumer groups and provider groups

In an effort to understand the great complexity of diverse health and illness beliefs, this book can, of necessity, only touch on the social and culturally related issues of our present population. The book presents the reader with an overview of the traditional health and illness beliefs and practices of the people who are health-care consumers and describes only a segment of their lives. The demographic trends described in this chapter indicate that efforts must be made now to prepare ourselves for the social changes to come. The problems that arose in the 1990s, particularly those related to health will continue for many decades, and as Hodgkinson emphasizes: "more effort should be placed on local prevention of social and medical problems, rather than their expensive and ineffective cures. Tomorrow is an extension of today's trends."[32]

An African proverb says that "to go back to tradition is the first step forward." This first step forward for those of us who will deliver health care in the 21st century is to be culturally aware and to make every effort to recognize and respect the traditional health beliefs and practices of our clients.

REFERENCES

1. Hollman, F. W. *United States Population Estimates, by Age, Sex, Race, and Hispanic Origin: 1980-1988.* (U.S. Department of Commerce, Bureau of the Census, January 1990); and U.S. Bureau of the Census, *1990 Census of the Population,* General Population Characteristics United States. Series 1990 CP-1-1 (Washington, D.C.: U.S. Government Printing Office, 1992), p. 23.
2. Hodgkinson, H. L. "Reform? Higher Education? Don't Be Absurd!" *Higher Education* (December, 1986): 273.
3. Ibid., p. 273.
4. Hodgkinson, H. L. *A Demographic Look at Tomorrow.* (Washington, D.C.: Institute for Educational Leadership, 1992), p. 2.
5. U.S. Department of Commerce, Bureau of the Census. *1980 Census of Population: Detailed Population Characteristics.* (Washington, DC: Government Printing Office, 1981), p. 1–47.
6. Sege, I. and Mashek, J. "Census Total Will Stand Despite Undercounting." *Boston Globe* 240, (July 16, 1991), p 1.
7. U.S. Bureau of the Census, *1990 Census of the Population,* p. 23.
8. Ibid.
9. Hodgkinson, *Demographic Look at Tomorrow,* p. 3.
10. Ibid., p. 5.
11. Ibid., p. 4.
12. U.S. Bureau of the Census. *1990 Census of the Population.* Education in the United States, Series 199CP-3-4. (Washington, D.C.: Government Printing Office, U.S. Department of Commerce. Bureau of the Census, January, 1994), p. 474.
13. U.S. Bureau of the Census. *1990 Census of the Population,* Education in the United States, p. 474.
14. U.S. Bureau of the Census, Current Population Reports, Series P-69, No. 181, *Poverty in the United States: 1991,* Series 199CP-3-4 (Washington, D.C.: U.S. Government Printing Office, 1992), p. 149.
15. U.S. Bureau of the Census. *1990 Census of the Population,* Education in the United States, p. 475.
16. U.S. Bureau of the Census. *1990 Census of the Population,* Social and Economic Characteristics American and Alaska Native Areas, Section 2 of 2, 1990 2-1. (Washington, D.C.: U.S. Government Printing Office, 1993), p. 1536.
17. Ibid., p. 475.
18. U.S. Bureau of the Census. *1990 Census of the Population,* Asians and Pacific Islanders in the United States. 1990 CP-3-5. (Washington, D.C.: U.S. Government Printing Office, 1993), p. 141.

19. U.S. Bureau of the Census. *1990 Census of the Population*, Education in the United States, p. 475.
20. U.S. Bureau of the Census. *1990 Census of the Population*, Poverty in the United States, p. 149.
21. U.S. Bureau of the Census. *1990 Census of the Population*, General Population Characteristics United States, Series 1990 CP-1-1 (Washington, D.C.: U.S. Government Printing Office, 1992), p. 4.
22. U.S. Bureau of the Census. *1990 Census of the Population*, Education in the United States, p. 475.
23. U.S. Bureau of the Census, *1990 Census of the Population*, Social and Economic Characteristics Persons of Hispanic Origin in The United States Series 1990 CP3-3. (Washington, D.C.: U.S. Government Printing Office, 1993), p. 153.
24. Gaines, J. R. Managing Editor, "The Numbers Game." *Time*, 142: (1993) 15.
25. Ibid.
26. Ibid., p. 16.
27. Ibid., p. 15.
28. Ibid., p. 16.
29. Ibid.
30. U.S. Bureau of the Census, *1990 Census of the Population*, Social and Economic Characteristics United States, Series 1990 CP-2-1 (Washington, D.C.: U.S. Government Printing Office, 1993), p. 14.
31. Hodgkinson. *Demographic Look at Tomorrow*, p. 11.
32. Ibid., p. 13.

unit

3

Selected Traditional Views of Health and Illness

The chapters in this unit will enable the reader to

1. Develop a level of awareness of the background and health problems of both the emerging majority and white ethnic populations

2. Understand some traditional beliefs of ethnic people with respect to health and illness

3. Understand the traditional pathways to health care and the relationship between these pathways and the American health-care system

4. Understand certain manpower problems of each of the communities discussed

5. Be more familiar with the available literature regarding each of these communities

The following exercises are appropriate to all chapters in Unit III.

1. Familiarize yourself with some literature of the given community, that is, read literature, poetry, or a biography of a member of each of these communities. (See Bibliographies for Chapters 9 through 14.)

2. Familiarize yourself with the history and sociopolitical background of each of these communities.

The questions that follow should be thoughtfully considered.

1. What are the traditional definitions of health and illness in each of these communities?

2. What are the traditional methods of maintaining health?

3. What are the traditional ways of preventing illness or protecting health?

4. What are the traditional ways of treating an illness?

5. What are traditionally thought to be the causes of an illness or restoring health?

6. Who are the traditional healers? What functions do they perform?

Health and Illness in African (Black) American Communities

... some people don't understand that it is the nature of the eye to have seen forever, and the nature of the mind to recall anything that was ever known.

—Alice Walker

African, or black, Americans are the nations largest emerging majority population, constituting 12% of the population of the United States.[1] Most members of the present African American community have their roots in Africa, and the majority descend from people who were brought here as slaves from the west coast of Africa.[2] The largest importation of slaves occurred during the 17th century, which means that black people have been living in the United States for many generations. Today, a number of blacks have immigrated to the United States voluntarily—from African countries, the West Indian islands, the Dominican Republic, Haiti, and Jamaica.

African Americans live in all regions of the country and are represented in every socioeconomic group; however, one third of this group lives in poverty, a rate three times that of the white population. Over half of black Americans live in urban areas surrounded by the symptoms of poverty—crowded and inadequate housing, poor schools, and high crime rates.[3] For example, Kotlowitz describes the Henry Horner Homes in Chicago as "16 high-rise buildings which stretch over eight blocks and at last census count housed 6,000 people, 4,000 of whom are children."[4] He goes on to present two facts about public housing: "Public housing served as a bulwark to segregation and as a kind of anchor for impoverished neighborhoods." and "It was

The author especially acknowledges those students who, over several years, have provided much of the data for this chapter.

built on the cheap—the walls are a naked cinder block with heating pipes snaking through the apartment; instead of closets, there are eight inch indentations in the walls without doors; and the heating system so storms out of control in the winter that it is 85 degrees."[5]

BACKGROUND

According to some sources, the first black people to enter this country arrived a year earlier than the Pilgrims, in 1619. Other sources claim that blacks arrived with Columbus in the 15th century.[6] In any event, the first blacks who came to the North American continent did not come as slaves, but between 1619 and 1860, more than 4 million people were transported here as slaves. One need only read a sampling of the many accounts of slavery to appreciate the tremendous hardships that the captured and enslaved people experienced during that time. Not only was the daily life of the slave very difficult, but the experience of being captured, shackled, and transported in steerage was devastating. Many of those captured in Africa died before they arrived here. The strongest and healthiest people were snatched from their homes by slave dealers and transported en masse in the holds of ships to the North American continent. In general, black captives were not taken care of or recognized as human beings and treated accordingly. Once here, they were sold and placed on plantations and in homes all over the country—it was only later that the practice was confined to the South. Families were separated; children were wrenched from their parents and sold to other buyers. Some slave owners bred their slaves much like farmer's breed cattle today, purchasing men to serve as studs and judging women based on whether they would produce the desired stock with a particular man.[7] Yet, in the midst of all this inhuman and inhumane treatment, the black family grew and survived. Gutman[8] in his careful documentation of plantation and family records traces the history of the black family from 1750 to 1925 and points out the existence of families and family or kinship ties before and after the Civil War, dispelling many of the myths about the black family and its structure. Despite overwhelming hardships and enforced separations, the people managed in most circumstances to maintain both a family and community awareness.

Ostensibly, the Civil War ended slavery, but in many ways, it did not emancipate blacks. Daily life after the war was fraught with tremendous difficulty, and black people—according to custom—were stripped of their civil rights. In the South, black people were overtly segregated, most living in conditions of extreme hardship and poverty. Those who migrated to the North over the years were subject to all the problems of fragmented urban life: poverty, racism, and covert segregation.[9]

The historic problems of the black community need to be appreciated by the health-care provider who attempts to juxtapose modern practices and traditional health and illness beliefs.

TRADITIONAL DEFINITIONS OF HEALTH AND ILLNESS

The traditional definition of health stems from the African belief about life and the nature of being. To the African, life was a process rather than a state. The nature of a person was viewed in terms of energy force rather than matter. All things, whether living or dead, were believed to influence one another. Therefore, one had the power to influence one's destiny and that of others through the use of *behavior,* whether proper or otherwise, as well as through *knowledge* of the person and the world. When one possessed health, one was in harmony with nature; illness was a state of disharmony. Traditional black belief regarding health did not separate the mind, body, and spirit.[10]

Disharmony, that is, illness, was attributed to a number of sources, primarily demons and evil spirits. These spirits were generally believed to act of their own accord, and the goal of treatment was to remove them from the body of the ill person. Several methods were employed to attain this result in addition to voodoo, which is discussed in the next section. The traditional healers, usually women, possessed extensive knowledge regarding the use of herbs and roots in the treatment of illness. Apparently, an early form of smallpox immunization was used by slaves. Women practiced inoculation by scraping a piece of cowpox crust into a place on a child's arm. These children appeared to have a far lower incidence of smallpox than those who did not receive the immunization.

The old and the young were cared for by all members of the community. The elderly were held in high esteem because African people believed that the living of a long life indicated that a person had the opportunity to acquire much wisdom and knowledge. Death was described as the passing from one realm of life to another[11] or as a passage from the evils of this world to another state. The funeral was often celebrated as a joyous occasion, with a party after the burial. Children were passed over the body of the deceased so that the dead person could carry any potential illness of the child away with him.

Many of the preventive and treatment practices of black Americans have their roots in Africa but have been merged with the approaches of Native Americans to whom the blacks were exposed and with the attitudes of whites among whom they lived and served. Then as today, illness was treated in a combination of ways. Methods found to be most useful were handed down through the generations.

TRADITIONAL METHODS OF HEALING

Voodoo

Voodoo is a belief system often alluded to but rarely described in any detail. At various times, patients may mention terms, such as "fix," "hex," or "spell." It is not clear whether voodoo is *fully* practiced today, but there is some evidence in the literature that there are people who still believe and practice it to some extent.[12] It also has been reported that many black people continue to fear voodoo and believe that when they become ill they have been "fixed." Voodoo involves two forms of magic: white magic, described as harmless, and black magic, which is quite dangerous. Belief in magic is, of course, ancient.[13]

Voodoo came to this country about 1724, with the arrival of slaves from the West African coast, who had been sold initially in the West Indies. The people who brought voodoo with them were "snake worshippers." *Vodu,* the name of their god, became with the passage of time *voodoo* (also *hoodoo*), an all-embracing term that included the god, the sect, the members of the sect, the priests and priestesses, the rites and practices, and the teaching.[14]

The sect spread rapidly from the West Indies. In 1782, the governor of Louisiana prohibited the importation of slaves from Martinique because of their practice in voodooism. (Despite the fact that gatherings of slaves were forbidden in Louisiana, small groups persisted in practicing voodoo.) In 1803, the importation of slaves to Louisiana from the West Indies was finally allowed, and with them came a strong influence of voodoo.[15] The practice entailed a large number of rituals and procedures. The ceremonies were held with large numbers of people, usually at night and in the open country. "Sacrifice and the drinking of blood were integral parts of all the voodoo ceremonies."[16] There were those who believed that this blood was from children. However, it was most commonly thought to be the blood of a cat or young goat. Such behavior evolved from primitive African rites, to which Christian rituals[17] were added to form the ceremonies that exist today. Leaders of the voodoo sect tended to be women, and stories abound in New Orleans about the workings of the sect and the women who ruled it —such as Marie Laveau.

In 1850, the practice of voodoo reached its height in New Orleans.[18] At that time, the beliefs and practices of voodoo were closely related to beliefs about health and illness. For example, many illnesses were attributed to a "fix" that was placed on one person out of anger. *Gris-gris,* the symbols of voodoo, were used to prevent illness or to give illness to others. Some examples of commonly used *gris-gris* follow.[19]

1. Good *gris-gris.* Powders and oils that are highly and pleasantly scented. The following are examples of good *gris-gris:* love powder, colored and scented with perfume; love oil, olive oil to which gardenia perfume has been added; luck water, ordinary water that is purchased in many shades (red is for success in love, yellow for success in money matters, blue for protection and friends).
2. Bad *gris-gris.* Oils and powders that have a vile odor. The following are examples of bad *gris-gris:* anger powder, war powder, and moving powder, which are composed of soil, gunpowder, and black pepper, respectively.
3. Flying devil oil is olive oil that has red coloring and cayenne pepper added to it.
4. Black cat oil is machine oil.

In addition to these oils and powders, a variety of colored candles are used, the color of the candle symbolizing the intention. For example, white symbolizes peace, red victory, pink love, yellow driving off enemies, brown attracting money, and black doing evil work and bringing bad luck.[20]

The following story exhibits the profound influence that belief in voodoo can have on a person. It was reported in Baltimore, Maryland, in 1967.

> The patient was a young, married black woman who was admitted to the hospital for evaluation of chest pain, syncope, and dyspnea. Her past history was one of good health. However, she had gained over 50 pounds in the past year and was given to eating Argo starch. She began to have symptoms 1 month before she was admitted. Her condition grew worse once in the hospital, and she was treated for heart failure and also for pulmonary embolism. She revealed that she had a serious problem. She had been born on Friday, the thirteenth, in the Okefenokee Swamp and was delivered by a midwife who delivered three children that day. The midwife told the mothers that the children were hexed and that the first would die before her 16th birthday, the second before her 21st birthday, and the third (the patient) before her 23rd birthday. The first girl was a passenger in a car involved in a fatal crash the day before her 16th birthday, the second girl was celebrating her 21st birthday in a saloon when a stray bullet hit and killed her. This patient also believed she was doomed. She, too, died—on August 12—a day before her 23rd birthday.[21]

There are a number of Catholic saints or relics to whom or which the practitioners of voodoo attribute special powers. Portraits of Saint Michael, who makes possible the conquest of enemies, Saint Anthony de Padua, who brings luck, Saint Mary Magdalene, who is popular with women who are in love, the Virgin Mary, whose presence in the home prevents illness, and the Sacred Heart of Jesus, which cures organic illness may be prominently displayed in the home of people who believe in voodoo.[22] These *gris-gris* are available today and can be purchased in stores in many American cities.

Other Practices

Many blacks believe in the power of some people to heal and help others, and there are many reports of numerous healers among the communities. This reliance on healers reflects the deep religious faith of the people. (Maya Angelou vividly describes this phenomenon in her book, *I Know Why the Caged Bird Sings.*[23]) For example, many blacks followed the Pentecostal movement long before its present more general popularity. Similarly, people often went to tent meetings and had an all-consuming belief in the healing powers of religion.

Another practice takes on significance when one appreciates its historical background: the eating of Argo starch. "Geophagy," or eating clay and dirt, occurred among the slaves, who brought the practice to this country from Africa. In *Roots*, Haley mentions that pregnant women were given clay because it was believed to be beneficial to both the mother and the unborn child.[24] In

TABLE 9–1. EXAMPLES OF CULTURAL PHENOMENA AFFECTING HEALTH CARE AMONG AFRICAN (BLACK) AMERICANS

Nations of Origin:	Many West African countries (as slaves) West Indian Islands Dominican Republic Haiti Jamaica
Environmental Control:	Traditional health and illness beliefs may continue to be observed by "traditional" people
Biological Variations:	Sickle cell anemia Hypertension Cancer of the esophagus Stomach cancer Coccidioidomycosis Lactose intolerance
Social Organization:	Family: many single-parent female-headed households Large, extended family networks Strong church affiliations within community Community social organizations
Communication:	National languages Dialect: Pidgin French, Spanish, Creole
Space:	Close personal space
Time Orientation:	Present over future

Adapted from: Spector, R. "Culture, Ethnicity, and Nursing," in Potter, P. and Perry, A. *Fundamentals of Nursing* (3rd. ed.), eds. (St. Louis: Mosby-Year Book, 1992), p. 101. Reprinted with permission.

fact, red clays are rich in iron. When clay was not available, dirt was substituted. In more modern times, when people were no longer living on farms and no longer had access to clay and dirt, Argo starch became the substitute.[25]

> It was my fortune, or misfortune to be born into a family that practiced geophagy (earth eating) and pica (eating Argo laundry starch). Even before I became pregnant I showed an interest in eating starch. It was sweet and dry, and I could take it or leave it. After I became pregnant, I found I wanted not only starch, but bread, grits, and potatoes. I found I craved starchy substances. I stuck to starchy substances and dropped the Argo because it made me feel sluggish and heavy.*

It is believed that anemia arose from this practice of substituting noniron-rich clays or starch for red clays that contain iron. Table 9–1 illustrates examples of cultural phenomena that affect health care among African (black) Americans.

---

*This experience was reported by a student, who consented to including her description in this book.

Black Muslims†

Many members of the black community are practicing Muslims. Religious beliefs are an important part of the Muslim lifestyle, and health-care providers should be familiar with them. Islamic dietary restrictions consist of eating a strictly kosher diet, and a newly admitted patient who refuses to eat should be asked if the hospital's ordinary diet interferes with his or her religious beliefs. "Kosher" means not eating pork or any pork products (such as nonbeef hamburger and ham) or any "soul foods" (such as black-eyed beans, kidney beans, ham hocks, bacon, and pork chops). Muslims consider such foods to be filthy and are taught that a "person is what he eats."

Islamic law teaches that certain foods affect the way a person thinks and acts. Therefore, one's diet should consist of food that has a clean, positive effect. Beans, such as black-eyed, kidney, and lima, are avoided because they are hard to digest and are meant for animal (not human) consumption. Muslims do not drink alcohol because they feel that it dulls the senses and causes illness.

Muslims fast for a 30-day period during September and October (fast of Ramadan), at which time they consume no meat of land animals and eat only one meal per day, in the evening. Nothing is taken by mouth from 5:00 AM until sundown, although ill Muslims, small children, and pregnant women are exempt from this rule.

The Muslim lifestyle is strictly regulated. According to those who have practiced the religion for many generations, this stems in part from the need for self-discipline, which many black people have not had because of living conditions associated with urban decay and family disintegration. Muslims believe in self-help and assist in uplifting each other. The Muslim lifestyle is not so rigid that the people do not have good times. Good times, however, are tempered with the realization that too much indulgence in sport and play can present problems. To Muslims, life is precious: if they need a transfusion to live, they will accept it. Because of their avoidance of pork or pork products, however, it is important to understand that a diabetic Muslim will refuse to take insulin that has a pork base. If the insulin is manufactured from the pancreas of a pig, it is considered unclean and will not be accepted.

Many Muslim subsects differ in their practice and philosophy of Islam. Members of some sects dress in distinctive clothing—for example, the women wear long skirts and a covering on the head at all times. Other sects are less strict about dress. Some adherents do not follow the kosher diet and are allowed to smoke and drink alcoholic beverages in moderation. In some sects, men practice polygamy and have a number of concubines.

---

†This material is adapted from a paper prepared by a student who is a practicing Muslim, who wanted to share her beliefs. She concluded: "I hope this will help a bit in understanding a Muslim who may be a patient."

CURRENT HEALTH PRACTICES

The following sections describe practices employed to prevent illness by maintaining and protecting health and to treat various types of maladies thereby restoring health. This discussion cannot encompass all of the types of care given to and by the members of the black community but instead presents a sample of the richness of the folk medicine that has survived over the years.

Prevention: Health Maintenance and Protection

Essentially, health is maintained with proper diet—that is, eating three nutritious meals a day, including a hot breakfast. Rest and a clean environment also are important. Laxatives were and are used to keep the system "running" or "open."

Asafetida—rotten flesh that looks like a dried-out sponge—is worn around the neck to prevent the contraction of contagious diseases. Codliver oil is taken to prevent colds. A sulfur and molasses preparation is used in the spring because it is believed that at the start of a new season people are more susceptible to illness. This preparation is rubbed up and down the back, not taken internally. A physician is not consulted routinely and is not generally regarded as the person to whom one goes for the prevention of disease.

Copper or silver bracelets may be worn around the wrist from the time a woman is a baby or young child. These bracelets are believed to protect the wearer as she grows. If for any reason these bracelets are removed, harm befalls the owner. In addition to granting protection, these bracelets indicate when the wearer is about to become ill: the skin around the bracelet turns black, alerting the woman to take precaution against the impending illness. These precautions consist of getting extra rest, praying more frequently, and eating a more nutritious diet.

Treatment of Illness: Health Restoration

The most common method of treating illness is prayer. The laying on of hands is described quite frequently. Rooting, a practice derived from voodoo, also is mentioned. In rooting, a person (usually a woman) is consulted as to the source of a given illness, and she then prescribes the appropriate treatment. Magic rituals often are employed.

The following home remedies have been reported by some black people as being successful in the treatment of disease.

1. Sugar and turpentine are mixed together and taken by mouth to get rid of worms. This combination can be used also to cure a backache when rubbed on the skin from the navel to the back.
2. Numerous types of poultices are employed to fight infection and inflammation. The poultices are placed on the part of the body that is painful or infected to draw out the cause of the affliction.

   One type of poultice is made of potatoes. The potatoes are sliced or grated and placed in a bag, which is placed on the affected area of the body. The potatoes turn black, and as this occurs, the disease goes away. It is believed that as these potatoes spoil, they produce a penicillin mold that is able to destroy the infectious organism. Another type of poultice is prepared from cornmeal and peach leaves that are cooked together and placed either in a bag or in a piece of flannel cloth. The cornmeal ferments and combines with an enzyme in the peach leaves to produce an antiseptic that destroys the bacteria and hastens the healing process. A third poultice, made with onions, is used to heal infections, and a flaxseed poultice is used to treat earaches.

3. Herbs from the woods are used in many ways. Herb teas are prepared—for example, from goldenrod root—to treat pain and reduce fevers. Sassafras tea frequently is used to treat colds. Other herbs that are boiled to make a tea include the root or leaf of rabbit tobacco.

4. Bluestone, a mineral found in the ground, is used as medicine for open wounds. The stone is crushed into a powder and sprinkled on the affected area. It prevents inflammation and is also used to treat poison ivy.

5. To treat a "crick" in the neck, two pieces of silverware are crossed over the painful area in the form of an X.

6. Nine drops of turpentine nine days after intercourse act as a contraceptive.

7. Cuts and wounds can be treated with sour or spoiled milk that is placed on stale bread, wrapped in a cloth, and placed on the wound.

8. Salt and pork (salt pork) placed on a rag also can be used to treat cuts and wounds.

9. A sprained ankle can be treated by placing clay in a dark leaf and wrapping it around the ankle.

10. A method for treating colds is hot lemon water with honey.

11. When congestion is present in the chest and the person is coughing, the chest is rubbed with hot camphorated oil and wrapped with warm flannel.

12. An expectorant for colds consists of chopped raw garlic, chopped onion, fresh parsley, and a little water, all mixed in a blender.

13. Hot toddies are used to treat colds and congestion. These drinks consist of hot tea with honey, lemon, peppermint, and a dash of brandy or whatever alcoholic beverage the person likes and is available. Vicks Vaporub also is swallowed.

14. A fever can be broken by placing raw onions on the feet and wrapping them in warm blankets.

15. Boils are treated by cracking a raw egg, peeling the white skin off the inside of the shell, and placing it on the boil. This brings the boil to a head.

16. Garlic can be placed on the ill person or in the room to remove the "evil spirits" that have caused the illness.

Folk Medicine

In the black community, folk medicine previously practiced in Africa is still employed. The methods have been tried and tested and are still relied on. Healers or voodoo practitioners make no class or status distinctions among their clients treating everyone fairly and honestly. This tradition of equality of care and perceived effectiveness accounts for the faith placed in the practices of the healer and in other methods. In fact, the home remedies used by some members of the black community have been employed for many generations. Another reason for their ongoing use is that hospitals are far away from people who live in rural areas. By the time they might get to the hospital they would be dead. Yet many of the people who continue to use these remedies live in urban areas in close proximity to hospitals—sometimes even world-renowned hospitals. Nonetheless, the use of folk medicine persists, and many people avoid the local hospital except in extreme emergencies.

CURRENT HEALTH-CARE PROBLEMS

Health Differences between Black and White Populations

Morbidity. The available data demonstrate a low use of health services by blacks and lower incidences of diseases. This is misleading, however, and can be attributed to such factors as the lack of access to the health services, low income, and a tendency to self-treat illness and to wait until symptoms are so severe that a doctor must be seen. When statistical adjustments are made for age, blacks exceed whites in the average number of days spent on bedrest and the number of days in restricted activity. In addition, blacks have a greater incidence of tooth decay than whites and have greater periodontal disease.[26] Adolescent pregnancy is a major concern with this group. The risk of infant mortality and low birth weight are also greater in this community.[27] The numbers of blacks suffering with mental illness is a greater percentage than the relative proportion of blacks in the overall population would predict.[28] In 1989, 703,000 adults with serious mental illness received government disability payment for their mental disorder. Of this population, 20.5% was white and 43.8% was black.[29]

Sickle Cell Anemia. The sickling of red blood cells is a genetically inherited trait that is hypothesized to have originally been an African adaptation to fight malaria. This condition occurs only in blacks and causes the normal disclike red blood cell to assume a sickle shape. Sickling results in hemolysis and thrombosis of red blood cells because these deformed cells do not flow properly through the blood vessels. Sickle cell disease comprises the following blood characteristics:

1. The presence of two hemoglobin-S genes (*Hb SS*)
2. The presence of the hemoglobin-S gene with another abnormal hemoglobin gene (*Hb SC, Hb SD,* etc.)
3. The presence of the hemoglobin-S gene with a different abnormality in hemoglobin synthesis

Some people (carriers) have the sickle cell trait (*HbSS, HbSC,* or others) but do not experience symptoms of the disease.

The clinical manifestations of sickle cell disease include hemolysis, anemia, and states of sickle cell crises in which severe pain occurs in the areas of the body where the thrombosed red cells are located. The cells also tend to clump in abdominal organs, such as the liver and the spleen. At present, statistics indicate that only 50% of children with sickle cell disease live to adulthood. Some children die before the age of 20, and some suffer complications during their lifetime that are chronic and irreversable.

It is possible to detect the sickle cell trait in healthy adults and to provide genetic counseling about their risk of bearing children with the disease. However, for many people, this is not an option.[30] The cost of genetic counseling, for example, may be prohibitive.

Mortality. Blacks born in 1991 in the United States will live, on average, 6.4 fewer years than whites. The life expectancy for whites is 76.4 years; for blacks, it is 70.0.[31]

The leading chronic diseases that are causes of death for African Americans are the same as those for whites, but the rates are greater. For example,

- Black men die from strokes at almost twice the rate of men in the white population.
- Coronary heart disease death rates are higher for African American women than for white women.
- Black men experience a higher risk of cancer than white men do.
- Diabetes is 33% more common among African Americans than among whites.
- African American babies are twice as likely as white babies to die before their first birthday.
- Homicide is the most frequent cause of death for African American men between the ages of 15 and 34. The homicide rate for those between ages 25 and 34 is seven times that for whites.
- The rate of AIDS among African American men generally is more than triple that for white men. Among women and children the gap is even wider.[32]

Table 9–2 lists the 10 leading causes of death for African American men in 1990. Table 9–3 further compares selected health problems and their manifestations in the white and black communities.

TABLE 9-2. THE 10 LEADING CAUSES OF DEATH FOR AFRICAN AMERICAN MALES: 1990

1. Diseases of the heart
2. Malignant neoplasms
3. Homicide and legal intervention
4. Unintentional injuries
5. Cerebrovascular diseases
6. Human immunodeficiency virus infection
7. Pneumonia and influenza
8. Chronic obstructive pulmonary diseases
9. Diabetes mellitus
10. Chronic liver disease and cirrhosis

From: Department of Health and Human Services. (1993) *Health United States 1992;* and *Healthy People 2000 Review.* (Washington, D.C.: United States Department of Health and Human Services, Public Health Service Centers for Disease Control and Prevention. DHHS Pub. No. (PHS) 93–1232, 1993), p. 49. Reprinted with permission.

TABLE 9-3. COMPARISON: SELECTED HEALTH PROBLEMS IN WHITE AND BLACK AMERICANS

Problem	Black Morbidity/Mortality Compared with White Morbidity/Mortality
Cardiovascular disease	Age-adjusted death rates for all causes were 60% higher in black men than in white men; 56% higher in black women than in white women.
Coronary artery disease (CHD)	CHD mortality rates in 1984 were similar among black and white men; women's rates are higher in blacks.
Cerebrovascular disease	Stroke is the single disease entity that accounts for most of the excess black mortality compared with whites.
Hypertension (HBP)	In blacks, HBP develops at a younger age and is more severe than in whites.
End-stage renal disease (ESRD)	Blacks are disproportionately represented in the total ESRD pool and in the number of new people who develop this problem each year. Currently, 25% of ESRD patients have functioning kidney transplants (30% of whites with ESRD and 13% of blacks have functioning transplants. 51% of whites are treated with dialysis, 74% of blacks.
Cancer	In 1989, the age-adjusted cancer incidence rate was 401.2/100,000 for blacks; 379.5 for whites. In 1990, the mortality rate was 182/100,000 for blacks compared with 131.5 for whites. The five-year survival rate for cancer in blacks diagnosed from 1983 to 1988 was about 38.3% and for whites, 53.5%.
Chronic obstructive pulmonary disease (COPD)	Between 1979 and 1990 the age-adjusted COPD mortality rate for blacks rose 52.3% and for whites, 34.9%. Studies have shown the adverse effects of pollution on the respiratory tract; blacks (59.7%) were more likely than whites (27%) to live in central cities where exposure to air pollution is greater.
Sickle cell disease (SCD)	The group of genetic disorders known as SCD is the most common genetic disorder within the black population: the incidence is 1 in every 500 live black births.
Opthalmology	The findings of numerous surveys indicate significantly higher incidences of blindness and visual impairment in blacks compared with whites.

TABLE 9–3. (*continued*)

Problem	Black Morbidity/Mortality Compared with White Morbidity/Mortality
AIDS	The HIV/AIDS epidemic and other sexually transmitted diseases threaten to decimate the black community. In AIDS cases among blacks, 78% have occurred in men, 19% in adult women, and 3% in children younger than 13 years. HIV-positive rates of 3.9/1,000 have been reported in black military recruits, compared with 0.9/1,000 in whites.
Sexually transmitted diseases (STDs)	There is a high incidence of STDs in the black community; for example, there has been a rapid increase of infectious primary and secondary syphilis among blacks since 1985.
Intentional injuries: homicide and suicides	*Homicide:* In recent years the homicide rate among blacks has exceeded that for all racial groups in the United States and may rank highest in the world. *Suicide:* Generally the suicide rate is lower in the black community than in the white community; but, young black males, who experience high rates of interpersonal violence, have a relatively high rate of suicide.
Unintentional injuries	Among black Americans, injuries were responsible for more deaths than any other cause in 1989; these included motor vehicle accidents (16.88/100,000), fires and burns (5.52), and drownings (4.22).
Chemical use	In general, alcohol and tobacco are the most used and abused substances in this country, particularly among blacks.
Infant mortality	The cause most associated with infant mortality is low birth weight; black American infants have the highest incidence (13% in 1988) of low birth weight among all ethnic groups—greater than twice the rate for whites (5.5%).

From: Livingston, I. L., ed. *Handbook of Black American Health.* (Westport, CT: Greenwood Publishing Group, 1994), pp. 3, 24, 33, 47, 60, 70, 78, 111, 117, 118, 125, 140, 160, 170, 179, 190, 205–206, and 219. Reprinted with permission.

Blacks and Health-Care Systems

To the black person, receiving health care is all too often a degrading and humiliating experience. In many settings, black patients continue to be viewed as beneath the white health-care giver. Quite often the insult is a subtle part of *experiencing* the health-care system. The insult may be intentional or unintentional. An intentional insult is, of course, a blatant remark or mistreatment. An unintentional insult is more difficult to define. A health-care provider may not *intend* to demean a person, yet an action or tone of voice may be interpreted as insulting. The provider may have some covert, underlying fears or difficulties in relating to blacks, but the patient quite often senses the difficulty. An unintentional insult may occur because the provider is not fully aware of the client's background and is unable to comprehend many of the client's beliefs and practices. The client, for example, may be afraid of the impending medical procedures and the possibility of misdiagnosis or mistreatment. It is not a secret among the people of the black community that those who receive care in public clinics and hospitals—and even in clinics of private institutions—are the "material" on whom students practice and on whom medical research is done.

Some blacks fear or resent health clinics. When they have a clinic appointment, they usually lose a day's work because they have to be at the clinic at an early hour and often spend many hours waiting to be seen by a physician. They often receive inadequate care, are told what their problem is in incomprehensible medical jargon, and are not given an identity, being seen rather as a body segment ("the appendix in treatment room A"). Such an experience creates a tremendous feeling of powerlessness and alienation from the system. In some parts of the country, segregation and racism are overt. There continue to be reports of hospitals that refuse admission to black patients. In one case, a black woman in labor was not admitted to a hospital because she had not "paid the bill from the last baby." There was not enough time to get her to another hospital, and she was forced to deliver in an ambulance. In light of this type of treatment, it is a small wonder that some black people prefer to use time-tested home remedies rather than be exposed to the humiliating experiences of hospitalization.

Another reason for the ongoing use of home remedies is poverty. Indigent people cannot afford the high costs of American health care. Quite often—even with the help of Medicaid and Medicare—the hidden costs of acquiring health services, such as transportation and child care, are a heavy burden. As a result, blacks may stay away from clinics or outpatient departments or receive their care with passivity while appearing to the provider to be evasive. Some black patients believe that they are being talked down to by health-care providers and that the providers fail to listen to them. They choose, consequently, to "suffer in silence." Many of the problems that blacks relate in dealing with the health-care system can apply to anyone, but the inherent racism within the health system cannot be denied. Currently, efforts are being made to overcome these barriers.

Since the 1960s, health-care services available to blacks and other people of color have improved. A growing number of community health centers have emphasized health maintenance and promotion. Community residents serve on the boards.

Among the services provided by community health centers is an effort to discover children with high blood levels of lead in order to provide early diagnosis of and treatment for lead poisoning. Once a child is found to have lead poisoning, the law requires that the source of the lead be found and eradicated. Today, only apartments free of lead paint can be rented to families with young children. Apartments that are found to have lead paint must be stripped and repainted with nonlead paint. Another ongoing effort by the community health centers is to inform blacks who are at risk of producing children with sickle cell anemia that they are carriers of this genetic disease. This program is fraught with conflict because many people prefer not to be screened for the sickle cell trait, fearing they may become labeled once the tendency is discovered.

Birth control is another problem that is recognized with mixed emotions. To some, especially women who want to space children or who do not want to have numerous children, birth control is a welcome development. People who believe in birth control prefer selecting the time when they will have children, how many children they will have, and when they will stop having children. To many other people, birth control is considered a form of "black genocide" and a way of limiting the growth of the community. Health workers in the black community must be aware of both sides of this issue and, if asked to make a decision, remain neutral. Such decisions must be made by the clients themselves.

HEALTHY PEOPLE 2000: SELECTED OBJECTIVES

The following are examples of the health objectives detailed in the U.S. Department of Health and Human Services' report, *Healthy People 2000,* that target members of the African American community.

1. Reduce growth retardation among low-income black children younger than age 1 to less than 10%. (Baseline: 15% in 1988.)
2. Reduce the prevalence of anemia to less than 20% among black, low-income pregnant women. (Baseline: 41% of those aged 15 through 44 in their third trimester in 1988.)
3. Reduce cigarette smoking to a prevalence of no more than 18% among blacks aged 20 and older. (Baseline: 34% in 1987.)
4. Reduce deaths from cirrhosis among black men to no more than 12 per 100,000. (Age-adjusted baseline: 22 per 100,000 in 1987.)
5. Reduce pregnancies among adolescent girls aged 15 through 19 to no more than 120 per 1,000. (Baseline: 186 per 1,000 for nonwhite adolescents in 1985.)
6. Reduce homicides among black men aged 15 through 34 to no more than 72.4 per 100,000. (Baseline: 90.5 per 100,000 in 1987.)
7. Reduce homicides among black women aged 15 through 34 to no more than 16.0 per 100,000. (Baseline: 20.0 per 100,000 in 1987.)
8. Increase years of healthy life among blacks to at least 60 years. (Baseline: an estimated 56 years in 1980.)
9. Reduce deaths among black males caused by unintentional injuries to no more than 51.9 per 100,000. (Age-adjusted baseline: 64.9 per 100,000 in 1987.)
10. Reduce asthma morbidity among blacks, as measured by a reduction in asthma hospitalizations to no more than 265 per 100,000. (Baseline: 334 per 100,000 blacks and other nonwhites in 1987.)[33]

Special Considerations for Black Health Care

White health-care providers know far too little about how to care for a black person's skin or hair, or how to understand both black nonverbal and verbal behavior.

Physiological Assessment. Examples of possible physiological problems include the following (in observing skin problems, it is important to note that skin assessment is best done in indirect sunlight).

1. *Pallor.* There is an absence of underlying red tones; the skin of a brown-skinned person appears yellow-brown, and that of a black-skinned person appears ashen gray. Mucous membranes appear ashen, and the lips and nailbeds are similar.
2. *Erythema.* Inflammation must be detected by palpation; the skin is warmer in the area, tight, and edematous, and the deeper tissues are hard. Fingertips must be used for this assessment, as with rashes, since they are sensitive to the feeling of different textures of skin.
3. *Cyanosis.* Cyanosis is difficult to observe in dark-colored skin, but it can be seen by close inspection of the lips, tongue, conjunctiva, palms of the hands, and the soles of the feet. One method of testing is pressing the palms. Slow blood return is an indication of cyanosis. Another sign is ashen gray lips and tongue.
4. *Ecchymosis.* History of trauma to a given area can be detected from a swelling of the skin surface.
5. *Jaundice.* The sclera are usually observed for yellow discoloration to reveal jaundice. This is not always a valid indication, however, since carotene deposits can also cause the sclera to appear yellow. The buccal mucosa and the palms of the hands and soles of the feet may appear yellow.[34]

Skin Problems. Several skin conditions are of importance in black patients.

1. *Keloids.* Keloids are scars that form at the site of a wound and grow beyond the normal boundaries of the wound. They are sharply elevated and irregular and continue to enlarge.
2. *Pigmentary disorders.* Pigmentary disorders, areas of either postinflammatory hypopigmentation or hyperpigmentation, appear as dark or light spots.
3. *Pseudofolliculitis.* "Razor bumps" and "ingrown hairs" are caused by shaving too closely with an electric razor or straight razor. The sharp point of the hair, if shaved too close, enters the skin and induces an immune response as to a foreign body. The symptoms include papules, pustules, and sometimes even keloids.

4. *Melasma.* The "mask of pregnancy," melasma is a patchy tan to dark brown discoloration of the face more prevalent in dark pregnant women.[35]

Hair-Care Needs. The care of the hair of blacks is not complicated, but special consideration must be given to help maintain its healthy condition.

1. The hair's dryness or oiliness must be assessed, as well as its texture (straight or extra curly) and the patient's hairstyle preference.
2. The hair must be shampooed as needed and groomed according to the person's preference.
3. Hair must be combed well, with the appropriate tools, such as a "pic" or comb with big teeth, before drying to prevent tangles.
4. If the hair is dry and needs oiling, the preparations that the person generally uses for this purpose ought to be on hand.
5. Once dry, the hair is ready to be styled (curled, braided, or rolled) as the person desires.[36]

CONSIDERATIONS FOR HEALTH-CARE PROVIDERS

When they enter the profession, the majority of the members of the health-care profession are steeped in a middle-class white value system. In clinical settings, these people are being helped to become familiar with and to understand the value systems of other ethnic socioeconomic groups. They are being taught to recognize the symptoms of illness in blacks and to provide proper skin and hair care. The following are guidelines that a health-care provider can follow in caring for members of the black community.

1. The education of an ever-increasing number of blacks in the health professions must continue to be encouraged.
2. The needs of the patient must be assessed realistically.
3. When a treatment or special diet is prescribed, every attempt must be made to ascertain whether it is consistent with the patient's physical needs, cultural background, income, and religious practices.
4. The patient's belief in and practice of folk medicine must be respected; the patient must not be criticized for these beliefs. Every effort should be made to assist the patient to combine folk treatment with standard Western treatment as long as the two are not antagonistic. Most people who have a strong belief in folk remedies continue to use them with or without medical sanction.
5. Providers should be familiar with formal and informal sources of help in the black community. The former sources consist of churches, social clubs, and community groups. The latter include

those women who provide care for members of their community in an informal way.

6. The beliefs and values of the health-care provider should not be forced on the client.
7. The treatment plan and the reasons for a given treatment must be shared with the patient.

Black-American Health-Care Manpower

The number of black Americans both enrolled in health programs and in practice in selected health professions is low. Tables 9–4 and 9–5 serve to illustrate this phenomenon. Efforts must be made to recruit and maintain more blacks in the health professions.

TABLE 9–4. PERCENTAGE OF NON-HISPANIC BLACKS ENROLLED IN SELECTED HEALTH PROFESSIONS SCHOOLS: 1990–1991

Program	Total Enrollment	Percentage Black
Allopathic medicine	65,163	6.5
Osteopathic medicine	6,792	3.2
Dentistry	15,770	6.0
Optometry	4,650	2.9
Pharmacy	18,325	5.7
Podiatry	2,226	10.6
Registered nursing	221,170	10.4
Veterinary medicine	8,420	2.3

From: U.S. Department of Health and Human Services. Health United States 1992; and Healthy People 2000 Review. (Washington, D.C.: United States Department of Health and Human Services, Public Health Service Centers for Disease Control and Prevention. DHHS Pub. No. (PHS) 93–1232, 1993), pp. 150–151.

TABLE 9–5. PERCENTAGE OF NON-HISPANIC BLACKS ENROLLED IN SCHOOLS FOR SELECTED HEALTH OCCUPATIONS COMPARED WITH NON-HISPANIC WHITES: 1990–1991

Profession	White (%)	Black (%)
Physicians (M.D. and D.O.)	73.5	6.5
Dentists	70.9	6.0
Optometrists	79.7	2.9
Pharmacists	80.5	5.7
Podiatrists	75.1	10.6
Registered nurses	82.8	10.4
Veterinarians	92.5	2.6

From: U.S. Department of Health and Human Services. Health United States 1992; and Healthy People 2000 Review. (Washington, D.C.: United States Department of Health and Human Services, Public Health Service Centers for Disease Control and Prevention. DHHS Pub. No. (PHS) 93–1232, 1993), pp. 150–151.

REFERENCES

1. U.S. Department of Health and Human Services. *Healthy People 2000 National Health Promotion and Disease Prevention Objectives—Full Report with Commentary.* (Boston: Jones and Bartlett, 1992), p. 32.
2. Bullough, B. and Bullough, V. L. *Poverty, Ethnic Identity, and Health Care* (New York: Appleton-Century-Crofts, 1972), pp. 39–41.
3. Department of Health and Human Services. *Healthy People 2000*, p. 32.
4. Kotlowitz A. "Breaking the Silence: Growing up in Today's Inner City," in *Resiliency in Ethnic Minority Families*, Vol. 2—*African-American Families.* McCubbin, H., Thompson, E. A., Thompson, A. I., et al. (Madison, WI: University of Wisconsin Center, 1995), pp. 5, 6.
5. Ibid.
6. Bullough and Bullough. *Poverty*, pp. 39–41.
7. Haley, A. *Roots* (New York: Doubleday, 1976).
8. Gutman, H. G. *The Black Family in Slavery and Freedom, 1750–1925* (New York: Pantheon, 1976).
9. Bullough and Bullough. *Poverty*, p. 43; and Kain, J. F. ed., *Race and Poverty* (Englewood Cliffs, NJ: Prentice-Hall, 1969), pp. 1–30.
10. Jacques, G. "Cultural Health Traditions: A Black Perspective," in *Providing Safe Nursing Care for Ethnic People of Color,* ed. Branch, M. and Paxton, P. P. (New York: Appleton-Century-Crofts, 1976), p. 116.
11. Ibid., p. 117.
12. Wintrob, R. "Hexes, Roots, Snake Eggs? M.D. vs. Occults." *Medical Opinion* 1(7) (1972):54–61.
13. Hughes, L. and Bontemps, A., eds. *The Book of Negro Folklore* (New York: Dodd, Mead, 1958), pp. 184–185.
14. Tallant, R. *Voodoo in New Orleans*, 7th printing (New York: Collier, 1946), p. 19.
15. Ibid., p. 21.
16. Ibid., p. 25.
17. Ibid., p. 38.
18. Ibid., p. 73.
19. Ibid., p. 226.
20. Ibid.
21. Letter. Dr. J. R. Krevans to Y. Webb, Feb 15, 1967. Reported in Webb, J. Y. *Superstitious Influence—VooDoo in Particular—Affecting Health Practices in a Selected Population in Southern Louisiana* (New Orleans: Author, 1971), pp. 1–3.
22. Tallant. *Voodoo*, p. 228.
23. Angelou, M. *I Know Why the Caged Bird Sings* (New York: Random House, 1970).
24. Haley. *Roots*, p. 32.
25. Dunstin, B. "Pica during Pregnancy," in *Current Concepts in Clinical Nursing* (St. Louis: Mosby, 1969), Chap. 26.
26. Department of Health and Human Services. *Healthy People 2000*, p. 597.
27. Ibid., p. 33.
28. Manderscheid, R. W. and Sonnenschein, M. A., eds. *Mental Health, United States, 1992.* (Washington, D.C.: Center for Mental Health Services and National Institute of Mental Health, 1992, Supt. of Docs., U.S., Government Printing Office DHHS Pub. No. (SMA)92–1942), p. 262.
29. Ibid., p. 265.

30. Bullock, W. H. and Jilly, P. N. "Hematology," in *Textbook of Black-Related Diseases*, ed. Williams, R. A. (New York: McGraw-Hill, 1975), pp. 234–272.
31. U.S. Department of Health and Human Services. (1993). *Health United States 1992; and Healthy People 2000 Review.* (Washington, D.C.: United States Department of Health and Human Services, Public Health Service Centers for Disease Control and Prevention. DHHS Pub. No. (PHS) 93–1232, 1993), p. 44.
32. U.S. Department of Health and Human Services. *Healthy People 2000*, p. 33.
33. Ibid., pp. 596–597.
34. Bloch, B. and Hunter, M. L. "Teaching Physiological Assessment of Black Persons." *Nurse Educator*, (January—February 1981):26; and Roach, L. B. "Color Changes in Dark Skin." *Nursing 77* (January 1977): 48–51.
35. Sykes, J., and Kelly, A. P. "Black Skin Problems." *American Journal of Nursing* (June 1979): 1092–1094.
36. Giles, S. F. "Hair: The Nursing Process and the Black Patient." *Nursing Forum* 11(1) (January 1972): 86.

ANNOTATED BIBLIOGRAPHY

Abraham, L. K. *Mama Might Be Better off Dead—The Failure of Health Care in Urban America.* Chicago: University of Chicago Press, 1993.

This book depicts the story of the "Banes family," an urban, black American family residing in Chicago from May 1989 to April 1990. It graphically illustrates their experiences in attempting to negotiate the health-care system when race and poverty are significant barriers.

Livingston, I. L., ed. *Handbook of Black American Health.* Westport, CT: Greenwood Press, 1994.

A mosaic of conditions, issues, policies, and prospects that affect the health status of black Americans. This book analyzes each of these factors and presents a description of the political and health-related consequences of poverty and racism.

McCall, N. *Makes Me Wanna Holler.* New York: Vintage Books, 1995.

This is the compelling story of a young black man growing up in America and the journey his life took from the streets, to prison, to journalism. It presents an honest and searching look at the perils of life and the consequences of racism.

FURTHER SUGGESTED READINGS

Articles

Airhihenbuwa, C. O. "Health Education for African Americans: A Neglected Task." *Health Education* 20 (1989): 9–14.

Alexander, G., Baruffi, G., Mor, J., et al. "Multiethnic Variations in the Pregnancy Outcomes of Military Dependents." *American Journal of Public Health.* 83(12) (1993): 1721–1725.

Allen, L. M., Graves, P. B., and Woodward, E. S. "Perceptions of Problematic Behavior by Southern Female Black Fundamentalists and Mental Health Workers." *Health Care for Women International* 6 (1/3) (1985): 87–104.

Allen, S., Serufilira, A., Gruber, V., et al. "Pregnancy and Contraceptive Use Among Urban Rwandan Women After HIV Testing and Counseling." *American Journal of Public Health.* 83(5) (1993): 705–710.

Ashmore, R. D., ed. "Black and White in the 1970's." *Journal of Social Issues.* 32(2) (1976).

Bell, M. E. *Roots and Remedies: Afro-American Folk Medicine in Rhode Island.* (Pamphlet produced as part of the Joint Project of the Rhode Island Heritage Society, St. Martin DePorres center, Rhode Island Folklife Project, and Brown University Long-Term Gerontology Center), undated.

Brims, H. "The Black Family: A Proud Reappraisal." *Ebony* (March 1974): 118–127.

Brunswick, A., Aidala, A., Dobkin, J., et al. HIV-1 Seroprevalence and Risk Behaviors in an Urban African-American Community Cohort. *American Journal of Public Health.* 83(10) (1993): 1390–1394.

Brunswick, A. F. "What Generation Gap? A Comparison of Some Generational Differences among Blacks and Whites." *Social Problems* 17 (1969–1970): 358–370.

Brunswick, A. F. and Josephson, E. "Adolescent Health in Harlem." *American Journal of Public Health* 62 (10), (a separate supplement to October 1972 issue).

Burke, G., Savage, P., Manolio, T., et al. "Correlates of Obesity in Young Black and White Women: The CARDIA Study." *American Journal of Public Health.* 92(12) (1992): 1621–1625.

Capers, C. F. "Nursing and the Afro-American Client." *Topics in Clinical Nursing* 7(3) (1985): 11–17.

Cappannari, S. C., Garn, S. M., and Clark, D. C. "Voodoo in the General Hospital: A Case of Regional Enteritis." 232 (2 June 1975): 938–940.

Carlton-Laney, I. "Elderly Black Farm Women: A Population at Risk." *Social Work.* 37(4) (1992): 517–523.

Clark, C., ed. "The White Researcher in Black Society." *Journal of Social Issues* 21 (1) (1973).

Clements, D., Wilfert, C., MacCormack, J. N., et al. "Pertussis Immunization in Eight-Month-Old Children in North Carolina." *American Journal of Public Health.* 80(6) (1990): 734–736.

Collins, J. W. and David, R. J. "The Differential Effect of Traditional Risk Factors on Infant Birthweight among Blacks and Whites in New York City." *American Journal of Public Health* 80 (1990): 679–684.

Crawford, S., McGraw, S., Smith, K., et al. "Do Blacks and Whites Differ in their Use of Health Care for Symptoms of Coronary Heart Disease?" *American Journal of Public Health.* 84(6) (1994): 957–964.

Croft, J., Strogatz, D., James, S., et al. "Socioeconomic and Behavioral Correlates of Body Mass Index in Black Adults: The Pitt County Study." *American Journal of Public Health.* 82(6) (1992): 821–826.

Curtin, P. "Public Health Then and Now: The Slavery Hypothesis for Hypertension among African Americans: The Historical Evidence." *American Journal of Public Health.* 82(12) (1992): 1681–1686.

Davis, D. "Growing Old Black." *Employment Prospects of Aged Blacks, Chicanos and Indians.* Washington, DC: National Council on the Aging, 1971, pp. 27–53.

DeBaun, M., Rowley, D., Province, M., et al. "Selected Antepartum Medical Complications and Very-Low-Birthweight Infants among Black and White Women." *American Journal of Public Health.* 84(9) (1994): 1495–1504.

De Cock, K., Lucas, S., Lucas, S., et al. "Clinical Research, Prophylaxis, Therapy, and Care for HIV Disease in Africa." *American Journal of Public Health.* 83(10) (1993): 1385–1388.

Del Giudice, M. "Voodoo, USA." *Boston Globe Magazine* (10 February 1980): 17–38.

Dempsey, P. A. and Gesse, T. "The Childbearing Haitian Refugee—Cultural Applications to Clinical Nursing." *Public Health Reports* 98(3) (1983): 261–267.

DuRant, R., Cadenhead, C., Pendergast, R., et al. "Factors Associated with the Use of Violence among Urban Black Adolescents." *American Journal of Public Health.* 84(4) (1994): 612–622.

Ell, K., Haywood, J., Sobel, E., et al. "Acute Chest Pain in African Americans: Factors in the Delay in Seeking Emergency Care." *American Journal of Public Health.* 84(6) (1994): 965–970.

English, P., Eskenazi, B., and Christianson, R. "Black-White Differences in Serum Cotinine Levels among Pregnant Women and Subsequent Effects on Infant Birthweight." *American Journal of Public Health.* 84(9) (1994): 1439–1442.

Fillenbaum, G., Hanlon, J., Corder, E., et al. "Prescription and Nonprescription Drug Use among Black and White Community-Residing Elderly." *American Journal of Public Health.* 83(11) (1993): 1577–1582.

Friedman, M. L. and Musgrove, J. A.: "Perceptions of Inner City Substance Abusers about Their Families." *Archives of Psychiatric Nursing.* (1994): 8(2):115–123.

Fruchter, R., Kamran, N., Remy J. C., et al. "Cervix and Breast Cancer Incidence in Immigrant Caribbean Women." *American Journal of Public Health.* 80(6) (1990): 722–724.

Garn, S. M. "Problems in the Nutritional Assessment of Black Individuals." *American Journal of Public Health* 66 (March 1976): 262–267.

Giles, S. F. "Hair: The Nursing Process and the Black Patient." *Nursing Forum* 11 (1) (January 1972): 79–89.

Grier, M. "Hair Care for the Black Patient." *American Journal of Nursing* 76 (November 1976): 1781.

Hess, G. "Racial Tensions: Barriers in Delivery of Nursing Care." *Journal of Nursing Administration* 5 (May–June 1972): 47–49.

"Higher Education of Minority Groups in the U.S." *Journal of Negro Education* 37 (Summer 1969): 291–303.

Icard, L., Schilling, R., El-Bassel, N., et al. "Preventing AIDS among Black Gay Men and Black Gay and Heterosexual Male Intravenous Drug Users." *Social Work.* 37(5) (1992): 440–445.

Jones-Webb, R. and Snowden, L. "Symptoms of Depression among Blacks and Whites." *American Journal of Public Health.* 83(2) (1993): 240–244.

Joyner, M. "Hair Care in the Black Patient." *Journal of Pediatric Health Care* 2 (1988): 281–287.

Kelly, C. "Health Care in the Mississippi Delta." *American Journal of Nursing* (April 1969): 759–63.

Killeen, M. R. "Parent Influences on Children's Self-esteem in Economically Disadvantaged Families." *Issues in Mental Health Nursing.* 14(4) 1993: 323–336.

Kochanek, K., Maurer, J., and Rosenberg, H. "Why Did Black Life Expectancy Decline from 1984 through 1989 in the United States?" *American Journal of Public Health.* 84(6) (1994): 938–944.

Levin, J. and Taylor, R. J. "Gender and Age Differences in Religiosity among Black Americans." *The Gerontologist.* 33(1) (1993): 16–23.

Lynds, B. G., Seyler, S. K., and Morgan, B. M. "The Relationship between Elevated Blood Pressure and Obesity in Black Children." *American Journal of Public Health* 70(2) (February 1980): 171–173.

McFarlane, J. M. "The Child with Sickle Cell Anemia—What His Parents Need to Know." *Nursing* 75 (May 1975): 29, 32.

National Heart, Lung, and Blood Institute Growth and Health Study Research Group. "Obesity and Cardiovascular Disease Risk Factors in Black and White Girls: The NHLBI Growth and Health Study." *American Journal of Public Health.* 82(12) (1992): 1613–1620.

Outlaw, F. H. "Stress and Coping: The Influence of Racism on the Cognitive Appraisal Processing of African Americans." *Issues in Mental Health Nursing* 14(4) (1993): 399–409.

Raczynski, J., Taylor, H., Cutter, G., et al. "Diagnoses, Symptoms, and Attribution of Symptoms among Black and White Inpatients Admitted for Coronary Heart Disease." *American Journal of Public Health.* 84(6) (1994): 951–956.

Ribadeneira, D. "Utilizing Mystical Forces: Haitians Regard Voodoo as Vital to Their Defense." *Boston Globe.* (July 13, 1994). pp. 1, 8.

Roach, L. B. "Assessing Skin Changes: The Subtle and the Obvious." *Nursing* 74(3) (March 1974): 64–67.

Roach, L. B. "Assessment: Color Changes in Dark Skin." *Nursing 77* (January 1977): 48–51.

Roark, A. C. "Witchcraft on the Rise in Africa: Modern Medicine Men Find Out Why." *Chronicle of Higher Education* (5 November 1979): 14.

Royce, J., Hymowitz, N., Corbett, K., et al., for the COMMIT Research Group. "Smoking Cessation Factors among African Americans and Whites." *American Journal of Public Health.* 83(2) (1993): 220–226.

Russell, N. K., Becker, D., Finney, C., et al. "The Yield of Cholesterol Screening in an Urban Black Community." *American Journal of Public Health.* 81(4) (1991): 448–451.

Samelson, E., Speers, M., Ferguson, R., et al. "Racial Differences in Cervical Cancer Mortality in Chicago." *American Journal of Public Health.* 84(6) (1994): 1007–1009.

Shea, S., Misra, D., Ehrlich, M., et al. "Correlates of Nonadherence to Hypertension Treatment in an Inner-City Minority Population." *American Journal of Public Health.* 82(12) (1992): 1607–1612.

Snow, L. F. "Folk Medical Beliefs and Their Implications for Care of Patients." *Annals of Internal Medicine* 81 (July 1974): 82–96.

Sorenson, S., Richardson, B., and Peterson, J. "Public Health Briefs: Race/Ethnicity Patterns in the Homicide of Children in Los Angeles, 1980 through 1989." *American Journal of Public Health.* 83(5) (1993): 725–727.

Staples, R. "Towards a Sociology of the Black Family: A Theoretical and Methodological Assessment." *Journal of Marriage and the Family* (February 1971): 119–138.

Sykes, J., Kelly, A. P., and Kenney, J. A., Jr. "Black Skin Problems." *American Journal of Nursing* (June 1979): 1092–1094.

Thomas, S., Quinn, S. C., Billingsley, A., et al. "The Characteristics of Northern Black Churches with Community Health Outreach Programs." *American Journal of Public Health.* 84(4) (1994): 575–586.

Thompson, M. S. and Peebles-Wilkins, W. "The Impact of Formal, Informal, and Societal Support Networks on the Psychological Well-Being of Black Adolescent Mothers." *Social Work.* 37(4) (1992): 322–328.

Timberlake, E. and Chipungu, S. S. "Grandmotherhood: Contemporary Meaning among African American Middle-Class Grandmothers." *Social Work.* 37(4) (1992): 216–222.

Tivnan, E. "The Voodoo that New Yorkers Do." *New York Times Magazine* (2 December 1979): 182–191.

Ware, D. R. "Task Force Seeks Multi-disciplinary Approach to Hypertension in Blacks." *Urban Health* (June 1979): 24, 29.

Watts, W. "Social Class, Ethnic Background, and Patient Care." *Nursing Forum* 17(2) (February 1967): 155–162.

White, E. H. "Giving Health Care to Minority Patients." *Nursing Clinics of North America* 12(1) (March 1977): 27–40.

Yankauer, A., ed. "Blood Pressure and Skin Color." *American Journal of Public Health* 68(12) (December 1978): 1170–1172.

RESOURCES

National Black Nurses Association, Inc.
    P.O. Box 1823
    Washington, D.C. 20013
    (202) 393–6870
    Publish: *Journal of the National Black Nurses Association*

University Microfilms International
    300 North Zeeb Road
    P.O. Box 1764
    Ann Arbor, MI 48106
    Publish: *Black Studies* A Catalog of Selected Doctoral Dissertation Research

Letteria Dalton Sigma Omega Foundation, Inc.
    P.O. Box 6479
    Cincinnati, OH 45206–0479
    This organization is a public foundation founded on the principle that the empowerment of the black family is necessary for a strong viable community.

Black Caucus
    American Public Health Association
    1015 Fifteenth Street, N.W.
    Washington, D.C. 20005

Additional Resources are included in Appendix VIII.

Chapter

Health and Illness in the American Indian, Aleut, and Eskimo Communities

To be an Indian in modern American society is in a very real sense to be unreal and antihistorical.

—Vine Deloria

The descendants of the original inhabitants of the North American continent now number 1.6 million and constitute the smallest of the emerging majority groups. This diverse group comprises numerous tribes and over 400 federally recognized nations, each with its own traditions and cultural heritage. Eskimos, Aleuts, and Indians residing in Alaska are referred to as Alaska Natives; those residing in other states are referred to as American Indians.[1]

To realize the plight of today's American Indian, it is necessary to journey back in time to the years when whites settled in this land. Before the arrival of Europeans, this country had no name but was inhabited by groups of people who called themselves *nations*. The people were strong both in their knowledge of the land and in their might as warriors. The Vikings reached the shores of this country about AD 1010. They were unable to settle on the land and left after a decade of frustration. Much later, another group of settlers, since termed the "Lost Colonies," were repulsed. More people came to these shores, however, and the land was taken over by Europeans. As the settlers expanded westward, they signed "treaties of peace" or "treaties of land cession" with the Indians. These treaties were similar to those struck between nations, although in this case the agreement was imposed by the "big" nation onto the "small" nation. One reason for treaties was to legitimize the takeover of the land that the Europeans had "discovered." Once the land was "discovered," it was divided among the Europeans, who set out to create a "legal" claim to it. The Indians signed the resultant treaties, ceding small amounts of their land to the settlers and keeping the rest for themselves. As time passed, the number of whites rapidly grew, and the number of Indians diminished because of wars and disease. As these events occurred, the treaties began to lose their meaning; the Europeans came to consider them as nothing but a joke. They decided that these "natives" had no real claim to the land and shifted them around like cargo from one reservation to another. Although the Indians tried to seek just settlements through the American court system, they failed to win back the land that had been taken from them through misrepresentation. For example, by 1831, the Cherokees were fighting in the courts to keep their nation in Georgia. They lost their legal battle, however, and, like other Indian nations since the time of the early European settlers, were forced to move westward. During this forced westward movement, many Indians died and all suffered. Today, many nations are seeking to reclaim their land through the courts.[2] Several claims, such as those of the Penebscot and Passamaquody tribes in Maine, have been successful.

As the Indians migrated westward, they carried with them the fragments of their culture. Their lives were disrupted, their land was lost, and many of their leaders and teachers had perished. Yet much of their history and culture somehow remain. Today, more and more Indians are seeking to know their history. The story of the colonization and settlement of the United States is being retold with a different emphasis.

Americans Indians live predominantly in 26 states (including Alaska), with most residing in the western part of the country as a result of the forced westward migration. Although many Indians remain on reservations and in rural areas, just as many of them live in cities, especially those on the West Coast. Oklahoma, Arizona, California, New Mexico, and Alaska have the largest numbers of Native Americans.[3] Today, more and more people are claiming to have American Indian roots. Since 1970, the Indian population has increased by 140%. By the year 2000, census officials project that there will be roughly 2.3 million Indians, or triple the number in 1970. Table 10–1 lists the 10 largest American Indian nations.[4]

TRADITIONAL DEFINITIONS OF HEALTH AND ILLNESS

Each American Indian nation or tribe had its own history and belief system regarding health and illness and the traditional treatment of illness. Yet some general beliefs and practices underlie the more specific tribal ideas. Certain specifics are noted, either in the text or in footnotes. The data—collected through a review of the literature and from interviews granted by members of the groups—come from the Navaho nation, the Hopis, the Cherokees, and Shoshones, and New England Indians with whom I have worked closely.

TABLE 10–1. THE TEN LARGEST AMERICAN INDIAN NATIONS

Nation	1990 Population
Cherokee	369,035
Navajo	225,298
Sioux	107,321
Chippewa	105,988
Choctaw	86,231
Pueblo	55,330
Apache	53,330
Iroquois	52,557
Lumbee	50,888
Cree	45,872

From: Zuckoff, M. "More and More Claiming American Indian Heritage." *Boston Globe.* April 18, 1995 p. 9. Reprinted with permission.

The traditional American Indian belief about health is that it reflects living in total harmony with nature and having the ability to survive under exceedingly difficult circumstances.[5] Humankind has an intimate relationship with nature.[6]* The earth is considered to be a living organism—the body of a higher individual, with a will and a desire to be well. The earth is periodically healthy and less healthy, just as human beings are. According to the American Indian belief system, a person should treat his or her body with respect, just as the earth should be treated with respect. When the earth is harmed, humankind is itself harmed, and, conversely, when humans harm themselves they harm the earth.[7] The earth gives food, shelter, and medicine to humankind, and for this reason, all things of the earth belong to human beings and nature. "The land belongs to life, life belongs to the land, and the land belongs to itself." In order to maintain health, Indians must maintain their relationship with Nature. "Mother Earth" is the friend of the Indian, and the land belongs to the Indian.[8]

According to Indian belief, as explained by a medicine man, Rolling Thunder, the human body is divided into two halves which are seen as plus and minus (yet another version of the concept that every whole is made of two opposite halves). There are also—in every whole—two energy poles: positive and negative. The energy of the body can be controlled by spiritual means. It is further believed that every being has a purpose and an identity. Every being has the power to control his or her own self, and from this force and the belief in its potency the spiritual power of a person in kindled.[9]

Many American Indians with traditional orientations believe there is a reason for every sickness or pain. They believe that illness is the price to be

*This philosophy was reiterated in a lecture at Boston College School of Nursing in April, 1975, by Will Basque, a Micmac Indian and former president of the Boston Indian Council.

paid, either for something that happened in the past or for something that will happen in the future. In spite of this conviction, a sick person must still be cared for. Everything is seen as being the result of something else, and this cause-and-effect relationship creates an eternal chain. American Indians do not subscribe to the germ theory of modern medicine. Illness is something that must *be*. Even the person who is experiencing the illness may not realize the reason for its occurrence,[10] but it may, in fact, be the best possible price to pay for the past or future event(s).

The Hopi Indians associate illness with evil spirits. The evil spirit responsible for the illness is identified by the medicine man, and the remedy for the malady resides in the treatment of the evil spirit.[11]

According to legend, the Navaho people originally emerged from the depths of the earth—fully formed as human beings. Before the beginning of time, they existed with holy people, supernatural beings with supernatural powers, in a series of 12 underworlds. The creation of all elements took place in these underworlds, and there all things were made to interact in constant harmony. A number of ceremonies and rituals were created at this time for "maintaining, renewing, and mending this state of harmony."[12]

When the Navaho people emerged from the underworlds, one female was missing. She was subsequently found by a search party in the same hole from which they had initially emerged. She told the people that she had chosen to remain there and wait for their return. She became known as death, sickness, and witchcraft. Because her hair was unraveled and her body was covered with dry red ochre, the Navahos today continue to unravel the hair of their dead and to cover their bodies with red ochre. Members of the Navaho nation believe that "witchcraft exists and that certain humans, known as witches, are able to interact with the evil spirits. These people can bring sickness and other unhappiness to the people who annoy them."[13]

Traditionally, illness, disharmony, and sadness are seen by the Navahos as the result of one or more combinations of the following actions: "(1) displeasing the holy people; (2) annoying the elements; (3) disturbing animal and plant life; (4) neglecting the celestial bodies; (5) misuse of a sacred Indian ceremony; or (6) tampering with witches and witchcraft."[14] If disharmony exists, disease can occur. The Navahos distinguish between two types of disease: (1) contagious diseases, such as measles, smallpox, diphtheria, syphilis, and gonorrhea, and (2) more generalized illnesses, such as "body fever" and "body ache." The notion of illness being caused by a microbe or other physiological agent is alien to the Navahos. The cause of disease, of injury to people or to their property, or of continued misfortune of any kind must be traced back to an action that should not have been performed. Examples of such infractions are breaking a taboo or contacting a ghost or witch. To the Navahos, the treatment of an illness, therefore, must be concerned with the external causative factor(s) and not with the illness or injury itself.[15]

TRADITIONAL METHODS OF HEALING

Traditional Healers

The traditional healer of Native America is the medicine man or woman, and the Indians, by and large, have maintained their faith in him or her over the ages. The medicine men and women are wise in the ways of the land and of nature. They know well the interrelationships of human beings, the earth, and the universe. They know the ways of the plants and animals, the sun, the moon, and the stars. Medicine men and women take time to determine first the cause of the illness and then the proper treatment. To determine the cause and treatment of an illness, they perform special ceremonies that may take up to several days.

As a specific example, Boyd describes the medicine man, Rolling Thunder, the spiritual leader, philosopher, and acknowledged spokesman of the Cherokee and Shoshone tribes, as being able to determine the cause of illness when the ill person does not himself know it. The "diagnostic" phase of the treatment often may take as long as three days. There are numerous causes of physical illness and a great number of reasons—good or bad—for having become ill. These causes are of a spiritual nature. When modern physicians see a sick person, they recognize and diagnose only the physical illness. Medicine men and women, on the other hand, look for the spiritual cause of the problem. To the American Indian, "every physical thing in nature has a spiritual nature because the whole is viewed as being essentially spiritual in nature."[16] The agents of nature, herbs, are seen as spiritual helpers, and the characteristics of plants must be known and understood. Rolling Thunder states that "we are born with a purpose in life and we have to fulfill that purpose."[17] The purpose of the medicine man or woman is to cure, and their power is not dying out.

The medicine man or woman of the Hopis uses meditation in determining the cause of an illness and sometimes even uses a crystal ball as the focal point for meditation. At other times, the medicine man or woman chews on the root of jimsonweed, a powerful herb that produces a trance. The Hopis claim that this herb gives the medicine man or woman a vision of the evil that caused a sickness. Once the meditation is concluded, the medicine man or woman is able to prescribe the proper herbal treatment. For example, fever is cured by a plant that smells like lightning; the Hopi phrase for fever is "lightning sickness."[18]

The Navaho Indians consider disease to result from breaking a taboo or the attack of a witch. The exact cause is diagnosed by divination, as is the ritual of treatment. There are three types of divination: motion in the hand (the most common form and often practiced by women), stargazing, and listening. The function of the diagnostician is first to determine the cause of the illness and then to recommend the treatment—that is, the type of chant that will be effective and the medicine man or woman who can best do it. A medicine man or woman may be called on to treat obvious symptoms, whereas the diagnostician is called on to ascertain the cause of the illness. (A person is considered wise if the diagnostician is called first.) Often, the same medicine man or woman can practice both divination (diagnosis) and the singing (treatment). When any form of divination is used in making the diagnosis, the diagnostician meets with the family and discusses the patient's condition and determines the fee.

The practice of motion in the hand includes the following rituals. Pollen or sand is sprinkled around the sick person, during which time the diagnostician sits with closed eyes and face turned from the patient. The hand begins to move during the song. While the hand is moving, the diagnostician thinks of various diseases and various causes. When the arm begins to move in a certain way, the diagnostician knows that the right disease and its cause have been discovered. He or she is then able to prescribe the proper treatment.[19] The ceremony of motion in the hand also may incorporate the use of sand paintings. (These paintings are a well-known form of art.) Four basic colors are used—white, blue, yellow, and black—and each color has a symbolic meaning. Chanting is performed as the painting is produced, and the shape of the painting determines the cause and treatment of the illness. The chants may continue for an extended time,[20] depending on the family's ability to pay and the capabilities of the singer. The process of motion in the hand can be neither inherited nor learned. It comes to a person suddenly, as a gift. It is said that people able to diagnose their own illnesses are able to practice motion in the hand.[21]

Unlike motion in the hand, stargazing can and must be learned. Sand paintings are often but not always made during stargazing. If they are not made, it is either because the sick person cannot afford to have one done or because there is not enough time to make one. The stargazer prays the star prayer to the star spirit, asking it to show the cause of the illness. During stargazing, singing begins and the star throws a ray of light that determines the cause of the patient's illness. If the ray of light is white or yellow, the patient will recover; if it is red, the illness is serious. If a white light falls on the patient's home, the person will recover; if the home is dark, the patient will die.[22]

Listening, the third type of divination, is somewhat similar to stargazing, except that something is heard rather than seen. In this instance, the cause of the illness is determined by the sound that is heard. If someone is heard to be crying, the patient will die.[23]

The traditional Navahos continue to use medicine men and women when an illness occurs. They use this service because, in many instances, the treatment they receive from these traditional healers is better than the treatment they receive from the health-care establishment. Treatments used by singers include massage and heat treatment, the sweatbath, and use of the yucca root—approaches similar to those common in physiotherapy.[24]

The main effects of the singer are psychological. During the chant, the patient feels cared for in a deeply personal way as the center of the singer's attention, since the patient's problem is the reason for the singer's presence. When the singer tells the patient recovery will occur and the reason for the illness, the patient has faith in what is heard. The singer is regarded as a distinguished authority and as a person of eminence with the gift of learning from the holy people. He is considered to be more than a mere mortal. The ceremony—surrounded by such high levels of prestige, mysticism, and power—takes the sick person into its circle, ultimately becoming one with the holy people by participating in the sing that is held in the patient's behalf. The patient once again comes into harmony with the universe and subsequently becomes free of all ills and evil.[25]

The religion of the Navahos is one of *good hope* when they are sick or suffer other misfortunes. Their system of beliefs and practices helps them through the crises of life and death. The stories that are told during ceremonies give the people a glimpse of a world that has gone by, which promotes a feeling of security because they see that they are links in the unbroken chain of countless generations.[26]

Many Navahos believe in witchcraft, and when it is considered to be the cause of an illness, special ceremonies are employed to rid the individual of the evil caused by the witches. Numerous methods are employed to manipulate the supernatural. Although many of these activities may meet with strong social disapproval, Navahos recognize the usefulness of blaming witches for illness and misfortune. Tales abound concerning witchcraft and how the witches work. Not all Navahos believe in witchcraft, but for those who do it provides a mechanism for laying blame for the overwhelming hardships and anxieties of life.

Such events as going into a trance can be ascribed to the work of witches. The way to cure a "witched" person is through the use of complicated prayer ceremonies that are attended by friends and relatives, who lend help and express sympathy. The victim of a witch is in no way responsible for being sick and is, therefore, free of any punitive action by the community if the illness causes the victim to behave in strange ways.[27] On the other hand, if an incurably "witched" person is affected so that alterations in the person's established role severely disrupt the community, the victim may be abandoned.

Traditional Remedies

American Indians practice an act of purification in order to maintain their harmony with nature and to cleanse the body and spirit. This is done by total immersion in water in addition to the use of sweat lodges, herb medicines, and special rituals. Purification is seen as the first step in the control of consciousness, a ritual that awakens the body and the senses and prepares a person for meditation. It is viewed by the participants as a new beginning.[28]

The basis of therapy lies in nature: hence the use of herbal remedies. Specific rituals are to be followed when herbs are gathered. Each plant is picked to be dried for later use. No plant is picked unless it is the proper one, and only enough plants are picked to meet the needs of the gatherers. Timing is crucial, and the procedures are followed meticulously. So deep is their belief in the harmony of human beings and nature that the herb gatherers exercise great care not to disturb any of the other plants and animals in the environment.[29]

One plant of interest, the common dandelion, contains a milky juice in its stem and is said to increase the flow of milk from the breasts of nursing mothers. Another plant, the thistle, is said to contain a substance that relieves the prickling sensation in the throats of people who live in the desert. The medicine used to hasten the birth of a baby is called "weasel medicine" because the weasel is clever at digging through and out of difficult territory.[30]

The following is a list of common ailments and herbal treatments used by the Hopi Indians.[31]

1. Cuts and wounds are treated with globe mallow. The root of this plant is chewed to help mend broken bones.
2. To keep air from cuts, piñon gum is applied to the wound. It is used also in an amulet to protect a person from witchcraft.
3. Cliff rose is used to wash wounds.
4. Boils are brought to a head with the use of sand sagebrush.
5. Spider bites are treated with sunflower. The person bathes in water in which the flowers have been soaked.
6. Snakebites are treated with the bladder pod. The bitter root of this plant is chewed and then placed on the bite.
7. Lichens are used to treat the gums. They are ground to a powder and then rubbed on the affected areas.
8. Fleabane is used to treat headaches. The entire herb is either bound to the head or infused and drunk as a tea.
9. Digestive disorders are treated with blue gillia. The leaves are boiled in water and drunk to relieve indigestion.
10. The stem of the yucca plant is used as a laxative. The purple flower of the thistle is used to expel worms.
11. Blanket flower is the diuretic used to provide relief from painful urination.
12. A tea is made from painted cup and drunk to relieve the pain of menstruation. Winter fat provides a tea from the leaves and roots and is drunk if the uterus fails to contract properly during labor.

The use of Indian cures and herbal remedies continues to be popular. Among the Oneida Indians, the following remedies are used:

Illness	Remedy
Colds	Witch hazel, sweet flag
Sore throat	Comfrey
Diarrhea	Elderberry flowers
Headache	Tansy and sage
Ear infection	Skunk oil
Mouth sores	Dried raspberry leaves[32]

Among the Micmac Indians of Canada, the following remedies are used:

Illness	Remedy
Warts	Juice from milkweed plant
Obesity	Spruce bark and water
Rheumatism	Juniper berries
Diabetes	Combination of blueberries and huckleberries
Insomnia	Eat a head of lettuce a day
Diarrhea	Tea from wild strawberry[33]

Table 10–2 summarizes the cultural phenomena affecting American Indians, Aleuts, and Eskimos.

TABLE 10–2. EXAMPLES OF CULTURAL PHENOMENA AFFECTING HEALTH CARE AMONG AMERICAN INDIANS, ALEUTS, AND ESKIMOS

Nations of Origin:	200 American Indian nations indigenous to North America Aleuts and Eskimos in Alaska
Environmental Control:	Traditional health and illness beliefs may continue to be observed by "traditional" people Natural and magicoreligious folk medicine tradition Traditional healer—medicine man or woman
Biological Variations:	Accidents Heart disease Cirrhosis of the liver Diabetes mellitus
Social Organization:	Extremely family-oriented to both biological and extended families Children are taught to respect traditions Community social organizations
Communication:	Tribal languages Use of silence and body language
Space:	Space is very important and has no boundaries
Time Orientation:	Present

Adapted from: Spector, R. "Culture, Ethnicity, and Nursing," in *Fundamentals of Nursing,* (3rd ed.) eds., Potter, P. and Perry, A. (St. Louis: Mosby-Year Book, 1992) p. 101. Reprinted with permission.

CURRENT HEALTH-CARE PROBLEMS

Today, American Indians are faced with a number of health-related problems. Many of the old ways of diagnosing and treating illness have not survived the migrations and changing ways of life of these people. Because these skills often have been lost and because modern health-care facilities are not always available, Indian peoples are frequently caught in limbo when it comes to obtaining adequate health care. At least one third of American Indians exist in a state of abject poverty. With this destitution come poor living conditions and attendant problems, as well as diseases of the poor—including malnutrition, tuberculosis, and high maternal and infant death rates. Poverty and isolated living serve as further barriers that keep American Indians from using limited health-care facilities even when they are available. Many of the illnesses that are familiar among white patients may manifest themselves differently in Indian patients.

MORBIDITY AND MORTALITY

A higher proportion of American Indian women have inadequate prenatal care and experience infant (particularly postnatal) deaths than do white women. American Indian youths are also more likely to be substance users and are more likely to die from firearm-related homicides than are whites.[34] The infant mortality rate in 1989 among American Indians was 9.7 per 1,000 live births; with a neonatal rate of 4.6 and a postnatal rate of 5.1. The percentage of mothers who received prenatal care in the third trimester or no prenatal care was 13.4 in 1989, and the maternal mortality rate was 7.1.[35] In 1991, 314 cases of AIDS (0.2% of the total number) were reported in this population, with 54.8% of these cases occurring in homosexual males; 203 cumulative deaths were reported.[36] Alcohol abuse remains an extremely critical health issue among American Indians as illustrated by an age-adjusted alcohol-related mortality rate of 33.9 per 100,000 people between the years 1986 and 1988. The rate for all races was 6.3.[37] Suicide rates are also high among American Indians: the rate in 1988 was 14.5 compared with the national rate of 11.4. The death rate for American Indian males aged 15 to 24 was 40.7, and that for those aged 25 to 34 was 49.6.[38] The homicide rate for American Indians is also higher than for the overall population. The 1988 rate was 14.1, about 1.6 times that of the national average (9.0) for that year. The rates of homicide-related deaths are the highest among males between ages 15 and 24 (32.1) and ages 25 to 34 (44.7).[39]

The leading causes of death for American Indians in Reservation states in 1987 were:

1. Diseases of the heart
2. Cancer
3. Injuries
4. Stroke
5. Liver disease
6. Diabetes
7. Pneumonia/Influenza
8. Suicide
9. Homicide
10. Chronic lung disease[40]

Alcohol Abuse

Mortality and morbidity rates for American Indians are directly affected by alcohol abuse. Alcohol abuse is the most widespread and severe problem in the American Indian community. It is extremely costly to the people and underlies many of their physical, mental, social, and economic problems, and the problem is growing worse. Hawk Littlejohn, the medicine man of the Cherokee Nation, Eastern band, attributes this problem, from a traditional point of view, to the fact that Native Americans have lost the opportunity to make choices. They can no longer choose how they live or how they practice their medicine and religion. He believes that once people return to a sense of identification within themselves, they begin to rid themselves of this problem of alcoholism. Whatever the solution may be the problem is indeed immense.[41]

Domestic Violence

Another problem related to alcohol abuse in the Native American peoples is domestic violence and the battering of women. A battered woman is one who is physically assaulted by her husband, boyfriend, or some significant other. The assault may range from a push to severe, even permanent, injury, to sexual abuse, to child abuse, and to neglect. Once the pattern of abuse is established, subsequent episodes of abuse tend to get worse. This abuse is not traditional in Native American life but has evolved. True Indian love is based on a tradition of mutual respect and the belief that men and women are part of an ordered universe that should live in peace. In the traditional Native American home, children were raised to respect their parents, and they were not corporally punished. Violence toward women was not practiced. In modern times, however, the sanctions and protections against domestic violence have decreased, and the women are far more vulnerable. Many women are reluctant to admit that they are victims of abuse because they believe that they will be blamed for the assault. Hence, the beatings continue. A number of services are available to women who are victims, such as safe houses and support groups. It is believed that the long-range solution to this problem lies in teaching children to love—to nurture children and give them self-esteem, to teach boys to love and respect women, and to give girls a sense of worth. Battering of women is not part of traditional Indian life.[42]

Domestic violence has a profound effect on the community and on the family. A pattern of abuse is easily established. It begins with tension: the female attempts to keep peace, but the male cannot contain himself, a fight erupts, and then the crisis arrives. The couple may make up, only to fight again. Attempts to help must be initiated, or the cycle escalates. The problem is extremely complex. Some of the services available to a household experiencing domestic violence include

1. Tribal health: direct services for physical and mental health
2. Law enforcement: police protection may be necessary

3. Legal assistance: assistance for immediate shelter and emergency food and transportation[43]

In addition to alcohol-related problems, recent studies indicate that incidences of both lung cancer in males and breast cancer in females are increasing.[44]

Urban Problems
More than 50% of American Indians live in urban areas; for example, in Seattle there are 15,000 Indians. Although this population is not particularly dense, its rates of diphtheria, tuberculosis, otitis media with subsequent hearing defects, alcohol abuse, inadequate immunization, iron deficiency anemia, childhood developmental lags, mental health problems (including depression, anxiety, and coping difficulties), and caries and other dental problems are high. As in all dysfunctional families, problems arise that are related to marital difficulties and financial strain, which usually are brought about by unemployment and the lack of education or knowledge of special skills. The tension often is compounded further by alcoholism.[45]

Between 5000 and 6000 Indians live in Boston. They experience the same problems as Native Americans in other cities, yet there is an additional problem. Few non-Indian residents are even aware that there is a Native American community in that city or that it is in desperate need of adequate health and social services.[46]

HEALTH-CARE PROVIDER SERVICES

Some historical differences in health care relate to geographical locations. Indians living in the eastern part of this country and in most urban areas are *not* covered by the services of the Indian Health Service, services which are available to Native Americans living on reservations in the West. In 1923, tribal government—under the control of the Bureau of Indian Affairs—was begun by the Navahos. Treaties were established by the Navahos with the United States government, but in the areas of health and education these treaties were not honored by the United States. Health services on the reservations were inadequate. Consequently, the people were sent to outside institutions for the treatment of illnesses, such as tuberculosis and mental health problems. As recently as 1930, the vast Navaho lands had only seven hospitals with 25 beds each. Not until 1955 were Indians finally offered concentrated services with modern physicians. Only since 1965 have more comprehensive services been available to the Navahos.[47]

Indian Health Service
The Indian Health Service provides inpatient facilities and outpatient clinics, among which are well-baby, prenatal, and diabetes clinics. In addition,

public-health nursing services are provided. Community health representatives who are tribal members serve in the community to identify health problems, to encourage people to use existing medical facilities, and to take people to the clinic when the need arises (Fig. 10–1 and Table 10–3).

The Indian Health Service also makes provision for health education. Paraprofessionals and professionals in the community work to educate the people, both formally and informally, in modern health practices. A section of the Indian Health Service is concerned with alcohol abuse and mental health problems. These mental health workers act as liaisons between the Indians and halfway houses, counselors, drug-prevention programs, and other agencies set up specifically to deal with the emotional problems of anxiety and depression. The Indian Health Service also maintains an otitis media program in view of the statistically established high incidence of this disorder among Native Americans. Young children are screened in an effort to begin early treatment so that deafness can be prevented. Figure 10–2 details many facts about the Indian Health Service.

Eligibility for Health Care

Proposals have been made to redefine eligibility for Indian Health Services that would significantly change the distribution of health-care services. Present regulations stipulate that people are eligible for services if they are of Indian descent and belong to an Indian community served by IHS. No distinction is made concerning the degree of Indian ancestry or specific tribal affiliation as long as the person lives in an area served by IHS. The proposed changes would stipulate that an Indian must (1) be a member or eligible for membership in a federally recognized tribe, (2) be of one quarter or more Indian or Alaska Native ancestry, and (3) reside in a designated health service delivery area. Indian blood quantum is made on the basis of proof of Indian blood by tribal origin, and the proof must be verified by the Bureau of Indian Affairs. The minimal blood quantum level is one fourth, and the numbers of people with this level or higher are declining.[48]

The ineligibility of Native Americans living on the East Coast to secure such services* has caused numerous difficulties for needy Indians. The providers of health care generally seem to think that Indians should receive health services from the Indian Health Service and try to send them there. Unfortunately, there simply is no Indian Health Service on the East Coast, so Native Americans tend to be shifted around among the regional health-care resources that are available.

Many providers of health-care and social services are not aware that many of the Indians on the East Coast have dual citizenship as a result of the Jay Treaty of 1794, which allows for international citizenship between the United States and Canada, a fact that raises questions about whether Indians can

---

*The situation stems from the Indian Renewal Act of 1840 and the Dawes Act of 1887, legislation that disbanded tribes east of the Mississippi and established reservations west of the Mississippi.

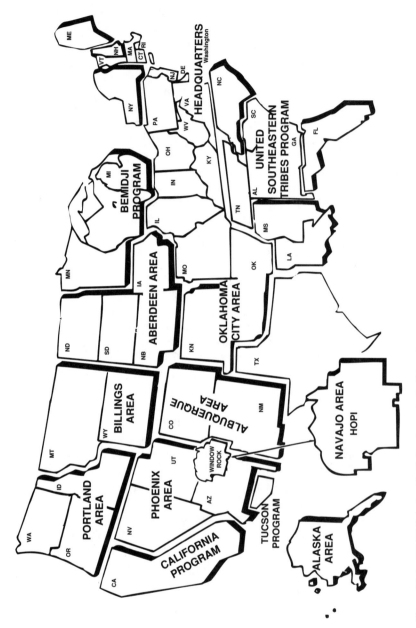

Figure 10–1. U.S.P.H.S. Indian Health Service major facilities. (Reprinted with permission from Indian Health Service. U.S. Department of Health and Human Services, Public Health Service Information Brochure. (1994).)

TABLE 10–3. MAJOR INDIAN HEALTH FACILITIES IN THE UNITED STATES

Aberdeen area		
Nebraska:	Hospital	
	Winnebago	
	Health Center	
	Macy	
North Dakota:	Hospitals	
	Belcourt	
	Fort Yates	
	Health Centers	
	Fort Totten	
	New Town	
	Trenton-Williston	
South Dakota:	Hospitals	
	Eagle Butte	
	Pine Ridge	
	Rapid City	
	Rosebud	
	Sisseton	
	Wagner	
	Health Centers	
	Chamberlain	
	McLaughlin	
	Wanblee	

Bemidji program

Michigan:	Health Centers
	Kincheloe
	L'Anse
Minnesota:	Hospitals
	Cass Lake
	Red Lake
	Health Centers
	Mille Lacs
	White Earth
Wisconsin:	Health Centers
	Menominee (Keshena)
	Lac du Flambeau
	Lac Courte Oreilles
	Oneida
	Stockbridge-Munsee

Alaska area

Hospitals
Alaska Native Med.
 (Anchorage)
Barrow
Yukon-Kuskowkim Delta
Bristol Bay Area
Kotzebue
Mt. Edgecumbe
Tanana
Health Centers
Ft. Wingate
Teec Nos Pos
Tohatchi

Health Centers
Fairbanks
Ft. Yukon
Juneau
Ketchikan
Metlakatla
St. Paul Island
St. George Island

Albuquerque area

Colorado:	Health Centers
	Ignacio
	Towaoc
New Mexico:	Hospitals
	Acoma-Cononcito-
	Laguna
	Albuquerque
	Mescalero
	Santa Fe
	Zuni
	Health Centers
	Alamo
	Dulce
	Taos

Billings area

Montana:	Hospitals
	Browning
	Crow
	Harlem
	Health Centers
	Lame Deer
	Poplar
	Rocky Boy's
	Wolfpoint
Wyoming:	Health Centers
	Arapahoe
	Fort Washakie

Navajo area

Arizona:	Hospitals
	Chinle
	Fort Defiance
	Tuba City
	Health Centers
	Kayenta
	Shonto
	Winslow
New Mexico:	Hospitals
	Crownpoint
	Gallup Medical Center
	Shiprock
	Health Centers
	Cibicue
	Peach Springs

TABLE 10–3. (*continued*)

		Nevada:	Hospitals
			Owyhee
Oklahoma City area			Schurz
Kansas:	Health Centers	Utah:	Health Center
	Holton		Roosevelt
	Lawrence		
Oklahoma:	Hospitals	**California program**	
	Claremore	Program Office at Sacramento	
	Clinton	**Tucson program**	
	Lawton	Arizona:	Hospital
	Ada		Sells
	Tahlequah		Health Center
	Talihina		San Xavier
	Health Centers		
	Anadarko	**Portland area**	
	Broken Bow	Idaho:	Health Centers
	Eufaula		Fort Hall
	Hugo		Northern Idaho
	Jay		(Lapwai)
	McAlester	Oregon:	Health Centers
	Miami		Chemawa
	Pawhuska		Umatilla
	Sapulpa		Warm Springs
	Shawnee	Washington:	Health Centers
	Tishomingo		Colville
	Watonga		Lummi
	White Eagle		Neah Bay
			Taholah
Phoenix area			Wellpinit
Arizona:	Hospitals		Yakima
	Keams Canyon		
	Parker	**United Southeastern Tribes Program**	
	Phoenix	Mississippi:	Hospital
	Sacaton		Pearl River
	San Carlos		(Philadelphia)
	Whiteriver	North Carolina:	Hospital
	Yuma		Cherokee

freely cross the border between the United States and Canada and whether those who live in the United States are eligible for welfare or Medicaid.

HEALTHY PEOPLE 2000: OBJECTIVES

The following are examples of selected objectives from *Healthy People 2000* that target American Indians and Alaska natives:

1. Reduce cigarette smoking to a prevalence of no more than 20% among American Indians and Alaska natives (Baseline: An estimated 42–70% for different tribes in 1979–1987).

2. Reduce death among American Indian and Alaska native men caused by alcohol-related motor vehicle crashes to no more than 44.8 per 100,000 (Age-adjusted baseline: 52.2 per 100,000 in 1987).

3. Reduce cirrhosis deaths among American Indian and Alaska natives to no more than 13 per 100,000 (Age-adjusted baseline: 25.9 per 100,000 in 1987).

4. Reduce suicides among American Indian and Alaska native men in reservation states to no more than 12.8 per 100,000 (Age-adjusted baseline: 15 per 100,000 in 1987).

5. Reduce homicides among American Indians and Alaska native men in reservation states to no more than 11.3 per 100,000 (Age-adjusted baseline: 14.1 per 100,000 in 1987).

6. Reduce deaths among American Indians and Alaska natives caused by motor vehicle crashes to no more than 9.2 per 100,000 (Age-adjusted baseline: 46.8 per 100,000 in 1987).

7. Reduce the infant mortality rate among American Indians and Alaska natives to no more than 8.5 per 1,000 live births (Baseline: 12.5 per 1,000 live births in 1984).

8. Reduce the incidence of fetal alcohol syndrome among American Indians and Alaska natives to no more than 2 per 1,000 live births (Baseline: 4 per 1,000 live births in 1987).

9. Increase to at least 90% the proportion of American Indian and Alaska native women who receive prenatal care in the first trimester of pregnancy (Baseline: 60.2% of live births in 1987).

10. Reduce tuberculosis among American Indians and Alaska natives to an incidence of no more than 5 cases per 100,000 (Baseline: 18.1 per 100,000 in 1988).[49]

Cultural and Communication Problems

A factor that inhibits the Indian use of white-dominated health services is a deep, cultural problem: Indians suffer disease when they come into contact with the white health-care provider.[†] Native Americans feel uneasy because for too many years they have been the victim of haphazard care and disrespectful treatment. All too often conflict arises between what the Native Americans perceive their illness to be and what the physician may diagnose. Native Americans, like most people, do not enjoy long waits in

---

[†]Dr. Red Horse explains the phenomenon of "Indian paranoia" that emerges in a predictable behavior: "It is *not* a sickness but an 'interactive reality' that Native Americans suffer whenever visits to non-Indian clinics are imminent. *Fear* is a variable and often when the fear is too great, help is not sought. For example, if a Native American child has a toothache, the parents may not take the child to the dentist because they fear the dentist's demeaning attitude."[50]

 DEPARTMENT OF HEALTH & HUMAN SERVICES   PUBLIC HEALTH SERVICE    INDIAN HEALTH SERVICE

Facts About the Indian Health Service

The Indian Health Service (IHS) provides comprehensive health care for almost 1.2 million American Indian and Alaska Natives. To achieve the IHS goal of raising the health status of American Indian and Alaska Native people to the highest possible level, efforts are dedicated to:

• Delivering high quality, comprehensive, and accessible health services;
• Providing increased opportunities for American Indian tribes and Alaska Native corporations to manage their own health programs; and
• Serving as a health advocate for American Indians and Alaska Natives.

Members of more than 500 federally recognized Indian tribes and Alaska Native corporations are eligible for health services provided by IHS, an agency of the U. S. Public Health Service in the Department of Health and Human Services.

In recognition of the disparity between the health status of American Indian and Alaska Native people and that of other U.S. citizens, and the desire of the Indian and Alaska Native people to have greater control over their own destiny, the Congress passed two landmark laws.

Public Law 93-638, the Indian Self-Determination ant Education Assistance Act of 1975. This law gives Indian tribes and Alaska Native groups the option of managing and operating health care programs in their communities.

The Indian Health Care Improvement Act Public Law 94-437 of 1976, amendment Public law 96-537 of 1980 and its latest amendment Public Law 101-630 of 1990. The purpose of this act, and its subsequent amendments, is to assist in elevating the health status of Indians and Alaska Natives to a level equal to that of the general population. Public Law 101-430 reauthorized Public Law 94-437 and directs IHS to establish a comprehensive mental health and treatment program. It also authorizes Indian tribes to develop and implement community based mental health programs.

The relationship between the Indian tribes and the federal government is one of government to government, as established through treaties, Executive Orders, and judicial decisions.

The IHS comprehensive delivery system is composed of two major systems:

1. a federal health care delivery system, administered by federal personnel; and
2. a tribal health care delivery system, administered by tribes.

Both systems include health care services provided directly by, and health services purchased from, over 2,000 private providers. In addition, there are 34 urban Indian health projects providing a wide variety of health and referral services.

The federally administered health care delivery system is made up of 42 hospitals, 7 service units, 65 health centers, 52 health stations, and four school health centers as of October 1, 1991. A priority of the federally administered program is health promotion and disease prevention.

The tribally administered program is made up of 8 hospitals, 61 service units, 93 health centers, 235 health stations, three school health centers, and 183 Alaska village clinics as of October 1,1991. Through self-determination contracts (P.L. 93-638), the tribal health pro grams continue the comprehensive preventive and curative service delivery systems initiated by the IHS. The IHS health programs are planned and carried out in cooperation with the Indian tribes.

Today, there are 34 Indian operated Urban Projects consisting of 28 health clinics and six facilities providing community services as of October 1, 1991.

IHS Components

IHS headquarters is located in Rockville, MD. Some of the headquarters' functions are conducted in IHS offices in Phoenix and Tucson, AZ, and

Figure 10–2. Facts about the Indian Health Service. (Reprinted with permission from Indian Health Service. U.S. Department of Health and Human Services, Public Health Service Information Brochure. (1994).

clinics, the separation from their families, the unfamiliar, regimented environment of the hospital, or the unfamiliar behavior of the nurses and physicians, who often display demeaning and demanding attitudes. Their response to this treatment varies. Sometimes it is silence; other times they

Albuquerque, NM. Eleven Area Offices are located in Aberdeen, SD; Anchorage, AK; Albuquerque, NM; Bemidji, MN; Billings, MT; Nashville, TN; Oklahoma City, OK; Phoenix, AZ; Portland, OR; Sacramento, CA; and Window Rock, AZ. IHS has about 14,000 employees. The medical staff is approximately 1,200 physicians and dentists, 100 physician assistants and 2,400 nurses. In addition, IHS employs allied health professionals such as nutritionists, health administrators, engineers, medical records staff and support staff.

The IHS is a large scale comprehensive health care delivery system whose closest counterparts in size and scope are the military and the Veterans Administration health services system.

Special Health Concerns

Tribes are located throughout the United States, including Alaska, from the most rural reservations to urban settings. Some of the most serious health-related problems are injuries, alcoholism, cancer, diabetes, nutritional deficiencies, poor dental health, and mental health problems. Other major health concerns are maternal and child health needs, unhealthy environmental conditions, and problems associated with aging. Two significant areas of health care improvement have been the infant mortality rates and the age-adjusted alcoholism mortality rates. For American Indians and Alaska Natives residing in the reservation states, infant mortality rates dropped 41 percent between 1976-78 and 1986-88. The number of deaths per 1,000 live births fell from 16.4 to 9.7. Likewise, alcohol related deaths declined 38 percent - from 54.5 deaths per 100,000 population in 1978 to 33.9 in 1988.

History

Federal health services for Indians began in the early nineteenth century when Army physicians took steps to curb smallpox and other contagious diseases among tribes living in the vicinity of military posts. Treaties committing the federal government to provide health services to Indians were introduced in 1832 when members of the Winnebago Tribe were promised physician care as partial payment for rights and property ceded to the U.S. government. Transfer of the Bureau of Indian Affairs (BIA) from the War Department to the Department of the Interior in 1849 extended physician services to Indians by emphasizing nonmilitary aspects of Indian administration and developing a corps of civilian field employees. The first federal hospital built to care for Indian people was constructed in the 1880s in Oklahoma Nurses were added to the staff in the 1890s. Professional medical supervision of health activities for Indians began in 1908 with the establishment of the BIA position of Chief Medical Supervisor. Dental services began in 1913. Pharmacy services were organized in 1953. In 1955, responsibility for the health of American Indians and Alaska Natives was transferred from the Department of the Interior's BIA to the Public Health Service (PHS) within the Department of Health, Education and Welfare (currently the Department of Health and Human Services). On January 4, 1988, the Indian Health Service was elevated to agency status and became the seventh agency in the PHS.

Figure 10–2 (*continued*)

leave and do not return. Many Native Americans request that if the ailment is not an emergency, they be allowed to see the medicine man first and then receive treatment from the physician. Often when a sick person is afraid of receiving the care of a physician, the medicine man encourages him to go to the hospital.[51]

Health-care providers must be aware of several factors when they communicate with Native Americans. One of them is recognition of the importance of nonverbal communication. Often Native Americans observe the provider and say very little. The patient may expect the provider to deduce the problem through instinct rather than by the extensive use of questions during history taking. In part, this derives from the belief that direct quoting is intrusive on individual privacy. When examining a Native American with an obvious cough, the provider might be well advised to use a declarative statement—"You have a cough that keeps you awake at night"—and then allow time for the client to respond to the statement.

It is Indian practice to converse in a very low tone of voice. It is expected that the listener will pay attention and listen carefully in order to hear what is being said. It is considered impolite to say, "Huh?" "I beg your pardon," or to give any indication that the communication was not heard. Therefore, an effort should be made to speak with clients in a quiet setting where they will be heard more easily.

Note taking is taboo. Indian history has been passed through generations by means of verbal story telling. Native Americans are sensitive about note taking while they are speaking. When one is taking a history or interviewing, it may be preferable to use memory skills rather than to record notes. This more conversational approach may encourage greater openness between the client and the provider.

Another factor to be considered is differing perceptions of time between the Native American client and the provider. Life on the reservation is not governed by the clock but by the dictates of need. When an Indian moves from the reservation to an urban area, this cultural conflict concerning time often exhibits itself as lateness for specific appointments. One solution would be the use of walk-in clinics.[52]

American Indian Health-Care Manpower

The number of Native Americans enrolled in most health programs in selected health professions is low. Tables 10–4 and 10–5 illustrate this phenom-

TABLE 10–4. PERCENTAGE OF AMERICAN INDIANS ENROLLED IN SELECTED HEALTH PROFESSIONS SCHOOLS: 1990–1991

Program	Total Enrollment	Percentage Native American
Allopathic medicine	65,163	0.4
Osteopathic medicine	6,792	0.5
Dentistry	15,770	0.3
Optometry	4,650	0.5
Pharmacy	22,764	0.3
Podiatry	2,226	0.3
Registered nursing	221,170	0.8
Veterinary medicine	8,420	0.5

From: U.S. Department of Health and Human Services. Health United States 1992; and Healthy People 2000, Review. (Washington, D.C.: United States Department of Health and Human Services, Public Health Service Centers for Disease Control and Prevention National Center for Health Statistics. DHHS Pub. No. (PHS) 93-1232, 1993), pp. 150–151. Reprinted with permission.

TABLE 10–5. PERCENTAGE OF AMERICAN INDIANS ENROLLED IN SCHOOLS FOR SELECTED HEALTH PROFESSIONS COMPARED WITH NON-HISPANIC WHITES: 1990–1991

Profession	Non-Hispanic White (%)	American Indian (%)
Physicians (M.D.)	73.5	0.4
Dentistry	88.5	0.3
Optometry	91.4	0.5
Pharmacy	88.6	0.3
Podiatry	91.3	0.3
Registered nurses	82.8	0.8
Veterinary	92.5	0.5

From: U.S. Department of Health and Human Services, Public Health Service, *Health United States 1992;* and *Healthy People 2000* Review. (Washington, D.C.: Centers for Disease Control and Prevention National Center for Health Statistics. DHHS Pub. No. (PHS) 93-1232, 1993), pp. 150–151. Reprinted with permission.

enon. Efforts must be made to recruit, maintain, and graduate more American Indians into the health professions.

REFERENCES

1. Department of Health and Human Services. *Healthy People 2000.* National Health Promotion and Disease Prevention Objectives—Full Report with Commentary. (Boston: Jones and Bartlett, 1992) p. 38.
2. Fortney, A. J. "Has White Man's Lease Expired?" *Boston Sunday Globe* (23 January 1977); Brown, D. *Bury My Heart at Wounded Knee* (New York: Holt, 1970); Deloria, V., Jr., *Custer Died for Your Sins* (New York: Avon Books, 1969); and Deloria, V., Jr., *Behind the Trail of Broken Treaties* (New York: Delacorte, 1974).
3. Primeaux, H. "American Indian Health Care Practices: A Cross-Cultural Perspective." *Nursing Clinics of North America* 12(1) (March 1977): 57.
4. Zuckoff, M. (1995). "More and More Claiming American Indian Heritage." *Boston Globe.* April 18, 1995, p. 9.
5. Ibid., p. 60.
6. Boyd, D. *Rolling Thunder* (New York: Random House, 1974), p. 96.
7. Ibid., p. 51.
8. Ibid., p. 96.
9. Ibid., p. 199.
10. Ibid., p. 123.
11. Leek, S. *Herbs: Medicine and Mysticism* (Chicago: Henry Regnery, 1975), p. 16.
12. Bilagody, H. "An American Indian Looks at Health Care," in *The Ninth Annual Training Institute for Psychiatrist-Teachers of Practicing Physicians,* eds. Feldman, R., and Buch, D. (Boulder, CO: WICHE, No. 3A30, 1969), p. 21.
13. Ibid., p. 22.
14. Ibid., p. 21.
15. Kluckhohn, C. and Leighton, D. *The Navaho,* rev. ed. (Garden City, NY: Doubleday, 1962), pp. 192–193.
16. Boyd. *Rolling Thunder,* p. 124.

17. Ibid., p. 263.
18. Leek. *Herbs,* p. 16.
19. Wyman, L. C. "Navaho Diagnosticians," in *Medical Care,* eds. Scott, W.R. and Volkhart, E. H. (New York: Wiley, 1966), pp. 8–14.
20. Kluckhohn and Leighton. *The Navaho,* pp. 209–218.
21. Wyman, "Navaho Diagnosticians," p. 14.
22. Ibid., p. 15.
23. Ibid., p. 16.
24. Kluckhohn and Leighton. *The Navaho,* p. 230.
25. Ibid., p. 232.
26. Ibid., p. 233.
27. Ibid., p. 244.
28. Boyd. *Rolling Thunder,* pp. 97–100.
29. Ibid., pp. 101–136.
30. Leek. *Herbs,* p. 17.
31. Ibid., pp. 17–26.
32. Knox, M. E. and Adams, L. "Traditional Health Practices of the Oneida Indian." Research report. College of Nursing, University of Wisconsin, Oshkosh, 1988.
33. Informational pamphlet. Boston, MA: Boston Indian Council, 1985.
34. Aday, L. A. *At Risk in America—The Health and Health Care Needs of Vulnerable Populations in the United States.* San Francisco: Jossey-Bass, 1993, p. 52.
35. Ibid., p. 55.
36. Ibid., p. 65.
37. Ibid., p. 79.
38. Ibid., p. 81.
39. Ibid., pp. 83–84.
40. Department of Health and Human Services, *Healthy People 2000,* p. 38.
41. Littlejohn, H. Interview. Boston State College, Boston, MA. June 1979.
42. American Indian Women of Minnesota, Inc., through a grant sponsored by the Department of Corrections, Minnesota State Task Force on Battered Women, Minnesota Council of Churches and the American Lutheran Church. "Battered Women—Definition," n.d., and "The Dakota View of Domestic Violence" in *The Circle Newspaper of the Boston Indian Council* (February/March 1984): 8–10.
43. Marshall, D. *Family Violence,* sponsored by ACTION Grant 137-0145/1, the Mental Health Association of North Dakota and the Abused Women's Resource Closet, n.d., pp. 9–11.
44. National Indian Health Board. *Reporter,* (Denver, CO, vol. 4 #8, April 1989) p. 8.
45. "What Are the Problems of Urban Native Americans?" (flyer distributed by the Seattle Indian Health Board, Seattle, WA, 1974).
46. Ginnish, J. "The Health Needs of the Boston Indian" (Lecture given at Boston College School of Nursing, 9 April 1975).
47. Bilagody. "Health Care" pp. 22–23.
48. Basherhshur, R., Steeler, W., and Murphy, T. "On Changing Indian Eligibility or Health Care." *American Journal of Public Health* 77 (May, 1989): 690–693.
49. Department of Health and Human Services, *Healthy People 2000,* pp. 602–604.
50. Red Horse, J. "Urban Native-American Health Care" (Minneapolis-St. Paul: unpublished paper, 1976), p. 3.
51. Bilagody. "Health Care," p. 22.
52. Bilagody. "Health Care," pp. 1–2.

ANNOTATED BIBLIOGRAPHY

Galloway, M. R. U., ed. *Aunt Mary, Tell Me a Story.* Cherokee, NC: Cherokee Commu-
nications, 1990.
  This book is a collection of Cherokee legends and tales. These stories were woven
into Galloway's life by her Aunt Mary as she grew up. They are the stories told by
the people of the Eastern band of the Cherokee nation who live in the Great Smokey
Mountains, in Cherokee, North Carolina.
Hauptman, L. M. and Wherry, J. D. *The Pequots in Southern New England—The Fall and
Rise of an American Indian Nation.* Norman, OK: University of Oklahoma Press, 1990.
  This collection of essays, originally presented in 1987, reveals the long-neglected
history of New England Indians.
Jilek W. G. *Indians Healing—Shamanic Ceremonialism in the Pacific Northwest Today.*
Blaine, WA: Hancock House, 1992.
  Jilek describes these ancient ceremonies in a new light. His goal is to dispel mis-
conceptions and negative opinions by showing that the traditional rituals have
well-defined therapeutic effects.
Knudtson, P. and Suzuki, D. *Wisdom of the Elders.* Toronto: Stoddart Publishing Co.,
Ltd., 1992.
  This book explores beliefs about the delicate relationship between humans, na-
ture, and the environment as held by two diametrically opposed forces: Western sci-
ence and the ancient wisdom of indigenous peoples around the world.
Kunitz, S. J. and Levy, J. E. *Navajo Aging—The Transition from Family to Institutional
Support.* Tucson: University of Arizona Press, 1991.
  This book chronicles the effects of social change on traditional Navajo people and
the social changes that have resulted.
Lake, M. G. *Native Healer Initiation into an Art.* Wheaton, IL: Quest Books, 1991.
  Lake, a healer and spiritual teacher, explains how a person is called to be a med-
icine man or woman and the trials and tests that person must undergo. He provides
the reader with a glimpse into the world of Native American healing.
Nerburn, K. and Mengelkoch, L., eds. *Native American Wisdom.* San Rafael, CA: New
World Library, 1991.
  This profound, enlightened, touching, and inspired book is a collection of words
and sayings compiled from American Indians. It speaks of the interconnectedness
of all nature and raises questions about the relationships and events of today.
Wall, S. and Arden, H. *Wisdomkeepers Meetings with Native American Spiritual Elders.*
Hillsboro, OR: Beyond Words Publishing Co., 1990.
  This beautifully illustrated and worded text takes the reader on a spiritual jour-
ney into the lives, minds, and natural world philosophy of Native American spiritual elders. It is a book that helps one understand the spiritual wisdom of elder
American Indians.

FURTHER SUGGESTED READINGS

Articles

Allen, J. R. "The Indian Adolescent: Psycho-Social Tasks of the Plains Indian of Western Oklahoma." *American Journal of Ortho-psychiatry* 43 (April 1973): 368–375.

Bashshur, R., Steeler, W., and Murphy, T. "On Changing Indian Eligibility for Health Care." *American Journal of Public Health* 77 (May 1989): 690–693.

Bell, R. "Prominence of Women in Navajo Healing Beliefs and Values." *Nursing and Health Care.* 15(5) (May, 1994): 232–240.

Bilagody, H. "An American Indian Looks at Health Care," in *The Ninth Annual Training Institute for Psychiatrist-Teachers of Practicing Physicians,* ed. Feldman, R. and Buch, D. (Boulder, CO: WICHE, No. 3A30, 1969), p. 21.

Bose, D. P., and Welsh, J. D. "Lactose Malabsorbtion in Oklahoma Indians." *American Journal of Clinical Nutrition* 26 (December 1973): 1320–1322.

Brosseau, J. D., et al. "Diabetes among the Three Affiliated Tribes: Correlation with Degree of Indian Inheritance." *American Journal of Public Health* 69(12) (December 1979): 1277–1278.

Colorado, P. "Wayfinding and the New Sun—Indigenous Science in the Modern World." *Noetic Sciences Review.* (Summer, 1992): 19–22.

Cohen, E. "After Wounded Knee: The Feeding of the American Indian." *Food Management,* (April 1974): 28–80.

Cress, J. N., and O'Donnell, J. P. "The Self-esteem Inventory and the Oglala Sioux: A Validation Study." *Journal of Social Psychology* 97 (October 1975): 135–136.

Crowell, S. "Life on the Largest Reservation: Poverty and Progress in the Navajo Nation." *Civil Rights Digest* 6 (Fall 1973): 3–9.

Farris, L. S. "Approaches to Caring for the American Indian Maternity Patient." *American Journal of Maternal Child Nursing* 1(2) (March/April 1976): 80–87.

Fortney, A. J. "Has White Man's Lease Expired?" *Boston Sunday Globe* (23 January 1977).

Fuchs, M. and Bashur, R. "Use of Traditional Indian Medicine among Urban Native Americans." *Medical Care* 13 (November 1975): 915–927.

Gillette, J. B. "Sweetgrass Saga," *Historic Preservation.* 46(5) (1994): 28–33.

Hagey, R. and Buller, E. "Drumming and Dancing: A New Rhythm in Nursing Care—Native Diabetes Project for Cree and Ojibway People in Toronto." *Canadian Nurse* 70(4) (April 1983): 28–31.

Hardy, M. K. and Burckhardt, M. A. "Nursing the Navaho." *American Journal of Nursing* 77 (January 1977): 95–96.

Hostetter, T. "Entering a Native American Community to Assess Nurses' Continuing Education Needs—in the Area of Mental Health." *Journal of Continuing Education in Nursing* 15(5) (September/October 1984): 188–190.

Johnson, C. -A. "A Case of a Psychotic Navaho Indian Male," in *Social Interaction and Patient Care,* ed. Skipper, J.K. Jr., and Leonard, R.C. Philadelphia: Lippincott, 1965, pp. 184–195.

King, D. H., ed. "Fading Voices." *Journal of Cherokee Studies,* Special Edition, XIV (1991): entire journal.

Kniep-Hardy, M. and Burkhardt, M. A. "Nursing the Navajo." *American Journal of Nursing* (January 1977): 95–96.

Knox, M. E. and Adams, L. "Traditional Health Practices of the Oneida Indian." Research report. College of Nursing, University of Wisconsin, Oshkosh, 1988.

Kunitz, S. J. "Navaho and Hopi Fertility 1971–1972." *Human Biology* 46 (September 1974): 435–451.

McCauley, M. A. "Indian Nurse Considers Cultural Traits." *American Journal of Nursing* (May 1975): 5, 15.

Maynard, E. "Negative Ethnic Image among Oglala Sioux High School Students." *Pine Ridge Research Bulletin* 6 (December 1968): 18–25.

Nagel, G. S. "American Indian Life: Unemployment, Ill Health, and Skid Rows." *Current* (January 1975): 34–42.

Native Peoples. A magazine that is dedicated to the sensitive portrayal of the arts and lifeways of American Indians and is published quarterly. It is affiliated with the National Museum of the American Indian, Smithsonian Institution.

Neumann, A. K. "American Indian Success Study: Factors Influencing Success in a Sample of Oklahoma Cheyenne and Arapaho Indians." Paper presented at the American Public Health Association Convention, 1988.

Nutting, P. A., Freeman, W. L., Risser, D. R., et al. "Cancer Incidence among American Indians and Alaska Natives, 1980 through 1987." *American Journal of Public Health,* 83(11) (1993): 1589–1598.

Peretti, P. O. "Enforced Acculturation and Indian-White Relations." *Indian Historian* 6 (Winter 1973): 38–52.

Primeaux, M. "American Indian Health Care Practices: A Cross-Cultural Perspective." *Nursing Clinics of North America* 12 (March 1977): 55–65.

Primeaux, M. "Caring for the American Indian Patient." *American Journal of Nursing* 77 (January 1977): 91–94.

Saland, J., McNamara, H., and Cohen, M. I. "Navaho Jaundice: A Variant of Neonatal Hyperbilirubinemia Associated with Breast Feeding." *Journal of Pediatrics* 85 (August 1974): 271–275.

Satz, K. J. "Integrating Navajo Tradition into Maternal–Child Nursing." *Image* 15(3) (October 1982): 89–91.

Sobralske, M. C. "Perceptions of Health: Navajo Indians." *Topics in Clinical Nursing* 7(3) (October 1985): 32–39.

Spencer, P .U. "A Native American Worldview." *Noetic Sciences Review.* (Summer 1990): 100–104.

Statz, K. J. "Integrating Navajo Tradition into Maternal–Child Nursing." *Image* 14(3) (October 1983): 89–91.

Sugarman, J. R., Soderberg, R., Gordon, J. E., et al. "Racial Misclassification of American Indians: Its Effect on Injury Rates in Oregon, 1989 through 1990." *American Journal of Public Health,* 83(5) (1993): 681–684.

Wauneka, A. D. "Helping a People to Understand." *American Journal of Nursing* 62(7) (July 1962): 88–90.

Webster, N. "WARN against Battering on the Reservations." *Guardian* (4 April 1984): 4.

Westermeyer, J. "The Drunken Indian: Myths and Realities." *Psychiatric Annals* 4(9) (November 1974): 29–35.

RESOURCES

The IHS Primary Care Provider—a monthly publication of the IHS Clinical Support Center. It can be obtained from:
Department of Health and Human Services
Indian Health Service/PHS
4212 North 16th Street
Phoenix, AZ 85016
(602) 263-1581

The NIHB Health Reporter—a monthly newsletter. It can be obtained from:
National Indian Health Board
50 S. Steele, Suite 500
Denver, CO 80209
(303) 394-3500

Department of Health and Human Services
Public Health Service
Health Services Administration
Indian Health Service
5600 Fishers Lane
Rockville, MD 20857

American Indian Health Care Association
245 East Sixth Street, Suite 499
St. Paul, MN 55101
(612) 293-0233

U.S. Department of Health and Human Services
Public Health Service
Alcohol, Drug Abuse, and Mental Health Administration

Prevention Resource Guide—American Indians and Native Alaskans
Office for Substance Abuse Prevention
1-800-729-6686

See Appendix VIII for further listings

11 Chapter

Health and Illness in the Asian/Pacific Islander American Community

"But when she arrived in the new country, the immigration officials pulled her swan away from her leaving the woman fluttering her arms and with only one swan feather for a memory."

—Amy Tan

The more than 11 million people who constitute the Asian and Pacific Islander communities are the nation's third largest emerging majority group. This group is characterized by its diversity: more than 30 different languages are spoken and there are a similar number of cultures.[1] The National Center for Health Statistics is now using the following categories to code this population:

Coded prior to 1992	*Expanded coding beginning with 1992*
Chinese	Vietnamese
Japanese	Asian Indian
Hawaiian	Korean
Filipino	Samoan
Other API	Guamanian
	Remaining API[2]

This chapter focuses on the traditional health and illness beliefs and practices of the Chinese Americans because those of many of the other Asians/Pacific Islanders are derived in part from the Chinese tradition.

BACKGROUND

Chinese immigration to the United States began over 100 years ago. In 1850, there were only 1000 Chinese inhabitants in this country; in 1880, there were well over 100,000. This rapid increase arose in part from the discovery of gold in California and in part from the need for cheap labor to build the transcontinental railroads. The immigrants were laborers who met the needs of the dominant society. Like many early immigrant groups, they came here intending only to stay as temporary workers. Mainly men came. They clung closely to their customs and beliefs and stayed together in their own communities. The hopes that many had for a better life when they came to the United States did not materialize. Subsequently, many of the workers and their kin returned to China before 1930. Part of the disharmony and disenchantment occurred because these immigrants were not white and did not have the same culture and habits as whites. For these reasons, they were not welcomed, and many jobs were not open to them. For example, Chinese immigrant workers were excluded from many mining, construction, and other hard-labor jobs even though the transcontinental railroad was constructed mainly by Chinese laborers. Between 1880 and 1930, the Chinese population declined by nearly 20%. One factor that helped perpetuate this decline in population was a series of exclusion acts halting further immigration. The people who remained behind were relegated to menial jobs, such as cooking and dishwashing. The Chinese workers first took these jobs in the West and later moved eastward throughout the United States. They tended to move to cities where they were allowed to let their entrepreneurial talents surface—their main pursuits included running small laundries, food shops, and restaurants.

The people settled in tightly knit groups in urban neighborhoods that took the name "Chinatown." Here they were able to maintain the ancient traditions of their homeland. They were hard workers, and in spite of the dull, menial jobs usually available to them, they were able to survive.

Both U.S. immigration laws and political problems in China had an effect on the nature of today's Chinese population. When the exclusion acts were passed, many men were left alone in this country without the possibility of their families joining them. For this reason, a great majority of the men spent many years alone. In addition, the political oppression experienced by the Chinese in the United States was compounded when, at a time immigration laws were relaxed here after World War II, people were unable to return to or leave China because of that country's restrictive new regulations. By 1965, however, a large number of refugees who had relatives here were able to come to this country. They settled in the Chinatowns of America, causing the population of these areas to swell. The rate of increase since 1965 has been 10% per year.

TRADITIONAL DEFINITIONS OF HEALTH AND ILLNESS

Chinese medicine teaches that health is a state of spiritual and physical harmony with nature. In ancient China, the task of the physician was to prevent illness. A first-class physician not only cured an illness but could also prevent disease from occurring. A second-class physician had to wait for patients to become ill before they could be treated. The physician was paid by the patient while the patient was healthy. When illness occurred, payments stopped. Indeed, the physician not only was not paid for his services when the patient became ill, but he also had to provide and pay for the needed medicine.[3]

To understand the Chinese philosophy of health and illness, it is necessary to look back at the age-old philosophies from which more current ideas have evolved. The foundation rests in the religion and philosophy of Taoism. Taoism originated with a man named Lao-Tzu, who is believed to have been born about 604 BC. The word *Tao* has several meanings: way, path, or discourse. On the spiritual level, it is the way of ultimate reality. It is the way of all nature, the primeval law that regulates all heavenly and earthly matters. To live according to the Tao, one must adapt oneself to the order of nature. Chinese medical works revere the ancient sages who knew the way and "led their lives in *Tao*."[4]

The Chinese view the universe as a vast, indivisible entity; each being has a definite function within it. No one thing can exist without the existence of the others. Each is linked in a chain that consists of concepts related to each other in harmonious balance. Violating this harmony is like hurling chaos, wars, and catastrophes on humankind—the end result of which is illness. Individuals must adjust themselves wholly within the environment. Five elements—wood, fire, earth, metal, and water—constitute the guiding principles of humankind's surroundings. These elements can both create and destroy each other. For example, "wood creates fire," "two pieces of wood rubbed together produce a spark," "wood destroys earth," "the tree sucks strength from the earth." The guiding principles arise from this "correspondences" theory[5] of the cosmos. Tables 11-1 and 11-2 highlight common elements of Asian/Pacific Island cultures and give examples of cultural phenomena affecting health care.

For a person to remain healthy, his or her actions must conform to the mobile cycle of the correspondences. The exact directions for achieving this were written in such works as the *Lu Chih Ch'un Ch'iu* (Spring and Autumn Annals) written by Lu Pu Wei, who died circa 230 BC.

The *holistic concept,* as explained by Dr. P. K. Chan,[6] is an important idea of traditional Chinese medicine in preventing and treating diseases. It has two main components.

TABLE 11–1. HIGHLIGHTS OF COMMON ELEMENTS OF ASIAN CULTURES

The teachings of Asian religions, including Confucianism and Buddhism, are complementary and have played a major role in the shaping of the cultural values in Asia.

Buddhism teaches:
- Harmony/nonconfrontation—(silence as a virtue)
- Respect for life
- Moderation in behavior, self-discipline, patience, humility, modesty, friendliness, selflessness, dedication, and loyalty to others
- Individualism devalued

Confucianism teaches:
- Achievement of harmony through observing the five basic relationships of society
  1. Ruler and ruled
  2. Father and son
  3. Husband and wife
  4. Older and younger brother
  5. Between friends
- Hierarchical roles, social class system, clearly defined behavioral code
- Importance of family
- Filial piety and respect for elders
- High regard for education and learning

Taoism teaches:
- Harmony between humans and nature
- Nature is benign because *yin* (evil) and *yang* (good) are in balance and harmony.
- Happiness and a long life
- Charity, simplicity, patience, avoidance of confrontation and an indirect approach to problems

Shamanism teaches:
- Emphasis on nature
- Everything in nature is endowed with a spirit

From: Romo, R. G. "Hispanic Health Traditions and Issues" presented at the Minnesota Health Educators Conference, *Health Education: Expanding Our Horizons,* May 3, 1995. Reprinted with permission.

1. A human body is regarded as an integral organism, with special emphasis on the harmonic and integral interrelationship between the viscera and the superficial structures in these close physiological connections, and their mutual pathological connection. In Chinese medicine, the local pathological changes always are considered in conjunction with other tissues and organs of the entire body, instead of considered alone.
2. Special attention is paid to the integration of the human body with the external environment. The onset, evolution, and change of disease are considered in conjunction with the geographic, social, and other environmental factors.[7]

Four thousand years before the English physician William Harvey described the circulatory system in 1628, *Huang-ti Nei Ching* (Yellow Emperor's Book of Internal Medicine) was written. This is the first known volume that

TABLE 11–2. EXAMPLES OF CULTURAL PHENOMENA AFFECTING HEALTH CARE AMONG AMERICANS OF ASIAN/PACIFIC ISLANDER HERITAGE

Nations of Origin:	China, Japan, Hawaii, the Philippines, Viet Nam, Asian India, Korea, Samoa, Guam, and the remaining Asian/Pacific islands
Environmental Control:	Traditional health and illness beliefs may continue to be observed by "traditional" people
Biological Variations:	Hypertension Liver cancer Stomach cancer Coccidioidomycosis Lactose intolerance Thalassemia
Social Organization:	Family—hierarchical structure, loyalty Large, extended family networks Devotion to tradition Many religions, including Taoism, Buddhism, Islam, and Christianity Community social organizations
Communication:	National language preference Dialects, written characters Use of silence Nonverbal and contextual cueing
Space:	Noncontact people
Time Orientation:	Present

Adapted from: Spector, R. "Culture, Ethnicity, and Nursing," in *Fundamentals of Nursing* eds. Potter, P. and Perry, A. (St. Louis: Mosby-Yearbook, 1992), p. 101. Reprinted with permission.

describes the circulation of blood. It described the oxygen-carrying powers of blood and defined the two basic world principles: *yin* and *yang*, powers that regulate the universe. *Yang* represents the male, positive energy that produces light, warmth, and fullness. *Yin* represents the female, negative energy—the force of darkness, cold, and emptiness. *Yin* and *yang* exert power not only over the universe but also over human beings.

Yin and *yang* were further explained by Dr. Chan as having been originally a philosophical theory in ancient China. Later, the theory was incorporated into Chinese medicine. The theory holds that "everything in the Universe contains two aspects—*yin* and *yang*, which are in opposition and also in unison. Hence, matters are impelled to develop and change."[8] In traditional Chinese medicine, the phenomena are further explained as follows:

- Matters that are dynamic, external, upward, ascending, and brilliant belong to *yang*.
- Those that are static, internal, downward, descending, dull, regressive, and hypoactive are *yin*.
- *Yin* flourishing and *yang* vivified steadily is the state of health. *Yin* and *yang* regulate themselves in the basic principle to promote the normal activities of life.

- Illness is the disharmony of *yin* and *yang*, a disharmony that leads to pathological changes, with excesses of one and deficiencies of the other, disturbances of vital energy and blood, malfunctioning of the viscera, and so forth.[9]

The various parts of the human body correspond to the dualistic principles of *yin* and *yang*. The inside of the body is *yin;* the surface of the body is *yang.* The front part of the body is *yin;* the back is *yang.* The five *ts'ang* viscera—liver, heart, spleen, lungs, and kidney—are *yang;* the six *fu* structures—gallbladder, stomach, large intestine, small intestine, bladder, and "warmer"—are *yin.* (The "warmer" is now believed to be the lymph system.) The diseases of winter and spring are *yin;* those of summer and fall are *yang.* The pulses are controlled by *yin* and *yang.* If *yin* is too strong, the person is nervous and apprehensive and catches colds easily. If the individual does not balance *yin* and *yang* properly, his or her life will be short. Half of the *yin* forces are depleted by age 40, at 40 the body is sluggish, and at 60 the *yin* is totally depleted, at which time the body deteriorates. *Yin* stores the vital strength of life. *Yang* protects the body from outside forces, and it too must be carefully maintained. If *yang* is not cared for, the viscera are thrown into disorder, and circulation ceases. *Yin* and *yang* cannot be injured by evil influences. When *yin* and *yang* are sound, the person lives in peaceful interaction with mind and body in proper order.[10]

Chinese medicine has a long history. The Emperor Shen Nung, who died in 2697 BC, was known as the patron god of agriculture. He was given this title because of the 70 experiments he performed on himself by swallowing a different plant every day and studying the effects. During this period of self-experimentation, Nung discovered many poisonous herbs and rendered them harmless by the use of antidotes, which he also discovered. His patron element was fire, for which he was known as the Red Emperor. The Emperor Shen Nung was followed by Huang-ti, whose patron element was earth. Huang-ti was known as the Yellow Emperor and ruled from 2697 BC to 2595 BC. The greater part of his life was devoted to the study of medicine. Many people ascribe to him the recording of the *Nei Ching,* the book that embraces the entire realm of Chinese medical knowledge. The treatments described in the *Nei Ching*—which became characteristic of Chinese medical practice—are almost totally aimed at reestablishing balances that are lost within the body when illness occurs. Disrupted harmonies are regarded as the sole cause of disease. Surgery was rarely resorted to, and when it was, it was used primarily to remove malignant tumors. The *Nei Ching* is a dialogue between Huang-ti and his minister, Ch'i Po. It begins with the concept of the Tao and the cosmological patterns of the universe and goes on to describe the powers of the *yin* and *yang.* This learned treatise discusses in great detail the therapy of the pulses and how a diagnosis can be made on the basis of alterations in the pulse beat. It also described various kinds of fevers and the use of acupuncture.[11]

The Chinese view their bodies as a gift given to them by their parents and forebears. A person's body is not his or her personal property. It must be cared for and well maintained. Confucius taught that "only those shall be truly revered who at the end of their lives will return their physical bodies whole and sound."

The body is composed of five solid organs (*ts'ang*), which collect and store secretions, and five hollow organs (*fu*), which excrete. The heart and liver are regarded as the noble organs. The head is the storage chamber for knowledge, the back is the home of the chest, the loins store the kidneys, the knees store the muscles, and the bones store the marrow.

The Chinese view the functions of the various organs as comparable to the functions of persons in positions of power and responsibility in the government. For example, the heart is the ruler over all other civil servants, the lungs are the administrators, the liver is the general who initiates all the strategic actions, and the gallbladder is the decision maker.

The organs have a complex relationship that maintains the balance and harmony of the body. Each organ is associated with a color. For example, the heart—which works in accordance with the pulse, controls the kidneys, and harmonizes with bitter flavors—is red. In addition, the organs have what is referred to as an "aura," the meaning of which, in the medical context, is health. The aura is determined by the color of the organ. In the balanced, healthy body, the colors look fresh and shiny.[12]

Disease is caused by an upset in the balance of *yin* and *yang*. The weather, too, has an effect on the body's balance and the body's relationship to *yin* and *yang*. For example, heat can be injurious to the heart, and cold is injurious to the lungs. Overexertion is harmful to the body. Prolonged sitting is harmful to the flesh and spine, and prolonged lying in bed can be harmful to the lungs.

Disease is diagnosed by the Chinese physician through inspection and palpation. During inspection, the Chinese physician looks at the tongue (glossoscopy), listens and smells (osphretics), and asks questions (anamnesis). During palpation, the physician feels the pulse (sphygmopalpation).

The Chinese believe that there are many different pulse types, which are all grouped together and must be felt with the three middle fingers. The pulse is considered the storehouse of the blood, and a person with a strong, regular pulse is considered to be in good health. By the nature of the pulse, the physician is able to determine various illnesses. For example, if the pulse is weak and skips beats, the person may have a cardiac problem. If the pulse is too strong, the person's body is distended.[13]

There are six different pulses, three in each hand. Each pulse is specifically related to various organs, and each pulse has its own characteristics. According to ancient Chinese sources, there are 15 ways of characterizing the pulses. Each of these descriptions accurately determines the diagnosis. There are seven *piao* pulses (superficial) and eight *li* pulses (sunken). An example of an illness that manifests with a *piao* pulse is headache; anxiety manifests with a *li* pulse. The pulses also take on a specific nature with various conditions.

For example, specific pulses are associated with epilepsy, pregnancy, and the time just before death.[14]

The Chinese physician is aided in making a diagnosis by the appearance of the patient's tongue. More than 100 conditions can be determined by glossoscopic examination. The color of the tongue and the part of the tongue that does not appear normal are the essential clues to the diagnosis.[15]

Breast cancer has been known to the Chinese since early times. "The disease begins with a knot in the breast, the size of a bean, and gradually swells to the size of an egg. After seven or eight months it perforates. When it has perforated, it is very difficult to cure."[16]

TRADITIONAL METHODS OF PREVENTION:
HEALTH MAINTENANCE AND PROTECTION

The Chinese often prepare amulets to prevent evil spirits. These amulets consist of a charm with an idol or Chinese character painted in red or black ink and written on a strip of yellow paper. These amulets are hung over a door or pasted on a curtain or wall, worn in the hair, or placed in a red bag and pinned on clothing. The paper may be burned and the ashes mixed in hot tea and swallowed to ward off evil. Jade is believed to be the most precious of all stones because it is seen as the giver of children, health, immortality, wisdom, power, victory, growth, and food. Jade charms are worn to bring health, and should they turn dull or break, the wearer will surely meet misfortune. The charm prevents harm and accidents. Children are kept safe with jade charms, and adults are made pure, just, humane, and intelligent by wearing them.[17]

TRADITIONAL METHODS OF HEALING:
HEALTH RESTORATION

Traditional Healers
The physician was the primary healer in Chinese medicine. Physicians who had to treat women encountered numerous difficulties because men were not allowed to touch directly women who were not family members. Thus, a diagnosis might be made through a ribbon that was attached to the woman's wrist. As an alternative to demonstrating areas of pain or discomfort on a woman's body, an alabaster figure was substituted. The area of pain was pointed out on the figurine.[18]

Not much is known about women doctors except that they did exist. Women were known to possess a large store of medical talent. There were also midwives and female shamans. The female shamans possessed gifts of prophecy. They danced themselves into ecstatic trances and had a profound effect on the people around them. As the knowledge that these women possessed was neither known nor understood by the general population, they were feared rather than respected. They were said to know all there was to know about life, death, and birth.[19]

Chinese Pediatrics

Babies are breastfed because neither cows' milk nor goats' milk is acceptable to the Chinese. Sometimes children are nursed for as long as four or five years.

Since early times, the Chinese have known about and practiced immunization against smallpox. A child was inoculated with the live virus from the crust of a pustule from a small pox victim. The crust was ground into a powder, and this powder was subsequently blown into the nose of the healthy child through the lumen of a small tube. If the child was healthy, he did not generally develop a full-blown case of smallpox but instead acquired immunity to this dreaded disease.[20]

Acupuncture

Acupuncture is an ancient Chinese practice of puncturing the body to cure disease or relieve pain. The body is punctured with special metal needles at points that are precisely predetermined for the treatment of specific symptoms. According to one source, the earliest use of this method was recorded between 106 BC and 200 AD. According to other sources, however, it was used even earlier. This treatment modality stems from diagnostic procedures described earlier. The most important aspect of the practice of acupuncture is the acquired skill and ability to know precisely where to puncture the skin. Nine needles are used in acupuncture, each with a specific purpose. The following is a list of the needles and their purposes.[21]

- Superficial pricking: arrowhead needle
- Massaging: round needle
- Knocking or pressing: blunt needle
- Venous pricking: sharp three-edged needle
- Evacuating pus: swordlike needle
- Rapid pricking: sharp, round needle
- Puncturing thick muscle: sharp, round needle
- Puncturing thick muscle: long needle
- Treating arthritis: large needle
- Most extensively used: filiform needle

The specific points of the body into which the needles are inserted are known as *meridians*. Acupuncture is based on the concept that certain meridians extend internally throughout the body in a fixed network. There are 365 points on the skin where these lines emerge. Since all of the networks merge and have their outlets on the skin, the way to treat internal problems is to puncture the meridians, which are also categorically identified in terms of *yin* and *yang*, as are the diseases. The treatment goal is to restore the balance of *yin* and *yang*.[22] The practice of this art is far too complex to explain in great detail in these pages. A suggested reading list on the subject is included in the bibliography at the end of the chapter.

Readers may find it interesting to visit acupuncture clinics in their area. After the therapist carefully explains the art and science of acupuncture, one may be able to grasp the fundamental concepts of this ancient treatment. The practice of acupuncture is based in antiquity, yet it took a long time for it to be accepted as a legitimate method of healing by practitioners of the Western medical system. Currently, numerous acupuncture clinics attract a fair number of non-Asians, and acupuncture is being used as a method of anesthesia in some hospitals.

Moxibustion

Moxibustion has been practiced for as long as acupuncture. Its purpose, too, is to restore the proper balance of *yin* and *yang*. Moxibustion is based on the therapeutic value of heat, whereas acupuncture is a cold treatment. Acupuncture is used mainly in diseases in which there is an excess of *yang*, and moxibustion is used in diseases in which there is an excess of *yin*. Moxibustion is performed by heating pulverized wormwood and applying this concoction directly to the skin over certain specific meridians. Great caution must be used in this application because it cannot be applied to all the meridians that are used for acupuncture. Moxibustion is believed to be most useful during the period of labor and delivery, if applied properly.[23]

Additional ancient forms of treatment, such as local and whole body massage and special exercises, are performed to prolong life.

Herbal Remedies

Medicinal herbs were used widely in the practice of ancient Chinese healing. Many of these herbs are available and in use today.

Herbology is an interesting subject. The gathering season of an herb was important for its effect. It was believed that some herbs were better if gathered at night and that others were more effective if gathered at dawn. The ancient sages understood quite well the dynamics of growth. It is known today that a plant may not be effective if the dew has been allowed to dry on its leaves.[24] The herbalist believes that the ginseng root must be harvested only at midnight in a full moon if it is to have therapeutic value. Ginseng's therapeutic value is due to its nonspecific action. The herb, which is derived from the root of a plant that resembles a man,* is recommended for use in more than two dozen ailments, including anemia, colics, depression, indigestion, impotence, and rheumatism.[25] It has maintained its reputation for centuries and continues to be a highly valued and widely used substance.

To release all the therapeutic properties of ginseng and to prepare it properly are of paramount importance. Ginseng must not be prepared in any-

---

*Early Chinese healers believed that if the name of a plant resembled the disease in question, the plant would be effective in the treatment of the disease.

thing made of metal because it is believed that some of the necessary con-
stituents are leeched out by the action of the metal. It must be stored in crock-
ery. It is boiled in water until only a sediment remains. This sediment is
pressed into a crock and stored. Some of the specific uses of ginseng are

- *To stimulate digestion*
  Rub ginseng to a powder, mix with the white of an egg, and take three
  times per day.
- *As a sedative*
  Prepare a light broth of ginseng and bamboo leaves.
- *For faintness after childbirth*
  Administer a strong brew of ginseng several times a day.
- *As a restorative for frail children*
  Give a dash of raw, minced ginseng several times per day.[26]

There are many Chinese medicinal herbs, but none is so famous as ginseng.

I had the opportunity to visit, with one of my Asian American students,
an import–export store in Boston's Chinatown where they sell Chinese
herbs—if one has the proper prescriptions. The front of the store is a gift shop
that attracts tourists. A room in the back is separated from the rest of the store.
We were allowed to enter this room when the student explained to the proprietor, in Chinese, that I was her teacher and that she had brought me to the
store to purchase herbs. We stayed there for quite a long time, observing the
people who came in with prescriptions. The man carefully weighed different
herbs, mixing them together, and dispensed them. We asked to purchase
some of the herbs that he took from the drawers lining the entire wall behind
him. He refused to sell us anything except some of the preparations that were
on the counter because a prescription was necessary to purchase any of the
herbal compounds that he prepared. Undaunted, we purchased a wide variety of herbs that could be used for indigestion, in addition to ointments and
liniments used for sore muscles and sprains.

In addition to herbs and plants, the Chinese use other products with
medicinal and healing properties. Some of these products were used also in
ancient Europe and are still used today. For example, in China, boys' urine
was used to cure lung diseases, soothe inflamed throats, and dissolve blood
clots in pregnant women. In Europe, it was used during the two world wars
as emergency treatment for open wounds. Urea is still used today as a treatment that promotes the healing of wounds. Other popular Chinese remedies
include[27]

- *Deer antlers*
  Used to strengthen bones, increase a man's potency, and dispel
  nightmares
- *Lime calcium*
  Used to clear excessive mucus
- *Quicksilver*
  Used externally to treat venereal diseases

- *Rhinoceros horns*
  Highly effective when applied to pus boils; an antitoxin for snakebites
- *Turtle shells*
  Used to stimulate weak kidneys and to remove gallstones
- *Snake flesh*
  Eaten as a delicacy to keep eyes healthy and vision clear
- *Seahorses*
  Pulverized and used to treat gout

CURRENT HEALTH PROBLEMS

In many instances, people who were born in the United States into families established here for generations are largely indistinguishable from the general population in their health-care beliefs. Other groups, however, especially new immigrants, differ from the general population on many social and health-related issues. National data do not cover population because it is relatively small; however, it is possible to determine group morbidity and mortality rates at state statistical levels. Most of the studies are conducted in California, which has the largest Asian/Pacific Islander population. The following are examples of the findings:

- The breast cancer incidence for Native Hawaiian women is 111 per 100,000 women compared with 86 per 100,000 white women.
- The lung cancer rate is 18% higher among Southeast Asian men than for the white men.
- The liver cancer rate is more than 12 times higher among Southeast Asians than within the white population.
- The incidence of tuberculosis is 40 times higher among Southeast Asians than for the total population.
- There are higher rates of hepatitis B among Southeast Asians.[28]

Poor health is found among the residents of Chinatowns partly because of poor working conditions. Many people work long hours in restaurants and laundries and receive the lowest possible wages for their hard work. Many cannot afford even minimal, let alone preventive, health care.[29]

Americans of Asian and Pacific Island heritage experience unique barriers, including linguistic and cultural differences, when they try to access the unfamiliar health care system.[30]

Language difficulties and adherence to native Chinese culture compound problems already associated with poverty, crowding, and poor health. Many people still prefer the traditional forms of Chinese medicine and seek help from Chinatown "physicians" who treat them with traditional herbs and other methods. Often, Asian people do not seek help from the Western system at all. Others use Chinese methods in conjunction with Western methods of health care, although the Chinese find many aspects of Western medicine distasteful. For example, they cannot understand why so many diagnostic tests, some of which are painful, are necessary. They do, however, accept the practice of immunization and the use of x-rays.

They are most upset by the practice of drawing blood. Chinese people cannot understand why the often frequent taking of blood samples considered routine in Western medicine are necessary. Blood is seen as the source of life for the entire body, and they believe that it is not regenerated. The Chinese people also believe that a good physician should be able to make a diagnosis simply by examining a person. Consequently, they do not react well to the often painful procedures used in Western diagnostic work-ups. Some people—because of their distaste for this procedure—leave the Western system rather than tolerate the pain. The Chinese have deep respect for their bodies and believe that it is best to die with their bodies intact. For this reason, many people refuse surgery or consent to it only under the most dire circumstances.[31] This reluctance to undergo intrusive surgical procedures has deep implications for those concerned with providing health care to Asian Americans. Even the Asian reluctance to have blood drawn for diagnostic tests may have its roots in the revered teachings of Confucius.

The hospital is an alien place to the Chinese. Not only are the customs and practices strange, but also the patients often are isolated from the rest of their people, which enhances the language barrier and feelings of helplessness. Something as basic as food creates another problem. Hospital food is strange to Asian patients and is served in an unfamiliar manner. The typical Chinese patient rarely complains about what bothers him or her. Often the only indication that there may be a problem is an untouched food tray and the silent withdrawal of the patient. Unfortunately, the silence may be regarded by the nurses as reflecting good, complacent behavior, and the health-care team exerts little energy to go beyond the assumption. The Chinese patient who says little and complies with all treatment is seen as stoic, and there is little awareness that deep problems may underlie this "exemplary" behavior. Ignorance on the part of health-care workers may cause the patient a great deal of suffering.

Much action has been taken in recent years to make Western health care more available and appealing to the Chinese. In Boston, for example, is a health clinic staffed primarily by Chinese-speaking nurses and physicians who work as paid employees and as volunteers. Most of the common health-related pamphlets have been translated into Chinese and are distributed to the patients. Booklets on such topics as breast self-examination and how to quit smoking are available. Since the language spoken in the clinic is mandarin Chinese, the problem of interpreters has been largely eliminated. The care is personal, and the clients are made to feel comfortable. Unnecessary and painful tests are avoided as much as possible. In addition, the clinic, which is open for long hours, provides social services and employment placements and is quite popular with the community. Although it began as a part-time, storefront operation, the clinic is now housed in its own building.[32]

TABLE 11–3. PERCENTAGE OF AMERICANS OF ASIAN/PACIFIC ISLANDER HERITAGE ENROLLMENT IN SELECTED HEALTH PROFESSIONS SCHOOLS: 1990–1991

Program	Total Enrollment	Percentage Asian
Allopathic medicine	65,163	12.9
Osteopathic medicine	6,792	8.6
Dentistry	15,770	16.0
Optometry	4,050	13.0
Pharmacy	22,764	9.4
Podiatry	2,226	7.3
Registered nursing	221,170	3.0
Veterinary medicine	8,420	1.5

From: U.S. Department of Health and Human Services. Health United States 1992; and Healthy People 2000 Review. (Washington, D.C.: United States Department of Health and Human Services, Public Health Service Centers for Disease Control and Prevention, National Center for Health Statistics, DHHS Pub. No. (PHS) 93-1232, 1993), p. 150. Reprinted with permission.

TABLE 11–4. PERCENTAGE OF AMERICANS OF ASIAN/PACIFIC ISLANDER HERITAGE ENROLLED IN SCHOOLS FOR SELECTED HEALTH PROFESSIONS COMPARED WITH NON-HISPANIC WHITES: 1990–1991

Profession	White (%)	Asian (%)
Physicians (M.D.)	73.5	12.9
Dentists	88.5	16.0
Optometrists	91.4	13.0
Pharmacists	88.6	9.4
Podiatrists	91.3	7.3
Registered nurses	82.8	3.0
Veterinarians	92.5	1.5

From: U.S. Department of Health and Human Services. Health United States 1992; and Healthy People 2000 Review. (Washington, D.C.: United States Department of Health and Human Services, Public Health Service Centers for Disease Control and Prevention, National Center for Health Statistics DHHS Pub. No. (PHS) 93-1232, 1993), p. 151. Reprinted with permission.

A resource list of selected health-related organizations for the Asian/ Pacific Islander communities may be found in Appendix VIII.

ASIAN-AMERICAN HEALTH MANPOWER

Asian Americans, a group that comprised 2.9% of the overall United States population in the 1990 census, is for the most part well represented in the health professions. Table 11-3 and Table 11-4 illustrate this phenomenon. Today, a person who desires to be a physician in China has the option of studying either Chinese or Western medicine. If he or she selects Western medicine, a limited amount of Chinese medicine is also taught. As Chinese traditional medicine is becoming better recognized and better understood in the United States, more doors are being opened to those who prefer or understand this mode of treatment.

HEALTHY PEOPLE 2000 OBJECTIVES

The following are samples of objectives for improving the health status of Americans of Asian/Pacific heritage.

1. Reduce growth retardation among low-income Asian/Pacific children aged 1 to less than 10% (Baseline: 14% in 1988).
2. Reduce growth retardation among low-income Asian/Pacific children aged 2 through 4 to less than 10% (Baseline: 16% in 1988).
3. Reduce cigarette smoking to a prevalence of no more than 20% among Southeast Asian men (Baseline: 55% in 1984–1988).
4. Reduce hepatitis B (HBV) among Asian/Pacific children to no more than 1,800 cases (Baseline: An estimated 8,900 cases in 1987).
5. Reduce tuberculosis among Asian/Pacific islanders to an incidence of no more than 15 cases per 100,000 (Baseline: 36.3 per 100,000 in 1988).[33]

REFERENCES

1. Martin, J. A. "Birth Characteristics for Asian or Pacific Islander Subgroups, 1992." *Monthly Vital Statistics Report,* National Center for Health Statistics, 43(10) (1995), p. 1.
2. Department of Health and Human Services. *Healthy People 2000* National Health Promotion and Disease Prevention Objectives—Full Report with Commentary. (Boston: Jones and Bartlett, 1992), p. 36.
3. Mann, F. *Acupuncture* (New York: Vintage Books, 1972), p. 222.
4. Smith, H. *The Religions of Man* (New York: Harper and Row, 1958), pp. 175–192.
5. Wallnöfer, H. and von Rattauscher, A. *Chinese Folk Medicine,* trans. M. Palmedo (New York: American Library, 1972), pp. 12–16, 19–21.
6. Personal interview: R. Spector with Dr. P. K. Chan, Herb Specialist. New York City, August 3, 1988. Dr. Chan prepared a supplemental written statement in Chinese and English for inclusion in this text.
7. Ibid.
8. Ibid.
9. Ibid.
10. Wallnöfer and von Rottauscher. *Chinese Folk Medicine,* pp. 12–16, 19–21.
11. Ibid., pp. 26–28.
12. Ibid., pp. 79–81.
13. Ibid., pp. 97–109.

14. Ibid., p. 99.
15. Ibid., p. 109.
16. Ibid., p. 115.
17. Morgan, H. T. *Chinese Symbols and Superstitions* (Detroit: Gale Research Co., 1972; originally published S. Pasadena, CA: Ione Perkins, 1942), pp. 133–134.
18. Dolan, J. *Nursing in Society: A Historical Perspective* (Philadelphia: W. B. Saunders, Co., 1973), p. 30.
19. Wallnöfer and von Rottauscher, *Chinese Folk Medicine,* pp. 39–40.
20. Ibid., p. 119.
21. Ibid., p. 126.
22. Ibid., pp. 127–128.
23. Ibid., pp. 135–138.
24. Ibid., p. 43.
25. Ibid., pp. 42–43.
26. Ibid., pp. 44–47.
27. Ibid., p. 71.
28. Department of Health and Human Services, *Healthy People 2000,* p. 36.
29. Li, F. P., Schlief, N. G., Chang, C., J., et al. "Health Care for the Chinese Community in Boston." *American Journal of Public Health* (April 1972): 537.
30. Department of Health and Human Services, *Healthy People 2000,* p. 36.
31. Ibid.
32. Ibid., p. 539.
33. Ibid., p. 601.

ANNOTATED BIBLIOGRAPHY

Leong, L. *Acupuncture: A Layman's View.* New York: Signet, 1974.
Acupuncture is, above all, preventive medicine, and the patient is treated as a whole—body, mind, and spirit being inseparable. The following precept applies to acupuncture as well as to all Chinese healing. The acupuncturist admonishes: "Curing is not so good as preventing, and preventing is not so good as taking care of oneself." Physicians are paid to keep people healthy; when clients fall ill, they stop payment.

Mann, F. *Acupuncture: The Ancient Chinese Art of Healing and How it Works Scientifically.* New York: Vintage Books, 1972.
This general book discusses the theories of acupuncture, the acupuncture points, the meridians, *yin* and *yang,* various diagnostic and therapeutic techniques, and preventive medicine.

Palos, S. *The Chinese Art of Healing.* New York: Herter and Herter, 1971.
Palos includes a history of the Chinese art of healing; a discussion of humankind and nature, *yin* and *yang,* and a description of the human body in ancient Chinese thought. The traditional methods of treatment discussed are acupuncture, moxibustion, remedial massage, and physiotherapy.

Shih-Chen, L. *Chinese Medicinal Herbs,* trans. Porter Smith, F. and Stuart, G. A., San Francisco: Georgetown Press, 1973.
Containing an alphabetical listing of numerous Chinese herbs, this book discusses the history and use of each herb. It also includes a glossary of terms. Excellent reference.

Wei-Kang, F. *The Story of Chinese Acupuncture and Moxibustion.* Peking: Foreign Languages Press, 1975.
    A booklet that vividly and precisely describes ancient Chinese medical techniques, this work also describes today's search in China for breakthroughs in medical science.

Wollnöffer, H. and von Rottauscher, A. *Chinese Folk Medicine,* trans. M. Palmedo. New York: American Library, 1972.
    This book discuses many treatments and alleged cures that were used in China for centuries. It describes the fundamentals of Chinese medicine and evaluates its approach to anatomy, physiology, and pathology.

FURTHER SUGGESTED READINGS

Articles

Anderson, J. "An Acculturation Scale for Southeast Asians," *Social Psychiatry and Psychiatric Epidemiology* 28(3) (1993): 134–141.

Aponte, G. E. "The Enigma of 'Bangungut'." *Annals of Internal Medicine* 52(6) (1960): 1258–1263.

Armstrong, M. E. "Acupuncture." *American Journal of Nursing* 72 (September 1972): 1582–1588.

Beare, J. "Parenthood in Other Cultures—Punjabi Speaking Asians." *Nursing* (Oxford) 17(1) (November 1983): 563–564.

Bersi, R. M. "In Search of Identity: Asians in America." Report of Activities, Asian American Research Project, California State College, Dominquez Hills, 1971.

Bourne, P. G. "Suicide among Chinese in San Francisco." *American Journal of Public Health* 63(8) (August 1973): 744–750.

Calhoun, M. A. "Providing Health Care to Vietnamese in America: What Practitioners Need to Know." *Home Healthcare Nurse* 4(5) (September–October 1986): 14–19, 22.

Campbell, T. and Chang, B. "Health Care of the Chinese in America." *Nursing Outlook* 21 (April 1973): 245–249.

Caringer, B. "Caring for the Institutionalized Filipino." *Journal of Gerontological Nursing* 3(5) (September–October 1977): 33–37.

Chae, M. "Older Asians." *Journal of Gerontological Nursing* 13(11) (November 1987): 10–17.

Charles, C. A. "A Midwife's Experience of the Asian Community." *Midwife Health Visitor and Community Nurse* 19(12) (December 1983): 471–473.

Chen, M. S., Jr. "The Indigenous Model and Its Application to Heart Health for Southeast Asians." *Health Education* 20 (1989): 48–51.

Choi, H. "Cultural and Noncultural Factors as Determinants of Caregiver Burden for the Impaired Elderly in South Korea." *The Gerontologist.* 33(1) (1993): 8–15.

Chung, H. J. "Understanding the Oriental Maternity Patient." *Nursing Clinics of North America* 12 (March 1977): 67–75.

Clayton, S., Yang, H., Guan, J., et al. "Hepatitis B Control in China: Knowledge and Practices among Village Doctors." *American Journal of Public Health* 83(12) (1993): 1685–1688.

Cruz, J. Z. "The Pathology of 'Bangungut'." *Journal of Philippines' Medical Association* 27 (1951): 476–481.

Cruz, L. "Professional Assertiveness toward Greater and More Effective Service to the Filipino People." *Philipine Journal of Nursing* 52 (1982): 22–23, 30.

Ellis, J. "Southeast Asian Refugees and Maternity Care: The Oakland Experience." *Birth: Issues in Prenatal Care and Education* 9(3) (Fall 1982): 191–194.

Erickson, R. V. and Hoang, G. N. "Health Problems among Indochinese Refugees." *American Journal of Public Health* 70 (September 1980): 1003–1006.

Friede, A., et al. "Transmission of Hepatitis B Virus from Adopted Asian Children to Their American Families." *American Journal of Public Health* 78 (January 1988): 26–30.

Frye, B. A. "Cultural Themes in Health-Care Decision Making among Cambodian Refugee Women." *Journal of Community Health Nursing* 8(1) (1991): 33–44.

Frye, B. A. and D'Avanzo, C. D. "Cultural Themes in Family Stress and Violence among Cambodian Refugee Women in the Inner City." *Advances in Nursing Science* 16(3) (1994): 64–77.

Frye, B. A. and D'Avanzo, C. D. "Themes in Managing Culturally Defined Illness in the Cambodian Refugee Family." *Journal of Community Health Nursing* 11(2) (1994): 89–98.

Gann, P., Nghiem, L., and Warner, S. "Pregnancy Characteristics and Outcomes of Cambodian Refugees." *American Journal of Public Health* 79 (November 1989): 1251–1256.

Gardner, J. H. "Asians in Britain—Some Cultural Considerations in Stomach Care." *Nursing (London): The Journal of Clinical Practice, Education, and Management* 3(21) (September 1987): 785–789.

Haenszel, W. "Studies of Migrant Populations." *American Journal of Public Health* 75 (February 1985): 225–226.

Helsel, D., Petitti, D., and Kunstadter, P. "Pregnancy among the Hmong: Birthweight, Age, and Parity." *American Journal of Public Health* 82(10) (1992): 1361–1364.

Henley, A. and Clayton, J. "Asians in Hospital—Illness and the Life Cycle. Some Aspects of Hinduism." *Health and Social Service Journal* 92(8) (August 1982): 972–974.

Hurh, W. M. and Kwang, C. K. "Adaptation Stages and Mental Health of Korean Male Immigrants in the United States." *International Migration Review* 24(3) (1990): 456–479.

Hurh, W. M. and Kwang, C. K. "Correlates of Korean Immigrants' Mental Health." *The Journal of Nervous and Mental Disease* 178(11) (1990): 703–711.

Jackson, M. V. V. "The Filipino Nurse in the Middle of Social, Economic, and Political Realities." *Philippine Journal of Nursing* 53(1987): 7–12.

Kemp, C. "Cambodian Refugee Health Care Beliefs and Practices." *Journal of Community Health Nursing* 2(1) (1985): 41–52.

Kim, B.-H. C. "Asian Americans: No Model Minority." *Social Work* (May 1973): 44–53.

Koplan, J. P., et al. "The Barefoot Doctor: Shanghai County Revisited." *American Journal of Public Health* 75 (June 1985): 768–770.

Kulig, J. C. "Conception and Birth Control Use: Cambodian Refugee Women's Beliefs and Practices." *Journal of Community Health Nursing* 5(4) (1988): 235–246.

Kulig, J. C. "Childbearing Beliefs among Cambodian Refugee Women." *Western Journal of Nursing Research* 12(1) (1990): 108–117.

Kulig, J. C. "Sexuality Beliefs among Cambodians: Implications for Health Care Professionals." *Health Care for Women International.* 15(2) (1994): 69–76.

La-Du, E. B. "Childbirth Care for Hmong Families." *American Journal of Maternal Child Nursing* 10(6) (November–December 1985): 382–385.

Lawson, J. S. and Lin, V. "Health Status Differentials in the People's Republic of China." *American Journal of Public Health* 84(5) (1994): 737–746.

Lee, R. V., D'Alauro, F., White L. M., et al. "Southeast Asian Folklore about Pregnancy and Parturition." *Obstetrics and Gynecology* 71(4) (1988): 643–645.

Li, D.-K., et al. "Secular Change in Birthweight among Southeast Asian Immigrants to the United States." *American Journal of Public Health* 80 (May 1990): 685–688.

Li, F. P., Schlief, N. Y., Chang, C. J., "Health Care for the Chinese Community in Boston." *American Journal of Public Health* 62 (April 1972): 536–539.

Lin, E. B., Carter, W. B., and Kleinman, A. M. "An Exploration of Somatization among Asian Refugees and Immigrants in Primary Care." *American Journal of Public Health* 75 (September 1985): 1080–1084.

Lipson, J. G. Afghan Refugees in California: Mental Health Issues, *Issues in Mental Health Nursing* 14(4) (1993): 411–423.

Louie, K. B. "Providing Health Care to Chinese Clients." *Topics in Clinical Nursing* 7(3) (October 1985): 18–25.

McKenzie, J. L., and Chrisman, N. J. "Healing Herbs, Gods, and Magic." *Nursing Outlook* 25(5) (May 1977): 326–329.

Montepio, S. N. "Magical Medicine and the Filipino Healer." *Folklore and Mythology Studies* 11–12 Special Issue (1987–1988): 36–46.

Muecke, M. A. "Caring for Southeast Asian Refugee Patients in the USA." *American Journal of Public Health* 73(4) (April 1983): 431–438.

Munger, R. G. "Sudden Death in Sleep of Laotian-Hmong Refugees in Thailand: A Case-Control Study." *American Journal of Public Health* 77 (October 1987): 1187–1190.

Nelson, C. C. and Hewitt, M. A. "An Indochinese Refugee Population in a Nurse-Midwife Service." *Journal of Nurse Midwifery* 28(5) (September–October 1983): 9–14.

Peang-Meth, A. "Understanding the Khmer." *Asian Survey* 31(5) (1991): 442–455.

Pearson, R. "Understanding the Vietnamese in Britain: Marriage, Death, and Religion, Part 2." *Health Visitor* 55(9) (September 1982): 477, 480–481, 483.

Phillips, K. "Asians in Britain." *Midwife, Health Visitor, and Community Nurse* 21(4) (April 1985): 116–118.

Pickwell, S. M. "Nursing Experiences with Indochinese Refugee Families." *Journal of School Health* 53(2) (February 1983): 86–91.

Pickwell, S. "The Incorporation of Family Primary Care for Southeast Asian Refugees in a Community-Based Mental Health Facility." *Archives of Psychiatric Nursing* 3(3) (June 1989): 173–177.

Pollick, H. F., Rice, A. N., and Echenberg, D. "Dental Health of Recent Immigrant Children in the Newcomer Schools, San Francisco." *American Journal of Public Health* 77 (1987): 731–732.

Poss, J. E. "Providing Healthcare for Southeast Asian Refugees." *Journal of the New York State Nurses' Association* 20(2) (June 1989): 4–6.

Shadick, K. M. "Development of a Transcultural Health Education Program for the Hmong." *Clinical Nurse Specialist* 7(2) (1993): 48–53.

Singh, G. and Yu, S. "Birthweight Differentials among Asian Americans." *American Journal of Public Health.* 84(9) (1994): 1444–1449.

Stehr-Green, J. K. and Schantz, P. M. "Trichinosis in Southeast Asian Refugees in the United States." *American Journal of Public Health* 76 (1986): 1239–1338.

Tao-Kim-Hai, A. M. "Orientals are Stoic," in *Social Interaction and Patient Care,* ed. Skipper, J. K., Jr., and Leonard, R. C., Philadelphia: Lippincott, 1965, pp. 143–53.

Thomas, R. B. and Tummiñia, P. A. "Maternity Care for Vietnamese in America." *Birth: Issues in Prenatal Care and Education* 9(3) (Fall 1982): 187–190.

Thompson, J. I. "Exploring Gender and Culture with Khmer Women: Reflections on Participatory Feminist Research." *Advances in Nursing Science* 13(3) (1991): 30–48.

Turrell, S. "Asian Expectations." *Nursing Times* 81(18) (May 1–7, 1985): 44–46.

Wadd, L. "Vietnamese Postpartum Practices: Implications for Nursing in the Hospital Setting." *Journal of Obstetric, Gynecologic, and Neonatal Nursing* 12(4) (July–August 1983): 252–258.

While, A. "A Place of Refuge—A Camp for Vietnamese Boat People in Hong Kong." *Nursing Mirror* 155(14) (October 1982): 34–35.

Williamson, D. and Foster, J. C. "American Childbirth Educators in China: A Transcultural Exchange." *Journal of Nurse-Midwifery* 27(5) (September–October 1982): 15–22.

Yu, E. and Liu, W. "U.S. National Health Data on Asian Americans and Pacific Islanders: A Research Agenda for the 1990's." *American Journal of Public Health* 82(12) (1992): 1645–1652.

Chapter

Health and Illness in European (White) American Communities

These are magic words. They'll make you feel better.

—P. Malpezzi

Members of European (white) American communities have been immigrating to this country ever since the very first settlers came to the shores of New England. The white population has diverse and multiple origins. The recent literature in the area of ethnicity and health has focused on people of color, and little has been written about the white ethnic communities. In this chapter, an overview of the differences, by ethnicity, is presented. Earlier chapters have focused on religious differences with respect to health and healing. The focus on this chapter is on ethnic differences. Given that we are talking about well over 75% of the American population, the enormity of the task of attempting to describe each difference is readily apparent. Instead, this chapter highlights some of the basic beliefs of selected groups (those groups with which I have had the greatest exposure). The overview includes not only library research but also firsthand interviews and observations of people in their daily experiences with the health-care delivery system, both as inpatients and as community residents receiving home care.

BACKGROUND

The major groups migrating to this country between 1820 and 1990 include people from Germany—15%, Italy—11%, United Kingdom—11%, Ireland—10%, Austro-Hungary—7%, Canada—8%, and Russia—7%: for a total of 69% of all the immigrants to arrive in this country.[1] The most populous group—that is, people who are foreign-born Americans or native-born Americans with at least one foreign-born parent—includes Italian, German, Canadian, British, and Poles.[2]

Ancestry refers to a person's nationality group, lineage, or the country in which the person or the person's parents or ancestors were born before they came to the United States. The 1980 census was the first to include a question about ancestry. The responses to the question were a reflection of the ethnic group(s) with which persons identified, and they were able to indicate their ethnic group regardless of how many generations they were removed from it.[3] The following indicates the most common European ancestries in the U.S. population:[4]

Ancestry	Numbers Identifying Themselves as of this Ancestry (millions)
German	58
Irish	39
English	33
Italian	15
French	10
Polish	9
Dutch	6

The following discussion focuses on several white ethnic groups and attempts to describe some of the history of their migration to America, the areas where they now live, the common beliefs regarding health and illness, some kernels of information regarding family and social life, and problems that members from a given group may have in interacting with health-care providers. The intention is not to create a vehicle for stereotyping but to whet the reader's appetite—to realize the vast differences among whites and to search out more information about the people the reader may be caring for from themselves. There are countless cultural phenomena affecting health care; Table 12–1 suggests a few.

ITALIAN AMERICANS

The Italian American community is made up of immigrants who came here from mainland Italy and from Sicily and Sardinia and other Mediterranean islands that are part of Italy. The number of Americans claiming Italian ancestry is 15 million.

Italian Americans indeed have a proud heritage in the United States, for America was "founded" by an Italian—Christopher Columbus, named for an Italian—Amerigo Vespucci, and explored by several Italian explorers, including Verrazano, Cabot, and Tonti.[5]

TABLE 12–1. EXAMPLES OF CULTURAL PHENOMENA AFFECTING HEALTH CARE AMONG EUROPEAN (WHITE) AMERICANS

Nations of Origin:	Germany, England, Italy, Ireland, Former Soviet Union, and all other European countries
Environmental Control:	Primary reliance on "modern, Western" health-care delivery system
	Remaining traditional health and illness beliefs and practices may be observed
	Some remaining traditional folk medicine
	Homeopathic medicine resurgent
Biological Variations:	Breast cancer
	Heart disease
	Diabetes mellitus
	Thalassemia
Social Organization:	Nuclear families
	Extended families
	Judeo-Christian religions
	Community and social organizations
Communication:	National languages
	Many learned English rapidly as immigrants
	Verbal, rather than nonverbal
Space:	Noncontact people—aloof, distant
	Southern countries—closer contact and touch
Time Orientation:	Future over present

Adapted from: Spector, R. "Culture, Ethnicity, and Nursing," in *Fundamentals of Nursing* (3rd. ed), Potter, P. and Perry, A., eds. (St. Louis: Mosby-Yearbook, 1992), p. 101. Reprinted with permission.

History of Migration

Between 1820 and 1990, over 5 million people from Italy[6] immigrated to the United States. The peak years were from 1901 to 1920, and only a small number of people are coming today. Italians came to this country to escape poverty and to search for a better life in a country where they expected to reap rewards for their hard labor. The early years were not easy, but people chose to remain in this country and not return to Italy. Italians tended to live in neighborhood enclaves, and these neighborhoods, such as the North End in Boston and Little Italy in New York, still exist as Italian neighborhoods. Although the younger generation may have moved out, they still return home to maintain family, community, and ethnic ties.[7]

The family has served as the main tie keeping Italian Americans together because it provides the person with the strength to cope with the surrounding world and produces a sense of continuity in all situations. The family is the primary focus of the Italian's concern, and Italians take pride in the family and the home. Italians are resilient, yet fatalistic, and they take advantage of the present. As mentioned, the home is a source of great pride, and it is a symbol of the family, not a status symbol per se. The church also is an important focus for the life of the Italian.[8] Many of the festivals and observances continue to exist today, and in the summer, the North End of Boston is alive each weekend with the celebration of a different saint (Fig. 12–1).

70th GRAND RELIGIOUS FEAST
IN HONOR OF THE PROTECTRESS
SAINT AGRIPPINA DI MINEO

THE THREE-DAY FEAST IS IN HONOR AND PRAISE OF SAINT AGRIPPINA, THE PROTECTRESS AND PATRON SAINT OF THE IMMIGRANTS FROM THE SMALL TOWN OF MINEO IN SICILY AND THEIR DESCENDANTS.

EACH YEAR FOR THE PAST 69 YEARS THIS GROUP OF DEVOTED 'PAESANI', NOW SCATTERED THROUGHOUT THE STATE, COME TOGETHER IN THE NORTH END SECTION TO PROCLAIM ANEW THEIR FAITH, AS WAS THE CUSTOM IN THEIR LAND OF ORIGIN. EACH YEAR EVERYONE IS INVITED TO PARTICIPATE AND WITNESS THE HONOR AND GLORY THAT IS BESTOWED TO THIS MARTYRED SAINT.

Advisory Consultant · Peter Tardo
Maestro di Banda · Gaetano Giaraffo
Capo di Banda · Stanley Pugliese

SANT'AGRIPPINA DI MINEO

A beautiful blonde maiden Saint'Agrippina was a princess by birth. This beautiful virgin martyr who was unmercifully scorged and tortured to death by the Emperor Valerion (256 AD). After her death, her relics were taken from Rome to Mineo by Saints Agatha Bassa and Paula.

The Greeks honor her in a lesser degree and claim to have relics of her. Also, in the city of Constantinople, they claim to have her body.

Saint Agrippina is the Patron Saint of thunderstorms, leprosy and evil spirits.

ST. AGRIPPINA PRAY FOR OUR DECEASED MEMBERS

A Tug of War will take place when the procession is over. The Saint is being carried by 20 men, namely Sicilians against the Romans.

Figure 12–1. Announcement of a North End (Boston) Festival. (*From the author's collection.*)

The father is the head of the Italian household, and the mother is said to be the heart of the household.

Italian Americans have tended to attain low levels of education in the United States, but their incomes are comparable to or higher than those of other groups.[9]

The Italian population falls into four generational groups: (1) the elderly, living in Italian enclaves, (2) a second generation, living both within the neighborhoods and in the suburbs, (3) a younger, well-educated group, living mainly in the suburbs, and (4) new immigrants.[10]

Health and Illness

Italians tend to present their symptoms to their fullest point and to expect immediate treatment for ailments. In terms of traditional beliefs, they may view the cause of illness to be one of the following: (1) winds and currents that bear diseases, (2) contagion or contamination, (3) heredity, (4) supernatural or human causes, and (5) psychosomatic interactions.

One such traditional Italian belief contends that moving air, in the form of drafts, causes irritation and then a cold that can lead to pneumonia. A belief an elderly person may express in terms of cancer surgery is that it is not a good idea to have surgery because surgery exposes the inner body to the air, and if the cancer is "exposed to the air the person is going to die quicker." Just as drafts are considered to be a cause of illness, fresh air is considered to be vital for the maintenance of health. Homes and the workplace must be well ventilated to prevent illness from occurring.

One sees the belief in contamination manifested in the reluctance of people to share food and objects with people who are considered unclean, and they will often not enter the homes of those who are ill. Traditional Italian women have a strong sense of modesty and shame, resulting in an avoidance of discussions relating to sex and menstruation.

Blood is regarded by some, especially the elderly, to be a "plastic entity" that responds to fluids and food and is responsible for many variable conditions. Various adjectives, such as "high" and "low" and "good" and "bad," are used to describe blood. Some of the "old superstitions" include the beliefs that

1. Congenital abnormalities can be attributed to the unsatisfied desire for food during pregnancy.
2. If a woman is not given food that she smells, the fetus will move inside, and a miscarriage will result.
3. If a pregnant woman bends or turns or moves in a certain way, the fetus may not develop normally.
4. A woman must not reach during pregnancy because reaching can harm the fetus.

Italians may also attribute the cause of illness to the evil eye (*malocchio*) or to curses (*castiga*). The difference between these two causes is that less serious illnesses, such as headaches, may be caused by *malocchio*, whereas more severe illness, which often can be fatal, may be attributed to more powerful *castiga*. Curses are sent either by God or by evil people. An example of a curse is the punishment from God for sins and bad behavior.[11]

It is recognized by Italians that illness can be caused by the suppression of emotions, as well as stress from fear, grief, and anxiety. If one is unable to find an emotional outlet, one well may "burst." It is not considered healthy to bottle up emotions.[12]

Often the care of the ill is managed in the home, with all members of the family sharing in the responsibilities. The use of home remedies ostensibly is decreasing, although several students have reported the continued use of rituals for the removal of the evil eye and the practice of leeching. One practice described for the removal of the evil eye was to take an egg and olive oil and to drip them into a pan of water, make the sign of the cross, and recite prayers. If the oil spreads over the water, the cause of the problem is the evil eye, and the illness should get better. Mineral waters are also used, and tonics are used to cleanse the blood. There is a strong religious influence among Italians, who believe that faith in God and the saints will see them through the illness. One woman that I worked with had breast cancer. She had had surgery several years before and did not have a recurrence. She attributed her recovery to the fact that she attended mass every single morning and that she had total faith in Saint Peregrine, whose medal she wore pinned to her bra by the site of the mastectomy. Italian people tend to take a fatalistic stance regarding terminal illness and death believing that it is God's will. Death often is not discussed between the dying person and the family members. I recall when caring for an elderly Italian man at home that it was not possible to have the man and his wife discuss his impending death. Although each knew that he was dying and would talk with the nurse, to each other he "was going to recover," and everything possible was done to that end.

Italian families observe numerous religious traditions surrounding death, and funeral masses and anniversary masses are observed. It is the custom for the widow to wear black for some time after her husband's death (occasionally for the remainder of her life), although this is not as common with the younger generations.

Health-Related Problems

Two genetic diseases commonly seen among Italians are (1) favism, a severe hemolytic anemia caused by deficiency of the X-linked enzyme glucose-6-phosphate dehydrogenase and triggered by the eating of fava beans, and (2) the thalassemia syndromes, also hemolytic anemias that include Cooley's anemia (or beta-thalassemia) and alpha-thalassemia.[13]

Language problems frequently occur when elderly or new Italian immigrants are seeking care. Often, due to modesty, people are reluctant to answer the questions asked through interpreters, and gathering of pertinent data is most difficult.

Problems related to time also occur. Physicians tend to diagnose emotional problems more often for Italian patients than other ethnic groups because of the Italian pattern of reporting more symptoms and reporting them more dramatically.[14]

In general, Italian Americans are motivated to seek explanations with respect to their health status and the care they are to receive. If instructions and explanations are well given, Italians tend to cooperate with health-care providers. It is often necessary to provide directions in the greatest detail and then to provide written instructions to ensure compliance with necessary regimens.

GERMAN AMERICANS

(The following material, relating to both the German American and Polish American communities, was obtained from research conducted in southeastern Texas in May 1982. It is by no means indicative of the health and ill-ness beliefs of the entire German American and Polish American communi-ties. It is included here to demonstrate the type of data that can be gleaned using an "emic"* approach to collecting data. It cannot be generalized, but it allows the reader to grasp the diversity of beliefs that surround us!)

Since 1830, more than 7 million Germans have immigrated[15] to the United States. There are, presently, 58 million Americans who claim German ancestry. The Germans represented a cross-section of German society and came from all social strata and walks of life. Some came to escape poverty, others came for religious or political reasons, and still others came to take ad-vantage of the opportunity to open up the new lands. Many were recruited to come here, as were the Germans who settled in the German enclaves in Texas. The immigrants represented all religions, including primarily Luther-ans, Catholics, and Jews. They represented the rich and the poor, the educated and the ignorant. The immigrants were of all ages. Present-day descendants are farmers, educators, artists, and so forth. The Germans brought to the United States the cultural diversity and folkways they observed in Germany. The festivals of Corpus Christi, Kinderfeste (children's feast), and Sangerfeste (singing festival) all originated in Germany.[16]

The Germans began to migrate to the United States in the 17th century and have contributed 15% of the total immigration population. They are the least visible ethnic group in the United States, and often people are surprised to discover there is such a large Germanic influence in this country. In some places, the German communities maintain strong identification with their German heritage. For example, the city of Fredericksberg, Texas, maintains an ambience of German culture and identity. Some people born there who are fourth generation and more, continue to learn German as their first spoken language.[17]

The German ethnic community is the second largest in the state of Texas and is exceeded only by the Mexican community. Germans have been immi-grating to Texas since 1840 and continue to arrive. They are predominantly Catholic, Lutheran, and Methodist. Many of these people have maintained their German identity. The major German communities in Texas are Victoria, Cuero, Gonzales, New Braunfels, and Fredericksberg.

During the European freedom revolutions of 1830 and 1848, Texas was quite popular, especially in Germany, and was seen as a "wild and fabulous land." For tradition-bound German families, however, the abandonment of the homeland was difficult. They were enticed, however, by the hopes of eco-nomic and social improvement and political idealism. An additional reason

---

*Emic: description of behavior dependent on the person's categorization of the action. *Etic:* de-scription of behavior based on categories created by the investigator and employed to compare phenomena cross-culturally. These are two forms of anthropological research described by Pelto, P. J. and Pelto, G. H. in *Anthropological Research: The Structure of Inquiry,* 2nd ed. (Cam-bridge: Cambridge University Press, 1978).

for the mass migration was the overpopulation of Germany and the immigrants' desire to escape an imminent European catastrophe. By the 1840s, several thousand northern Germans had come to Texas, and another large migration occurred in 1890. This second cluster of people came because there was a severe crop failure in Russian-occupied Germany, and the Russian language had become a required subject in German schools. Other German migrations occurred from 1903 to 1905.

The Germans found pleasure in the small things of everyday life. They were tied together by the German language because it bound them to the past, entertaining them with games, riddles, folk songs and literature, and folk wisdom. The greatest amusement was singing and dancing. Religion for the Lutherans, Catholics, and Methodists was a part of everyday life. The year was measured by the church calendar; observance of church ritual paced the milestones of the life cycle. The Germans believed that each individual was a "part of the fabric of humanity," that "history was a continued process," and "everything had a purpose as mankind strove to something better."[18]

The Germans had a penchant for forming societies and clubs, the longest lasting of which are the singing societies. The first was organized in 1850 and exists still today. The Germans brought with them their customs and traditions, their cures, curses, and recipes, and their tools and ways of building.[19]

Health and Illness

Among the Germans, health is described as more than not being ill but as a state of well-being—physically and emotionally; the ability to do your duty, positive energy to do things, and the ability to do and think and act the way you would like, to go and congregate, to enjoy life. Illness may be described as the absence of well-being: pain, malfunction of body organs, not being able to do what you want, a blessing from God to suffer, and a disorder of body, imbalance.

Causes of Illness

Most German Americans believe in the germ theory of infection and in stress-related theories. Other causes of illness are identified, however, such as drafts, environmental changes, and belief in the evil eye and punishment from God.

The methods of maintaining health include the requirement of dressing properly for the season, proper nutrition, and the wearing of shawls to protect oneself from drafts—also, the taking of cod-liver oil, exercise, and hard work. Methods for preventing illness include wearing an asafetida bag around the neck in the winter to prevent colds, wearing scapulars, religious practices, sleeping with the windows open, and cleanliness.

The use of home remedies to treat illness continues to be practiced. Table 12–2 gives examples of commonly used home remedies.

TABLE 12–2. ILLNESS SYMPTOMS AND REMEDIES AMONG GERMAN AMERICANS

Gastrointestinal Problems

Symptom	Remedy
Constipation	Castor oil
	Black draught
Diarrhea or vomiting	Do not eat for 24 hours
	Chicken soup
Stomachache	Peppermint tea
	Tea and toast
	Berries, elderberries

Respiratory Problems

Symptom	Remedy
Cold	Wet compress around throat—cover with wool
	Lemon juice and whiskey
	Apply chopped onions in a sack to the soles of the feet
	Olbas oil (made in Germany)
Cough	Goose fat—rub on chest
	Honey and milk
	Tausend Gülden Kraut (thousand golden cabbage)—rum
Earache	Put warm oil in ear
	Warm towels
	Bitter geranium leaves
Sore throat	Put camphor on a wet rag—wind around the throat
	Gargle with salt water
	Onion compress
	Chicken soup
	Liniments

Physical Injuries

Symptom	Remedy
Bumps	Hard knife (cold metal), place on bump
Cuts	Iodine—clean well
Puncture wound (nail)	Soak in kerosene
Wounds	Clean well with water—apply iodine

Miscellaneous Problems

Symptom	Remedy
Aches and pains	Kytle's liniment
	Olbas oil
	Volcanic oil
	Salves and liniments
Arthritis	Warm water soaks
	Honey, vinegar, and water soaks
Boils	"Capital water"—sulfur water—drink this (this is available at the Texas capital)
Clean body after winter	Kur (similar to hot springs) drink
Fever	Cold compress on head—fluids
Headache	Iced cloth on head
Menstrual cramps	Cardui

TABLE 12–2.—Continued

Miscellaneous Problems—Continued	
Symptom	*Remedy*
Rheumatism	Aloe vera—rub on sore area
	Cod-liver oil—massage
	Apply fig juice
Ringworm	Camomile tea compress
Stye	One half of hard-boiled egg—apply warm white on eye
Toothache	Cloves
	Salbec tea
	Olbas oil
Warts	Apply fig juice and fig leaf milk

From: Spector, R.E. "A Description of the Impact of Medicare on Health-Illness Beliefs and Practices of White Ethnic Senior Citizens in Central Texas" Ph.D. diss. University of Texas at Austin School of Nursing, 1983; Ann Arbor, MI: University Microfilms International, 1983. Reprinted with permission.

Current Health Problems

There do not appear to be any unusual health problems particular to German Americans.[20]

POLISH AMERICANS

The first people immigrating to this country from Poland came with Germans in 1608 to Jamestown, Virginia, to help develop the timber industry. Since that time, Poland, too, has given America one of its largest ethnic groups, with over 9 million people claiming Polish ancestry. The peak year for Polish immigration was 1921, and well over 578,875 people immigrated here.[21] Many of the people arriving before 1890 came for economic reasons. Those coming here since that time have come for both economic and political reasons and for religious freedom. Polish heroes include Casimir Pulaski and Thaddeus Kosciuszko, who were heroes in the American Revolution. The major influx of Poles to the United States began in 1870 and ended in 1913. The people who arrived were mainly peasants seeking food and release from the political oppression of three foreign governments in Poland. The immigrants who came both before and after this mass migration were better educated and not as poor. In the United States, Polish immigrants lived in poor conditions either because they had no choice or because that was the way they were able to meet their own priorities. They were seen by other Americans to live as animals and were often mocked and called stupid. Quite often, the Polish people spoke and understood several European languages but had difficulty learning English and were therefore scorned. Polish people shared the problem as a community and banded together in tight enclaves called "Polonia." They attempted to be as self-sufficient as possible. They worked at preserving their native culture, and voluntary Polish ghettos grew up in close proximity to the parish church.[22]

An example of the Polish experience in the United States is that of the Polish immigrants in Texas. The first Poles came to Texas in the second half of the 19th century, and most of them settled in Victoria, San Antonio, Houston, and Bandera. The first Polish colonies in America were located in Texas, the oldest being Panna Maria (Virgin Mary) in Karnes County, 50 miles southeast of San Antonio. Unlike other Poles who wanted to return to Poland, the colonists who arrived in Texas after 1850 came to settle permanently and had no intention of returning to their homeland. Although these people came to Texas for economic, political, and religious reasons, severe poverty was their major reason for leaving Poland.

The first collective Polish immigration to America was in 1854, when 100 families came to Texas. They landed in Galveston where a few in the party remained. The rest traveled in a procession northwestward, bringing with them a few belongings, such as featherbeds, crude farm implements, and a cross from their parish church. Their dream was to live in the fertile lands of Texas and raise crops, speak their own language, educate their children, and worship God as they pleased. This dream did not materialize, and members of the band grew discouraged. Some of the immigrants remained in Victoria and others went to San Antonio.

The people who went to San Antonio continued to travel, and on Christmas Eve, 1854, they stopped at the junction of the San Antonio and Cibolo rivers. Here, under a live oak tree, they celebrated mass and founded Panna Maria. In 1855, 1856, and 1857, others followed this small group in moving to this part of Texas.

These settlers were exposed to many dangers from nature, such as heat, drought, snakes, and insects. The Polish settlers were not accepted by the other settlers in the area because their language, customs, and culture were different, but the immigrants survived, and many moved to settle other areas near Panna Maria. Today, the people of Panna Maria continue to live simple lives close to nature and God and speak mainly Polish.

Much of the history of the Polish people in Texas is written around the founding and the location of the various church parishes. For example, in 1873 the Parish of the Nativity of the Blessed Virgin Mary was begun in Cestohowa. Within this church above the main altar is a large picture of the Virgin Mary of Czestohowa. This picture was taken to the church from Panna Maria. It is a copy of the famous Black Madonna of Czestohowa, Poland, a city 65 miles east of where the immigrants to Texas originated. The Black Madonna is a beloved, miraculous image and a source of faith to the Polish people. The shrine of Our Lady in Czestohowa, Poland, is one of the largest shrines in the world. Since the 14th century, that picture had been the object of veneration and devotion of Polish Catholics. It is claimed to have been painted by Saint Luke the Evangelist. Its origin is traced to the fifth or sixth century and is the oldest picture of the Virgin in the world. The scars on the face date from 1430 when bandits struck it with a sword. The history, traditions, and miracles of Czestohowa are the heritage of the Polish people.[23] One woman I interviewed said she had been ill with a fatal disease. The entire time that she lay close to death she prayed to the Virgin. When she finally did recover, she made a pilgrimage back to her homeland in Poland and visited the shrine to give thanks to the Virgin. The woman was positive that this was the source of her recovery.

Health and Illness

The definitions of health among the Polish people I interviewed included: feeling O.K.—as a whole—body, spirit, everything a person cannot separate; happy, until war, do not need doctor, do not need medicine; active, able to work, feel good, do what I want to do; and good spirit, good to everybody, never cross. The definitions for illness may include: something wrong with body, mind, or spirit; one wrong affects them all; not capable of working, see the doctor often; not right, something ailing you; not active; feeling bad; and opposite of health, not doing what I want to do. The methods for maintaining health include maintaining a happy home, being kind and loving, eating healthy food, remaining pure, walking, exercising, wearing proper clothing, (sweaters), eating a well-balanced diet, trying not to worry, having faith in God, being active, dressing warmly, going to bed early, and working hard. The methods for preventing illness include: cleanliness, the wearing of scapulars, avoiding drafts, following the proper diet, not gossiping, keeping away from people with colds, and wearing medals because "God is with you all the time to protect you and take care of you." Other ideas about illness include the beliefs that illnesses are caused by poor diets and that the evil eye may well exist as a causative factor (but not really sure). This belief was attributed to the older generations and is not regarded as prevalent among younger Polish Americans.

The home remedies listed in Table 12–3 were described by and were in common use among Polish Americans.

Health-Care Problems

The Polish community has not tended to have any major problems with the health-care deliverers. Language may be a barrier if members of the older generation do not speak English, and the taking of health histories is complicated when the providers cannot communicate directly with the informant. Again, problems may develop when there is difficulty finding someone who is conversant in Polish, whom the informant can trust to reveal personal matters to, and who can translate medical terms accurately.[24]

In Poland, there is a shortage of medical supplies, so the people tend to use faith healers and believe in miracle workers. On the main street of Warsaw all sorts of folk-medicine and miracle-worker paraphernalia are on sale:

TABLE 12–3. ILLNESS SYMPTOMS AND REMEDIES AMONG POLISH AMERICANS

Gastrointestinal Problems	
Symptom	*Remedy*
Colic	Tea—peppermint or camomile
	Sugar, water, vinegar, and soda, makes soda water
	Bess-plant tea
	Homemade sauerkraut
Constipation	Epsom salts—teaspoon in water—cleans out stomach
	Cascara
	Castor oil
	Senna-leaf tea
Cramps	Camomile tea
Diarrhea	Paregoric
	Cinnamon tea
	Dried blueberries
	Chew coffee beans
Gas	Drink soda water
Indigestion	Aloes vulgaris—juniper and elderberries
	Peppermint and spearmint teas
	Blackberries

Respiratory Problems	
Symptom	*Remedy*
Cold	Castor oil—mentholatum
	Flaxseed or mustard poultice on chest
	Dried raspberries and tea with wine
	Mustard plaster
	Oatmeal poultice—hot bricks to feet
	Cupping
	Camphor salve
	Oxidine
	Rub goose fat on chest
Cough	Honey and hot water; bedrest
	Hot lemonade with whiskey; honey
	Few drops of turpentine and sugar
	"Gugel Mugel"—warm milk with butter, whiskey, and honey
	Honey and warm milk
	Milk with butter and garlic
	Mustard plaster
	Linden tea
	Onion poultice
Croup	Few drops of kerosene and sugar
Sore throat	Honey
	Warm water, salt—gargle
	Goose grease around throat covered with dry rag
	Paint throat with kerosene
	Goose fat in milk

TABLE 12-3.—Continued

Physical Injury

Symptom	Remedy
Burns	Aloe vera
Cuts	Vinegar, water, flour paste
	Clean with urine
	Carbolic salve
Puncture wounds (nail)	Turpentine and liniment
	Put salt pork on wound and soak in hot water
	Hunt's lightning oil
Frostbite	Put snow on frozen place
Scratches, sores	Liniment
	Moss
	Spider webs
Sprains	Liniments—Sloan's Volcanic

Miscellaneous Problems

Symptom	Remedy
Earache	Hot water bottle to ear
	Camphor on cotton—place in ear
Fever	Camomile tea
Flu	Novak oil—rub on head
	Knorr's Green Drops
Headache	Vinegar on a cloth applied to head
	Steam kettle—cover head and inhale
High blood pressure	Cooked garlic
	Garlic oil
Lice	Cover head with kerosene
Toothache	Hot salt compress
Neuralgia	Bedrest
Pyorrhea	Drink yarrow tea
Rheumatism	Lemon juice—rub on sore places
Trouble urinating	Juice of pumpkin seeds made into a tea
	Swamp root medicine

From: Spector, R.E. "A Description of the Impact of Medicare on Health-Illness Beliefs and Practices of White Ethnic Senior Citizens in Central Texas." Ph.D. diss. University of Texas at Austin School of Nursing, 1983; Ann Arbor, Mich.: University Microfilms International, 1983. Reprinted with permission.

divining rods, cotton sacks filled with herbs to be worn over an ailing heart or liver, coils of copper wire to be placed under food to rid it of poisons, and pendulums.[25]

In this chapter I have attempted to open the door to the enormous diversity in health and illness beliefs that exists in European American (white) communities. I have only opened the door and peeked inside. There is a richness of knowledge to be gained. It is for you to acquire it as you care for all patients. Ask them what they believe about health and illness and what their practices and remedies may be. The students that I am working with find this to be a most enlightening experience.

REFERENCES

1. Lefcowitz, E. *The United States Immigration History Timeline* (New York: Terra Firma Press, 1990), p. 6.
2. Bernardo, S. *The Ethnic Almanac* (New York: Doubleday, 1981), p. 474.
3. U.S. Department of Commerce, Bureau of the Census. *1980 Census of Population—* Ancestry of the Population by State: 1980 (Washington, DC: Government Printing Office, 1983), p. 6.
4. Gaines, J. R. The New Face of America. *TIME*. 142, #21, (1993) p. 14.
5. Bernardo. *Ethnic Almanac*, p. 26.
6. Lefcowitz, *Timeline*, p. 6.
7. Nelli, H. S. "Italians," in *Harvard Encyclopedia of American Ethnic Groups,* ed. Thernstrom, S. (Cambridge, MA: Harvard University Press, 1980), pp. 545–560.
8. Rotunno, M. and McGoldrick, M. "Italian Families," in *Ethnicity and Family Therapy,* ed. McGoldrick, M., Pearce, J. K., and Giordano, J. (New York: Guilford Press, 1982), p. 341.
9. Ibid., p. 344.
10. Ragucci, A. T. "Italian Americans," in *Ethnicity and Medical Care,* ed. Harwood, A. (Cambridge, MA: Harvard University Press, 1981), p. 216.
11. Ibid., pp. 223–232.
12. Ibid., p. 232.
13. Ibid., p. 222.
14. Rotunno and McGoldrick. "Italian Families," p. 350.
15. Lefcowitz, *Timeline*, p. 6.
16. Conzen, K. N. "Germans," in *Harvard Encyclopedia of American Ethnic Groups,* ed. Thernstrom, S. (Cambridge, MA: Harvard University Press, 1980), pp. 405–425.
17. Spector, R. E. "A Description of the Impact of Medicare on Health-Illness Beliefs and Practices of White Ethnic Senior Citizens in Central Texas." Ph.D. diss. University of Texas at Austin School of Nursing, 1983; Ann Arbor, MI: University Microfilms International, 1983.
18. Lich, G. E. *The German Texans* (San Antonio: University of Texas Institute of Texan Cultures, 1982), pp. 33–72.
19. Ibid., p. 81.
20. Spector. "Impact of Medicare," pp. 120–133.
21. Lefcowitz, *Timeline*, p. 6.
22. Green, V. "Poles," in *Harvard Encyclopedia of American Ethnic Groups,* ed. Thernstrom, S. (Cambridge, MA: Harvard University Press, 1980), pp. 787–803.
23. Dworaczyk, E. J. *The First Polish Colonies of America in Texas* (San Antonio: Naylor Co., 1979); Grzelonski, B. *Poles in the United States: 1776–1865* (Warsaw: Interpeirs, 1976).
24. Spector. "Impact of Medicare," pp. 120–133.
25. "Letter from Poland—of Faith Healers and Miracle Workers." *Boston Globe* (21 August 1983).

ANNOTATED BIBLIOGRAPHY

Bernardo, S. *The Ethnic Almanac*. New York: Doubleday, 1981.
    Bernardo describes the customs, culture, and traditions of numerous ethnic groups in America. She also provides pertinent information regarding the numbers

of people in various ethnic groups, the states where they live, and interesting facts about the contributions members have made to American life.

Hand, W. D., ed. *American Folk Medicine: A Symposium.* Berkeley: University of California Press, 1976.

A description of the practice of folk medicine in the United States, this symposium covers such topics as folk medicine among the Amish, the powwow in Pennsylvania, and folk medicine among French Canadians.

Harney, R. F. and Troper, H. *Immigrants.* Toronto: Van Nostrand Reinhold, 1975.

This well-illustrated text provides a history of the ethnic groups who immigrated to Canada.

Harwood, A., ed. *Ethnicity and Medical Care.* Cambridge, MA: Harvard University Press, 1981.

This book covers the health and illness beliefs and practices among the Italian Americans in addition to the beliefs of various ethnic groups of color.

McGoldrick, M., Pearce, J. K., and Giordano, J., eds. *Ethnicity and Family Therapy.* New York: Guilford Press, 1982.

In this excellent text, the experiences of several family therapists working with families of diverse backgrounds are described. Among the ethnic groups included are the Greeks, Irish, Germans, Iranians, and Polish. It is one of the few sources that contains background information to any great extent on white ethnic groups.

McLemore, S. D. *Racial and Ethnic Relations in America.* Boston: Allyn and Bacon, 1980.

McLemore describes theories of Americanization and the experiences of various groups in socializing to the American culture.

Thernstrom, S., ed. *Harvard Encyclopedia of American Ethnic Groups.* Cambridge, MA: Harvard University Press, 1980.

This outstanding text provides information about all aspects of immigration and the immigrants in terms of their social and cultural backgrounds. It is a valuable library resource for every nursing school.

FURTHER SUGGESTED READINGS

Allison, D. *Bastard out of Carolina.* (New York: Plume, 1992).

Andrews, E. D. *The People Called Shakers.* (New York: Dover, 1953).

Boney, W. *The French Canadians Today.* (London: J. M. Dent and Sons, 1939).

Bracq, J. C. *The Evolution of French Canada.* (New York: Macmillan Co., 1924).

Candill, H. M. *Night Comes to the Cumberlands.* (Boston: Little, Brown and Co., 1962).

Conde, M. *I, Tituba, Black Witch of Salem.* (New York: Ballantine Books, 1992).

Crispino, J. A. *Assimilation of Ethnic Groups: The Italian Case.* (Newark: New Jersey Center for Migration, 1980).

Gambino, R. *Blood of My Blood: The Dilemma of Italian-Americans.* (Garden City, NY: Doubleday, 1974).

Frost, M. *The Shaker Story.* (Canterbury, NH: Canterbury Shakers.)

Greeley, A. M. *The Irish Americans.* (New York: Harper and Row, 1981).

Hughes, H. S. *The United States and Italy.* (Cambridge, MA: Harvard University Press, 1953).

Hufford, D. J. *American Healing Systems: An Introduction and Exploration. Conference Booklet.* (Philadelphia: University of Pennsylvania, 1984).

Iorizzo, L. J. *Italian Immigration and the Impact of the Padrone System.* (New York: Arno Press, 1980).

Johnson, C. L. *Growing Up and Growing Old in Italian-American Families.* (New Brunswick, NJ: Rutgers University Press, 1985).

Kmit, A., Luciow, L. L., Luciow, J., and Perchyshyn, L. *Ukrainian Easter Eggs and How We Make Them.* (Minneapolis: Ukrainian Gift Shop, 1979).

Malpezzi, F. M. and Clement, W. M. *Italian American Folklore.* (Little Rock: August House Publishers, 1992).

Martin, J. L. and Nelson S. J. *They Had Stories, We Had Chores.* (Hastings, MN: Caragana Press, 1995).

Martin, J. L. and Nelson, S. J. *They Glorified Mary, We Glorified Rice.* (Hastings, MN: Caragana Press, 1994).

Martin, J. and Todnem, A. *Cream and Bread.* (Hastings, MN: Redbird Productions, 1984).

Miner, H. *St. Denis: A French Canadian Parish.* (Chicago: University of Chicago Press, 1939).

Morgan, M. *Mutant Message Downunder.* (Lees Summit, MO: MM CO, 1991).

Nelli, H. S. *From Immigrants to Ethnics: The Italian Americans.* (Oxford: Oxford University Press, 1983).

Null, G., and Stone, C. *The Italian-Americans.* (Harrisburg, PA: Stackpole Books, 1976).

Reneaux, J. J. *Cajun Folktales.* (Little Rock: August House Publishers, 1992).

Shepard, R. F., and Levi, V. G. *Live and Be Well.* (New York: Ballantine Books, 1982).

Tomasi, S. M., ed. *National Directory of Research Centers. Repositories and Organizations of Italian Culture in the United States.* (Torino, Italy: Fondazione Giovanni Agnelli, 1980).

Wade, M. *The French-Canadian Outlook.* (New York: Viking Press, 1946).

Wade, M. *The French Canadians, 1876–1945.* (New York: Macmillan Co., 1955).

Chapter 13

Health and Illness in Hispanic American Communities

... AIDS haunts East Harlem. The neighborhood, north of 96th Street and east of Fifth Avenue is home to mostly poor Hispanics. On these streets, about 1 of every 35 adults has AIDS.

—Felicia R. Lee[1]

The second largest emerging majority group in the United States is composed of the Hispanic subgroups. In this chapter, the term *Hispanic Americans* refers to people who were born in or whose predecessors came from (even generations ago) Mexico, Puerto Rico, Cuba, Central and South America, Spain, and other Spanish-speaking communities and who now live in the United States. The term is then used to represent the diversity of the populations. These people constituted 9% of the population in the 1990 census and are the fastest growing group. Over 70% of the people within this group were born in the United States.[2]

THE CHICANOS

Who are the Chicanos? In answering this question, we hope to discover who the Mexican Americans are. What should these people be called? Depending on socioeconomic status, immigration or citizenship status, age, and the area in which this person lives, a member of this large minority group refers to him or herself as either Mexican American, Spanish American, Latin American, Latin, Latino or Mexican.[3] The term *Chicano* is used as an "identifying

279

umbrella that identifies all Americans of Mexican descent."[4] Hence the term is used here to refer to this particular cultural and ethnic group.

Americans of Hispanic origin, according to the 1990 census, number at least 13,600,190 people and of this number 7,225,591 are of Mexican origin.[5] This figure is known to be an underenumeration. This population is rapidly increasing because of a high birthrate and both legal and illegal immigration.[6]

> We came to California long before the Pilgrims landed at Plymouth Rock. We settled California, and all the Southwestern part of the United States, including the States of Arizona, New Mexico, Colorado, and Texas. We built the missions and cultivated the ranches.[7]

The Chicanos have been in the United States for a long time, moving from Mexico and later intermarrying with Indians and Spanish people in the southwestern parts of what is now the United States. Santa Fe, New Mexico, was settled in 1609. Most of the descendants of these early settlers now live in Arizona, California, Colorado, New Mexico, and Texas. A large number of Chicanos also live in Illinois, Indiana, Kansas, Michigan, Missouri, Nebraska, New York, Ohio, Utah, Washington, and Wisconsin. Most Chicanos arrived in these latter states as migrant farm workers. While located there as temporary farm workers, they found permanent jobs and stayed.[8] Contrary to the popular views that Chicanos live in rural areas, most live in urban areas.[9] Chicanos are employed in all types of jobs. Few, however, have high-paying or high-status jobs in labor or management. The majority work in factories, mines, and construction; others are employed in farm work and service areas. At present, only a small—though growing—number of the people are employed in clerical and professional areas. The number of unemployed in this group is high (estimated to be between 25 and 30%), and the earnings of those employed are well below the national average. The education of Chicanos, like that of most minorities in the United States, lags behind that of most of the population. Many Chicanos fail to complete high school. In the past few years, this situation has changed, and Chicano children are being encouraged to stay in school, go on to college, and enter the professions.[10]

Traditional Definitions of Health and Illness

There are conflicting reports about the traditional meaning of health among Chicanos. Some sources maintain that health is considered to be purely the result of "good luck" and that a person loses his or her health if that luck changes.[11] Some Chicanos describe health as a reward for good behavior. Seen in this context, health is a gift from God and should not be taken for granted. People are expected to maintain their own equilibrium in the universe by performing in the proper way, eating the proper foods, and working the proper amount of time. The prevention of illness is an accepted practice that is accomplished with prayer, the wearing of religious medals or amulets, and keeping relics in the home. Herbs and spices can be used to enhance this form of prevention, as can exemplary behavior.[12] Illness is seen as an imbalance in an individual's body or as punishment meted out for some wrongdoing. The causes of illness can be grouped into five major categories.

The Body's Imbalance. Imbalance may exist between "hot" and "cold" or "wet" and "dry." The theory of hot and cold was brought to Mexico by Spanish priests and was fused with Aztec beliefs.[13] The concept actually dates back to the early Hippocratic theory of disease and four body humors. The disrupted relationship among these humors is often mentioned by Chicanos as the cause of disease.

There are four body fluids, or humors: (1) *blood,* hot and wet, (2) *yellow bile,* hot and dry, (3) *phlegm,* cold and wet, and (4) *black bile,* cold and dry. When all four humors are balanced, the body is healthy. When any imbalance occurs, an illness is manifested.[14] These concepts, of course, provide one way of determining the remedy for a particular illness. For example, if an illness is classified as hot, it is treated with a cold substance. A cold disease, in turn, must be treated with a hot substance. Food, beverages, animals, and people possess the characteristics of hot and cold to various degrees. Hot foods cannot be combined; they are to be eaten with cold foods. There is no general agreement as to what is a hot disease or food and what is a cold disease or food. The classification varies from person to person, and what is hot to one person may be cold to another.[15] Therefore, if a Chicano patient refuses to eat the meals offered to him in the hospital, it is wise to ask precisely what he can eat and what combinations of foods he thinks would be helpful for the existing condition. It is important to note that *hot* and *cold* do not refer to temperature but are descriptive of a particular substance itself.

For example, after a woman delivers a baby, a hot experience, she cannot eat pork, which is considered a hot food. She must eat something cold to restore her balance. Penicillin is a hot medication; therefore, it cannot be used to treat a hot disease.[16] The major problem for the health-care provider is to *know* that the rules, so to speak, of hot and cold vary from person to person. If health-care providers understand the general nature of the hot and cold imbalance, they will be able to help the patient reveal the nature of the problem from the patient's perspective.

Dislocation of Parts of the Body. Two examples of "dislocation" are *empacho* and *caida de la mollera.*[17]

Empacho is believed to be caused by a ball of food clinging to the wall of the stomach. Common symptoms of this illness are stomach pains and cramps. This ailment is treated by rubbing and gently pinching the spine. Prayers are recited throughout the treatment. Another, more common, cause of such illness is thought to be lying about the amount of food consumed.[18]

A 20-year-old Hispanic woman experienced the acute onset of sharp abdominal pain. She complained to her friend, and together they diagnosed the problem as *empacho* and treated it by massaging her stomach and waiting for the pain to dissipate. It did not, and they continued folk treatment for 48 hours. When the pain did not diminish, they sought help in a nearby hospital. The diagnosis was "acute appendicitis." The young woman nearly died and was quite embarrassed when she was scolded by the physician for not seeking help sooner.

Caida de la mollera is a more serious illness. It occurs in infants and young children aged under 1 year who are dehydrated for some reason (usually because of diarrhea or severe vomiting) and whose anterior fontanelle is depressed below the contour of the skull.[19] Much superstition and mystery surrounds this problem. Some of the poorly educated and rural people, in particular, believe that it is caused by a nurse's or physician's having touched the head of the baby. This can be understood if we take into account that (1) the fontanelle of an infant does become depressed if the infant is dehydrated and (2) when physicians or nurses measure an infant's head they do touch this area. If a mother brings her baby to a physician for an examination and sees the physician touch the child's head, and if the baby gets sick thereafter with *caida de la mollera*, it might be very easy for this woman to believe it is the fault of the physician's or nurse's touch. Unfortunately, epidemics of diarrhea are common in the rural and urban areas of the Southwest, and a number of children tend to be affected. One case of severe dehydration that leads to *caida de la mollera* may create quite a stir among the people. The folk treatment of this illness has not been found to be effective. Unfortunately, babies are rarely brought to the hospital in time, and the mortality rate for this illness is high.[20]

Magic or Supernatural Causes Outside the Body. Witchcraft or possession is considered to be culturally patterned role playing, a safe vehicle for restoring oneself. Witchcraft or possession legitimizes acting out bizarre behavior or engaging in incoherent speech.[21]

A lesser disease that is caused from outside the body is *mal ojo. Mal ojo* means "bad eye," and it is believed to result from excessive admiration on the part of another. General malaise, sleepiness, fatigue, and severe headache are the symptoms of this condition. The folk treatment is to find the person who has caused the illness by casting the "bad eye" and have him care for the afflicted person.[22]

Strong Emotional States. *Susto* is described as an illness arising from fright. It afflicts many people—males and females, rich and poor, rural dwellers and urbanities. It involves *soul loss:* the soul is able to leave the body and wander freely. This can occur while a person is dreaming or when a person experiences a particularly traumatic event. The symptoms of the disease are (1) restlessness while sleeping, (2) listlessness, anorexia, and disinterest in personal appearance when awake, including disinterest in both clothing and personal hygiene, (3) loss of strength, depression, and introversion. The person is treated by a *curandero* (a folk healer, discussed in the section on *curanderismo*) who coaxes the soul back into the person's body. During the healing rites, the person is massaged and made to relax.[23]

Envidia. *Envidia,* or envy, also is considered to be a cause of illness and bad luck. Many people believe that to succeed is to fail. That is, when one's success provokes the envy of friends and neighbors, misfortune can befall the person and his or her family. For example, a successful farmer, just when he is able to purchase extra clothing and equipment, is stricken with a fatal illness. He may well attribute the cause of this illness to the envy of his peers. A number of social scientists have, after much research, concluded that the "low" economic and success rates of the Chicano can ostensibly be attributed to belief in *envidia.*[24]

Religious Rituals

Magicoreligious practices are quite common among the Chicano population. The more severe an illness, the more likely these practices are observed. There are four types of practices: (1) making promises, (2) visiting shrines, (3) offering medals and candles, and (4) offering prayers.[25] It is not unusual for the people residing near the southern border of the continental United States to return home to Mexico on religious pilgrimages. The film mentioned in Chapter 7, "We Believe in Niño Fedencio," demonstrates how these pilgrimages are conducted. The lighting of candles also is a frequently observed practice. These beautiful candles made of beeswax and tallow can be purchased in many stores, particularly grocery stores and pharmacies that are located in Chicano neighborhoods (Figs. 13–1 and 13–2). Many homes have shrines with statues and pictures of saints. The candles are lit here and prayers are recited. Some homes have altars with statues and pictures on them and are the focal point of the home. Some Chicanos are devoted to the Virgin de San Juan del Valle and make pilgrimages to the shrine in San Juan, Texas (Fig. 13–3).

Curanderismo

There are no specific rules for knowing who in the community uses the services of the folk healers. Not all Chicanos do, and not all Chicanos believe in their precepts. Initially, it was thought that only the poor used a folk healer, or *curandero,* because they were unable to get treatment from the larger, institutionalized health-care establishments. It now appears, however, that the use of healers occurs widely throughout the Chicano population. Some people try to use healers exclusively, whereas others use them along with institutionalized care. The healers do not advertise, but they are well known throughout the population because of informal community and kinship networks.

Curanderismo is defined as a medical system.[26] It is a coherent view with historical roots that combine Aztec, Spanish, spiritualistic, homeopathic, and scientific elements.

The *curandero* is a holistic healer. The people who seek help from him or her do so for social, physical, and psychological purposes. The *curandero(a)*

Figure 13–1. A traditional community resource (Yerberia) in Mission, Texas, where a person seeking traditional remedies and amulets may purchase them. *(Photograph by R. Spector, 1993.)*

can be either a male or female, a "specialist" or a "generalist," a full-time or part-time practitioner. Chicanos who believe in *curanderos* consider them to be religious figures.

A *curandero* may receive the "gift of healing" through three means. (1) He or she may be "born" to heal. In this case it is known from the moment of a *curandero*'s birth that something unique about this person means he or she is destined to be a healer. (2) He or she may learn by apprenticeship—that is, a person is taught the ways of healing, especially the use of herbs. (3) He or she may receive a "calling" through a dream, trance, or vision by which contact is made with the supernatural by means of a "patron" (or "caller"), who may be a saint. The "call" comes either during adolescence or during the midlife crises. This "call" is resisted at first. Later the person becomes resigned to his or her fate and gives in to the demands of the "calling."

Treatment

The most popular form of treatment used by folk healers involves herbs, especially when used as teas. The *curandero* knows what specific herbs to use for a problem. This information is revealed in dreams in which the "patron" gives suggestions.

A

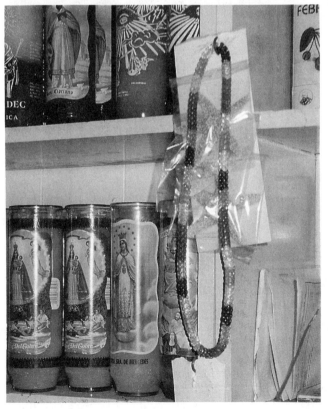

B

Figure 13–2. Samples of amulets, (**A**) and candles, (**B**) sold in Sr. Garcia's Yerberia. *(Photographs by R. Spector, 1993.)*

Figure 13–3 A person is giving thanks to the Virgin of San Jaun de la Valle for the recovery of a loved one. (*Source: Spector Collection, R. Spector photograph.*)

Because the *curandero* has a religious orientation, much of the treatment includes elements of both the Catholic and Pentecostal rituals and artifacts: offerings of money, penance, confession, lighting candles, wooden or metal offerings in the shape of the afflicted anatomical parts (*milagros*), and laying on of hands. Massage is used in illnesses, such as *empacho* (discussed in the section on body imbalance).

Cleanings, or *limpias,* are done in two ways. The first is by passing an unbroken egg over the body of the ill person. The second method entails passing herbs tied in a bunch over the body. The back of the neck, which is considered a vulnerable spot, is given particular attention.

In contrast to the depersonalized care Chicanos expect to receive in medical institutions, their relationship with and care by the *curandero* are uniquely personal, as demonstrated in Table 13–1. This special relationship between the Chicano and the *curandero* may well account for this folk healer's popularity. In addition to the close, personal relationship between patient and healer, other factors may explain the continuing belief in *curanderismo.*

TABLE 13–1. COMPARISONS BETWEEN CURANDERO AND PHYSICIAN

Curandero	Physician
1. Maintains informal, friendly, affective relationship with entire family	1. Businesslike, formal relationship; deals only with the patient
2. Comes to house day or night	2. Patient must go to physician's office or clinic, and only during the day; may have to wait for hours to be seen; home visits are rarely made
3. For diagnosis, consults with head of house, creates a mood of awe, talks to all family members, is not authoritarian, has social rapport, builds expectation of cure	3. Rest of family is usually ignored; deals solely with the ill person, and may deal only with the sick part of the patient; authoritarian manner creates fear
4. Is generally less expensive than physicians	4. More expensive than *curanderos*
5. Has ties to the "world of the sacred"; has rapport with the symbolic, spiritual, creative, or holy force	5. Secular; pays little attention to the religious beliefs or meaning of a given illness
6. Shares the world view of the patient—that is, speaks the same language, lives in the same neighborhood or in some similar socioeconomic conditions, may know the same people, understands the lifestyle of the patient	6. Generally does not share the world view of the patient—that is, may not speak the same language, does not live in the same neighborhood, does not understand the socioeconomic conditions or lifestyle of the patient

1. The mind and body are inseparable.

2. The central problem of life is to maintain harmony, including social, physical, and psychological aspects of the person.

3. There must be harmony between the hot and cold, wet and dry. The treatment of illness should restore the body's harmony, which has been lost.

4. The patient is the passive recipient of disease when the disease is caused by an external force. This external force disrupts the natural order of the internal person, and the treatment must be designed to restore this order. The causes of disharmony are evil and witches.

5. A person is related to the spirit world. When the body and soul are separated, "soul loss can occur." This loss is sometimes caused by *susto*, a disease or illness resulting from fright, which may afflict individuals from all socioeconomic levels and lifestyles.

6. The responsibility for recovery is shared by the ill person, the family, and the *curandero.*

7. The natural world is not clearly distinguished from the supernatural world. Thus, the *curandero* can coerce, curse, and appease the spirits. The *curandero* places more emphasis on his or her connections with the sacred and the gift of healing than on personal properties. (Such personal properties might include, for example, social status, a large home, and expensive material goods.)

TABLE 13–2. CLASSIFICATION OF SELECTED EMOTIONAL ILLNESSES IN SEGMENTS OF THE HISPANIC POPULATION

Disease type	Common cause	Specific diseases
Mental illness	Heredity	Epilepsy (*epilepsia*)
	Hex	Evil eye (*mal ojo*)
		Witchcraft (*hechiceria*)
	Worry	Anxiety (*tirisia*)
	Fright	Hysteria (*histeria*)
	(*Susto*)	Nervous breakdown (*ataque de nervios*)
	Blow to the head	Craziness (*locura*)
Moral illness	Vice	User of—drugs (*drogadicto*)
		—Marijuana (*marijuanero*)
	Character weakness	Alcoholism (*alcoholismo*)
	Emotions	Jealousy (*celos*)
		Rage (*coraje*)

From: Spencer, R. T., Nichols, L. W., Lipkin, G. B., et al. *Clinical Pharmacology and Nursing Management* (4th ed.). (Philadelphia: Lippincott, 1993), p. 133. Reprinted with permission.

TABLE 13–3. ETHNOPHARMACOLOGIC TEAS COMMONLY USED TO TREAT MENTAL AILMENTS

Language name	English name	Botanical name	Ailment treated
Manzanilla	Camomile	*Matricaria chamomilla*	Cure fright (*susto*)
Yerba buena	Spearmint	*Mentha spicata*	Nervousness
Te de narranjo	Orange leaves	*Citrus aurantium*	Sedative, nervousness
Albacar	Sweet basil	*Ocimum basilicum*	Treat *susto*; ward off evil spirits

From: Spencer, R. T., Nichols, L. W., Lipkin, G. B. et al. *Clinical Pharmacology and Nursing Management* (4th ed.). (Philadelphia: Lippincott, 1993), p. 133. Reprinted with permission.

Several examples of emotional illnesses (Table 13–2) are found in the Hispanic, and frequently in Chicano, populations. These are further divided into mental illness (in which the illness is not judged) and moral illness (in which others can judge the victim). Ethnopharmacologic teas may be used to treat these maladies. (Table 13–3).

PUERTO RICANS

Puerto Rican migrants to the United States mainland are American citizens, albeit with a different language and culture. They are neither immigrants nor aliens. According to the 1990 census, at least 1,895,981[27] Puerto Ricans live on the mainland. They live mostly on the East Coast, with the greatest number living in New York City and metropolitan New Jersey. Most Puerto Ricans migrate to search for a better life or because relatives, particularly spouses and parents, have migrated previously. Life on the island of Puerto Rico is difficult because there is a high level of unemployment. Puerto Ricans are not well known or understood by the majority of people in the continental United States. Little is known about their cultural identity. Mainlanders tend to forget that Puerto Rico is, for the most part, a poor island whose people have many problems. When many Puerto Ricans migrate to the mainland, they bring many of their problems—especially those with poor health and social circumstance.[28]

Puerto Ricans, along with Cubans, constitute the most recent major immigration group to these shores. They cover the spectrum of racial differences and have practiced racial intermarriage. Many are Catholic, but some belong to Protestant sects.

Puerto Ricans and Chicanos perceive health and illness and use of folk healers and remedies in some similar ways, but there are also differences. Most studies on health and illness beliefs and healing have been conducted on Chicanos. It is not easy to find information about the beliefs of Puerto Ricans. Much of the information presented here was gleaned from students and patients. Both groups feel that their beliefs should be known by health-care deliverers. One student, whose mother is a healer and is teaching her daughter the art, corroborated much of the following material.

Common Folk Diseases and Their Treatment

Table 13–4 lists a number of folk diseases and the usual source and type of treatment.* Many of these diseases or disharmonies have been mentioned in the section on Chicano approaches. Nonetheless, there are subtle differences in the ways folk diseases are perceived by Chicanos and Puerto Ricans. For example, although diseases are classified as hot and cold, treatments—that is, food and medications—are categorized as hot (*caliente*), cold (*frío*), and cool (*fresco*). Cold illnesses are treated with hot remedies; hot diseases are treated with cold or *cool* remedies. Table 13–5 lists the major illnesses, foods, and medicines and herbs associated with the hot–cold system as it is applied among Puerto Ricans in New York City.

A number of activities are carried out to maintain the proper hot–cold balance in the body. The following list was prepared by a patient.

1. *Pasmo,* a form of paralysis, usually is caused by an upset in the hot–cold balance. For example, if a woman is ironing (hot) and then steps out into the rain (cold), she may get facial or other paralysis.

---

*The data contained in Table 13–4 were provided by Puerto Rican students and patients who were interviewed carefully several times.

TABLE 13–4. FOLK DISEASES

Name	Description	Treatment	Source of Treatment
Susto	Sudden fright, causing shock	Relaxation	Relative or friend
Fatique	Asthma-like symptoms	Oxygen; medications	Western health-care system
Pasmo	Paralysis-like symptoms, face or limbs	Prevention; massage	Folk
Empacho	Food forms into a ball and clings to the stomach, causing pain and cramps	Strong massage over the stomach; medication; gently pinching and rubbing the spine	Folk
Mal ojo	Sudden, unexplained illness in a usually well child or person	Prevention; babies wear a special charm	Depends on the severity of the symptoms; usually home or folk
Ataque	Screaming, falling to ground, wildly moving arms and legs	None—ends spontaneously	

TABLE 13–5. THE HOT–COLD CLASSIFICATION AMONG PUERTO RICANS

	Frio (cold)	Fresco (cool)	Caliente (hot)
Illness or bodily conditions	Arthritis Menstrual period Joint pains	Colds	Constipation Diarrhea Pregnancy Rashes Ulcers
Medicine and herbs		Bicarbonate of soda Linden flowers Milk of magnesia Nightshade Orange flower water Sage Tobacco	Anise Aspirin Castor oil Cinnamon Cod liver oil Iron tablets Penicillin Vitamins
Foods	Avocado Banana Coconut Lima beans Sugar cane White beans	Barley water Whole milk Chicken Fruits Honey Raisins Salt cod Watercress Onions Peas	Alcoholic beverages Chili peppers Chocolate Coffee Corn meal Evaporated milk Garlic Kidney beans

From: Schilling, B. and Brannon, E. "Health Related Dietary Practices," Cross-Cultural Counseling—A Guide for Nutrition and Health Counselors. (Alexandria, VA: United States Department of Agriculture, United States Department of Health and Human Services, Nutrition and Technical Services Division, September, 1986), p. 5. Reprinted with permission.

2. A person who is hot cannot sit under a mango tree (cold) because he or she can get a kidney infection or "back problems."
3. A baby should not be fed a formula (hot), as it may cause rashes; whole milk (cold) is acceptable.
4. A man who has been working (hot) must not go into the coffee fields (cold), or he could contract a respiratory illness.
5. A hot person must not drink cold water, as it could cause colic.

There is often a considerable time lag between disregarding these precautions and the occurrence of illness. A patient who had injured himself while lifting heavy cartons in a factory revealed that the "true" reason he was now experiencing prolonged back problems was because as a child he often sat under a mango tree when he was "hot" after running. This childhood habit had significantly damaged his back so that, as an adult, he was unable to lift heavy objects without causing injury.

Table 13–6 summarizes some of the behaviors a patient may manifest with certain illnesses thought to be caused by the hot–cold imbalance.

Puerto Ricans also share with others of Hispanic origin a number of beliefs in spirits and spiritualism. They believe that mental illness is caused primarily by evil spirits and forces. People with such disorders are preferably treated by a "spiritualist medium."[29] The psychiatric clinic is known as the place where *locos* go. This attitude is exemplified in the Puerto Rican approach to visions and the like. The social and cultural environment encourages the acceptance of having visions and hearing voices. In the dominant culture of the continental United States, when one has visions or hears voices, one is encouraged to see a psychiatrist. When a Puerto Rican regards this experience as a problem, he or she may seek help through *santeria*.[30]

Santeria is the form of Latin American magic that had its birth in Nigeria, the country of origin of the Yoruba people, who were brought to the new

TABLE 13–6. EXPECTED PATIENT BEHAVIOR WHEN THE HOT–COLD THEORY IS FOLLOWED

Condition	Expected Behavior
Pregnancy	Avoid hot foods and medicines—take cool medicines
Postpartum and menstruation	Avoid cool foods and medicine
Infant formulas containing evaporated milk (hot-classified)	Baby fed cold—classified whole milk or baby is given cool substance after formula (May be a diuretic)
Penicillin prescription (hot-classified symptoms)	May not take for diarrhea, constipation, rash (Hot medication)
Diuretic prescribed—needs to supplement with bananas or raisins	May not eat these cold-classified foods if problem is a cold or cold condition (This includes menses)
Diarrhea, rash, ulcers	Will not take hot-classified medicines
Cold, arthritis	Will not take cold-classified medicines, takes those which are hot-classified

Adapted from: Harwood, A. "The Hot-Cold Theory of Disease: Implications for Treatment of Puerto Rican Patients," *Journal of the American Medical Association* 216 (1971): 1154–1155. Reprinted with permission.

world as slaves over 400 years ago. The *santeria*, or *santero*, may use story telling as a way of helping people cope with day-to-day difficulties.[31] They brought with them their traditional religion, which was in time synthesized with Catholic images. The believers continue to worship in the traditional way, especially in Puerto Rico, Cuba, and Brazil. The Yorubas identified their gods—*orishas*—with the Christian saints and invested in these saints the same supernatural powers of gods. The *orishas*/saints related to health situations include the following:

Orisha	Saint	Health Problem
Chango	Saint Barbara	Violent death
Babalu-Aye	Saint Lazarus	Sickness
Bacoso	Saint Christopher	Infections
Ibeyi	Saints Cosmos and Damian	Infant illnesses
Ifa	Saint Anthony	Fertility
Yemaya	Our Lady of Regla	Maternity[32]

Santeria is a structured system consisting of *espiritismo*, which is practiced by gypsies and mediums who claim to have *facultades*. These special *facultades* provide them with the "license" to practice. The positions of the practitioners form a hierarchy: the head is the *babalow*, a male, second is the *presidente*, the head medium, and third are the *santeros*. Novices are the "believers." The *facultades* are given to the healer from protective Catholic saints, who have African names and are known as *protecciones*. *Santeria* can be practiced in storefronts, basements, homes, and even college dormitories. *Santeros* dress in white robes for ceremonies and wear special beaded bracelets as a sign of their identity.[33]

Puerto Ricans are able to accept much of what Anglos may judge to be idiosyncratic behavior. In fact, behavioral disturbances are seen as symptoms of illness that are to be treated, not judged. Puerto Ricans make a sharp distinction between "nervous" behavior and being *loco*. To be *loco* is to be bad, dangerous, evil. It also means losing all of one's social status. Puerto Ricans who seek standard American treatment for mental illness are castigated by the community. They understandably prefer to get help for the symptoms of mental illness from the *santero*, who accepts the symptoms and attributes the cause of the illness to spirits outside the body. Puerto Ricans have great faith in this system of care and maintain a high level of hope for recovery.[34]

The *santero* is an important person, respecting the patient and not gossiping about either the patient or his or her problems. Anyone can "pour his or her heart out" with no worry of being labeled or judged. The *santero* is able to tell a person what the problem is, prescribe the proper treatment, and tell the person what to do, how to do it, and when to do it. A study in New York found that 73% of the Puerto Rican patients in an outpatient mental health

TABLE 13–7. EXAMPLES OF CULTURAL PHENOMENA AFFECTING HEALTH AND HEALTH CARE AMONG HISPANIC AMERICANS

Nations of Origin:	Hispanic countries: Spain, Cuba, Mexico, Central and South America, Puerto Rico
Environmental Control:	Traditional health and illness beliefs may continue to be observed by "traditional" people.
	Folk medicine tradition
	Traditional healers:
	Curandero, Espiritista, Partera, Senora
Biological Variations:	Diabetes mellitus
	Parasites
	Coccidioidomycosis
	Lactose intolerance
Social Organization:	Nuclear families
	Large, extended family networks
	Compadrazzo (godparents)
	Strong church affiliations within community
	Community social organizations
Communication:	Spanish or Portuguese are the primary languages
Space:	Tactile relationships: touch, handshakes, embrace
	Value physical presence
Time Orientation:	Present

Adapted from: Spector, R. "Culture, Ethnicity, and Nursing," in *Fundamentals of Nursing,* (3rd. ed.), eds. P. Potter, and A. Perry, (St. Louis: Mosby-Yearbook, 1992), p. 101. Reprinted with permission.

clinic reported having visited a *santero.*[35] Often a sick person is taken to a psychiatrist by his family to be "calmed down" and prepared for treatment by a *santero*. Families may become angry if the psychiatrist does not encourage belief in God and prayer during the psychiatrist's work with the patient.[36] Because of cultural differences and beliefs, a psychiatrist often may diagnose as illness what Puerto Ricans may define as health. Frequently, a spiritualist treats the "mental illness" of a patient as *facultades,* which makes the patient a "special person." Thus, esteem is granted to the patient as a form of treatment.[37] A number of cultural phenomena affect the health and health care of Hispanic Americans (Table 13–7).

Entry into Mainland Health Systems

Puerto Ricans living in New York City and other parts of the northern United States experience a high rate of illness and hospitalization during their first year on the mainland,[38] as do other people of Hispanic origin. It is worthwhile considering the vast differences between living in New York and living in Puerto Rico. In Puerto Rico, winter weather is unheard of. The winters in the north can be bitter cold, and adjustment to climate change in itself is extremely difficult. Migrant people may be forced to live in crowded living quarters with poor sanitation.

Puerto Ricans seeking health care may go to a physician or to a folk practitioner or to both. The general progression of seeking care is as follows:

1. The person seeks advice from a daughter, mother, grandmother, or neighbor woman. These sources are consulted because the women of this culture are the primary healers and dispensers of medicine on the family level.
2. If the advice is not sufficient, the person may seek help from a *senoria* (a woman who is especially knowledgeable about the causes and treatment of illness).
3. If the *senoria* is unable to help, the person goes to a more sophisticated folk practitioner, an *espiritista* or a *curandera*. If the problem is "psychiatric," a *santero* may be consulted. These names describe similar people—those who obtain their knowledge from spirits and treat illness according to the instructions of the spirits. Herbs, lotions, creams, and massage often are used.
4. If the person is still not satisfied, he or she may go to a physician.
5. If the results are not satisfactory, the person may return to a folk practitioner. He or she may seek medical help sooner than Step 4 or may go back and forth between the two systems.

Not all Puerto Ricans use the folk system. Health-care providers should remember that people who appear to have delayed seeking health care have most likely counted on curing their illness through the culturally known and well-understood folk process. Often when people disappear—or elope from the established health system—they may have elected to return to the folk system. Those who elope from the larger, institutionalized medical system may visit *botanica*. In these small *botanicas*, one can purchase herbs, potents, Florida water, ointments, and incense prescribed by the spiritualists. Some of these *botanicas* are so busy that each customer is given a number and is assisted only after the number is called.[39] There are 24 *botanicas* located in one small area of New York City. A Spanish-speaking colleague and I visited a *botanica* in Boston that was similar to a pharmacy. The door was locked, but the proprietor admitted us when we revealed our identity. He explained the various remedies that were for sale. We were allowed to purchase only a few items because we did not have a spiritualist's prescription for herbs. The store also sold candles, religious statues, cards, medals, and relics.

A limited number of *santerias* place advertisements in local Spanish daily newspapers. Some of the more industrious ones distribute flyers in the New York City subways. Others maintain a low profile, and patients visit them because of their well-established reputations.

Current Health Problems

The Hispanic health profile is marked by diversity, and people of the Hispanic community experience perhaps the most varied set of health issues encountered by any of the emerging majority populations. The diversity in

TABLE 13–8. THE 10 LEADING CAUSES OF DEATH FOR HISPANICS IN 18 STATES AND THE DISTRICT OF COLUMBIA: 1987

Hispanics	Percentage	Rank	White Non-Hispanics	(%)
Heart disease	25	1	Heart disease	37
Cancer	17	2	Cancer	23
Injuries	9	3	Stroke	7
Stroke	6	4	Chronic lung disease	4
Homicide	5	5	Injuries	4
Liver disease	3	6	Pneumonia/influenza	4
Pneumonia/influenza	3	7	Diabetes	2
Diabetes	3	8	Suicide	2
HIV infection	3	9	Atherosclerosis	1
Perinatal conditions	3	10	Liver disease	1

Note: National death rate data are unavailable for Hispanics.
From: Department of Health and Human Services. Healthy People 2000, National Health Promotion and Disease Prevention Objectives—Full Report with Commentary. (Boston: Jones and Bartlett, 1992), p. 35. Reprinted with permission.

health problems is intertwined with the effects of socioeconomic status, and with geographic and cultural differences. The most important health issues for Hispanics are related to these demographic facts: the population is young and has a high birth rate.[40]

Mexican Americans have low rates of cerebrovascular disease; yet stroke rates among Puerto Ricans in New York are high. Infant mortality rates vary from group to group. The leading causes of death among Hispanic Americans illustrate differences between their health experiences and those of the total population, as can be seen in Table 13–8.

Hispanics experience a number of barriers when seeking health care. The most obvious one is language. In spite of the fact that Spanish-speaking people constitute one of the largest minority groups in this country, very few health-care deliverers speak Spanish. This is especially true in communities in which the number of Spanish-speaking people is relatively small. Hispanics who live in these areas experience tremendous frustration because of the language barrier. Even in large cities, there are far too many occasions when a sick person has to rely on a young child to act not only as a translator but also as interpreter. One way of sensitizing young nursing students to the pain of this situation is to ask them to present a health problem to a person who does not speak or understand a word of English. Needless to say, this is extremely difficult; it is also embarrassing. People who try this rapidly comprehend and appreciate the feelings experienced by patients who are unable to speak or understand English. (After this experience, two of my students decided to take a foreign-language elective.) Language will continue to be a problem until (1) there are more physicians, nurses, and social workers from the Spanish-speaking communities and (2) more of the present deliverers of health care learn to speak Spanish.

A second crucial barrier that Hispanic people encounter is poverty. The diseases of the poor—for example, tuberculosis, malnutrition, and lead poisoning—all have high incidences among Spanish-speaking populations.

A final barrier to adequate health care is the time orientation of Hispanic Americans. To Hispanics, time is a relative phenomenon. Little attention is given to the *exact* time of day. The frame of reference is wider, and the issue is whether it is day or night.[41] The American health-care system, on the other hand, places great emphasis on promptness. Health-care providers demand that clients arrive at the exact time of the appointment—despite the fact that clients are often kept waiting. Health-system workers stress the client's promptness rather than their own. In fact, they tend to deny responsibility for the waiting periods by blaming them on the "system." Many facilities commonly schedule all appointments for 9:00 AM, when it is clearly known and understood by the staff members that the doctor will not even arrive until 11:00 AM or later. The Hispanic person frequently responds to this practice by coming late for appointments or failing to come at all. They prefer to attend walk-in clinics, where the waits are shorter. They also much prefer going to traditional healers.

HEALTHY PEOPLE 2000: SELECTED OBJECTIVES

The following are examples of the health objectives from *Healthy People 2000* that target members of the Hispanic American community:

1. Reduce growth retardation among low-income Hispanic children younger than age 1 to less than 10% (Baseline: 13% in 1988).
2. Reduce cigarette smoking to a prevalence of no more than 18% among Hispanics aged 20 and older (Baseline: 33% in 1982–1984).
3. Reduce pregnancies among Hispanic adolescent girls aged 15 through 19 to no more than 105 per 1,000 (Baseline: 158 per 1,000 in 1985).
4. Reduce the prevalence of infertility among Hispanic couples to no more than 9% (Baseline: 12.4% of married couples with wives aged 25–44 in 1988).
5. Reduce homicides among Hispanic men aged 15 through 34 to no more than 42.5 per 100,000 (Baseline: 53.1 per 100,000 in 1987).
6. Increase years of healthy life among Hispanics to at least 65 years (Baseline: an estimated 62 years in 1980).
7. Reduce the infant mortality rate among Puerto Ricans to no more than 8 per 1,000 live births (Baseline: 12.9 per 1,000 live births in 1984).
8. Reduce the neonatal mortality rate among Puerto Ricans to no more than 5.2 per 1,000 live births (Baseline: 8.6 per 1,000 live births in 1984).

9. Confine annual incidence of diagnosed AIDS cases among Hispanics to no more than 18,000 (Baseline: An estimated 7,000–8,000 cases diagnosed in 1989).
10. Reduce tuberculosis among Hispanics to an incidence of no more than 5 cases per 100,000 Hispanics (Baseline: 18.3 per 100,000 in 1988).[42]

Hispanic American Health-Care Manpower

The number of Americans of Hispanic origin who are enrolled in health programs or who in practice in selected health professions is low. Tables 13–9 and 13–10 illustrate this phenomenon. Efforts must be made to recruit and maintain more Hispanics in the health professions.

TABLE 13–9. PERCENTAGE OF HISPANICS ENROLLED IN SELECTED HEALTH PROFESSIONS SCHOOLS: 1990–1991

Program	Total Enrollment	Percentage Hispanic
Allopathic medicine	66,163	5.4
Osteopathic medicine	6,792	0.5
Dentistry	15,770	6.8
Optometry	4,650	4.0
Pharmacy	22,764	4.2
Podiatry	2,226	6.6
Registered nursing	221,170	3.0
Veterinary medicine	7,787	2.9

From: U.S. Department of Health and Human Services. *Health United States 1992;* and *Healthy People 2000* Review. (Washington, D.C.: United States Department of Health and Human Services, Public Health Service Centers for Disease Control and Prevention. DHHS Pub. No. (PHS) 93–1232, 1993), pp. 150–151. Reprinted with permission.

TABLE 13–10. PERCENTAGE OF HISPANICS ENROLLED IN SELECTED HEALTH PROFESSIONS SCHOOLS COMPARED WITH WHITES: 1991

Profession	Non-Hispanic White (%)	Hispanic (%)
Physicians	73.5	5.4
Dentists	70.9	6.8
Optometrists	79.7	4.0
Pharmacists	80.5	4.2
Podiatrists	75.1	6.6
Registered nurses	82.8	3.0
Veterinarians	92.5	2.9

From: U.S. Department of Health and Human Services. *Health United States 1992;* and *Healthy People 2000* Review. (Washington, D.C.: United States Department of Health and Human Services, Public Health Service Centers for Disease Control and Prevention. DHHS Pub. No. (PHS) 93–1232, 1993), pp. 150–151. Reprinted with permission.

REFERENCES

1. Lee, F. R. "In El Barrio, Another Cycle of Suffering." *New York Times* (May 28, 1995), p. 29.
2. Department of Health and Human Services. *Healthy People 2000,* National Health Promotion and Disease Prevention Objectives—Full Report with Commentary. Boston: Jones and Barlett, 1992, p. 34.
3. Simmen, E., ed. *Pain and Promise: The Chicano Today* (New York: New American Library, 1972), p. 35.
4. Ibid., p. 36.
5. U.S. Bureau of the Census. *1990 Census of the Population,* General Population Characteristics United States, Series 1990 CP-1-1 (Washington, D.C.: U.S. Government Printing Office, 1992), p. 23.
6. Russell, G. "It's Your Turn in the Sun." *Time* (16 October 1978), p. 48.
7. Simmen, E. "Anonymous, Who Am I?" in *Educating the Mexican American,* ed. Johnson, H. S. and Hernandez–M, W. J. (Valley Forge, PA: Judson Press, 1970), p. 38.
8. Simmen, E. and Bureau of the Census. "We Mexican Americans," in *Educating the Mexican American,* ed. Johnson, H. S. and Hernandez–M, W. J. (Valley Forge, PA: Judson Press, 1970), pp. 45–47.
9. Ibid., p. 47.
10. Ibid., pp. 49–52.
11. Welch, S., Comer, J., and Steinman, M. "Some Social and Attitudinal Correlates of Health Care among Mexican Americans." *Journal of Health and Social Behavior* 14 (September 1973): 205.
12. Lucero, G. "Health and Illness in the Chicano Community" (lecture given at Boston College School of Nursing, March 1975).
13. Ibid.
14. Currier, R. L. "The Hot–Cold Syndrome and Symbolic Balance in Mexican and Spanish-American Folk Medicine." *Ethnology* 5 (March 1966): 251–263.
15. Saunders, L. "Healing Ways in the Spanish Southwest," in *Patients, Physicians, and Illness,* ed. E. G. Jaco (Glencoe, IL: Free Press, 1958), p. 193.
16. Ibid.
17. Nall, F. C., II and Spielberg, J. "Social and Cultural Factors in the Responses of Mexican-Americans to Medical Treatment." *Journal of Health and Social Behavior* 8 (1967): 302.
18. Ibid.
19. Dorsey, P. R. and Jackson, H. Q. "Cultural Health Traditions: The Latino/Chicano Perspective," in *Providing Safe Nursing Care for Ethnic People of Color,* ed. Branch, M. F. and Paxton, P. P. (New York: Appleton-Century-Crofts, 1976), p. 56.
20. Lucero. "Health and Illness."
21. Ibid.
22. Nall and Spielberg. "Responses of Mexican-Americans," p. 302.
23. Rubel, A. J. "The Epidemiology of a Folk Illness: Susto in Hispanic America." *Ethnology* 3(3) (July 1964): 270–271.
24. Lucero. "Health and Illness."
25. Nall and Spielberg. "Responses of Mexican-Americans," p. 303.
26. Maduro, R. J. *"Curanderismo:* Latin American Folk Healing" (Conference, "Ways of Healing, Ancient and Modern." San Francisco, January 1976); Kiev, A. *Curan-*

derismo: Mexican-American Folk Psychiatry (New York: Free Press, 1968); Lucero. "Health and Illness."

27. U.S. Bureau of the Census. *1990 Census of the Population,* 1992, p. 23.
28. Cohen, R. E. "Principles of Preventive Mental Health Programs for Ethnic Minority Populations: The Acculturation of Puerto Ricans to the United States." *American Journal of Psychiatry* 128(12) (June 1972): 79.
29. Ibid.
30. Mumford, E. "Puerto Rican Perspectives on Mental Illness." *Mount Sinai Journal of Medicine* 40(6) (November–December 1973): 771.
31. Flores, Y. "Santero in Los Angeles, California," Personal Interview, 10 June, 1991.
32. Gonzalez–Wippler, M. *Santeria—African Magic in Latin America.* (Bronx, NY: Original Publications, 1987), pp. 1–30; Riva, A. *Devotions to the Saints.* (Los Angeles: International Imports, 1990), pp. 91–93.
33. Mumford. "Puerto Rican Perspective."
34. Ibid.
35. Ibid., p. 772.
36. Ibid., p. 773.
37. Ibid., p. 771.
38. Ibid.
39. Ibid., p. 772.
40. Department of Health and Human Services. *Healthy People 2000,* p. 34.
41. Lucero. "Health and Illness."
42. Department of Health and Human Services, *Healthy People 2000,* pp. 599–601.

ANNOTATED BIBLIOGRAPHY

Butler, H. *Doctor Gringo.* New York: Rand McNally, 1967.
   This is the story of a young physician who practices modern medicine in a remote village in Mexico. It aptly describes the differences between the cultural beliefs of the people and standard American medicine.
Kiev, A. *Curanderismo: Mexican-American Folk Psychiatry.* New York: Free Press, 1968.
   Kiev presents an in-depth study of Mexican-American folk psychiatry in San Antonio, Texas. In this study, the folk healer's sensitivity to the nuances and subtleties of psychopathology among members of this group are examined.
Lewis, O. *The Children of Sanchez: Autobiography of a Mexican Family.* New York: New American Library, 1961.
Lewis, O. *A Death in the Sanchez Family.* New York: Random House, 1966.
Lewis, O. *Five Families: Mexican Case Studies in the Culture of Poverty.* New York: New American Library, 1959.
Lewis, O. *La Vida: A Puerto Rican Family in the Culture of Poverty.* New York: Random House, 1966.
   The works of Oscar Lewis, each in its own way, portray a "slice of life" of the people he observed. The books are very relevant and helpful in the context of cultural diversity in health care.
Padilla, E. *Up from Puerto Rico.* New York: Columbia University Press, 1958.
   This book describes the Puerto Rican migration to New York City and explores the issues inherent in a large migration of people.

Rand, C. *The Puerto Ricans*. New York: Oxford University Press, 1958.
    The contrasts between living in New York City and living in Puerto Rico are explored in this book.
Rogler, L. H. *Migrant in the City*. New York: Basic Books, 1972.
    Rogler relates the story of a Puerto Rican action group and how it involved people who came from Puerto Rican slums to New York.
Simmen, E., ed. *Pain and Promise: The Chicano Today*. New York: New American Library, 1972.
    Vivid, sensitive accounts of the reawakening of a proud and oppressed people are presented. The book consists of numerous essays—written mainly by Chicanos—that explore the identity and life of the people.
Steiner, S. *Al Raza: The Mexican Americans*. New York: Harper and Row, 1969.
    This book consists of essays, short stories, and poetry illustrating the life and beliefs of the Chicano people.
Thomas, P. *Down These Mean Streets*. New York: Signet, 1958.
Thomas P. *Savior, Savior, Hold My Hand*. Garden City, NY: Doubleday, 1972.
    Both these books depict life in the streets of Harlem as experienced by the writer.

FURTHER SUGGESTED READINGS

Articles

Abril, I. "Mexican American Folk Beliefs That Affect Health Care." *Arizona Nurse* 28 (May–June 1975): 14–20.
Aguirre, L. R. "The Meaning of the Chicano Movement," in *We Are Chicanos,* ed. Orrego, P. D. New York: Washington Square, 1973.
Allinger, R. L. "Beliefs about Treatment of Hypertension among Hispanic Older Persons." *Topics in Clinical Nursing* 7(3) (October 1985): 26–31.
Alonso, J., Anto, J. M., and Moreno, C. "Spanish Version of the Nottingham Health Profile: Translation and Preliminary Validity." *American Journal of Public Health* 80, 5 (1990): 704–708.
American Journal of Public Health (Supplement). *Hispanic Health and Nutrition Examination Survey, 1982–1984: Findings on Health Status and Health Care Needs* (1990). 80.
Baca, J. "Some Health Beliefs of the Spanish-speaking." *American Journal of Nursing* (October 1969): 2172–2176.
Baca, J. E. "Some Health Beliefs of the Spanish-speaking." *American Journal of Nursing* (October 1972): 1852–1854.
Becerra, J., Atrash, H., Perez, N., et al. "Low Birthweight and Infant Mortality in Puerto Rico." *American Journal of Public Health.* 83(11) (1993): 1572–1576.
Becerra, J. and Smith, J. "Breastfeeding Patterns in Puerto Rico." *American Journal of Public Health.* 80(6) (1990): 694–697.
Canino, G., Anthony, J., Freeman, D., et al. "Drug Abuse and Illicit Drug Use in Puerto Rico." *American Journal of Public Health.* 83(2) (1993): 194–200.
Cohen, R. "Principles of Preventive Mental Health Programs for Ethnic Minority Populations: The Acculturation of Puerto Ricans to the United States." *American Journal of Psychiatry* 128 (June 1972): 79–83.
Coler, M. S. "An Axial Representation of Community Mental Health Nursing Diagnoses of a Country at War: El Salvador." *Nursing Diagnosis* 4(2) (1993): 63–69.

Darabi, K. F. and Ortiz, V. "Childbearing among Young Latino Women in the United States." *American Journal of Public Health* 77 (January 1987): 25–28.

Dean, C. "Problems Encountered by the Aged Mexican-American in Health Care and Hospitalization." *Kansas Nurse* 59(1) (January 1984): 8–10.

Diede, N. R. "Transcultural Nursing in a Migrant School." *Home Healthcare Nurse* 4(5) (September–October 1986): 39–43.

Foreman, J. T. "Susto and the Health Needs of the Cuban Refugee Population—Symptoms of Depression and Withdrawal from Normal Social Activity." *Topics in Clinical Nursing* 7(3) (October 1985): 40–47.

Garrison, V. "Doctor, *Espiritista,* or Psychiatrist? Health-seeking Behavior in a Puerto Rican Neighborhood in New York City." *Medical Anthropology* 1 (January 1977): 65–180.

Garrison, V. "The 'Puerto Rican Syndrome' in Psychiatry and *Espiritismo,*" in *Case Studies in Spirit Possession,* ed. Crapanzano, V. and Garrison, V. New York: Wiley, 1977.

Guendelman, S. "Developing Responsiveness to the Health Needs of Hispanic Children and Families." *Social Work in Health Care* 8(4) (Summer 1983): 1–15.

Guendelman, S. and Abrams, B. "Dietary Intake among Mexican-American Women: Generational Differences and a Comparison with White Non-Hispanic Women." *American Journal of Public Health* 85(1) (1995): 20–25.

Harwood, A. "The Hot–Cold Theory of Disease." *Journal of the American Medical Association* 216 (17 May 1971): 1153–1158.

Hayes-Bautista, D. E. "Identifying Hispanic Populations: The Influence of Research Methodology upon Public Policy." *American Journal of Public Health* 70(4) (April 1980): 353–358.

Hayes-Bautista, D. E. and Chapa, J. "Latino Terminology: Conceptual Bases for Standardized Terminology." *American Journal of Public Health* 77 (1987): 61–72.

Hoppe, S. K. and Heller, P. L. "Alienation, Familism, and the Utilization of Health Services by Mexican Americans." *Journal of Health and Social Behavior* 16 (September 1975): 304–314.

Johnson, C. A. "Mexican-American Women in the Labor Force and Lowered Fertility." *American Journal of Public Health* 66(12) (December 1976): 1186–1188.

Lauria, A., Jr. " 'Respeto,' 'Rela Jo' and Interpersonal Relations in Puerto Rico." *Anthropological Quarterly* 5 (April 1964): 53–67.

Lawrence, T. F. L., Bozzetti, L., and Kane, T. J. "Curanderas: A Unique Role for Mexican Women." *Psychiatric Annals* 2 (February 1976): 65–73.

Litwin, B. "Clinical Consideration in Treating Minority Patients, Part 3." *Clinical Management in Physical Therapy* 2(3) (Fall 1982): 6–7.

Markides, K. S., Coreil, J., and Ray, L. A. "Smoking among Mexican Americans: A Three-Generation Study." *American Journal of Public Health* 775 (1987): 708–712.

Markides, K. S., Krause, N., and Mendes de Leon, C. F. "Acculturation and Alcohol Consumption among Mexican Americans: A Three-Generation Study." *American Journal of Public Health* 7810 (1988): 1178–1186.

Marks, G., et al. "Health Behavior of Elderly Hispanic Women: Does Cultural Assimilation Make a Difference?" *American Journal of Public Health* 77 (December 1987): 1315–1324.

Martaus, T. M. "The Health-Seeking Process of Mexican-American Migrant Farmworkers." *Home Healthcare Nurse* 4(5) (September–October 1986): 32–38.

Martinez, C. and Martin, H. "Folk Diseases among Urban Mexican Americans." *Journal of the American Medical Association* 196 (11 April 1966): 147–150.

Martinez, R. and Wetli, C. "Santeria: A Magico-Religious System of Afro-Cuban Origin." *American Journal of Social Psychiatry.* 2(3) (1982): 32–38.

Mumford, E. "Puerto Rican Perspectives on Mental Health." *Mount Sinai Journal of Medicine* 40 (November–December 1973): 768–779.

Nall, F. C., II and Speilberg, J. "Social and Cultural Factors in the Responses of Mexican-Americans to Medical Treatment." *Journal of Health and Social Behavior* 8 (1967): 299–308.

Notzon, F., Bobadilla, J., and Coria, I. "Birthweight Distributions in Mexico City and among U.S. Southwest Mexican Americans: The Effect of Altitude." *American Journal of Public Health.* 82(7) (1992): 1014–1017.

O'Brien, M. E. "Pragmatic Survivalism: Behavior Patterns Affecting Low-Level Wellness among Minority Group Members." *Advances in Nursing Science* (April 1982): 13–26.

Ortiz, J. S. "The Prevalence of Intestinal Parasites in Puerto Rican Farm Workers in Western Massachusetts." *American Journal of Public Health* 70(10) (October 1980) 1103–1105.

Pasquali, E. A. "Santeria: A Religion That Is a Health Care System for Long Island Cuban-Americans." *Journal of the New York State Nurses' Association* 17(1) (March 1986): 12–15.

Perez-Stable, E., Marin, G., and VanOss Martin, B. "Behavioral Risk Factors: A Comparison of Latinos and Non-Latino Whites in San Francisco." *American Journal of Public Health.* 84(6) (1994): 971–976.

Phillipos, M. J. "Successful and Unsuccessful Approaches to Mental Health Services for an Urban Hispano American Population." *American Journal of Public Health* 61 (April 1971): 820–830.

Pick de Weiss, S., and David, H. P. "Illegal Abortion in Mexico: Client Perceptions." *American Journal of Public Health* 80 (June 1990): 715–716.

Reinhert, B. R. "The Health Care Beliefs and Values of Mexican-Americans." *Home Healthcare Nurse* 4(5) (September–October 1986): 23, 26–27.

Roberts, R. E. "The Health of Mexican-Americans: Evidence from the Human Population Laboratory Studies." *American Journal of Public Health* 70(4) (April 1980): 375–384.

Rodriquez, J. "Mexican Americans—Factors Influencing Health Practices." *Journal of School Health* 53(2) (February 1983): 136–139.

Rogler, L. D. and Hollingshead, A. B. "The Puerto Rican Spiritualist as a Psychiatrist." *American Journal of Sociology* 5 (July 1961): 17–21.

Romaine, M. E. "Clinical Management, of the Spanish-speaking Patient, Part 4." *Clinical Management in Physical Therapy* 2(3) (Fall 1982): 9–10.

Rubel, A. J. "Concepts of Disease in Mexican-American Culture." *American Anthropologist* 62 (October 1960): 795–814.

Rubel, A. J. "The Epidemiology of a Folk Illness: Susto in Hispanic America." *Ethnology* 6 (July 1964): 268–282.

Russell, G. "It's Your Turn in the Sun." *Time* 112(16) (16 October 1978): 48–61.

Sabagh, G. "Fertility Planning Status of Chicano Couples in Los Angeles." *American Journal of Public Health* 70(1) (January 1980): 56–61.

Santiago, E. "A Puerto Rican Stew," *New York Times* Magazine, (December 18, 1994): 34–36.

Saunders, L. "Healing Ways in the Spanish Southwest," in *Patients, Physicians, and Illness,* ed. Jaco, E. G. Glencoe, IL: Free Press, 1958.

Shiono, P. H. and Klebanoff, M. A. "Ethnic Differences in Preterm and Very Preterm Delivery." *American Journal of Public Health* 76 (December 1986): 1317–1322.

Simmons, L. W. "Cultural Patterns in Childbirth." *American Journal of Nursing* 52(8) (August 1952): 989–991.

Smith, K., McGraw, S., Crawford, S., et al. "HIV Risk among Latino Adolescents in Two New England Cities." *American Journal of Public Health.* 83(10) (1993): 1395–1399.

Staton, R. D. "A Comparison of Mexican and Mexican-American Families." *Family Co-ordinator* 21 (July 1972): 325–329.

Weaver, J. L. "Mexican American Health Care Behavior: A Critical Review of the Literature." *Social Science Quarterly* 54 (June 1973): 85–102.

Welch, S., Comer, J., and Steinman, M. "Some Social and Attitudinal Correlates of Health Care among Mexican Americans." *Journal of Health and Social Behavior* 14 (September 1975): 205–213.

Wendeborn, J. D. "Administrative Considerations in Treating Hispanic Patient, Part 2." *Clinical Management in Physical Therapy* 2(3) (Fall 1982): 8–9.

Whiteside, R. "Six Chiles, PRN—A Patient's Cultural Beliefs about Health." *Nursing* 13(5) (May 1983): 32.

William, G. A. and Zimmerman, R. "Patterns of Drug Use among Cuban-American, African-American, and White Non-Hispanic Boys." *American Journal of Public Health.* 83(2) (1993): 257–262.

Wolf, E. R. "The Virgin of Guadalupe: A Mexican National Symbol," in *Introduction to Chicano Studies,* eds. Duran, L. I. and Bernard, H. R. New York: Macmillan, 1973, pp. 246–252.

Yankauer, A. "Hispanic/Latino—What's in a Name?" *American Journal of Public Health* 771 (1987): 15–17.

Zepeda, M. "Selected Maternal–Infant Care Practices of Spanish Speaking Women." *Journal of Obstetric, Gynecologie and Neonatal Nursing* (November–December 1982): 371–374.

RESOURCES

National Coalition of Hispanic Health and Human Services (COSSMHO)
1030 15th Street, N.W.
Suite 1053
Washington, DC 20005

Latino Caucus
American Public Health Association
1015 15th Street, N.W.
Washington, DC 20005

National Association of Hispanic Nurses
2300 West Commerce
Suite 304
San Antonio, TX 78207
(512) 226–9743

Most recent publication is the *Hispanic Health and Nutrition Examination Survey,* 1982–1984; "Findings on Health Status and Health Care Needs," supplement to December 1990 *American Journal of Public Health.*

CSAP Prevention and Resource Guide
U.S. Department of Health and Human Services
Public Health Service Substance Abuse and Mental Health Services Administration
Prevention Material for Hispanic Americans
DHHS Pub. No. (ADM) 1959
For further information call 1–800–729–6686

Chapter 14

The Use of *Parteras* in the Rio Grande Valley, Texas

A Case Study*

January 2, 1925

Malone Duggan, M.D.
State Health Officer
Capital Station
Austin, Texas

Dear Sir:

. . . The conclusions, based on a study (of the midwife situation in Texas) and information gained by contact and correspondence during the past sixteen months, are:

1. That the midwives have practiced without restraint and have practically ignored state laws.
2. That the midwives have no training, not even in the simplest rudiments of surgical cleanliness.
3. That many of the midwives are not capable of being trained.
4. That many deaths and much disability both of mothers and babies, are directly traceable to the lack of proper care.
5. That despite the above enumerated conclusions, the midwife is still a necessity in some communities. . . .

Respectfully submitted,
H. Garst, M.D.
Director, Bureau of Child Hygiene

---

*This final chapter is an example of two health-care systems—modern and traditional—existing side by side. It is an edited and abridged edition of a paper originally published as Working Paper Number 23, The Lyndon B. Johnson School of Public Affairs, The University of Texas at Austin, 1983. It represents one outcome of the U.S–Mexican Border Maternal and Child Health

INTRODUCTION

The preceding letter—written more than 7 decades ago—illustrates well an aspect of the current paradoxical view the medical and public health professions take of the practicing lay midwife, especially the *partera*.[†]

Midwifery, one of the oldest female professions, is the art and practice of attending women during childbirth, and the practice has been recognized throughout the history of humankind. *Midwife* means "with women," and until the 17th century, midwives were women. Women have always been healers—passing on skills and knowledge from one to another.[3]

Female healers were called "wise women" by the populace—witches or charlatans by the authorities.[4] As the male physician ascended to power over the centuries, women were more and more excluded from the healing profession, first by the suppression of "witches" in medieval Europe and later by the rise of male medical professionals. In the United States, male physicians began to include the delivery of babies in their medical practice during the 18th century. The number of hospital deliveries has increased rapidly over the years, and the number midwife deliveries have in turn decreased. It is only recently that a change has been seen in this trend, and the demand for female-attended births is increasing.[5]

In Mexico, too, there is a long history of the use of midwives—*parteras*. The practice of midwifery predates Cortes. The goddess Tlozoteotl was the goddess of childbirth, and the midwives were known as "Tlamatqui-Tuti." They cared for the pregnant woman, attended the delivery, and cared for the newborn.[6]

OVERVIEW OF THE BORDERLANDS

"The United States–Mexico border presents a unique situation of human interdependence in a bi-national, multi-social-cultural and economic world."[7]

Care Project. The overall project was directed by Drs. David C. Warner, Chandler Stolp, and Bernard Portnoy. The project was conducted under a contract with the American Academy of Pediatrics and funded by a grant from the Robert Wood Johnson Foundation, the Hogg Foundation, the Lyndon B. Johnson Foundation, and the Henry J. Kaiser Family Foundation. The original research was conducted in 1981 and 1982. It has been updated for this edition with the assistance of Jennifer Dailey-Vail, RN, MS, in 1990 and Sister Mary Nicholas Vincelli, RN MS, in 1993–1995.

[†]The following definitions are presented to clarify terms:

Lay midwife, a person who practices lay midwifery.

Lay midwifery, assisting childbirth for compensation.[1]

Partera, a Mexican American or Mexican lay midwife, is a member of the indigenous health-care system of the Mexican American and Mexican communities.[2] Because the majority of lay midwives residing in the Texas border counties are Mexican American, or Mexican, the term *partera* is used here. The only occasion for using the term midwife is in a discussion of state birth certificates because there is no way of isolating the *parteras* from the midwife category. It is assumed that in the counties along the United States–Mexico border, the midwives are predominantly *parteras*.

The border extends for 2000 miles from Brownsville, Texas, and Matamoros, Mexico, in the east to San Diego, California, and Tijuana, Mexico, in the west. The border is one of the most rapidly developing areas in the United States. In Mexico, the population is growing even more rapidly than in the United States. More than 4 million people live along the Mexican side of the border, most in extreme poverty. Many of the people cross the border legally on a daily basis for work—many more cross the border illegally and disperse throughout the United States. In fact, illegal immigration, with few exceptions,[8] continues to be a major issue in the borderlands and also in the entire country. A study of the costs of illegal immigration released in 1994 affirmed that illegal immigrants cost states more than they contribute in taxes.[9] On the other hand, it was also found that illegal immigrants who are young, poor, and inexperienced may over time adjust and go on to become legal immigrants. Legal immigrants have a higher average household income than native-born Americans within 10 years of residency in the United States. The passage of California's Proposition 187 in November, 1995, attempting to limit services to illegal immigrants could well represent a backlash from this phenomenon.[10]

I am most familiar with the lower Rio Grande Valley and focus on this part of the border. The South Texas border area is one of contrasts, containing as it does the very rich and the very poor, the migrant and rural farm workers. Many of the poor live in *colonias* (Fig. 14–1). In 1995, the Texas Water Development Board reported more than 1,400 *colonias* with 340,000 residents. The residents are mainly impoverished Mexican immigrants who desire their own home. The mortgage payments for the land and shacks thereon range from $50 to $200 a month. The living conditions for most of the residents can be described as "horrible" as there is frequently no sewage and no running water.[11] Some minimal improvement has been made, however, in older *colonias* in the form of paved roads and a sewage system.[12] Diseases, such as hepatitis and measles, are endemic.[13] The United States side of the border is bicultural—nearly 80% of the population is either bilingual or speaks only Spanish, and Mexican customs are observed. The major industry in the Valley is agriculture—oranges, grapefruit, and vegetables. The other important industry is tourism. Several small factories have also been developed along the border.

The water supply in the valley is of a poor quality, being contaminated with insecticides and other agricultural runoffs.[14] In addition, at times the water is in critically short supply. Large amounts of water are lost to irrigation upriver. To add to the problem the local population nearly doubles each fall when the migrant workers return to their base camps.[15]

The major health problems in the valley's children are a high incidence of neural-tube defects, lack of immunization, anemia, gastroenteritis, conjunctivitis, lack of parental health education,[16] parental discipline by threat, late identification of developmental problems, and lack of basic health-care needs, such as eye glasses.[17] The major barrier to health-care services is

Figure 14–1. Homes in a *colonia*. (Photograph by R. Spector, 1993.)

poverty.[18] In the present climate of health-care reform, services are being cut or shifted and the maze of health care is becoming increasingly complex for clients to negotiate.[19]

In 1981, Mr. E. Garcia, the clinic manager of the McAllen Family Health Center in McAllen, Texas, and Mr. R. Garza, clinic director of *Su Clinica Familiar* in Harlingen, Texas, believed lack of money led to an increased use of *parteras* (lay midwives) and *curanderas* (folk healers) to treat childhood illnesses. Both herbal and prescription medications are readily available over the counter in Mexico. In 1990, Mr. R. Campman, director of planning in *Su Clinica Familiar*, disagreed, stating that he believed that "the lack of money was not the predominant reason for the use of *parteras*, who charge from \$400 to 500 for a delivery."[20] In 1993, the charge for a *partera* delivery rose to at least \$700.[21] Perhaps this population's preference for the traditional healers is related to issues of the accessibility, flexibility, and sensitivity of these providers. This is in contrast to the fact that *Su Clinica Familiar* offers affordable prenatal care that can be obtained for as low as \$335 and begins prior to 28 weeks gestation[22] Many Mexican women come to the United States side, especially Brownsville, for the delivery of their babies by *parteras*. The children are thereby United States citizens by birth and eligible for numerous benefits. Several problems have developed from this practice, such as the sale of illegal birth certificates and an unusually low neonatal mortality rate in Brownsville.[23] If a baby dies in Mexico, its death is not recorded in the United States. There were two maternal deaths in Hidalgo county in 1981, and both women were delivered by *parteras*. One woman died from a hemorrhage due to a retained placenta, the other from eclampsia.[24] At least 23 maternal deaths were reported in the border counties between 1982 and 1991,[25] but it has not been possible to determine the causes of these deaths or by whom these women were delivered. The neonatal mortality rate in these counties ranged between 2.4 and 11.4, but data were not available on the cause of death and person who delivered the infant. Also, in Hidalgo County, a mother who was not immunized against tetanus delivered a baby who developed tetanus of the umbilical cord. The baby survived.[26]

In the spring of 1981, there was a large measles epidemic in the valley. Several hundred children contracted measles, and one died. Many of the children who developed measles were between the ages of 6 and 15 months. The practice of delaying measles immunization until 18 months was changed, and babies are now immunized at 5 to 6 months. A door-to-door immunization program was initiated, and 98% of the children were immunized against the measles. It had been estimated that 92% of the resident children were immunized against all childhood communicable diseases.[27] In 1990, it was reported that 70% or better of children less than 1 year of age were immunized in all vaccine categories, 86% or better of 1 to 4 year olds, and 99% or better of school-age children enrolled in public school.[28] Preschool children and those attending private schools were less likely to be fully immunized because day care and private schools are not monitored as closely by the Department of Human Services as the public schools.[29]

PARTERAS

The Background of *Parteras*

Definition. The *partera*, or midwife, is viewed as a healer by many members of the Mexican American and Mexican communities. She is described as "an individual who is recognized in her community as having the ability to heal."[30] *Parteras* are almost always female and are described as outgoing, warm, gentle, caring, and cooperative.

Function and Role. A *partera's* duties include (1) giving advice to the pregnant woman, (2) giving physical aid, such as treating any illness the woman may experience during pregnancy, (3) guiding the woman through her pregnancy in terms of nutrition or activities she can and cannot do, and (4) being in attendance during labor and delivery.[31]

Profile. The following description of *parteras* has been developed from L. L. Philpott's dissertation[32] based on data collected in 1977 from *partera* interviews (Table 14–1). The *parteras* Philpott studied practiced in the Rio Grande Valley of Texas, 6 in Cameron County, 25 in Hidalgo County, and 1 in Willacy County. Thirty-one of the *parteras* had Spanish surnames, 21 (65.6%) were United States citizens, and 11 (34.4%) were Mexican citizens residing in the United States. Spanish was the primary language for 31 of the women, and 1, an Anglo, stated that English was her primary language. All had been married, 19 still were. All had given birth to children, the mean being 5.1 and the range 1 to 21. The mean age of the *parteras* was 60.5 years, with a range of 38 to 80 years. The mean number of years that the *parteras* had been residing in the United States was 35.4, with a range of 3 to 78. Most of the *parteras* were themselves attended by *parteras* when they delivered their babies. Several of the present lay midwives are Mexican physicians who cross the border to practice midwifery in the valley and register as lay midwives.[33]

The homes the *parteras* lived in were rated as "nice," which meant a clean, comfortable, relatively modern edifice. Of the homes visited, 5 were described as beautiful, 10 very nice, 5 as nice, 10 not nice, and 1 was an apartment.

Education. The educational background of the *parteras* was diverse. The numbers of years spent in school ranged from 0 to 17; 7 were found to be illiterate, 11 had no education, 10 had from 1 to 6 years of school, 7 had from 7 to 12 years, and 4 women had 12 or more years. One woman was a registered nurse, and one had attended two years of medical school in Mexico.

In terms of "training," they all had many years of experience. Many of them began their practice as young women, 3 before the age of 20, 15 between the ages of 20 and 30 years, 8 between 30 and 40 years old, and the remainder when they were over 40. The average number of years in practice was 30. The traditional midwife has no "formal" training, but rather learns her craft from a family member or under the tutelage of an older midwife. One of the *parteras* reported that she was out on a delivery with another midwife. The other woman left her alone with the woman in labor while she ran an errand. While the "teacher" was gone, the woman delivered. The younger woman assisted in the birth and began her practice at that time.

Many of the *parteras* came from families with three to four generations of *parteras*. "My mother, grandmother, aunt—all were midwives." Another claimed that as a child she knew that she would be a midwife. One woman reported that she had observed several deliveries and that she "just went out and delivered babies." Several of the midwives did have formal nursing or practical nursing education. As mentioned, one was a nurse, another attended medical school for two years.

The Functioning of *Parteras*

Use. Patients are most often referred to the *parteras* by their friends or relatives. "A *partera* with a good reputation is always busy." Several *parteras*

TABLE 14–1. PROFILE SUMMARY: 32 *PARTERAS* IN THE LOWER RIO GRANDE VALLEY, TEXAS

Characteristic	Number	Percentage	Range	Mean
Spanish surname	31	97.0		
U.S. citizen	21	65.6		
Mexican citizen residing in U.S.	11	34.4		
Primary language: Spanish	31	97.0		
Number of children			1–21	5.1
Age (years)			38–50	60.5
Years residing in U.S.			3–78	35.4
Living conditions				
Beautiful	5	16.0		
Very nice	10	31.0		
Nice	5	16.0		
Not very nice	10	31.0		
Apartment	1	3.0		
Missing	1	3.0		
Years in school			0–17	
No education	11	34.3		
1–6 years	10	31.3		
7–12 years	7	21.9		
More than 12 years	4	12.5		
Years in practice				30
Age beginning practice				
Before 20	3	9.3		
20–30	15	46.9		
30–40	8	25.0		
40+	6	18.8		
Cost of delivery			$185–300	
Place where delivered				
Mother's home only	10	31.0		
Partera's home only	8	25.0		
Choice of location	14	44.0		
Emergency actions				
Refer to hospital	21	65.6		
Call M.D. first	11	34.3		
Record keeping	24	75.0		
Experienced stillbirths	14	44.0		
Practice within a religious context	11	34.3		
Herbalists	11	34.3		
Use home remedies	18	56.0		

Information compiled from: Philpott, L. L. "A Descriptive Study of Birth Practices and Midwifery in the Lower Rio Grande Valley of Texas" (Ph.D. diss., U of Texas Health Sciences Center in Houston School of Public Health, 1979).

claimed that they received referrals from the health department they were registered with, one advertised in the local newspaper, another in the telephone book, and several had signs on their homes.

Costs. The cost of a *partera* delivery has risen from an average of $175 in 1977 to a range of $400 to $500 in 1990[34] and $700 in 1993.[35] The *parteras* purchase their own supplies, such as cotton and maternity pads. Birth certificates are filed by them.

The *parteras*, in general, believe that the women come to them because they are poor and cannot afford a hospital delivery. There are other reasons, however. For example, some *parteras* believed that the mothers have more confidence in them than in the doctors because they speak Spanish, understand modesty, and work within the mother's cultural and religious context.

Facilities. Many of the *parteras* have birthing rooms in their own homes or in birthing clinics (Fig. 14–2). In fact, eight of the *parteras* only deliver in their homes. Ten of the *parteras* deliver only in the mother's home, and the rest deliver where the mother wants. Most of the *parteras* do have a contact with a doctor whom they can call if they have a problem. In case of an emergency, 21 (65.6%) of the *parteras* send the mother to the hospital, and 11 (34%) call a doctor first. Several reported that they felt "the doctors do not want to help. I guess they think that we are going to take their job away." All of the *parteras* who had been interviewed for the Philpott study were registered with the county (Cameron, Hidalgo, or Willacy) health departments.

Practice. The *parteras* avoid delivering women with high blood pressure, anemia, a history of diabetes, multiple babies, and transverse presentations. Several *parteras* also prefer to send women with breech presentations to the hospital. If an unfamiliar woman in labor appears at their door "in the middle of the night" who is very poor with no place to go to deliver, most claim they will "take her in."

Seventy-five percent (24) of the *parteras* keep records of their deliveries. Included in these records are such data as the name of the mother, date, time of admission, stage of labor, time in labor, contractions, time of delivery, presenting part, time of delivery and condition of placenta, and the physical condition of the mother and baby.

Several of the midwives reported that they had delivered stillborn babies. Eighteen reported, however, that they had never had a stillborn. A study by Sanchez in 1971 reported that many midwives in South Texas had delivered defective children. The midwives that he interviewed differentiated between physically defective children and mentally defective children. He reported that the *parteras* were "aware of the problems of defective children, and some felt that much more effort was needed in this area to eliminate the causes of defective children and to help those already born." Sanchez also reported that a majority of the *parteras* he interviewed had beliefs (folk) about

A

B

Figure 14–2 (**A** and **B**) Signs for *partera* facilities. (Photograph by R. Spector, 1993.)

the causes of birth defects that included "eclipses" or "punishment from God." Others expressed concern about blood problems and syphilis.

Prenatal Care. The amount of prenatal care the *parteras* deliver ranges from "a lot to a little." In general, the mothers seek assistance during their third or fourth month of pregnancy. When the *partera's* assistance is sought, the mother is sent either to the health department or to a doctor for blood work. The *partera* is able to follow the mother's case and gives her advice and massages and may charge $1 to $3 for this prenatal care. Sanchez found that one important service that the midwife performed was the repositioning of the fetus in the womb through massaging.[36]

A *partera* may give several forms of advice to the pregnant woman. For example, she may advise the woman who is experiencing pica (the craving for and ingestion of nonfood substances, such as clay and laundry starch) to purchase solid milk of magnesia in Mexico. The milk of magnesia tastes like clay, thereby satisfying the pica, and is not considered harmful. The mother with food cravings is advised to satisfy them. The mothers also are instructed not to lift heavy objects, to take laxatives to prevent constipation, to exercise often by walking frequently, and not to cross their legs or bathe in hot water. The reason for the last two admonitions is the belief that crossing the legs and taking hot baths can cause the baby to assume the breech position.

If the *partera* knows the exact date of the mother's last period, she is able to accurately estimate when the woman is going to deliver by calculating eight lunar months and 27 days from the onset of the last period.

Labor and Delivery Care. With the onset of labor, the mother contacts the *partera*. She goes to the home of the *partera*, or the *partera* comes to her home. The mother is examined vaginally to determine how far along in labor she is and the position of the baby. She is instructed to shower and to empty her bowels, with an enema, if necessary. She is encouraged to walk and move around until the delivery is impending. Some of the *parteras* elect to shave the pubic hair, others trim it, and others simply clean the area with a disinfectant.

The mother is helped to relax and is kept walking. Once she is ready to deliver, she is put to bed. Most of the mothers are delivered lying down in bed. If the mother chooses to do so, however, she is delivered in a squatting or sitting position.

Several home remedies are used during labor. *Comino* (cumin seed) tea or *canela* (cinnamon) tea may be used to stimulate labor. Occasionally, oxytocin (Pitocin) is given to speed labor, and ergonovine maleate (Ergotrate) is given to prevent hemorrhage after delivery. These medications are purchased in Mexico. However, dispensing them in Texas without a prescription is illegal, and most of the *parteras* claimed *not* to use them. Olive oil is used to lubricate the abdomen during massage, and oil is later massaged on the perineum to prevent tearing. It is believed that the gentle touch of the *partera* in massaging the abdomen and later the perineum helps the mother to relax during her labor.

Many of the *parteras* will deliver a woman who has had a previous cesarean section. Twelve of the *parteras* work alone and require no assistance during the delivery; six require assistance occasionally. Many state that they depend on "the Virgin or Saint Raymond, the patron saint of *parteras*" for help.

Equipment. A *partera's* equipment consists of gloves (the majority use gloves while delivering the baby), umbilical cord ties, scissors, eyedrops (they instill silver nitrate eyedrops that are procured at the health department), a scale, alcohol, gauze and cotton, a bulb syringe (to suction mucus from the newborn's mouth), hemostats (to clamp the cord), and plastic bags, to place the placenta in. The *partera* washes her hands and dons gloves for the delivery.

Care of the Baby and Mother. The baby is stimulated if needed, and the mucus is removed from the mouth and nose as needed with the use of a bulb syringe. The cord is clamped, tied with cord ties, and cut with scissors that have been boiled and soaked in alcohol. The stump is then treated with merbromin (Mercurochrome), alcohol, or a combination of the two. The baby is weighed, and some time after the delivery, it is bathed. Most of the *parteras* bind both the mother and the baby. The baby may be fed oregano or cumin tea right after birth or later to help it spit up the mucus. Other *parteras* give the baby sugar water, weak *comino* tea, or boiled water. Eyedrops are instilled in the baby's eyes, in compliance with state laws (silver nitrate is used most frequently).

The *partera* stays at the mother's home for several hours after the delivery and then returns to check her and the baby the next day. If the mother delivers at the home of the *partera*, she generally stays 12 to 14 hours.

Disposal of the Placenta. There are several ways of disposing of the placenta. It may just be placed in a plastic bag and thrown in the trash, or it may be buried in the yard. Some placentas are buried with a religious or folk ceremony.

There are several folk reasons given for the burial of the placenta. The reason given for not burning it was that it was like "burning a person." The placenta must be buried so that the animals will not eat it. If it is eaten by a dog, the mother will not be able to bear any more children. If it is thrown in the trash, the mother's womb may become "cold." Another reason given for the burial of the placenta is that to do so prevents the mother from having pain. If the baby is a girl, the placenta is buried near the home so the daughter will not go far away. If it is a boy, it is buried far away.

Folk Beliefs. Several of the *parteras* who were interviewed discussed the following folk beliefs.

The pregnant woman is "hot," and she must avoid "hot" foods. There was also mention, primarily in Sanchez's study, of such folk beliefs as *mal de ojo* (evil eye), *susto* (shock or fright), eclipse (the viewing of the moon at the wrong time of the month, thus causing birth defects), *empacho* (food not passing through the stomach), *latido* (chronic lack of appetite causing emaciation), and *bilis* (nervous tension and fatigue caused by extreme anger). Eleven of the *parteras* claimed that they practiced within a religious context, 11 claimed to be herbalists, and 18 used home remedies.

Cross-Check: *Partera* Visit

In order to verify the findings of Philpott and to answer questions she did not deal with, we visited a *partera* in Weslaco, Texas. The following is a description of that visit and the *partera's* answers to the questions that were discussed. This woman had been described by the public health nurse as a *partera* who "loves her work, does the job well, and is one to whom people come back because she is able to establish excellent rapport with her clients."

We visited this *partera* shortly after 1:00 PM on a sunny December afternoon. We turned off the superhighway onto a small unpaved road and drove up to a yellow house that was surrounded by a neatly trimmed lawn, with flowers and statues. A small sign on the front of the house had a stork painted on it, the word "*partera*," and a telephone number.

We were greeted at the door by a 4-year-old boy who invited us in and said that his grandmother would help us in a moment. When the *partera* came, we explained the purpose of the visit and were invited to come in and sit down. The home was well furnished and decorated for Christmas, which was in two weeks. The woman was warm, friendly, and receptive. She spoke no English but was willing to talk slowly and was able to understand our Boston-accented Spanish.

She was 51 years old, had studied some nursing in Mexico, had previously practiced for 10 years in Victoria, Texas, 3 years in Reynosa, Mexico, and had been practicing in Weslaco for 4 years. She had established a good relationship with the nurses in the county and also with the doctors.

The women who come to her are from Rio Grande, McAllen, San Juan, Weslaco, and Donna, Texas. Some also come from Mexico. She is very popular and delivers from five to nine babies a month. She charges $185 a delivery. She sends her patients to the public health department for prenatal care. The ages of the women she sees are 15 to 42. Most come to her during their fourth or fifth month of pregnancy. She will not accept as a patient a woman who is anemic, has high blood pressure, has a history of diabetes or other medical problems, or indicates a malpresentation, which she feels is a major problem. If the baby is in a transverse presentation, she will not deliver it and sends the mother to a doctor. She is cautious with breech presentations and has delivered twins.

She then took us to her birthing room in the back of the house. The home had appeared small from the outside. It went straight back for quite a distance, however, and we passed several rooms, including a dining room, several bedrooms, and a kitchen, on the way to the birthing room. The home was extremely clean, well furnished, and comfortable. The walls were adorned with family and religious pictures.

The birthing room consisted of two single beds, an examining table, an instrument table with a scale on it, and the following equipment: hemostats and scissors (soaking in basins filled with alcohol), cotton, gauze, gloves, and eye medications. There were also a sphygmomanometer and stethoscope. In the back corner of the room were a washing machine and dryer and a large carton of maternity pads. There was a statue of the Virgin with a candle in front of her on the washing machine and religious pictures on the walls. The room was clean, and both beds were neatly made up. There was a separate entrance into the room from outside. There was also one small window covered with a colorful curtain.

The *partera* explained that she keeps the mothers active until they are ready to deliver. When the woman comes to her house, she examines her to determine how far along she is in labor. If this is her first baby and she has not started to dilate and everything appears normal, the *partera* sends her home with instructions to return when the "labor" comes more often or if "her water breaks." If the mother is in more active labor or if this is more than her first child, the mother stays. The *partera* keeps the mother active by, for example, walking in the neighborhood until her labor is quite active. When the delivery appears imminent, that is, when the head begins to crown, she puts the mother to bed. If the baby's head is in a posterior position, she rests the mother's hips on rolled towels or a bedpan to elevate her hips and lower back. She massages the mother's abdomen and perineum with oil. The abdomen is massaged to relax the mother, and the perineum is massaged to prevent tearing. She cleanses the perineum with soap, water, and then Mercurochrome. If needed, she shaves the mother. She may also give the mother an enema earlier in labor if it is needed. Before the baby is delivered, she washes her hands and puts on gloves. She does not wear a mask or special clothes but does wear an apron. She works alone but prays to the Virgin for assistance.

Once the baby is delivered, she suctions it with the bulb syringe to remove excess mucus. She clamps the cord with the hemostats, cuts it with the scissors, and ties it with the cord ties. She instills silver nitrate in the baby's eyes. She wraps the baby and places it with the mother and waits for the placenta. She related that if she has difficulty delivering the placenta, she has the mother blow into a coke bottle and the placenta then "pops out." The placenta is disposed of in accordance with the patient's wishes.

She encourages the father of the baby to remain with the mother, or else she has some other relative stay with the mother. She wants them to see what she does and to be aware of the "good job" that she does. She keeps the mother in her home for 8 hours after the delivery.

She also assumes the responsibility for registering the baby's birth at the county courthouse.

MIDWIFE DELIVERIES IN THE TEXAS–MEXICO BORDER AREA

Statistical Background

Midwives, or *parteras* deliver a high percentage of babies along the Texas–Mexico border. Cameron County has both the greatest number of registered *parteras* and the greatest number of *partera* deliveries. In 1993 there were 45 lay midwives in Cameron County, 31 in Brownsville; and 40 in Hidalgo County compared with 1988, when there were 33 lay midwives in Cameron County and 13 in Hidalgo.[37] (Table 14–2). In 1977, the city of Brownsville passed a strict city ordinance to control the midwives. An examination was given, and passage was required to practice within the city limits. Several of the midwives were unable to pass the new requirements and moved outside the city limits.[38] In 1993, however, there were 37 lay midwives in Brownsville.[39] In 1993, state legislation was passed making it mandatory for midwives to take a midwifery course, pass a C.P.R. course, and take continuing education. Birthing centers had to be licensed.[40]

Over the span of years between 1980 and 1993 the overall number of lay midwife deliveries had decreased, as indicated by birth occurrence in Cameron and Hidalgo Counties. For example, in 1980 the percentage of midwife deliveries by occurrence in Cameron County was 31%, and in Hidalgo County it was 13%. In 1988, the percentage for Cameron County was 20% and for Hidalgo County it was 17%; by 1993 the percentage was 10% in Cameron County and 11% in Hidalgo County. As shown in Table 14–3 and Figure 14–3, the percentage of lay midwife deliveries declined until 1986 and then began to climb, declining again by 1993.[41] The decline may be due to changes in legislation, the need for licensure, and changes in the emergency Medicaid program.[42]

Midwifery: Issues and Problems

The following are examples of issues and problems that have been raised about the practice of lay midwifery.

TABLE 14–2. REGISTERED LAY MIDWIVES, CAMERON AND HIDALGO COUNTIES AND BROWNSVILLE, TEXAS: 1977, 1988, 1993

Location	1977	1988	1993
Brownsville	30	25	37
Cameron County	39	33	8
Hildalgo County	31	13	40
Total	100	71	85

From: Salazar Texas Department of Public Health, Bureau of Vital Statistics June 11, 1980, Personal Correspondence with J. Dailey-Vail and Sister Mary Nicholas Vincelli.

TABLE 14-3. PERCENTAGE OF MIDWIFE DELIVERIES IN THE RIO GRANDE VALLEY, TEXAS, COUNTIES 1979-1993 BY OCCURRENCE

Total Number of Births

County	1979	1980	1981	1982	1983	1984	1985	1986	1987	1988	1989	1990	1991	1992	1993
Cameron	6,387	6,927	7,082	6,616	6,232	6,053	6,198	6,155	6,484	6,915	7,408	7,978	8,551	9,276	9,436
Willacy	236	259	256	231	237	217	162	125	8	—	6	8	9	3	2
Hidalgo	7,881	8,538	8,642	8,327	7,907	7,923	8,388	8,513	8,693	9,399	10,319	10,945	11,233	11,559	12,676
Zapata	1	—	—	—	2	2	1	—	—	—	2	1	1	3	5

Total Number of Midwife Deliveries

County	1979	1980	1981	1982	1983	1984	1985	1986	1987	1988	1989	1990	1991	1992	1993
Cameron	2,035	2,131	2,350	1,798	1,807	1,697	1,538	1,226	1,149	1,361	1,301	1,137	1,104	1,054	956
Willacy	34	57	25	19	9	8	15	14	4	2	3	2	2	2	0
Hidalgo	1,042	1,075	1,135	1,055	1,188	1,053	838	1,095	1,238	1,583	1,796	1,801	1,718	1,576	1,443
Zapata	—	—	—	—	—	—	—	—	—	—	—	—	—	1	—

Percentage of Midwife Deliveries

County	1979	1980	1981	1982	1983	1984	1985	1986	1987	1988	1989	1990	1991	1992	1993
Cameron	32	31	33	27	29	28	25	20	18	20	18	14	13	11	10
Willacy	14	22	10	8	4	4	9	11	15	25	50	25	22	66	—
Hidalgo	13	13	13	15	15	13	10	13	14	17	17	16	15	14	11
Zapata	100	—	—	—	—	—	—	—	—	—	—	—	—	33	—

From: Texas Department of Health, Bureau of Vital Statistics, Austin, Texas, 1979–1993. Reprinted with permission.

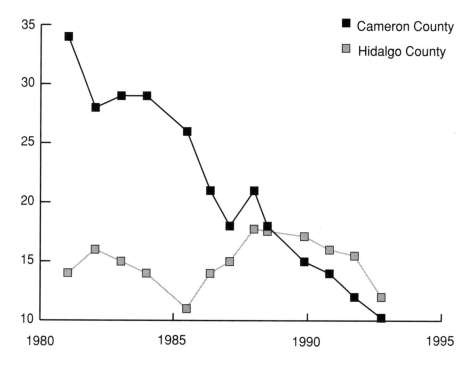

Figure 14–3. Percentage of *partera* deliveries in Cameron and Hidalgo Counties, Texas, by occurrence: 1980–1993. (Reprinted with permission from Texas Department of Health, Bureau of Vital Statistics, Austin, Texas, 1980–1993.)

Birth Practices. The Philpott study reported that

1. Midwives often administered medications without consulting a physician.
2. Substandard sanitary conditions existed in midwives' clinics or homes.
3. Many of the midwives did not use silver nitrate in the baby's eyes, in violation of the law.
4. Many of the midwives did not know or practice sterile technique.
5. Folk medications and folk remedies were used often in the midwife's care of the mother and baby.[43]

Maternal Mortality. In 1980, a maternal death was reported in Hidalgo County. The mother, a 24-year-old gravida 1, was a Mexican national. She was delivered by a *partera* in Mission, Texas. The cause of death was found to be related to

1. Severe shortness of breath on exertion during pregnancy, causing limitation of activities

2. Severe abdominal pain two hours after delivery
3. A hemoglobin of 8 grams per deciliter on admission to the hospital[44]

In 1981, another maternal death occurred in Hidalgo county—this mother was 48 years-old, gravida 4, and para 3. She, too, was a Mexican national. With her last pregnancy she had been advised to "have no more children." The family was very poor, and she had had no prenatal care. The mother arrived at the *partera's* home at the "last moment" with no records of blood tests and prenatal care. The *partera* attempted to refuse to take care of her but was unable to refuse her because of the advanced stage of labor. The woman was pushing, and it was too late to send her elsewhere. The baby was delivered, and the cord was greenish yellow. The placenta did not deliver; after 20 to 30 minutes the woman began to bleed. The *partera* attempted to stop the bleeding and to get an ambulance to come to take the woman to the hospital. There were a number of delays, and two hours passed before the woman got to the hospital. She was dead on arrival. The death was most likely due to a postpartum hemorrhage.[45] Two maternal deaths were reported in 1984 and three in 1985 in Hidalgo County. In 1991, three maternal deaths occurred in rural Hidalgo county.[46]

Infant Morbidity. An infant developed tetanus of the cord in 1981. This baby was delivered by a *partera* who had been delivering babies since the early 1950s. The *partera* had been defensive about visits by the public health nurses, and she was reluctant to allow them into her home. She was illiterate and had a vision impairment.

According to the mother, the *partera* had cut the baby's cord with scissors that she removed from her instrument bag and tied the cord with string that she cut from a ball of string. In other words, neither the scissors nor the cord ties were sterile. The baby was treated and recovered with some residual neurological damage. The mother, who did not know if she had received tetanus immunization, was immunized.[47] Throughout this area, the occurrence of neural tube defects has continued to be higher than expected. A birth defects registry has been established in Harlingen, Texas to determine the cause of the defect and to determine the efficacy of giving the mother prepregnancy and prenatal folic acid.[48]

Crossover Births. Crossover births, that is, births to women from Mexico who cross over the border to deliver, represent a large share of the number of *partera* deliveries. These births have caused numerous problems in the communities along the border. Many of the mothers do not receive adequate or any prenatal care. There are problems with welfare and food stamps and immigration practices and policies. In some areas along the border, for example, Cameron County, Texas, the number of crossover births is large. In other areas, the numbers are smaller, either because there are no *parteras* to deliver the mothers or because the United States hospitals are able to return the women to Mexico.

As of June, 1995, the National Commission on Immigration Reform was developing recommendations to reduce legal immigration to the United States. Current immigration policy on crossover births is

1. All people born in the United States are citizens of the United States.
2. The policy of allowing a child born in the United States to attend public school at the United States place of residence is being re-examined.
3. A policy change is being considered to prevent parents of children born as United States citizens from legally immigrating here until their children purchase health insurance for them.[49]

Associated Problems. Additional, tangential issues surround *partera* deliveries.

1. The extreme poverty of large numbers of people residing along the border who are migrant workers or unemployed.
2. The practice of hospitals of not accepting patients without pre-payment. Several hospitals were cited for turning away patients, and in several places, the practice of sending women in labor back to Mexico to deliver still exists.
3. The alleged issuance of false birth certificates by some *parteras* for babies born in Mexico. Several *parteras* have been indicted for these charges.[50]

Although problems have existed for many years in *partera* deliveries, serious medical problems have been reported in only a few cases.

Research and Policy Recommendations

To improve the quality of maternal and child health care, the following recommendations are offered.

Conduct a Community Survey. In addition to the training of TBAs (traditional birth attendants), the United Nations has developed a program for surveying people in the community, including mothers, about their needs for maternal and child health care. Such a survey should be made along the United States–Mexico border, primarily in the Texas area, because of the prevalence of traditional midwives. Most people state that poverty is the chief reason why women elect to be delivered by *parteras*, but this may not be the only reason. Only a survey of the mothers who choose to go to either the doctor or a *partera* will shed light on this situation.

An example of a community survey is the study "Use of a Maternity Center as a Birthing Alternative in the El Paso–Juarez Area," by Eastman and Loustaunau. The study was undertaken from October 1980 through January

1981. The researchers discovered that women who used the maternity center in El Paso "strongly endorsed it as their first choice of location for birthing and overwhelmingly supported the use of female midwives." This preference for a female birth attendant fits in with the Mexican American and Mexican culture. The researchers also found that the main reason for using this center was not cost—the women did not want a hospital birth. A third finding was that 66% of those using the center were Mexican nationals, whereas the amount of Anglo women using the center was 8%. The reason offered for the high use of this clinic by Mexican nationals was the guarantee of United States citizenship for their children. Finally, the researchers found that a large percentage of women using this clinic had no family doctor or gynecologist.[51]

Each society has its own customs, beliefs, values, and practices regarding childbirth and the care of mothers and children, and these vary from society to society. Prior to making policy, it is necessary to be aware of and sensitive to the practices within the society. In an area that includes a heterogeneous society, such as the United States–Mexico border, one must be cognizant—before legislation is enacted—of the role the *partera* plays in the community she serves. Legislation to both license lay midwives and birthing centers was passed in Texas in 1993[52]. It is important for the policy makers to

1. Monitor and identify aspects of traditional practice that need to be changed.
2. Determine the extent to which the *parteras* need retraining.
3. Determine the incentives that may be needed to obtain their cooperation.
4. Monitor the rituals, techniques, and procedures used in the management of labor and delivery—that is, the scope of the *parteras'* practice.
5. Monitor how the people in the community feel about *parteras*.
6. Be sensitive to existing language barriers. The training programs must be in a language that the *parteras* understand and understand both the connotations and denotations of words. If the *partera* is illiterate, other forms of learning besides the written word must be devised. This also holds true for testing. The *parteras* ought to be tested in the language they understand, either spoken or written.
7. Monitor the use of *parteras* over time to determine the efficacy of the legislation.

Use the Spanish Language. Those who deliver health services to Mexican and Mexican American mothers must speak and understand Spanish. Health education materials—films, books, pamphlets, and posters—must be available in Spanish.

Establish Collaboration. Close collaboration between the public health nurses and the *parteras* is vital. An example of this collaboration is found in Hidalgo

County, where public health nurses recognize that the *parteras* will not change their ways. The nurses are able to work with the *parteras*, however, by insisting that they do certain things, such as register the births within the correct time and instill eyedrops in the baby's eyes. The nurses in the Hidalgo County Health Department have been able to upgrade the care that indigent prenatal patients receive by ensuring that every woman has prenatal blood work done regardless of when she seeks the service, that each woman has a prenatal physical examination done by a nurse midwife, and that health education play a predominant role in their maternal–child health program. It has been observed that women are seeking the services of the health department maternity nurses earlier in their pregnancy.

A goal of health policy must be to improve maternal–child health care by developing cooperative and collaborative relationships among the various parties (physicians, nurses, certified nurse midwives, and lay midwives) who deliver maternal–child health care.

CONCLUSION

This chapter has focused primarily on the *parteras* who practice midwifery in Texas along the United States–Mexico border. Their background and practice, the issues and problems related to their practice, present regulation, and research and policy recommendations have all been described.

The practice of midwifery is ancient—the role of women in the birthing process continues to be popular in this geographic region. Observation of the practice of *parteras*, interviews with the leading characters, the midwives and health-care providers, and literature reviews, have led to the conclusion that given safeguards (adequate prenatal care and prenatal screening, and adequate medical backup, such as access to the hospital for emergencies), the practice of the *partera* can be safe and effective. It provides women with a *choice*—the choice to be delivered by someone who (1) speaks their language, (2) shares a similar culture or religious world view, and (3) is willing to deliver them in the privacy of their home or in a birthing center. Alternatively, the woman has the choice of delivering in the hospital and being delivered by a physician or certified nurse midwife. In these circumstances, the pregnant women is not constrained by only one choice: that of the hospital way of childbirth.

Problems have occurred with midwife deliveries, and several of these problems have been discussed. It should be noted that iatrogenic problems also continue to occur in hospital deliveries, a fact that should be kept in mind by those who criticize midwife births. Childbirth in itself involves risks, and often problems are inherent in the nature of the event. For the normal healthy woman, however, who is delivering a child in an uncomplicated delivery (about 97% of all births) many of the interventions espoused by the medical professionals may not be necessary.

It is important for public policy discussion, decision making, and legislation, as well as for the major deliverers of health care, to understand the intricacies of midwifery. The goal of health care has been to provide safe and adequate services to all recipients. Only with the mutual collaboration and respect of health-care providers and midwives can the prenatal and perinatal care of the indigent and others desiring traditional birthing services be sustained and upgraded.

The situation described by Dr. Garst in 1925 may also exist today. He recognized then that the "midwife is still a necessity in some communities." These words are still true today. Avenues of collaboration and mutual respect must be explored and followed.

The practice of the *partera* in the Rio Grande Valley is the life of the past, the present, and of the future: "a way of life *de ayer, hoy y mañana*".[53]

REFERENCES

1. Trotter, R. T., II and Chavira, J. A. "*Curanderismo*: An Emic Theoretical Perspective of Mexican-American Folk Medicine." *Medical Anthropology* (Fall 1980): 423–487.
2. Uribe, H. Texas S. B. 1093, 1981.
3. Forbes, T. R. *The Midwife and the Witch* (New Haven: Yale University Press, 1966); Donegan, J. B. *Women and Men Midwives: Medicine, Morality, and Misogyny in Early America* (Westport, CT: Greenwood Press, 1978).
4. Ehrenreich, B. and English, D. *Witches, Midwives, and Nurses: A History of Women Healers* (2nd ed.) (Old Westbury, NY: Feminist Press, 1973).
5. Litoff, J. B. *American Midwives 1860 to the Present* (Westport, CT: Greenwood Press, 1978).
6. Kelly, I. *Folk Practice in North Mexico Birth Customs, Folk Medicine, and Spiritualism in the Laguna Zone* (Austin: University of Texas Press, 1965).
7. Zavaleta, A. N., ed., "Mexican American Health Status: Selected Topics from the Borderlands." *Borderlands Journal—Special Issue* 4(1) (Fall 1980):1.
8. Brinkley, J. "A Success at the Border Earned Only a Shrug." *New York Times*. (September 14, 1994) pp. A1, A14.
9. Sontag, D. "Illegal Aliens Put Uneven Load on States, Study Says." *New York Times*. (September 15, 1994) p. A14.
10. Ibid.
11. Myerson, A. R. "This is the House That Greed Built." *New York Times*. (April 2, 1995) pp. 3–1, 3–14.
12. Vincelli, M. N., director of nursing, Hidalgo County Health Department, Edinburg, TX, Personal interview, 22 June, 1993.
13. Garcia, E., clinic manager, McAllen Family Health Center, McAllen, TX: Personal interview, 19 November, 1981.
14. Garza, R., clinic director, *Su Clinica Familiar*, Harlingen, TX: Personal interview, 18 November, 1981.
15. Shenkin, B. N. *Health Care for Migrant Workers: Policies and Politics* (Cambridge MA: Ballinger Publishing Co., 1974).
16. Vincelli, Personal interview, 1993.

17. Ibid.
18. Ibid.
19. Vincelli, M. N., director of nursing, Hidalgo County Health Department, Edinburg, TX: Personal interview, 2 June, 1995.
20. Personal telephone interview. Dailey-Vail, J. with Campman, R., director of planning, *Su Clinica Familiar,* Harlingen, TX, June 14, 1990.
21. Vincelli interview, 1993.
22. Ibid.
23. Chapman interview, 1990.
24. Vincelli interview, 1993.
25. Texas Department of Public Health, 1991 TDH/MCH/NBSI/GENETICS Infant, Neonatal, Fetal, Perinatal, and Maternal Deaths—1992.
26. Texas Department of Health. "Infant and Maternal Mortality in Five Selected Texas Counties." 1982–1988.
27. Garcia and Garza interviews.
28. Texas Department of Health Immunization Records, 1988.
29. Vincelli interview, 1993.
30. Trotter and Chavira. *"Curanderismo."*
31. Kay, M. A. "The Mexican American," in *Culture, Child Bearing, Health Professionals,* ed. Clark, A. (Philadelphia: F. A. Davis, 1978).
32. Philpott, L. L. "A Descriptive Study of Birth Practices and Midwifery in the Lower Rio Grande Valley of Texas" (Ph.D. diss., University of Texas Health Science Center at Houston, School of Public Health, 1979).
33. Vincelli interviews, 1993 and 1995.
34. Campman interview.
35. Vincelli interview, 1993.
36. Sanchez, A. R. "An Exploratory Study of Mexican American Midwives' Attitudes, Practices, and Beliefs Regarding Children Born with Congenital Defects" (Master's thesis, University of Texas at Austin, 1971).
37. Texas Department of Health. Midwife Roster for Cameron County and Harlingen County, 1993.
38. Chavez, B., director of the Brownsville Health Department, Brownsville, TX: Personal interview, 19 November, 1981.
39. Texas Midwife Roster.
40. Vincelli interview, 1993.
41. Texas Department of Health. Bureau of Vital Statistics, Live Births by Occurance: 1980–1993.
42. Vincelli interview, 1995.
43. Philpott. "Descriptive Study."
44. Vincelli interview, 1993.
45. Ibid.
46. Texas Department of Public Health, 1991.
47. Vincelli interview, 1993.
48. Vincelli interview, 1995.
49. Puente, M. "Panel to Urge Reductions in Immigration." *U.S.A. Today* (June 6, 1995) p. 3A.
50. Vincelli interview, 1995.
51. Eastman, K. and Loustaunau, M. "Use of a Maternity Center as a Birthing Alternative in the El Paso-Juarez Area" (1982).

52. Vincelli interview, 1995.

53. Castillo, J. director, Division of Health Related Professions. Personal letter of 6 April, 1982.

ANNOTATED BIBLIOGRAPHY

Alvarez, H. R. *Health without Boundaries.* Mexico: United States–Mexico Border Public Health Association, 1975.

In this extensive report, Alvarez describes the unique, 30-year-old public health center that serves the United States–Mexico border area. The author stresses the point that "health problems do not recognize boundaries between two countries." Numerous factors—biological, social, cultural, economic, and geographic—that contribute to health problems are described in depth. Alvarez also compares morbidity and mortality rates for the two countries over the past 30 years. He describes health areas where change is desperately needed, such as in the area of maternal–child care in Mexico. He also describes several joint projects in which cooperation has led to better health conditions, such as a sanitation project in Baja, California, and Tijuana. This report provides the reader with a broad, general awareness of the scope of health problems on the United States–Mexico border.

Clark, M. *Health in the Mexican-American Culture* (2nd ed.). Berkeley: University of California Press, 1970.

In this book, Clark describes the traditional health and illness beliefs and practices of Mexican Americans in California. The book is based on a study designed to secure sociocultural information helpful to health workers. Clark describes such phenomena as family life, attitudes and beliefs relating to health and illness, and specifically to pregnancy and childbirth. For example, she describes the specific practices of *la cuarentena* (40 days after delivery) and the diet during and after pregnancy in great detail. In addition, she describes the traditional beliefs and practices relating to infant care, such as feeding practices, the fondling of babies, and the methods of protecting the babies from *mal d'ojo,* "evil eye." The descriptive and anecdotal information in this book is valuable for health-care providers who work in the Mexican American community. This book is well written and documented and is considered a classic in the early work done in medical sociology and anthropology.

Kessner, D. M. *Infant Death: An Analysis by Maternal Risk and Health Care.* Washington, DC: Institute of Medicine, 1973.

Kessner's theme throughout this book is that one cannot discuss health care without first realizing that those who are receiving the health care have basic needs—food and water, clothing, and shelter—met first. He vividly describes the social risks—maternal age, birth order of children, maternal education, and the given legitimacy status of each child—that affect infant morbidity and mortality. Kessner also describes the medical risks—the time of the first prenatal visit, the time spent in receiving medical care both in pregnancy and labor, and the early detection of complications—and their relationship to maternal morbidity and mortality rates and the effect on infant morbidity and mortality. He illustrates this presentation with numerous case studies that point out the need for comprehensive maternity care. The contents of this book provide not only an in-depth understanding of the medical risks related to infant mortality but also an analysis of the social conditions that relate to the phenomena. In addition, this book facilitates the reader's understanding of the role that the poverty in the peoples living along the United States–Mexico border plays in the higher-than-expected infant mortality rates.

Landmann, R. S., ed. *The Problem of the Undocumented Worker.* Albuquerque: Latin American Institute, University of New Mexico, 1981.

This series of 13 articles deals with one of the most sensitive and pressing issues facing today's immigration policy makers—the monumental problems of undocumented workers and their families. The anthology represents a spectrum of scholarly opinion on the illegal migration of Mexicans to the United States, and it explores this issue from several dimensions, such as

1. Why do people come to the United States illegally?
2. What is the effect of illegal migration on labor?
3. What are the human rights of the migrants?

In general, the present literature relating to this topic is fragmented and not in consensus. There is confusion about the extent of the social, political, economic, and health consequences of the undocumented workers and their families. The United States–Mexico border is the focal point of this problem—hence, the importance of this document (or other related literature) for the acquisition of knowledge in this area. This particular document provides the reader with an in-depth analysis. To begin to understand the complexities of the maternal–child health issues on the border, one must be knowledgeable about the issues discussed in this anthology.

Louv, R. *Southwind: The Mexican Migration.* San Diego: San Diego Union, 1980.

In this book, Louv attempts to describe the life of the undocumented alien. Louv discusses issues, such as the history of migration, the people who are coming to the United States from Mexico, the numbers of illegals, the underground railroad, and other aspects of this complex problem. He paints a vivid picture, in personal terms, of lives enmeshed in poverty and exploitation. The book is designed to provide answers to the questions of human rights and economic and political problems. It is a much more personal account than the Landmann anthology and presents another facet of this complex problem. It, too, helps to enhance one's understanding of the United States–Mexico border area and the maternal–child health problems that exist there.

Shenkin, B. N. *Health Care for Migrant Workers: Policies and Politics.* Cambridge, MA: Ballinger Publishing Co., 1974.

In this book, Shenkin describes migrant workers in the United States. A migrant is a person who moves far away from home to work in the fields. Included in Shenkin's description of the migrants are three major streams: who are they? where do they originate? and where do they journey to? In addition to a sociological description, he provides a comprehensive description of the health of the migrant workers and their families. He states that "valid health statistics of migrants and of the rural poor are hard to find, but that despite these limited figures a strong case can be made to demonstrate that the health status is generally *wretched.* Poor people are sicker than nonpoor people in the United States. The sicker groups get less medical care." Shenkin describes, in depth, several health programs that have been created to provide health services to the migrants, yet, despite these attempts, their health status remains poor. Several reasons, such as mobility, the fact that services do not extend far enough, and health education and motivation are deficient, explain this ongoing problem. Several solutions are proposed: alleviation of poverty, alleviation of discrimination, and increasing the capacity of the rural medical-care delivery system. In summary, this book is highly informative about the overall health conditions of a large number of residents in the border area.

Silver, G. A. *Child Health: America's Future Generation.* Germantown, MD: Aspen Systems Corp., 1978.

Silver states that "the future of social policy is embodied in child health." He focuses on the belief that children's health is more a matter of protection and prevention than adult health is. The author argues that the United States child health services are not operating at their peak, and he describes several reasons for this failure. Silver documents that 40% of children from poverty areas (urban and rural) are not immunized. He further demonstrates that these children receive inadequate prevention and curative services. "The value of children is reflected in the care they receive." In summary, this book presents a comprehensive description of the care that children ought to receive and examples of where this care does not exist.

Tidemann, M. "Maternal/Child Health: Background Paper for a Border Health Research Agenda Development Conference." (Paper presented September 20, 1981, at the Border Health Focused Research Agenda Development Conference, Westwood Look Resort, Tucson, Arizona, 20–22 September 1981.)

In this paper, Tidemann reviews the status of maternal and child health care problems on both sides of the United States–Mexico border. The first issue that the author describes is that of infant mortality rates. These rates ranged from 32.8 to 52.1/1000 births in Northern Mexico in 1974 and from 5.1 to 40.3/1000 births in the United States border counties. Second, she describes the child-bearing practices of women in the border area. Traditionally, women bear children early, and families of 12 to 16 children are not uncommon. Third, children of the poor in this area are "extremely" vulnerable to infectious diseases because of poor nutrition. Tidemann also introduces the plight of migrant workers, undocumented aliens, environmental problems, and cultural problems. She concludes her presentation by describing the nature of the problems on the border as "historic." She believes that an approach to their resolution must be "creative and acknowledge the interrelationships among the multiple groups of problems."

Trotter, R. T., II and Chavira, J. A. "*Curanderismo*: An Emic Theoretical Perspective of Mexican-American Folk Medicine." *Medical Anthropology* (Fall 1980): 423–87.

In this outstanding, highly informative article, Trotter and Chavira describe the actual practice of *curanderismo*, Mexican American folk medicine, as a systematic body of healing theories. *Curanderismo* is practiced at three levels, each demanding a higher degree of learning. This article is unique in that it describes in great detail how the *curandero* actually carries out the rituals. The underlying meanings of rituals are also explained. The informants were several *curanderos* in South Texas. The information was collected through participant-observation methods over a span of four years. (The *curanderos* were informed of the purpose of the research and gave their consent to be observed.) The authors describe the relationship of the *curandero* to the patient and the family, the methods the *curandero* uses in the prevention, detection, and healing of illness, and the underlying unity of the perception of illness. The use of *curanderos* and other traditional healers, such as *parteras* (midwives), is widespread along the United States–Mexico border. Their advice and services are sought throughout the life cycle of family members, including during pregnancy and the child-rearing years.

Warner, D. *The Health of Mexican-Americans in South Texas.* Austin: LBJ School of Public Affairs, University of Texas at Austin, 1979.

In this report on the physical and mental health of Mexican Americans, Warner describes the following situations in great depth.

1. Socioeconomic and health conditions
2. Morbidity and mortality rates
3. Living conditions in urban and rural areas of South Texas
4. Nutritional, mental health services, and migrant health services
5. Folk medicine

This report is a well-executed study of the area.

Zavaleta, A. N., ed. "Mexican-American Health Status: Selected Topics from the Borderlands." *Borderlands Journal—Special Issue* 4(1) (Fall 1980).

The material contained in this journal is similar to other material presented thus far, but for this quote: Zavaleta states "The United States–Mexico border presents a unique situation of human interdependence in a bi-national, multi-social-cultural- and economic world."

Epilogue

Why must health-care deliverers—nurses, physicians, public health and social workers, and other health-care professionals—study ethnicity, culture, and cultural sensitivity? Why must they know the difference between "hot" and "cold" and *yin* and *yang*? Why must they be concerned with the consumer's failure to practice what professionals believe to be good preventive medicine or with the consumer's failure to comply with a given treatment regimen or with the consumer's failure to seek medical care during the initial phase of an illness? Is there a difference between *curing* and *healing*?

There is little disagreement that health-care services in this country are unevenly distributed and that the poor and the emerging majority get the short end of the stick in terms of the care they receive (or do not receive). There is the need to understand new immigrants as more and more people come to this country. Yet it is often maintained that when such care *is* provided, these same people fail to use it or use it inappropriately. Why is this seeming paradox so?

The major focus of this book has been on the provider's and the consumer's differing perceptions of health and illness. These differences may account for the health-care provider's misconception that services are used inappropriately and that people do not care about their health. What to the casual observer appears to be "misuse" may represent our failure to understand and to meet the needs and expectations of the consumer. This possibility may well be difficult for health-care providers to face, but careful analysis of the available information seems to indicate that this may—at least in part—be the case. How, then, can health-care providers change their method of operations and provide both safe and effective care for the emerging majority and, at the same time, for the population at large? The answer to this question is not an easy one, and some researchers think we are not succeeding.[1] A number of measures can and must be taken to ameliorate the current situation. Multicultural health care and the educational preparation leading to this is a process, one that becomes a way of life and must be recognized as such. The changing of one's personal and professional ideas and stereotypes does *not* occur overnight, and the process, quite often, is neither direct nor easy. It is a multistep process, in which one must:

- Explore his or her own cultural identity and heritage and confront biases and stereotypes.
- Develop an awareness and understanding of the complexities of the modern health-care delivery system—its philosophy and problems, biases, and stereotypes.
- Develop a keen awareness of the socialization process that brings the provider into this complex system.
- Develop the ability to "hear" things that transcend language, foster an understanding of the client and his or her cultural heritage and the resilience found within the culture that supports family and community structures.

Given, the processes of acculturation, assimilation, and modernism, this is often difficult and painful. Yet, once the journey of exploring one's own cultural heritage and prejudices is undertaken, the awareness of the cultural needs of others becomes more subtle and understandable. This is well accomplished by using the umbrella of health traditions as the point of entry.

A student I once taught described the journey this way:

> I was born in 1973 to fourth-generation Japanese American parents. I understood Japanese culture and the way of thinking and did not question when my parents told me to eat noodles on New Year's Day to bring long life. Then I changed schools and went to the Caucasian school. I came to *hate* my heritage and wanted to scream that "I'm as white on the inside as you are." I was bitter and embarrassed by my heritage and blamed my family, who was proud of their ancestry. When my parents tried to teach me about Japanese American history, I was not interested. I came to know, understand, and hate racism. On the inside I felt as "white American" as everyone else but I soon realized what I felt inside was not what other people saw. I now acknowledge who I am and I accept myself.

The voice of this young student speaks for many. In the course of having to explore the family's traditional health beliefs and practices, the student began to see, think through, understand, and accept herself.

Although curricula in professional education are quite full, multicultural health studies must be taken by all people who wish to deliver health care. It is no longer sufficient to teach a student in the health professions to "accept patients for who they are." The question arises: who is the patient? Introductory sociology and psychology courses fail to provide this information. It is learned best by meeting with the people themselves and letting them describe who they are from their own perspective. I have suggested two approaches to the problem. One is to have people who work as patient advocates or as nurses and physicians come to the class setting and explain how people of their ethnic group view health and illness and describe the given community's health traditions. Another approach is to send students out into communities where they will have the opportunity to meet with people in their own settings. It is not necessary to memorize all the available lists of herbs, hot–cold imbalances, folk diseases, and so forth. The objective is to become more sensitive to the crucial fact that multiple factors underly given patient behaviors. One, of course, is that the patient may well *perceive* and *understand* health and illness from quite a different perspective than that of the health-care provider. Each person comes from a unique culture and a unique socialization process.

The health-care provider must be sensitive to his or her own perceptions of health and illness and the practices he or she employs. Even though the perceptions of most health professionals are based on a middle-class and medical-model viewpoint, providers must realize that there are other ways of regarding health and illness. The early chapters of this book are devoted to consciousness raising about self-treatment. It is always an eye-opening experience to publicly scrutinize ourselves in this respect. Quite often we are amazed to see how far we stray from the system's prescribed methods of keeping healthy. The journals confirm that we, too, delay in seeking health care and fail to comply with treatment regimens. Often our ability to comply rests on quite pragmatic issues, such as "What is it doing for me?" and "Can I afford to miss work and stay in bed for two days?" As we gain insight into our own health–illness attitudes and behaviors, we tend to be much more sympathetic to and empathetic with the person who fails to come to the clinic or who hates to wait for the physician or who delays in seeking health care.

The health-care provider should be aware of the complex issues that surround the delivery of health care from the patient's viewpoint. Calling the medical society for the name of a physician (because a "family member has a health problem") and visiting and comparing the services rendered in an urban and a suburban emergency room are exercises that can enable us to better appreciate some of the difficulties that the poor, the emerging majority, and the population at large all too often experience when they attempt to obtain health care. Members of the health-care team have a number of advantages in gaining access to the health-care system. For example, they can choose a physician whom they know because they work with him or her or because someone they work with has recommended this physician. Health-care providers must never forget, however, that most people do not have these advantages. It is indeed an unsettling, anxiety-provoking, and frustrating experience to be forced to select a physician from a list. It is an even more frustrating experience to be a patient in an unfamiliar location—for example, an urban emergency room, where, quite literally, anything can happen.

Another barrier to adequate health care is the financial burden imposed by treatments and tests. There are other issues as well. For example, a Chinese patient—who traditionally does not believe that the body replaces the blood taken for testing purposes—should have as little blood work as necessary, and the reasons for the tests should be explained carefully. A Hispanic woman who believes that taking a Pap smear is an intrusive procedure that will bring shame to her should have the procedure performed by a female physician or nurse. When this is not possible, she should have a female chaperone with her for the entire time that the male physician or nurse is in the room.

More members of the emerging majority must be represented in the health-care professions. Multiple issues are related to the problem of underrepresentation. Many of the programs designed to increase the number of emerging majority students in the health-care team have failed. Difficulties surrounding successful entrance into and completion of professional education programs are complex and numerous, having their roots in impoverished community structures and early educational deprivation. Although society is in some ways dealing with such issues—for example, initiating improvements in early education—we are faced with an *immediate* need to bring more emerging majority people into health-care services.

One method would be the more extensive use of patient advocates and outreach workers from the given ethnic community who may be recognized there as healers. These people can provide an overwhelmingly positive service to both the provider and the consumer in that they can serve as the bridge in bringing health-care services to the people. The patient advocate can speak to the client in language that the client understands and in a manner that is acceptable. Advocates also are able to coordinate medical, nursing, social, and even educational services to meet the patient's needs as the patient perceives them. In settings where advocates are employed, many problems are resolved to the convenience of both the health-care member and, more importantly, the client!

The nettlesome issue of language bursts forth with regularity. There is always a problem when a non-English-speaking person tries to seek help from the English-speaking majority. The more common languages, French, Italian, and Spanish, ideally should be spoken by at least some of the professional people who staff hospitals, clinics, neighborhood health-care centers, and home health agencies. The use of an interpreter is always difficult because the interpreter generally "interprets" what he or she translates. To bring this thought home, the reader should recall the childhood game of "gossip": a message is passed around the room from person to person, and by the time it gets back to the sender, its content is usually substantially changed. This game is not unlike trying to communicate through an interpreter, and the situation is even more frustrating when—as can often be the case in urban emergency rooms—the interpreter is a six-year-old child. It is, obviously, far more satisfying and productive if the patient, nurse, and physician can all speak the same language.

Health services must be made far more accessible and available to members of the emerging majority. I believe that one of the most important events in this modern era of health-care delivery is the advent of neighborhood health centers. They are successful essentially because people who work in them know the people of the neighborhood. In addition, the people of the community can contribute to the decision-making involved in governing and running the agency so that services are tailored to meet the needs of the clients. Concerned members of the health-care team have a moral obligation to support the increased use of health-care centers and *not* their decreased use, as currently tends to occur because of cutbacks in response to allegations (frequently politically motivated) of too-high costs or the misuse of funds. These neighborhood health-care centers provide greatly needed personal services in addition to relief from the widespread depersonalization that occurs in larger institutions. When health-care providers who are genuinely concerned face this reality, perhaps they will be more willing to fight for the survival of these centers and strongly urge their increased funding rather than acquiesce in their demise. In rural areas, the problem is even greater, and far more comprehensive health planning is needed to meet patient needs.

I should like to reiterate that this book was written with the hope that by sharing the material I have taught over the years, some small changes will be made in the thinking of all health-care providers who read it. There is nothing new in these pages. Perhaps it is simply a recombination of material with which the reader is familiar, but I hope it serves its purpose: the sharing of beliefs and attitudes, and the stimulation of lots of consciousness raising concerning issues of vital concern to health-care providers who must confront the needs of clients with diverse cultural backgrounds.

REFERENCES

1. Pope-Davis, D.B., Eliason, M.J., and Ottavi, T.M. "Are Nursing Students Multiculturally Competent? An Exploratory Investigation." *Journal of Nursing Education.* 33(1) (1994): 31–33.

FURTHER SUGGESTED READING

Articles

Baker, A.W. "Stress, Adaptation, and the Black Individual: Implications for Nursing Education." *Journal of Nursing Education* 22(6) (June 1983): 237–242.

Blakeney, A.B. "Appalachian Values: Implications for Occupational Therapists." *Occupational Therapy in Health Care* 4(1) (Spring 1987): 57–72.

Branch, M. "Faculty Development to Meet Minority Group Needs: Recruitment, Retention, and Curriculum Change, 1971–1974." Western Interstate Commission for Higher Education, no. 2060.

Burrows, A. "Patient-Centered Nursing Care in a Multi-Racial Society: The Relevance of Ethnographic Perspectives in Nursing Curricula." *Journal of Advanced Nursing* 8(6) (November 1983): 477–485.

Calabretto, H. "Interpreting the Needs of Migrants." *Australian Nurses Journal* 12(3) (September 1982): 41 –42.

Claerbaut, D. "The Black Nursing Student at the Liberal Arts College: A Study in Alienation." *Nursing Forum* 15(2) (February 1976): 211–218.

Cofer, A. "Autobiography of a Black Nurse." *American Journal of Nursing* (October 1974): 1836–1838.

Crosbie, J.M., "LTC in the Third World—Long-term care." *Journal of Gerontological Nursing* 15(3) (March 1989): 6 –10.

Felder, E. "From Cultural Conflict to Cultural Relevant Care: A Cultural Diversity Practice Model." Paper presented. First Annual International Interdisciplinary Conference—Spiritual Dimensions of Health: Transcultural Perspectives. University of Windsor, Windsor, Ontario, Canada, June 1990.

Group, T.M. "If a Nurse Is to Help in Ghettos." *American Journal of Nursing* 69 (December 1969): 2635–2636.

Harvey, L.H. "Educational Problems of Minority Group Nurses." *Nursing Outlook* 18(9) (September 1970): 48–50.

Henderson, G. and Primeaux, M. "How We See it—Nursing Career Talks with Transcultural Nursing Experts." *Nursing Careers—Continuing Education in Nursing* 3(60) (July–August 1982): 8–10.

Hodgkinson, H.L. *All One System: Demographics of Education—Kindergarten through Graduate School.* Washington, DC: Institute for Educational Leadership, 1985.

Kanitsaki, O. "Acculturation—A New Dimension in Nursing." *Australian Nursing Journal* 13(5) (November 1983): 42–45, 52.

Kegley, C.F. and Saviers, A.N. "Working with Others Who Are Not Like Me." *Journal of School Health* 53(2) (February 1983): 81–85.

Kiu, Y.C. "China: Traditional Healing and Contemporary Medicine." *International Nursing Review* 31(4/256) (July–August 1984): 110–114.

La Fargue, J. "Role of Prejudice in Rejection of Health Care." *Nursing Research* 21 (January–February 1972): 53–58.

Leininger, M. "Transcultural Nursing: An Overview." *Nursing Outlook* 32(2) (March–April 1984): 72–73.

Leininger, M. "Transcultural Nursing Education: A Worldwide Imperative." *Nursing and Health Care.* 15(5) (1994): 254 –257.

Lowe, A.G. "The Counterpart System in International Nursing." *Pediatric Nursing* 9(4) (July–August 1983): 259–261.

Lukasik, C. "International Nursing with Project HOPE." *Pediatric Nursing* 9(4) (July–August 1983): 267–268.

MacFadyen, J.S. "CE Needs: American Nurses Working Overseas." *Journal of Continuing Education in Nursing* 14(5) (September–October 1983): 28–31.

McGinley, M. "In the Best of Traditions? To Balance Western Practices with Traditional Midwifery and Healing in the Villages of Panama." *Nursing Mirror* 157(18) (November 2, 1983): viii–xi.

Milio, N. "Values, Social Class, and Community Health Services." *Nursing Research* 16 (Winter 1967): 26–31.

Miller, M.H. "On Blacks Entering Nursing." *Nursing Forum* 11(3) (March 1972): 248–263.

Mills, A.C. "Saudi Arabia: An Overview of Nursing and Health Care." *Focus on Critical Care* 13(1) (February 1986): 50–56.

Morse, J.M. and English, J. "The Incorporation of Cultural Concepts into Basic Nursing Texts." *Nursing Papers: Perspectives in Nursing* 18(2) (Summer 1986): 69–76.

Nance, T.A. "Intercultural Communication: Finding Common Ground." *Journal of Obstetric, Gynecologic, and Neonatal Nursing.* 24(3) (1995): 249–255.

Paxton, P. and Robinson, S.P. "Continuing Education Needs of Nurses Serving Minorities and the Poor." *Journal of Continuing Education in Nursing* 5 (March–April 1974): 12–17.

Pfeiffer, B.A. and Frey, M.F. "A Transcultural Nursing Project on the Campus." *Health Values* 7(3) (May–June 1983): 28–30.

Piero, P. "Black White Crises." *American Journal of Nursing* 74 (February 1974): 280–281.

Price, J.L. and Cordell, B. "Cultural Diversity and Patient Teaching." *Journal of Continuing Education in Nursing.* 25(4) (1994): 163–1166.

Richeck, H.G. "A Note on Prejudice in Prospective Professional Helpers." *Nursing Research* 19 (March–April 1970): 172–175.

Rojas, D. "Leadership in a Multicultural Society." *Nursing and Health Care.* 15(5) (1994): 258–261.

Rorabaugh, M.L. "The Pediatric Nurse Practitioner in South East Asia: A Personal Account." *Pediatric Nursing* 9(4) (July –August 1983): 263–266.

Rosella, J.D., Regan-Kubinski, M.J., and Albrecht, S.A. "The Need for Multicultural Diversity among Health Professionals." *Nursing and Health Care.* 15(5) (1994): 242–253.

Segall, M. "Letter from Aswan—A Nurse Consultant Working in Egypt." *Nursing Outlook* 31(4) (July–August 1983): 220–224.

Sellers, R.V. "The Black Health Worker and the Black Health Consumer—New Roles for Both." *American Journal of Public Health* 60(11) (November 1970): 2154–2170.

Smith, G.R. "From Invisibility to Blackness: The Story of the Black Nurses' Association." *Nursing Outlook* 23(4) (April 1975): 225–229.

Smith-Campbell, B. "Haiti: An International Nursing Experience." *Kansas Nurse* 63(3) (March 1988): 4–5.

Stone, A.C. "Nursing in the Third World: from Problem to Passport." *Pediatric Nursing* 9(4) (July–August 1983): 251–254.

Tripp-Reimer, T., Brink, P.J., and Saunders, J.M. "Cultural Assessment: Content and Process." *Nursing Outlook* 32(2) (March–April 1984): 78–82.

Viers-Henderson, V. "The Nurse and Minority Health Problems in the United States." *Imprint* 63(30) (April–May 1983): 60–63.

RESOURCES

CULTURGRAM
Brigham Young University
David M. Kennedy Center for International Studies
Publication Services
280 HRCB
Provo, UT 84602
(801) 378-6528

The American Story
Anti-Defamation League of B'nai B'rith
823 United Nations Plaza
New York, NY 10017
(They also publish *Education and Society*)

Multicultural Studies Catalog
10200 Jefferson Blvd.
P.O. Box 802
Culver City, PA 90232-0802

Office of Minority Affairs
U.S. Department of Health and Human Services
Public Health Service
Room 118-F
HHH Building
200 Independence Ave., SW
Washington, DC 20201

Bibliography

Abraham, L. K. *Mama Might be Better off Dead—The Failure of Health Care in Urban America.* Chicago: University of Chicago Press, 1993.

Abrahams, P. *Tell Freedom: Memories of Africa.* New York: Knopf, 1954.

Achebe, C. *Things Fall Apart.* Greenwich, CT: Fawcett Crest, 1959.

Achebe, C. *Anthills of Savannah.* New York: Anchor Press/Doubleday, 1987.

Achterberg, J., Dossey, B., and Kolkmeier, L. *Rituals of Healing—Using Imagery for Health and Wellness.* New York: Bantam Books, 1994.

Aday, L. A. *At Risk in America—The Health and Health Care Needs of Vulnerable Populations in the United States.* San Francisco: Jossey-Bass, 1993.

Aiken, L. G. *Health Policy and Nursing Practice.* New York: McGraw-Hill, 1981.

Aiken, R. *Mexican Folk Tales from the Borderland.* Dallas: Southern Methodist University Press, 1980.

Albrecht, G. L. and Higgens, P. C., eds. *Health, Illness, and Medicine.* Chicago: Rand McNally, 1979.

Alcott, W. A. *The House I Live In; or The Human Body.* Boston: George W. Light, 1839.

Allende, I. *The House of the Spirits.* New York: Bantam Books, 1993.

Allison, D. *Bastard out of Carolina.* New York: Plume, 1992.

Allport, G. W. *The Nature of Prejudice* (abridged). Garden City, NY: Doubleday and Co., 1958.

Alvarez, H. R. *Health without Boundaries.* Mexico: United States–Mexico Border Public Health Association, 1975.

Alvarez, J. *How the Garcia Girls Lost Their Accents.* New York: Plume, 1992.

Ameer Ali, S. *The Spirit of Islam.* Delhi, India: IDARAH-I-ADABIYAT-I-DELLI, 1922, 1978.

American Nurses' Association. *A Strategy for Change.* Papers presented at the conference of the Commission on Human Rights, Albuquerque, NM, 9–10 June 1979.

Anderson, E. T. and McFarlane, J. M. *Community as Client.* Philadelphia: J. B. Lippincott, 1988.

Anderson, J. Q. *Texas Folk Medicine.* Austin: Encino Press, 1970.

Andrade, S. J. *Chicano Mental Health: The Case of Cristal.* Austin: Hogg Foundation for Mental Health, 1978.

Andrews, E. D. *The People Called Shakers.* New York: Dover, 1953.

Andrews, M. M. and Boyle, J. S. *Transcultural Concepts in Nursing Care* (2nd. ed.). Philadelphia: J. B. Lippincott, 1995.

Angelou, M. *I Know Why the Caged Bird Sings.* New York: Random House, 1970.

Annas, G. J. *The Rights of Hospital Patients.* New York: Avon, 1975.

Apple, D., ed. *Sociological Studies of Health and Sickness: A Source Book for the Health Professions.* New York: McGraw-Hill, Blakiston Division, 1960.

Appelfeld, A. *The Healer.* New York: Grove Weidenfeld, 1990.

Archer, S. E. and Fleshman, R. P. *Community Health Nursing* (3rd ed.). Monterey: Wadsworth, 1985.

Arnold, M. G. and Rosenbaum, G. *The Crime of Poverty.* Skokie, IL: National Textbook Co., 1973.

Ashely, J. *Hospitals, Paternalism, and the Role of the Nurse.* New York: Teachers College Press, 1976.

Aurand, A. M., Jr. *The Realness of Witchcraft in America.* Lancaster, PA: The Aurand Press, undated.

Ausubel, N. *The Book of Jewish Knowledge.* New York: Crown Publishers, 1964.

Bahti, T. *Southwestern Indian Ceremonials.* Las Vegas: KC Publications, 1974.

Bahti, T. *Southwestern Indian Tribes.* Las Vegas: KC Publications, 1975.

Bakan, D. *Disease, Pain and Sacrifice: Toward a Psychology of Suffering.* Chicago: University of Chicago Press, 1968.

Baker, G. C. *Planning and Organizing for Multicultural Instruction* (2nd. ed.). Menlo Park, CA: Addison-Wesley, 1994.

Balch, J. F. and Balch, P. A. *Prescription for Nutritional Healing.* Garden City Park, NY: Avery Publishing, 1990.

Baldwin, R. *The Healers.* Huntington, IN: Our Sunday Visitor Publishing Division, 1986.

Banks, J. A., ed. *Teaching Ethnic Studies.* Washington, DC: National Council for Social Studies, 1973.

Bannerman, R. H., Burton, J., and Wen-Chieh, C. *Traditional Medicine and Health Care Coverage.* Geneva: World Health Organization, 1983.

Barden, T. E., ed. *Virginia Folk Legends.* Charlottesville: University Press of Virginia, 1991.

Bauwens, E. F. *The Anthropology of Health.* St. Louis: C. V. Mosby, 1979.

Becerra, R. M. and Shaw, D. *The Elderly Hispanic A Research and Reference Guide.* Lanham, MD: University Press of America, 1984.

Becker, M. H. *The Health Belief Model and Personal Health Behavior.* Thorofare, NJ: Slack, 1974.

Benedict, R. *Patterns of Culture.* New York: Penguin Books, 1946.

Benjamin, G. G. *The Germans in Texas.* 1910. Reprint. Austin: Jenkins Publishing Co., 1974.

Bennett, C. I. *Comprehensive Multicultural Education* (2nd ed.). Boston: Allyn and Bacon, 1990.

Berg, D. J., ed. *Homestead Hints.* Berkeley. CA: Ten Speed Press, 1986.

Berg, P. S., ed. *An Entrance to the Tree of Life.* Jerusalem, Israel: Research Center for Kabbalah, 1977.

Berman, E. *The Solid Gold Stethoscope.* New York: Macmillan Co., 1976.

Bermann, E. *Scapegoat.* Ann Arbor: University of Michigan Press, 1973.

Bernardo, A., trans. Rand, P. T. *Lourdes: Then and Now.* Lourdes, France: Etablissements Estrade, undated.

Bernardo, S. *The Ethnic Almanac.* Garden City, NY: Doubleday and Co., 1981.

Berwick, D. M., Godfrey, A. B., and Roessner, J. *Curing Health Care.* San Francisco: Josey-Bass, 1990.

Bienvenue, R. M., and Goldstein, J. E. *Ethnicity and Ethnic Relations in Canada* (2nd ed.). Toronto: Butterworths, 1979.

Birnbaum, P. *Encyclopedia of Jewish Concepts.* New York: Hebrew Publishing Co., 1988.

Bishop, G. *Faith Healing: God or Fraud?* Los Angeles: Shervourne Press, 1967.

Bohannan P. *We, the Alien* Prospect Heights IL: Waveland Press, Inc., 1992.

Boney, W. *The French Canadians Today.* London: J. M. Dent and Sons, 1939.

Bonfanti, L. *Biographies and Legends of the New England Indians.* Wakefield, MA: Pride, 1974: vol. iv.

Bonfanti, L. *Strange Beliefs, Customs, & Superstitions of New England.* Wakefield, MA: Pride Publications, 1980.

Bottomore, T. B. *Classes in Modern Society.* New York: Vintage Books, 1968.

Bowen, E. S. *Return to Laughter.* Garden City, NY: Doubleday, 1964.

Boyd, D. *Rolling Thunder.* New York: Random House, 1974.

Boyle, J. S. and Andrews, M. M. *Transcultural Concepts in Nursing Care.* Glenview, IL: Scott, Foresman/Little, Brown College Division, 1989.

Bracq, J. C. *The Evolution of French Canada.* New York: Macmillan Co., 1924.

Bradley, C. J. "Characteristics of Women and Infants Attended by Lay Midwives in Texas, 1971: A Case Comparison Study." (Master's thesis, University of Texas Health Science Center at Houston, School of Public Health, 1980).

Branch, M. F. and Paxton, P. P. *Providing Safe Nursing Care for Ethnic People of Color.* New York: Appleton-Century-Crofts, 1976.

Brand, J. *The Life and Death of Anna Mae Aquash.* Toronto: James Lorimer, 1978.

Brink, P. J., ed. *Transcultural Nursing: A Book of Readings.* Englewood Cliffs, NJ: Prentice-Hall, 1976.

Brink, J. and Keen, L. *Feverfew.* London: Century, 1979.

Brown, D. *Bury My Heart at Wounded Knee.* New York: Holt, Rinehart and Winston, 1970.

Brown, D. *Creek Mary's Blood.* New York: Holt, Rinehart and Winston, 1980.

Browne, K. and Freeling, P. *The Doctor–Patient Relationship.* Edinburgh: E & S Livingstone, 1967.

Browne, G., Howard, J., and Pitts, M. *Culture and Children.* Austin, TX: University of Texas Press, 1985.

Brownlee, A. T. *Community, Culture and Care: A Cross Cultural Guide for Healthworkers.* St. Louis: C. V. Mosby, 1979.

Bruchac, J. *Iroquois Stories Heroes and Heroines Monsters and Magic.* Freedom, CA: The Crossing Press, 1985.

Bryant, C. A. *The Cultural Feast: An Introduction to Food and Society.* St. Paul: West, 1985.

Buchman, D. D. *Herbal Medicine: The Natural Way to Get Well and Stay Well.* New York: Gramercy, 1979.

Budge, E. A. W. *Amulets and Superstitions.* New York: Dover, 1978.

Bullough, B. and Bullough, V. L. *Poverty, Ethnic Identity and Health Care.* New York: Appleton-Century-Crofts, 1972.

Bullough, V. L., and Bullough, B. *Health Care for Other Americans.* New York: Appleton-Century-Crofts, 1982.

Buxton, J. *Religion and Healing in Mandari.* Oxford: Clarendon Press, 1973.

Cafferty, P. S. J., Chiswick, B. R., Greeley, A. M., et al. *The Dilemma of American Immigration: Beyond the Golden Door.* New Brunswick: Transaction Books, 1983.

Cahill, R. E. *Olde New England's Curious Customs and Cures.* Salem, MA: Old Saltbox Publishing House, 1990.

Cahill, R. E. *Strange Superstitions.* Salem, MA: Old Saltbox Publishing House, 1990.

Calhoun, M. *Medicine Show.* New York: Harper and Row, 1976.

Califano, J. *Radical Surgery.* New York: Random House, 1994.

Campos, E. *Medicina Popular—Supersticione Credios E Meizinhas* (2nd ed.). Rio de Janeiro: Livraria—Editora da Casa. 1955.

Candill, H. M. *Night Comes to the Cumberlands.* Boston: Little, Brown and Co., 1962.

Carnegie, M. E. *The Path We Tread: Blacks in Nursing 1854–1984.* Philadelphia: J. B. Lippincott, 1987.

Carson, V. B., ed. *Spiritual Dimensions of Nursing Practice.* Philadelphia: W. B. Saunders, 1989.

Catalog 70 and 75. *Immigration and Ethnic Studies.* Austin: The Austin Book Shop.

Chafets, Z. *Devil's Night and Other Tales of Detroit.* New York: Vintage Books, 1990.

Chan, L. S., McCandless, R., Portnoy, B., et al. *Maternal and Child Health on the U.S.-Mexico Border.* Austin: The University of Texas, 1987.

Chavira, L. *Curanderismo: An Optional Health-Care System.* Edinburg, TX: Pan American University, 1975.

Chenault, L. R. *The Puerto Rican Migrant in New York City.* New York: Columbia University Press, 1938.

Chiba, R. *The Seven Lucky Gods of Japan.* Rutland, VT: Charles E. Tuttle Co., 1966.

Choron, J. *Death and Modern Man.* New York: Collier Books, 1964.

Chute, C. *The Beans of Egypt, Maine.* New York: Ticknor & Fields, 1985.

Clark, A. L. *Culture and Child Rearing.* Philadelphia: F. A. Davis Co., 1981.

Clark, A. *Culture, Childbearing Health Professionals.* Philadelphia: F. A. Davis Co., 1978.

Clark, M. *Health in the Mexican-American Culture: A Community Study.* Berkeley: University of California Press, 1959.

Comas-Diaz, L. and Griffith, E. E. H. *Clinical Guidelines in Cross-Cultural Mental Health.* New York: John Wiley and Sons, 1988.

Committee on Medical Care Teaching, eds. *Readings in Medical Care.* Chapel Hill, NC: University of North Carolina Press, 1958.

Conde, M. *I, Tituba, Black Witch of Salem.* New York: Ballantine Books, 1992.

Conway, M. *Rise Gonna Rise.* New York: Anchor Books, 1974.

Corish, J. L. *Health Knowledge.* New York: Domestic Health Society, 1923; vol. 1.

Cornacchia, H. J. *Consumer Health.* St. Louis: C. V. Mosby, 1976.

Council on Cultural Diversity in Nursing Practice. *Proceedings of the Invitational Meeting Multicultural Issues in the Nursing Workforce and Workplace.* Washington, D.C.: American Nurses' Association, 1994.

Cowan, N. M. and Cowan, R. S. *Our Parent's Lives.* New York: Basic Books, 1989.

Cramer, M. E. *Divine Science and Healing.* Denver: Colorado College of Divine Science, 1923.

Crichton, M. *Five Patients.* New York: Alfred A. Knopf, 1970.

Crispino, J. A. *Assimilation of Ethnic Groups: The Italian Case.* Newark, NJ: New Jersey Center for Migration, 1980.

Culpeper, N. *Culpeper's Complete Herbal.* London: W. Foulsham, 1889.

Curry, M. A., project director. *Access to Prenatal Care: Key to Preventing Low Birth-weight.* Kansas City, MO: American Nurses' Association, 1987.

Cutter, C. *First Book on Anatomy, Physiology, and Hygiene, for Grammar Schools and Families.* Boston: Benjamin B. Mussey, 1850.

Davis, F., ed. *The Nursing Profession: Five Sociological Essays*. New York: John Wiley and Sons, 1966.

DeBella, S., Martin, L., and Siddall, S. *Nurses' Role in Health Care Planning*. Norwalk, CT: Appleton-Century-Crofts, 1986.

De Castro, J. *The Black Book of Hunger*. Boston: Beacon Press, 1967.

Delaney, J., Lupton, M. J., and Toth, E. *The Curse: A Cultural History of Menstruation*. Chicago: University of Chicago Press, 1988.

Deller, B., Hicks, D., and MacDonald, G., coordinators. *Stone Boats and Lone Stars*. Hyde Park, Ontario: Middlesex County Board of Education, 1979.

Deloria, V., Jr. *Custer Died for Your Sins—An Indian Manifesto*. New York: Avon Books, 1969.

DeLys, C. *A Treasury of American Superstitions*. New York: Philosophical Library, 1948.

Densmore, F. *How Indians Use Wild Plants for Food, Medicine, and Crafts*. New York: Dover, 1974.

Deren, M. *Divine Horseman—The Living Gods of Haiti*. New York: McPherson & Co., 1953.

Dey C. *The Magic Candle*. Bronx, NY: Original Publications, 1982.

Dickison, R., ed. *Causes, Cures, Sense, and Nonsense*. Sacramento, CA: Bishop Publishing Co., 1987.

Dinnerstein, L. and Reimers, D. M. *Ethnic Americans* (3rd ed.). New York: Harper & Row, 1988.

Doane, N. L. *Indian Doctor Book*. Charlotte, NC: Aerial, 1985.

Donegan, J. B. *Women and Men Midwives: Medicine, Morality and Misogyny in Early America*. Westport, CT: Greenwood Press, 1978.

Donin, H. H. *To Be a Jew*. New York: Basic Books, 1972.

Dorson, R. H. D., ed. *Folklore and Folklife*. Chicago: University of Chicago Press, 1972.

Dresser N. *Our Own Stories: Cross-cultural Communication Practice*. White Plains, NY: Longman, 1993.

Dubos, R. J. *Man Adapting*. New Haven: Yale University Press, 1965.

Dubos, R. *Man, Medicine and Environment*. New York: Mentor, 1968.

Dubos, R. *Mirage of Health*. Garden City, NY: Anchor Books, Doubleday and Co., 1961.

Dworaczyk, E. J. *The First Polish Colonies of America in Texas*. San Antonio: The Naylor Company, 1979.

Ehrenreich, B. and Ehrenreich, J. *The American Health Empire: Power, Profits, and Politics*. New York: Random House, Vintage Books, 1970.

Ehrenreich, B. and English, D. *Witches, Midwives, and Nurses: A History of Women Healers* (2nd ed.). Old Westbury, NY: Feminist Press, 1973.

Ehrlich, P. R. *The Golden Door: International Migration, Mexico and the United States*. New York: Wideview Books, 1979.

Eichler, L. *The Customs of Mankind*. Garden City, NY: Doubleday, Page & Co., 1923.

Eisenberg, D. *Encounters with Qi*. New York: W. W. Norton, 1985.

Elling, R. H. *Socio-Cultural Influences on Health and Health Care*. New York: Springer Co., 1977.

Elworthy, R. T. *The Evil Eye: The Origins and Practices of Superstition*. New York: Julian Press, 1958 (originally published by John Murray, London, 1915).

Epstein, C. *Effective Interaction in Contemporary Nursing*. Englewood Cliffs, NJ: Prentice-Hall, 1974.

Evans, E. F. *The Devine Law of Cure*. Boston: H. H. Carter & Co., 1881.

Farge, E. J. *La Vida Chicana: Health Care Attitudes and Behaviors of Houston Chicanos*. San Francisco: R and E Research Associates, 1975.

Feagin, J. R. *Subordinating the Poor—Welfare and American Beliefs*. Englewood Cliffs, NJ: Prentice-Hall, 1975.

Feagin, J. R. and Feagin, C. B. *Discrimination American Style*. Englewood Cliffs, NJ: Prentice-Hall, 1978.

Feldman, D. M. *Health and Medicine in the Jewish Tradition*. New York: Crossroads Publishing, 1986.

Finney, J. C., ed. *Culture Change, Mental Health and Poverty*. New York: Simon and Schuster, 1969.

Fleming, A. S., chairman, U.S. Commission on Civil Rights. *The Tarnished Golden Door—Civil Rights Issues on Immigration*. Washington, DC: Government Printing Office, 1980.

Flores-Pena, Y. and Evanchuk, R. J. *Santeria Garments and Alters*. Jackson, MS: University of Mississippi Press, 1994.

Forbes, T. R. *The Midwife and the Witch*. New Haven: Yale University Press, 1966.

Ford, P. S. *The Healing Trinity: Prescriptions for Body, Mind, and Spirit*. New York: Harper and Row, 1971.

Foy, F. A., ed. *Catholic Almanac*. Huntington, IN: Our Sunday Visitor, 1980.

Frankel, E. and Teutsch, B. P. *The Encyclopedia of Jewish Symbols*. Northvale, NJ: Jason Aronson, Inc., 1992.

Frazer, J. G. *Folklore in the Old Testament*. New York: Tudor Publishing, 1923.

Freedman, L. *Public Housing: The Politics of Poverty*. New York: Holt, Rinehart, Winston, 1969.

Freeman, H., Levine, S., and Reeder, L. G., eds. *Handbook of Medical Sociology* (2nd ed.). Englewood Cliffs, NJ: Prentice-Hall, 1972.

Freidson, E. *Profession of Medicine*. New York: Dodd, Mead and Co., 1971.

Freire, P. *Pedagogy of the Oppressed*, trans. M. B. Ramos. New York: Seabury Press, 1970.

Frost, M. *The Shaker Story*. Canterbury, NH: Canterbury Shakers, undated.

Fuentes, C. *The Old Gringo*. New York: Farrar, Straus, Giroux, 1985.

Fuller, J. G. *Arigo: Surgeon of the Rusty Knife*. New York: Pockett Books, 1974.

Galloway, M. R. U., ed. *Aunt Mary, Tell Me a Story*. Cherokee, NC: Cherokee Communications, 1990.

Gambino, R. *Blood of My Blood: The Dilemma of Italian-Americans*. Garden City, NY: Doubleday and Co., 1974.

Gans, H. J. *The Urban Villagers*. New York: The Free Press, 1962.

Garcia, C. *Dreaming in Cuban*. New York: Ballantine Books, 1992.

Garner, J. *Healing Yourself* (6th ed.). Vashon, WA: Crossing Press, 1976.

Gaver, J. R. *Sickle Cell Disease*. New York: Lancer Books, 1972.

Gaw A, ed: *Cross-cultural Psychiatry*, Boston: John Wright, 1982.

Geissler, E. M. *Cultural Assessment*. St. Louis: Mosby, 1993.

Gelfond, D. E. and Kutzik, A., eds. *Ethnicity and Aging: Theory, Research and Policy*. New York: Springer, 1979.

Genovese, E. D. *Roll, Jordan, Roll*. New York: Vintage Books, 1972.

Gibbs, J. T., Huang, L. N., Nagata, D. K., et al. *Children of Color*. San Francisco: Jossey-Bass, 1988.

Giger, J. N. and Davidhizar, R. E. *Transcultural Nursing Assessment and Intervention*. 2nd ed. St. Louis: Mosby, 1995.

Giordano, J. and Giordano, G. P. *The Ethno-Cultural Factor in Mental Health*. New York: New York Institute of Pluralism and Group Identity, 1977.

Glazer, N. and Moynihan, D., eds. *Ethnicity: Theory and Experience.* Cambridge: Harvard University Press, 1975.

Goldberg B. *Alternative Medicine—The Definitive Guide,* Puyallup, WA: Future Medicine Publishing, Inc., 1993.

Gonzalez-Wippler, M. *Santeria—African Magic in Latin America.* Bronx, NY: Original Publications, 1987.

Gonzalez-Wippler, M. *Tales of the Orishas.* New York: Original Publications, 1985.

Gonzalez-Wippler, M. *The Santeria Experience.* Bronx, NY: Original Publications, 1982.

Gordon, A. F. and Kahan, L. *The Tribal Beads a Handbook of African Trade Beads.* New York: Tribal Arts Gallery, 1976.

Gordon, D. M. *Theories of Poverty and Underemployment.* Lexington, MA: D. C. Heath and Co., 1972.

Gordon, F. *Role Theory and Illness.* New Haven, CT: College and University Press, 1966.

Goswami, S. D. *Prabhupada: He Built a House in Which the Whole World Can Live.* Los Angeles: The Bhaktivedanta Book Trust, 1983.

Greeley, A. M. *The Irish Americans.* New York: Harper and Row, 1981.

Greeley, A. M. *Why Can't They Be Like Us? America's White Ethnic Groups.* New York: E. P. Dutton, 1975.

Grier, W. H. and Cobbs, P. M. *Black Rage.* New York: Bantam Books, 1968.

Griffin, J. H. *Black Like Me.* New York: Signet, 1960.

Gruber R. *Rescue: The Exodus of the Ethiopian Jews.* New York: Atheneum, 1987.

Gutman, H. G. *The Black Family in Slavery and Freedom, 1750–1925.* New York: Pantheon Books, 1976.

Hailey, A. *Strong Medicine.* Garden City, NY: Doubleday & Co., 1984.

Haley, A. *Roots.* Garden City, NY: Doubleday and Co., 1976.

Hammerschlag, C. A. *The Dancing Healers.* San Francisco: Harper & Row, 1988.

Hand, W. D. *Magical Medicine.* Berkeley: University of California Press, 1980.

Hand, W. D. *American Folk Medicine: A Symposium.* Berkeley: University of California Press, 1973.

Harney, R. F. and Troper, H. *Immigrants: A Portrait of Urban Experience 1890–1930.* Toronto: Van Nostrand Reinhold, 1975.

Harrington, C. and Estes, C. L. *Health Policy and Nursing.* Boston: Jones and Bartlett, 1994.

Harris, L. *Holy Days: The World of a Hasidic Family.* New York: Summit Books, 1985.

Harwood, A., ed. *Ethnicity and Medical Care.* Cambridge: Harvard University Press, 1981.

Haskins, J. *Voodoo and Hoodoo.* Bronx, NY: Original Publications, 1978.

Hauptman, L. M. and Wherry, J. D. *The Pequots in Southern New England—The Fall and Rise of an American Indian Nation.* Norman, OK: University of Oklahoma Press, 1990.

Hawkins, J. B. W. and Higgins, L. P. *Nursing and the Health Care Delivery System.* New York: The Tiresias Press, 1983.

Hecker, M. *Ethnic American, 1970–1977.* Dobbs Ferry, NY: Oceana Publications, 1979.

Henderson, G. and Primeaux, M., eds. *Transcultural Health Care.* Menlo Park, CA: Addison-Wesley, 1981.

Hernandez, C. A., Haug, M. J., and Wagner, N. N. *Chicanos' Social and Psychological Perspectives.* St. Louis: C. V. Mosby, 1976.

Herzlich, C. *Health and Illness—A Social Psychological Analysis,* trans. D. Graham. New York: Academic Press, 1973.

Hiatt, H. H. *America's Health in the Balance: Choice or Chance?* New York: Harper and Row, 1987.

Hickel, W. J. *Who Owns America?* New York: Paperback Library, 1972.

Himmelstein, D. U. and Woolhandler, S. *The National Health Program Book—A Source Guide for Advocates.* Monroe, ME: Common Courage Press, 1994.

Hirsch, E. D. *Cultural Literacy: What Every American Needs to Know.* Boston: Houghton Mifflin, 1987.

Hongo, F. M., general ed. *Japanese American Journey: The Story of a People.* San Mateo, CA: JACP, 1985.

Honychurch P. N. *Caribbean Wild Plants and Their Uses.* London: Macmillan Publishers, Ltd., 1980.

Howard M. *Candle Burning* (2nd ed.). Weingborough, Northamptonshire, England: Aquarian Press, 1980.

Howe, I. *World of Our Fathers.* New York: Harcourt Brace Jovanovich, 1976.

Hufford, D. J. *American Healing Systems: An Introduction and Exploration.* Conference Booklet, Philadelphia: University of Pennsylvania, 1984.

Hughes, H. S. *The United States and Italy.* Cambridge, MA: Harvard University Press, 1953.

Hughes, L., and Bontemps, A., eds. *The Book of Negro Folklore.* New York: Dodd, Mead, 1958.

Hunter, J. D. *Culture Wars—The Struggle to Define America.* New York: Basic Books, 1991.

Hunter, J. D. *Before the Shooting Begins—Searching for Democracy in America's Culture War.* New York: Free Press, 1994.

Hurmence, B., ed. *My Folks Don't Want Me to Talk about Slavery.* Winston-Salem, NC: John F. Blair, 1984.

Hutchens, A. R. *Indian Herbalogy of North America.* Windsor, Ontario: Meico, 1973.

Hutton, J. B. *The Healing Power.* London: Leslie Frewin, 1975.

Illich, I. *Medical Nemesis: The Expropriation of Health.* London: Marion Bogars, 1975.

Illich, I., Zola, I. K., McKnight, J., et al. *Disabling Professions.* Salem, NH: Boyars, 1977.

Iorizzo, L. J. *Italian Immigration and the Impact of the Padrone System.* New York: Arno Press, 1980.

Jaco, E. G., ed. *Patients, Physicians, and Illness: Sourcebook in Behavioral Science and Medicine.* Glencoe, IL: Free Press, 1958.

Jacobs, H. A. *Incidents in the Life of a Slave Girl.* London: Oxford University Press, 1988.

Jacobs, L., ed. *The Jewish Mystics.* London: Kyle Cathie Ltd., 1990.

Jangl, A. M. and Jangl, J. F. *Ancient Legends of Healing Herbs.* Coeuor D'Alene, ID: Prisma Press, 1987.

Jarvis, D. C. *Folk Medicine: A Vermont Doctor's Guide to Good Health.* New York: Henry Holt and Co., 1958.

Jilek W. G. *Indian Healing—Shamanic Ceremonialism in the Pacific Northwest Today.* Blaine, WA: Hancock House, 1992.

Johnson, C. L. *Growing Up and Growing Old in Italian-American Families.* New Brunswick, NJ: Rutgers University Press, 1985.

Johnson, E. A. *To the First Americans—The Sixth Report on the Indian Health Program of the U.S. Public Health Service.* Washington, DC: DHEW Publication (HSA) 77-1000, 1976.

Jonas, S. *Health Care Delivery in the United States* (2nd ed.). New York: Springer, 1982.

Jordan, B. and Heardon, S. *Barbara Jordan: A Self-Portrait.* Garden City, NY: Doubleday & Co., 1979.

Jung, C. G., ed. *Man and His Symbols.* Garden City, NY: Doubleday and Co., 1964.

Kain, J. F., ed. *Race and Poverty: The Economics of Discrimination.* Englewood Cliffs, NJ: Prentice-Hall, 1969.

Kaptchuk, T. and Croucher, M. *The Healing Arts.* New York: Summit Books, 1987.

Karolevitz, R. F. *Doctors of the Old West.* New York: Bonanza Books, 1967.

Katz, J. H. *White Awareness.* Norman, OK: University of Oklahoma Press, 1978.

Kaufman, B. N. and Kaufman, S. L. *A Land Beyond Tears.* Garden City, NY: Doubleday, 1982.

Kavanagh, K. H. and Kennedy, P. H. *Promoting Cultural Diversity: Strategies for Health Care Professionals.* Newbury Park, CA: Sage, 1992.

Keith, J. *Old People as People—Social and Cultural Influences on Aging and Old Age.* Boston: Little, Brown, 1982.

Keith, J. *Old People New Lives.* Chicago: The University of Chicago Press, 1982.

Kekahbah, J. and Wood, R., eds. *Life Cycle of the American Indian Family.* Norman, OK: AIANA Publishing Co., 1980.

Kelly, I. *Folk Practice in North Mexico. Birth Customs, Folk Medicine and Spiritualism in the Laguna Zone.* Austin: University of Texas Press, 1965.

Kelsey, M. T. *Healing and Christianity.* New York: Harper and Row, 1973.

Kennedy, E. M. *In Critical Condition: The Crises in America's Health Care.* New York: Simon and Schuster, 1972.

Kennett, F. *Folk Medicine, Fact and Fiction.* New York: Crescent Books, 1976.

Kiev, A. *Curanderismo: Mexican-American Folk Psychiatry.* New York: Free Press, 1968.

Kiev, A. *Magic, Faith and Healing: Studies in Primitive Psychiatry Today.* New York: Free Press, 1964.

Killens, J. O. *The Cotillion.* New York: Ballantine, 1988.

Kilner, W. J. *The Human Aura.* Secaucus, NJ: Citadel Press, 1965.

Kincaid, J. *A Small Place.* New York: Farrar, Straus, Giroux, 1988.

King, D. H. *Cherokee Heritage.* Cherokee, NC: Cherokee Communications, 1988.

Kingston, M. H. *Tripmaster Monkey: His Fake Book.* New York: Knopf, 1989.

Kirkland, J., Matthews, H. F. M., Sullivan, C. W., III, et al. eds. *Herbal and Magical Medicine—Traditional Healing Today.* Durham, NC: Duke University Press, 1992.

Klein, A. M. *Sugarball, The American Game, the Dominican Dream.* New Haven: Yale University Press, 1991.

Klein, J. W. *Jewish Identity and Self-Esteem: Healing Wounds through Ethnotherapy.* New York: Institute on Pluralism and Group Identity, 1980.

Kluckhohn, C. *Navaho Witchcraft,* Boston: Beacon Press, 1944.

Kluckhohn, C. and Leighton, D. *The Navaho* (rev. ed.). Garden City, NY: Doubleday and Co., 1962.

Kmit, A., Luciow, L. L., Luciow, J., et al. *Ukrainian Easter Eggs and How We Make Them.* Minneapolis: Ukrainian Gift Shop, 1979.

Knudtson, P. and Suzuki, D. *Wisdom of the Elders.* Toronto: Stoddart Publishing Co. Ltd., 1992.

Knutson, A. L. *The Individual, Society and Health Behavior.* New York: Russell Sage Foundation, 1965.

Komisar, L. *Down and Out in the USA—A History of Social Welfare.* New York: New Viewpoints, 1974.

Kordel, L. *Natural Folk Remedies.* New York: G. P. Putnam's Sons, 1974.

Kosa, J., and Zola, I. K. *Poverty and Health—A Sociological Analysis* (2nd ed.). Cambridge, MA: Harvard University Press, 1976.

Kotelchuck, D., ed. *Prognosis Negative*. New York: Vintage Books, 1976.

Kotz, N. *Let Them Eat Promises*. Garden City, NY: Doubleday and Co., 1971.

Kovner, A., ed. *Health Care Delivery in the United States* (4th ed.). New York: Springer, 1990.

Kramer, R. M. *Participation of the Poor*. Englewood Cliffs, NJ: Prentice-Hall, 1969.

Kraut, A. M. *Silent Travelers: Germs, Genes, and the Immigrant Menace*. New York: Basic Books, 1994.

Kreiger, D. *The Therapeutic Touch*. Englewood Cliffs, NJ: Prentice-Hall, 1979.

Krippner, S. and Villaldo, A. *The Realms of Healing*. Millbrae, CA: Celestial Arts, 1976.

Kronenfeld, J. J. *Controversial Issues in Health Care Policy*. Newbury Park, CA: SAGE Publications, 1993.

Kunitz, S. J. and Levy, J. E. *Navajo Aging—The Transition from Family to Institutional Support*. Tucson: University of Arizona Press, 1991.

Lake, M. G. *Native Healer Initiation into an Art*. Wheaton, IL: Quest Books, 1991.

Landmann, R. S., ed. *The Problem of the Undocumented Worker*. Albuquerque: Latin American Institute, University of New Mexico, 1981.

Last, J. M. *Public Health and Human Ecology*. Norwalk, CT: Appleton, 1987.

Laveau, M. *Black and White Magic—Burning of Candles, Use of Roots and Oils, Powders, and Incenses*. Purchased in New Orleans, LA, in 1990.

Lavelle, R., ed. *America's New War on Poverty—A Reader for Action*. San Francisco: KQED Books, 1995.

Lawless, E. J. *God's Peculiar People*. Lexington, KY: University of Kentucky Press, 1988.

Lee, P. R. and Estes, C. L., eds. *The Nation's Health* (4th ed.). Boston: Jones and Bartlett, 1994.

Leek, S. *Herbs: Medicine and Mysticism*. Chicago: Henry Regnery Co., 1975.

Leff, S. and Leff, V. *From Witchcraft to World Health*. New York: Macmillan Co., 1957.

Leininger, M. *Nursing and Anthropology: Two Worlds to Blend*. New York: John Wiley and Sons, 1970.

Leininger, M. *Transcultural Nursing: Concepts, Theories and Practices*. New York: John Wiley and Sons, 1978.

Lerner, M. *Choices in Healing*. Cambridge, MA: MIT Press, 1994.

Lesnoff-Caravaglia, G., ed. *Realistic Expectations for Long Life*. New York: Human Sciences Press, 1987.

Lewis, O. *The Children of Sanchez: Autobiography of a Mexican Family*. New York: Random House, 1961.

Lewis, O. *A Death in the Sanchez Family*. New York: Random House, 1966.

Lewis, O. *Five Families: Mexican Case Studies in the Culture of Poverty*. New York: New American Library Basic Books, 1959.

Lewis, O. *La Vida: A Puerto Rican Family in the Culture of Poverty—San Juan and New York*. New York: Random House, 1966.

Lewis, T. H. *The Medicine Men—Oglala Sioux Ceremony and Healing*. Lincoln, NE: University of Nebraska Press, 1990.

Lich, G. E. *The German Texans*. San Antonio: The Institute of Texan Cultures, 1981.

Lieban, R. W. *Cebuano Sorcery*. Berkeley: University of California Press, 1967.

Linck, E. S. and Roach J. G. *Eats—A Folkhistory of Texas Foods*. Fort Worth: Texas Christian University Press, 1989.

Litoff, J. B. *American Midwives 1860 to the Present.* Westport, CT: Greenwood Press, 1978.

LittleDog, P. *Border Healing Woman—The Story of Jewel Babb* (2nd ed.). Austin: University of Texas Press, 1994.

Livingston, I. L., ed. *Handbook of Black American Health.* Westport, CT: Greenwood Press, 1994.

Logan, P. *Irish Country Cures.* Dublin: Talbot Press, 1981.

Louv, R. *Southwind: The Mexican Migration.* San Diego: San Diego Union, 1980.

Lovering, A. T. *The Household Physician.* Boston: Woodruff, 1923; vol. I.

Lovering, A. T. *The Household Physician.* Boston: Woodruff, 1923; vol. II.

Lum, D. *Social Work Practice and People of Color—A Process-Stage Approach* (2nd ed.). Pacific Grove, CA: Brooks/Cole, 1992.

Lynch, L. R., ed. *The Cross-Cultural Approach to Health Behavior.* Rutherford, NJ: Fairleigh Dickenson University Press, 1969.

Mackintosh, J. *Principles of Pathology and Practice of Physic* (3rd ed.). Philadelphia: Key & Biddle, 1836; vol. I.

MacNutt, F. *Healing.* Notre Dame, IN: Ave Maria Press, 1974.

MacNutt, F. *The Power to Heal.* Notre Dame, IN: Ave Maria Press, 1977.

Malinowski, B. *Magic, Science and Religion.* Garden City, NY: Doubleday and Co., 1954.

Maloney, C., ed. *The Evil Eye.* New York: Columbia University Press, 1976.

Malpezzi, F. M. and Clement, W. M. *Italian American Folklore.* Little Rock: August House Publishers, 1992.

Mandell, B. R., ed. *Welfare in America: Controlling the "Dangerous Classes."* Englewood Cliffs, NJ: Prentice-Hall, 1975.

Manderschied, R. W. and Sonnenschein, M. A., eds: Center for Mental Health Services and National Institute of Mental Health *Mental Health, United States, 1992.* Washington, D.C.: Supt. of Docs., U.S. Government Printing Office DHHS Pub. No. (SMA)92-1942, 1992.

Mann, F. *Acupuncture—The Ancient Chinese Art of Healing and How It Works Scientifically.* New York: Vintage Books, 1972.

Marquez, G. G. *Love in the Time of Cholera.* New York: Alfred A. Knopf, 1998.

Marsella, A. B. and Pedersens, P. B., eds. *Cross Cultural Counseling and Psychotherapy.* New York: Pergamon, 1981.

Marsella, A. J. and White G. M., eds. *Cultural Conceptions of Mental Health Therapy.* London: D. Reidel Publishing Co., 1982.

Martin, J. and Todnem, A. *Cream and Bread.* Hastings, MN: Redbird Productions, 1984.

Martin, J. L. and Nelson, S. J. *They Glorified Mary, We Glorified Rice.* Hastings, MN: Caragana Press, 1994.

Martin, J. L. and Nelson, S. J. *They Had Stories, We Had Chores.* Hastings, MN: Caragana Press, 1995.

Martin, L. C. *Wildflower Folklore.* Charlotte, NC: East Woods Press, 1984.

Martinez, R. A., ed. *Hispanic Culture and Health Care.* St. Louis: C. V. Mosby, 1978.

Matsumoto M. *The Unspoken Way.* Tokyo: Kodansha International, 1988.

Matthiessen, P. *In the Spirit of Crazy Horse.* New York: Viking Press, 1980.

McCall, N. *Makes Me Wanna Holler.* New York: Vintage Books, 1995.

McClain, M. *A Feeling for Life: Cultural Identity, Community and the Arts.* Chicago: Urban Traditions, 1988.

McCubbin, H. I., Thompson, E. A., Thompson, A. I., et al. *Resiliency in Ethnic Minority Families Native and Immigrant American Families* (Vol. 1). Madison, WI: University of Wisconsin-Madison, 1994.

McCubbin, H. I., Thompson, E. A., Thompson, A. I., et al. *Sense of Coherence and Resiliency.* Madison, WI: University of Wisconsin-Madison, 1994.

McCubbin, H., Thompson, E. A., Thompson, A. I., et al. *Resiliency in Ethnic Minority Families* (Vol. 2)—African-American Families. Madison, WI: The University of Wisconsin Center, 1995.

McGill, O. *The Mysticism and Magic of India.* South Brunswick, NJ, and New York: A. S. Baines and Co., 1977.

McGoldrick, M., Pearce, J. K., and Giordano, J. *Ethnicity and Family Therapy.* New York: Guilford Press, 1982.

McGregor, J. H. *The Wounded Knee Massacre from the Viewpoint of the Sioux.* Rapid City, SD: Fenwyn Press, 1940.

McLemore, S. D. *Racial and Ethnic Relations in America.* Boston: Allyn and Bacon, 1980.

Mechanic, D. *Medical Sociology: A Selective View.* New York: Free Press, 1968.

Menchu, R. trans. Wright, A. *I, Rigoberta Menchu.* London: Verso, 1983.

Merrill, F. E. *Society and Culture.* Englewood Cliffs, NJ: Prentice-Hall, 1962.

Metraux, A. *Voodoo in Haiti.* New York: Schocken Books, 1972.

Meyer, C. E. *American Folk Medicine.* Glenwood, IL: Meyerbooks, 1985.

Milio, N. *The Care of Health in Communities: Access for Outcasts.* New York: Macmillan Co., 1975.

Millman, M. *The Unkindest Cut.* New York: William Morrow and Co., 1977.

Mindel, C. H. and Habenstein, R. W., eds. *Ethnic Families in America.* New York: Elsevier, 1976.

Miner, H. *St. Denis, A French Canadian Parish.* Chicago: University of Chicago Press, 1939.

Montagu, A. *Touching.* New York: Harper & Row, 1971.

Montgomery, R. *Born to Heal.* New York: Coward, McCann, and Geoghegan, 1973.

Moody, R. A. *Life after Life.* New York: Bantam, 1976.

Mooney, J. *Myths of the Cherokee and Sacred Formulas of the Cherokees.* Nashville, TN: Charles and Randy Elder—Booksellers and Cherokee, NC: Museum of the Cherokee Indian, 1982.

Morgan, M. *Mutant Message Downunder.* Lees Summit, MO: MM CO, 1991.

Morgenstern, J. *Rites of Birth, Marriage, Death and Kindred Occasions among the Semites.* Chicago: Quadrangle Books, 1966.

Morley, P. and Wallis, R., eds. *Culture and Curing.* Pittsburgh: University of Pittsburgh Press, 1978.

Morrison, T. *Beloved.* New York: Knopf/Random House, 1987.

Morrison, T. *Tar Baby.* New York: Alfred A. Knopf, 1981.

Murray, P. *Song in a Weary Throat: An American Pilgrimage.* New York: Harper & Row, 1987.

Mushkin, S. V. *Consumer Incentives for Health Care.* New York: Prodist, 1974.

Nelli, H. S. *From Immigrants to Ethnics: The Italian Americans.* Oxford: Oxford University Press, 1983.

Nelson, D. *Food Combining Simplified.* Santa Cruz, CA: The Plan, 1985.

NemetzRobinson, G. L. *Crosscultural Understanding.* New York: Prentice Hall, 1988.

Nerburn, K. and Mengelkoch, L., eds. *Native American Wisdom.* San Rafael, CA: New World Library, 1991.

Neugrossschel, J. *Great Tales of Jewish Occult and Fantasy.* New York: Wings Books, 1991.

Newman, K. D. *Ethnic American Short Stories.* New York: Pocket Books, 1975.

Norman, J. C., ed. *Medicine in the Ghetto.* New York: Appleton-Century-Crofts, 1969.

North, J. H. and Grodsky, S. J. compiled. *Immigration Literature: Abstracts of Demographic, Economic, and Policy Studies.* Washington, DC: US Department of Justice, Immigration & Naturalization Service, 1979.

Novak, M. *The Rise of the Unmeltable Ethnics.* New York: Macmillan Co., 1972.

Null, G. and Stone, C. *The Italian-Americans.* Harrisburg, PA: Stackpole Books, 1976.

O'Berennan, J. and Smith, N. *The Crystal Icon.* Austin: Galahad Press, 1981.

Opler, M. K., ed. *Culture and Mental Health.* New York: Macmillan Co., 1959.

Orlando, L. *The Multicultural Game Book.* New York: Scholastic Professional Books, 1993.

Orque, M. S., Block, B., and Monrray, L. S. A. *Ethnic Nursing Care: A Multi-Cultural Approach.* St. Louis: C. V. Mosby, 1983.

Osofsky, G. *Harlem: The Making of a Ghetto.* New York: Harper and Row, 1963.

Overfield, T. *Biologic Variation in Health and Illness.* Menlo Park, CA: Addison-Wesley, 1985.

Padilla, E. *Up From Puerto Rico.* New York: Columbia University Press, 1958.

Paley, V. G. *White Teacher.* Cambridge, MA: Harvard University Press, 1979.

Pappworth, M. H. *Human Guinea Pigs: Experimentation on Man.* Boston: Beacon Press, 1967.

Parsons, T. and Clark, K. B. *The Negro American.* Boston: Beacon Press, 1965.

Paul, B., ed. *Health, Culture, and Community: Case Studies of Public Reactions to Health Programs.* New York: Russell Sage Foundation, 1955.

Pearsall, M. *Medical Behavior Science: A Selected Bibliography of Cultural Anthropology, Social Psychology, and Sociology in Medicine.* Louisville: University of Kentucky Press, 1963.

Pelto, P. J. and Pelto, G. H. *Anthropological Research: The Structure of Inquiry* (2nd ed.). Cambridge: Cambridge University Press, 1978.

Pelton, R. W. *Voodoo Charms and Talismans.* New York: Popular Library, 1973.

Petry, A. *The Street.* Boston: Beacon Press, 1985.

Philpott, L. L. "A Descriptive Study of Birth Practices and Midwifery in the Lower Rio Grande Valley of Texas." (Ph.D. diss., University of Texas Health Science Center at Houston School of Public Health, 1979).

Pierce, R. V. *The People's Common Sense Medical Advisor in Plain English, or Medicine Simplified* (12th ed.). Buffalo: World's Dispensary, 1883.

Piven, F. F. and Cloward, R. A. *Regulating the Poor: The Functions of Public Welfare.* New York: Vintage Books, 1971.

Plotkin, M. J. *Tales of a Shaman's Apprentice.* New York: Viking, 1993.

Popenoe, C. *Wellness.* Washington, DC: YES!, 1977.

Powell, C. A. *Bound Feet.* Boston: Warren Press, 1938.

Power, S. *The Grass Dancer.* New York: Putnam, 1994.

Prabhupada, A. C. *Bhaktivedanta Swami. KRSNA: The Supreme Personality of Godhead.* Los Angeles: The Bhaktivedanta Book Trust, 1970; vol. 1.

Prose, F. *Marie Laveau.* New York: Berkeley, 1977.

Rand, C. *The Puerto Ricans.* New York: Oxford University Press, 1958.

Read, M. *Culture, Health and Disease.* London: Javistock Publications, 1966.

Rector-Page, L. G. *Healthy Healing—An Alternative Healing Reference* (9th ed.). CA: Healthy Healing Publications, 1992.

Redman, E. *The Dance of Legislation.* New York: Simon and Schuster, 1973.

Reichard, G. A. *Navajo Medicine-Man Sandpaintings.* New York: Dover, 1977.

Reneaux, J. J. *Cajun Folktales.* Little Rock: August House Publishers, 1992.

Rist, R. C. *Desegregated Schools—Appraisals of an American Experiment.* New York: Academic Press, 1979.

Riva, A. *Devotions to the Saints.* Los Angeles: International Imports, 1990.

Riva, A. *Magic with Incense and Powders.* N. Hollywood, CA: International Imports, 1985.

Riva, A. *The Modern Herbal Spellbook.* N. Hollywood, CA: International Imports, 1974.

Rivera, J. R. *Puerto Rican Tales.* Mayaquez, Puerto Rico: Ediciones Libero, 1977.

Roby, P., ed. *The Poverty Establishment.* Englewood Cliffs, NJ: Prentice-Hall, 1974.

Rodriquez, C. E. *Puerto Ricans Born in the U.S.A.* Boulder: Westview Press, 1991.

Roemer, M. I. *An Introduction to the U.S. Health Care System* (2nd ed.). New York: Springer, 1990.

Rogler, L. H. *Migrant in the City.* New York: Basic Books, 1972.

Rohde, E. S. *The Old English Herbs.* New York: Dover, (1922, 1971).

Rose, P. I. *They and We: Racial and Ethnic Relations in the United States* (3rd ed.). New York: Random House, 1981.

Rosen, P. *The Neglected Dimension—Ethnicity in American Life.* Notre Dame-London: University of Notre Dame Press, 1980.

Rosenbaum, B. Z. *How to Avoid the Evil Eye.* New York: St. Martin's Press, 1985.

Ross, N. W. *The World of Zen.* New York: Vintage Books, 1960.

Rossbach, S. *Interior Design with Feng Shui.* New York: Arkana, 1987.

Rude, D., ed. *Alienation: Minority Groups.* New York: John Wiley and Sons, 1972.

Russell, A. J. *Health in His Wings.* London: Metheun and Co., 1937.

Ryan, W. *Blaming the Victim.* New York: Vintage Books, 1971.

S., E. M. *The House of Wonder—A Romance of Psychic Healing.* London: Rider and Co., 1927.

Santillo, H. *Herbal Combinations from Authoritative Sources.* Provo, UT: NuLife, 1983.

Santoli A. *New Americans.* New York: Ballantine, 1988.

Sargent, D. A. *Health, Strength, & Power.* New York: HM Caldwell, 1904.

Saunders, L. *Cultural Difference and Medical Care: The Case of the Spanish-Speaking People of the Southwest.* New York: Russell Sage Foundation, 1954.

Saunders, R. *Healing through the Spirit Agency.* London: Hutchinson and Co., 1927.

Schneider, M. *Self Healing—My Life and Vision.* New York: Routledge & Kegan Paul, 1987.

Scholem, G. G. *Major Trends in Jewish Mysticism.* NY: Schocken Books, 1941.

School, B. F. *Library of Health Complete Guide to Prevention and Cure of Disease.* Philadelphia: Historical Publishing Co., 1924.

Schrefer, S., ed. *Quick Reference to Cultural Assessment.* St. Louis: Mosby, 1994.

Scott, W. R. and Volkart, E. H. *Medical Care.* New York: John Wiley & Sons, 1966.

Senior, C. *The Puerto Ricans, Strangers—Then Neighbors.* Chicago: Quadrangle Books, 1961.

Serinus, J., ed. *Psychoimmunity and the Healing Process.* Berkeley: Celestial Arts, 1986.

Sexton, P. C. *Spanish Harlem.* New York: Harper and Row, 1965.

Shaw, W. *Aspects of Malaysian Magic.* Kuala Lumpur, Malaysia: Naziabum Nigara, 1975.

Sheinkin, D. *Path of the Kabbalah.* New York: Paragon House, 1986.

Shelton, F. *Pioneer Comforts and Kitchen Remedies—Oldtime Highland Secrets from the Blue Ridge and Great Smoky Mountains.* High Point, NC: Hutcraft, 1965.

Shelton, F., ed. *Pioneer Superstitions.* High Point, NC: Hutcraft, 1969.

Shenkin, B. N. *Health Care for Migrant Workers: Policies and Politics.* Cambridge, MA: Ballinger Publishing Co., 1974.

Shepard, R. F. and Levi, V. G. *Live and Be Well.* New York: Ballantine Books, 1982.

Shih-Chen, L. *Chinese Medicinal Herbs,* trans. Smith, F. P. and Stuart, G. A. San Francisco: Georgetown Press, 1973.

Shor, I. *Culture Wars: School and Society in the Conservative Restoration 1969–1984.* Boston: Routledge & Kegan Paul, 1986.

Shostak, A. B., Van Til, J., and Van Til, S. B. *Privilege in America: An End to Inequality?* Englewood Cliffs, NJ: Prentice-Hall, 1973.

Silver, G. *A Spy in the House of Medicine.* Germantown, MD: Aspen Systems Corp., 1976.

Silverman, D. *Legends of Safed.* Jerusalem: Gefen, Ltd., 1989.

Silverstein, M. E., Chang, I-L., and Macon, N., trans. *Acupuncture and Moxibustion.* New York: Schocken Books, 1975.

Simmen, E., ed. *Pain and Promise: The Chicano Today.* New York: New American Library, 1972.

Simmons, A. G. *A Witch's Brew.* Coventry, CT: Caprilands Herb Farm, undated.

Skelton, R. *Talismanic Magic.* York Beach, ME: Samuel Weiser, Inc., 1985.

Slater, P. *The Pursuit of Loneliness.* Boston: Beacon Press, 1970.

Smith, H. *The Religions of Man.* New York: Harper and Row, 1958.

Smith, L. *Killers of the Dream.* Garden City, NY: Doubleday and Co., 1963.

Smith, P. *The Origins of Modern Culture, 1543–1687.* New York: Collier Books, 1962.

Sowell, T. *Ethnic America.* New York: Basic Books, 1981.

Spann, M. B. *Literature-Based Multicultural Activities.* New York: Scholastic Professional Books, 1992.

Spector, R. E. "A Description of the Impact of Medicare on Health-Illness Beliefs and Practices of White Ethnic Senior Citizens in Central Texas." (Ph.D. diss. University of Texas at Austin School of Nursing, 1983); Ann Arbor, MI: University Microfilms International, 1983.

Spicer, E., ed. *Ethnic Medicine in the Southwest.* New York: Russell Sage Foundation, 1977.

Stack, C. B. *All Our Kin.* New York: Harper and Row, 1974.

Starr, P. *The Social Transformation of American Medicine.* New York: Basic Books, 1982.

Steele, J. D. *Hygienic Physiology.* New York: A. S. Barnes, 1884.

Steinberg, M. *Basic Judaism.* New York: Harcourt, Brace and World, 1947.

Steinberg, S. *The Ethnic Myth—Race, Ethnicity, and Class in America.* Boston: Beacon Press, 1989.

Steiner, S. *La Raza: The Mexican Americans.* New York: Harper and Row, 1969.

Stephan, W. G. and Feagin, J. R. *School Desegregation Past, Present, Future.* New York: Plenum, 1980.

Stevens, A. *Vitamins and Remedies.* High Point, NC: Hutcraft, 1974.

Stewart, J., ed. *Bridges Not Walls.* Reading, MA: Addison-Wesley, 1973.

Stoll, R. I. *Concepts in Nursing: A Christian Perspective,* Madison, WI: Intervarsity Christian Fellowship, 1990.

Stone, E. *Medicine among the American Indians.* New York: Hafner Publishing Co., 1962.

Storlie, F. *Nursing and the Social Conscience.* New York: Appleton-Century-Crofts, 1970.

Storm, H. *Seven Arrows.* New York: Ballantine Books, 1972.

Strauss, A. and Corbin, J. M. *Shaping a New Health Care System.* San Francisco: Josey-Bass, 1988.

Styron, W. *The Confessions of Nat Turner.* New York: Random House, 1966.

Swazey, J. P. and Reeds, K. *Today's Medicine, Tomorrow's Science.* Washington, DC: U.S. Government Department of Health, Education, and Welfare, 1978.

Sweet, M. *Common Edible Plants of the West.* Happy Camp, CA: Naturegraph, 1976.

Szasz, T. S. *The Myth of Mental Illness.* New York: Dell, 1961.

Takaki, R. *A Different Mirror—A History of Multicultural America.* Boston: Little Brown and Company, 1993.

Tallant, R. *Voodoo in New Orleans.* New York: Collier Books, 1946.

Tan, A. *The Joy Luck Club.* New York: Ivy Books, 1989.

Te Selle, S., ed. *The Rediscovery of Ethnicity: Its Implications for Culture and Politics in America.* New York: Harper and Row, 1973.

ten Boom, C. *The Hiding Place.* Washington Depot, CT: Chosen Books, 1971.

Thernstrom, S., ed. *Harvard Encyclopedia of American Ethnic Groups.* Cambridge: Harvard University Press, 1980.

Thomas, C. *They Came to Pittsburgh.* Pittsburgh: *Post-Gazette,* 1983.

Thomas, P. *Down These Mean Streets.* New York: Signet Books, 1958.

Thomas, P. *Savior, Savior, Hold My Hand.* Garden City, NY: Doubleday and Co., 1972.

Tierra, M. *The Way of Herbs.* New York: Pocket Books, 1990.

Titmuss, R. M. *The Gift Relationship.* New York: Vintage, 1971.

Tomasi, S. M., ed. *National Directory of Research Centers, Repositories and Organizations of Italian Culture in the United States.* Torino: Fondazione Giovanni Agnelli, 1980.

Tompkins, P. and Bird C. *The Secret Life of Plants.* New York: Avon, 1973.

Tooker, E., ed. *Native American Spirituality of the Eastern Woodlands.* New York: Paulist Press, 1979.

Torres, E. *Green Medicine—Traditional Mexican-American Herbal Remedies.* Kingsville, TX: Nieves Press, 1982.

Torres-Gill, F. M. *Politics of Aging among Elder Hispanics.* Washington, DC: University Press of America, 1982.

Touchstone, S. J. *Herbal and Folk Medicine of Louisiana and Adjacent States.* Princeton, LA: Folk-Life Books, 1983.

Trachtenberg, J. *The Devil and the Jews.* Philadelphia: The Jewish Publication Society of America, 1983. (Original publication, New Haven: Yale University Press, 1945).

Trachtenberg, J. *Jewish Magic and Superstition.* New York: Behrman House, Inc., 1939.

Trattner, W. I. *From Poor Law to Welfare State: A History of Social Welfare in America.* New York: Free Press, 1974.

Trotter, R., II and Chavira, J. A. *Curanderismo—Mexican American Folk Healing.* Athens, GA: University of Georgia Press, 1981.

Tucker, G. H. *Virginia Supernatural Tales.* Norfolk: The Donning Co., 1977.

Tula, M. T. *Hear My Testimony.* Boston: South End Press, 1994.

Twining, M. A. and Baird, K. E., eds. *Sea Island Roots: African Presence in the Carolinas and Georgia.* Trenton, NJ: Africa World Press, 1991.

Unger, S., ed. *The Destruction of American Indian Families.* New York: Association on American Indian Affairs, 1977.

U.S. Commission on Civil Rights. *Mexican Americans and the Administration of Justice in the Southwest.* Washington, DC: Government Printing Office, 1970.

U.S. Commission on Civil Rights. *Fulfilling the Letter and Spirit of the Law.* Washington, DC: U.S. Government Printing Office, 1976.

U.S. Department of Commerce, Bureau of the Census. *Ancestry of the Population by State: 1980.* Washington, DC: Government Printing Office, 1980.

U.S. Department of Commerce, Bureau of the Census. *Population Profile of the United States: 1981.* "Population Characteristics," ser. 20, no. 374, September 1982.

U.S. Department of Health, Education, and Welfare. *Health in America: 1776–1976.* DHEW pub. (HRA) 76-616, 1976.

U.S. Department of Health and Human Services. *Healthy People 2000 National Health Promotion and Disease Prevention Objectives—Full Report with Commentary.* Boston: Jones and Bartlett, 1992.

U.S. Department of Health and Human Services. *Health United States 1992* and *Healthy People 2000 Review.* Washington, D.C.: United States Department of Health and Human Services, Public Health Service Centers for Disease Control and Prevention. DHHS Pub. No. (PHS) 93-1232, 1993.

U.S. Department of Justice. Immigration and Naturalization Service. *Immigration Literature: Abstracts of Demographic Economic and Policy Studies.* Washington, DC: Government Printing Office, 1979.

Valentine, C. A. *Culture and Poverty.* Chicago: University of Chicago Press, 1968.

Wade, M. *The French-Canadian Outlook.* New York: Viking Press, 1946.

Wade, M. *The French-Canadians, 1876–1945.* New York: Macmillan Co., 1955.

Walker, A. *The Temple of My Familiar.* New York: Harcourt, Brace, Jovanovich, 1989.

Wall, S. and Arden, H. *Wisdomkeepers Meetings with Native American Spiritual Elders.* Hillsboro, OR: Beyond Words Publishing Co., 1990.

Wallnöfer, H. and von Rottauscher, A. *Chinese Folk Medicine,* trans. M. Palmedo. New York: New American Library, 1972.

Warner, D. *The Health of Mexican Americans in South Texas.* Austin: Lyndon Baines Johnson School of Public Affairs, University of Texas at Austin, 1979.

Warren, N., ed. *Studies in Cross-Cultural Psychology.* New York: Academic Press, 1980.

Weible, W. *Medjugore—The Message.* Orleans, MA: Paraclete Press, 1983.

Wei-kang, F. *The Story of Chinese Acupuncture and Moxibustion.* Peking: Foreign Languages Press, 1975.

Weil, A. *Health and Healing.* Boston: Houghton Mifflin Co., 1983.

Weinbach, S. *Rabbenu Yisrael Abuchatzira: The Story of His Life and Wonders.* Brooklyn, NY: ASABA-FUJIE publication, 1991.

Weinberg, R. D. *Eligibility for Entry to the United States of America.* Dobbs Ferry, NY: Oceana Publications, 1967.

Weiss, G. and Weiss, S. *Growing and Using the Healing Herbs.* New York: Wings Books, 1985.

Wheelwright, E. G. *Medicinal Plants and Their History.* New York: Dover, 1974.

Wilen, J. and Wilen, L. *Chicken Soup and Other Folk Remedies.* New York: Fawcett Columbine, 1984.

Williams, R. A., ed. *Textbook of Black-Related Diseases.* New York: McGraw-Hill, 1975.

Williams, S. J., and Torrens, P. R. *Introduction to Health Services* (3rd ed.). New York: John Wiley & Sons, 1990.

Wilson, F. A. and Neuhauser, D. *Health Services in the United States* (2nd ed.). Cambridge, MA: Ballinger, 1982.

Wilson, S. G. *The Drummer's Path—Moving the Spirit with Ritual and Traditional Drumming.* Rochester, VT: Destiny Books, 1992.

Winkler, G. *Dybbuk.* New York: Judaica Press, 1981.

Wright, E. *The Book of Magical Talismans.* Minneapolis, MN: Marlar Publishing, Co., 1984.

Wright, R. *Black Boy.* New York: Harper and Brothers, 1937.

Wright, R. *Native Son*. New York: Grosset and Dunlop, 1940.

Wright-Hybbard, E. *A Brief Study Course in Homeopathy*. Philadelphia: Formur, Inc., 1977–1992.

Young, J. H. *The Medical Messiahs*. Princeton: Princeton University Press, 1967.

Zambrana, R. E., ed. *Work, Family, and Health—Latina Women in Transition*. New York: Fordham University, 1982.

Zborowski, M. *People in Pain*. San Francisco: Jossey-Bass, 1969.

Zeitlin, S. J., Kotkin, A. J., and Baker, H. C. *A Celebration of American Family Folklore: Tales and Traditions from the Smithsonian Collection*. New York: Pantheon Books, 1977.

Zolla, E. *The Writer and the Shaman*. New York: Harcourt Brace Jovanovich, 1969.

Zook, J. and Zook, J. *Hexology*. Paradise, PA: Zook, 1978.

Zook, J. *Exploring the Secrets of Treating Deaf-Mutes*. Peking: Foreign Languages Press, 1972.

Zook, J. *Your New Life in the United States*. Washington, DC: Center for Applied Linguistics, 1972.

Zook, J. *Oneida, The People of the Stone. The Church's Mission to the Oneidas*. Oneida Indian Reservation, Wisconsin, 1899.

Appendix

Selected Key Terms Related to Cultural Diversity in Health and Illness

Acculturation   The process of adapting to another culture. To acquire the majority group's culture.

Acupuncture   The traditional Chinese medical way of restoring the balance of *yin* and *yang* that is based on the therapeutic value of cold. Cold is used in a disease where there is an excess of *yang*.

Alien   Every person applying for entry to the United States. Anyone who is not a U.S. citizen.

Allopathic   Health beliefs and practices that are derived from current scientific models and involve the use of technology and other modalities of present-day health care, such as immunization, proper nutrition, and resuscitation.

Alternative health system   A system of health care a person may use that is not predicated within their traditional culture, but is not allopathic.

Amulet   An object with magical powers, such as a charm, worn on a string or chain around the neck, wrist, or waist to protect the wearer from both physical and psychic illness, harm, and misfortune.

Anamnesis   The traditional Chinese medical way of diagnosing a health problem by asking questions.

Aromatherapy   Ancient science that uses essential plant oils to produce strong physical and emotional effects in the body.

Assimilation   To become absorbed into another culture and to adopt its characteristics. To develop a new cultural identity.

Ayurvedic   Four-thousand-year-old method of healing originating in India, the chief aim of which is longevity and quality of life. The most ancient existing medical system that uses diet, natural therapies, and herbs.

Biofeedback   The use of an electronic machine to measure skin temperatures. The patient controls responses that are usually involuntary.

Biological variations   Biological differences that exist among races and ethnic groups in body structure, skin color, biochemical differences, susceptibility to disease, and nutritional differences.

Caida de la mollera   (Fallen fontanel) Traditional Hispanic belief that the fontanel falls if the baby's head is touched.

Care   Factors that assist, enable, support, or facilitate a person's needs to maintain, improve, or ease a health problem.

Charm   Objects that combine the functions of both amulets and talismans but consist only of written words or symbols.

Chinese doctor   Physician educated in China who uses traditional herbs and other therapeutic modalities in the delivery of health care.

Conjure   To effect magic.

Culture   Nonphysical traits, such as values, beliefs, attitudes, and customs, that are shared by a group of people and passed from one generation to the next. A meta-communication system.

Culture shock   Disorder that occurs in response to transition from one cultural setting to another. Former behavior patterns are ineffective in such a setting and basic cues for social behavior are absent.

Curandero   Traditional Hispanic holistic healer.

Curing*   Two-dimensional phenomena that results in ridding the body or mind (or both) of a given disease.

Decoction   A simmered tea made from the bark, root, seed, or berry, of a plant.

Demography   The statistical study of populations, including statistical counts of people of various ages, sexes, and population densities for specific locations.

Disadvantaged background   Both educational and economic factors that act as barriers to an individual's participation in a health professions program.

Discrimination   Denying people equal opportunity by acting on a prejudice.

Divination   Traditional American Indian practice of calling on spirits or other forces to determine a diagnosis of a health problem.

Dybbuk   Wandering, disembodied soul that enters another person's body and holds fast.

Emerging majority People of color—blacks; Asian/Pacific Islanders; American Indians, Eskimos, or Aleuts; and Hispanics—who are expected to constitute a majority of the American population by the year 2020.

Emic Person's way of describing an action or event, an inside view.

Empacho Traditional Hispanic belief that a ball of food is stuck in the stomach.

Envidia Traditional Hispanic belief that the envy of others can be the cause of illness and bad luck.

Environmental control Ability of a person from a given cultural group to actively control nature and to direct factors in the environment.

Epidemiology The study of the distribution of disease.

Ethnicity Cultural group's sense of identification associated with the group's common social and cultural heritage.

Ethnocentrism Tendency of members of one cultural group to view the members of other cultural groups in terms of the standards of behavior, attitudes, and values of their own group. The belief that one's own cultural, ethnic, professional, or social group is superior to that of others.

Ethnomedicine Health beliefs and practices of indigenous cultural development. Not practiced in many of the tenants of modern medicine.

Etic The interpretation of an event by someone who is not experiencing that event, an outside view.

Evil eye Belief that someone can project harm by gazing or staring at another's property or person.

Exorcism Ceremonious expulsion of an evil spirit from a person.

Faith Strong beliefs in a religious or other spiritual philosophy.

Folklore Body of preserved traditions, usually oral, consisting of beliefs, stories, and associated information of people.

Geophagy Eating of nonfood substances, such as starch.

Glossoscopy Traditional Chinese medical way of diagnosing a health problem by examining the tongue.

Gris-gris Symbols of voodoo. They may take numerous forms and be used either to protect a person or harm that person.

Haragei Japanese art or practice of using nonverbal communication.

Healing* Holistic, or three-dimensional, phenomenon that results in the restoration of balance, or harmony, to the body, mind, and spirit; or between the person and the environment.

Health* A state of balance between the body, mind, and spirit.

Heritage consistency   Observance of the beliefs and practices of one's traditional cultural belief system.

Heritage inconsistency   Observance of the beliefs and practices of one's acculturated belief system.

Hex   Evil spell, misfortune, or bad luck that one person can impose on another.

Homeopathic   Health beliefs and practices derived from traditional cultural knowledge to maintain health, prevent changes in health status, and restore health.

Homeopathy   System of medicine based on the belief that a disease can be cured by minute doses of a substance that, if given to a healthy person in large doses would produce the same symptoms that the person being treated is experiencing.

Hoodoo   A form of conjuring and a term that refers to the magical practices of voodoo outside New Orleans.

Hypnotherapy   The use of hypnosis to stimulate emotions and control involuntary responses such as blood pressure.

Illness*   State of imbalance among the body, mind, and spirit; a sense of disharmony both within the person and with the environment.

Immigrant   Alien entering the United States for permanent (or temporary) residence.

Indigenous   People native to an area.

Lay midwife   A person who practices lay midwifery.

Lay midwifery   Assisting childbirth for compensation.

Limpia   Traditional Hispanic practice of cleansing a person.

Macrobiotics   Diet and lifestyle from the Far East adapted for the United States by Michio Kushif. The principles of this vegetarian diet consist of balancing *yin* and *yang* energies of food.

Magicoreligious folk medicine   Use of charms, holy words, and holy actions to prevent and cure illness.

Mal ojo   (Bad eye) Traditional Hispanic belief that excessive admiration by one person can bring harm to another person.

Massage therapy   Use of manipulative techniques to relieve pain and return energy to the body.

Medically underserved community   Urban or rural population group that lacked or lacks adequate health care services.

Melting pot   The social blending of cultures.

Meridians   Specific points of the body into which needles are inserted in the traditional Chinese medical practice of acupuncture.

Metacommunication system   Large system of communication that includes both verbal language and nonverbal signs and symbols.

Miracle   Supernatural, unexplained event.

Modern   Present-day health and illness beliefs and practices of the providers within the American, or Western, health-care delivery system.

Motion in the hand   An example of a traditional American Indian practice of moving the diagnostician's hands in a ritual of divination.

Moxibustion   Traditional Chinese medical way of restoring the balance of *yin* and *yang* that is based on the therapeutic value of heat. Heat is used in a disease where there is an excess of *yin*.

Multicultural nursing   Pluralistic approach to understanding relationships between two or more cultures to create a nursing practice framework for broadening nurses' understanding of health-related beliefs, practices, and issues that are part of the experiences of people from diverse cultural backgrounds.

Mysticism   Aspect of spiritual healing and beliefs.

Natural folk-medicine   Use of the natural environment and use of herbs, plants, minerals, and animal substances to prevent and treat illness.

Nonimmigrant   People who are allowed to enter the country temporarily under certain conditions, such as crewmen, students, and temporary workers.

Occult folk medicine   The use of charms, holy words, and holy actions to prevent and cure illness.

Osphretics   Traditional Chinese medical way of diagnosing a health problem by listening and smelling.

Overheating therapy (Hyperthermia)   Used since the time of the Ancient Greeks, the natural immune system is stimulated with heat to kill pathogens.

Partera   A Mexican American or Mexican lay midwife.

Pasmo   Traditional Hispanic disease of paralysis.

Pluralistic society   A society comprising people of numerous ethnocultural backgrounds.

Poultice   A hot, soft, moist mass of herbs, flour, mustard, and other substances spread on muslin and placed on a sore body part.

Pow wow   A form of traditional healing practiced by German Americans.

Prejudice   Negative beliefs or preferences that are generalized about a group and that leads to "prejudgment."

Racism   The belief that members of one race are superior to those of other races.

Rational folk medicine   Use of the natural environment and use of herbs, plants, minerals, and animal substances to prevent and treat illness.

Raza-Latina   A popular term used as a reference group name for people of Latin American descent.

Reflexology   Natural science that manipulates the reflex points in the hands and feet that correspond to every organ in the body in order to clear the energy pathways and the flow of energy through the body.

Religion   Belief in a divine or superhuman power or powers to be obeyed and worshipped as the creator(s) and ruler(s) of the universe.

Resident alien   A lawfully admitted alien.

Restoration   Process used by a given person to return health.

Santeria   A syncretic religion comprising both African and Catholic beliefs.

Santero   Traditional priest in the religion of *santeria*.

Sexism   Belief that members of one sex are superior to those of the other sex.

Singer   A type of traditional American Indian healer who is able to practice singing as a form of treating a health problem.

Social organization   Patterns of cultural behavior related to life events, such as birth, death, child rearing, and health and illness, that are followed within a given social group.

Socialization   Process of being raised within a culture and acquiring the characteristics of the given group.

Soul loss   Belief that a person's soul can leave the body, wander around, and then return.

Space   Area surrounding a person's body and the objects within that area.

Spell   A magical word or formula or a condition of evil or bad luck.

Sphygmopalpation   Traditional Chinese medical way of diagnosing a health problem by feeling pulses.

Spirit   The noncorporeal and nonmental dimension of a person that is the source of meaning and unity. The source of the experience of spirituality and every religion.

Spirit possession   Belief that a spirit can enter people, possess them, and control what they say and do.

Spiritual   Ideas, attitudes, concepts, beliefs, and behaviors that are the result of the person's experience of the spirit.

Spirituality   The experience of meaning and unity.

Stargazing*   Example of a traditional American Indian practice of praying the star prayer to the star spirit as a method of divination.

Stereotype   Notion that all people from a given group are the same.

Superstition   Belief that performing an action, wearing a charm or amulet, or eating something, will have an influence on life events. These beliefs are upheld by magic and faith.

Susto (Soul loss)*   Traditional Hispanic belief that the soul is able to leave a person's body.

Taboo   A culture-bound ban that excludes certain behaviors from common use.

Talisman   Consecrated religious object that confers power of various kinds and protects people who wear, carry, or own them from harm and evil.

Tao   Way, path, or discourse. On the spiritual level, the way to ultimate reality.

Time   Duration, interval of time; also instances, points in time.

Traditional   Ancient, ethnocultural–religious beliefs and practices that have been handed down through the generations.

Traditional epidemiology   Belief in agents—other than those of a scientific nature, causing disease.

Undocumented alien   Person of foreign origin who has entered the country unlawfully by bypassing inspection or who has overstayed the original terms of admission.

Voodoo*   A religion that is a combination of Christianity and African Yoruba religious beliefs.

Witched*   Example of a traditional American Indian belief that a person is harmed by witches.

Xenophobia   Morbid fear of strangers.

*Yang**   Male, positive energy that produces light, warmth, and fullness.

*Yin**   Female, negative energy; the force of darkness, cold, and emptiness.

---

*These terms are defined with their traditional connotations, rather than with modern denotations. Source: Compiled over time by R. Spector.

Appendix

Suggested Course Outline

NU301. CULTURAL DIVERSITY IN HEALTH AND ILLNESS*

The purpose of this course is to bring the student into a direct relationship with health-care consumers from various cultural backgrounds—white, black, Asian, Hispanic, American Indian. The course content includes discussion of the following topics:

- The perception of health and illness among health-care providers and consumers
- The cultural and institutional factors that affect the consumers' access to and use of health-care resources
- Health-care providers' ways of coping with illness and related problems
- The manner in which people of different backgrounds and their problems have been depicted in the literature (e.g., the works of Lewis, Kiev, Clark) and the implications of historical treatment for nursing practice and health-care delivery.

Goal

The goal of this course is to broaden the student's perception and understanding of health and illness and the variety of meanings these terms carry for members of differing groups.

Objectives

On completion of this course, the student should be able to

1. Understand more fully the perception and meaning of health and illness among various health-care consumers

---

†From the Boston College School of Nursing, Chestnut Hill, Massachusetts 02167.

2. Enter into dialogue with people who have experienced problems in dealing with the American health-care system
3. Understand the conflicts between the consumer and the American health-care system and the effect of those conflicts on nursing practice and action
4. Develop ideas about what nursing practice can do to intervene in this conflict and diminish it

Texts

The following texts should be read in total: Spector, R.E. *Cultural Diversity in Health and Illness*, 4th ed. (Stanford, CT: Appleton & Lange, 1996). Starr, P. *The Social Transformation of American Medicine*. New York: Basic Books, 1982.

Assignments and Evaluation

1. Weekly readings, class attendance, preparedness, and participation	15%
2. Health interviews	5%
3. Health diaries	10%
4. Reaction papers	20%

The purpose of the reaction papers is to express the student's response to the assigned readings and to the classroom discussion.

5. Term paper (maximum 8 to 10 pages)   25%

The term paper must deal with the problems and issues presented in class and the student's interpretation of how professional nurses must cope with them in practice. All papers must be submitted in proper Turabian format, typed and double-spaced.

6. Term project   25%

The term project should be a class presentation, with a small group, on perspectives of health and illness in one of the four communities studied. The class presentation must include the following data:

1. History of ethnic group in the United States
2. Traditional perceptions of health and illness
3. Traditional healing methods
4. Current health-care problems

Sources for the term project must include a bibliography, interviews with people within the given community, and personal observations.

COURSE OUTLINE

Week I **Course Introduction: Discussion of General Concepts of Health**
> Assignments for Class II:
> 1. Interview an older member of your family to determine
>   (a) what practices were used to prevent illness and maintain health
>   (b) what was done to treat illness
> 2. Begin a daily diary of your health status for 1 month. (Both assignments must be handed in.)

Week II **Discussion: Concepts of Illness and Practices for Maintaining Health and Preventing Illness**
> Readings:[†]
> • Spector, *Cultural Diversity*, Chapters 1 and 2
> Dubos, *Mirage of Health*
> Dubos, *Man Adapting*

Week III **The Delivery of Health Care in the United States**
> Readings:
> • Spector, *Cultural Diversity*, Chapter 5
> • Starr, *Social Transformation*, pp. 198–232, 379–419
> • Califano, *Radical Surgery—What's Next for America's Health Care*

Week IV **Culture: Its Effect on the Perception of Health and Illness**
> Readings:
> • Spector, *Cultural Diversity*, Chapters 3 and 4
> • Zola, "Culture and Symptoms: An Analysis of Patients Presenting Complaints"

Week V **Poverty and Its Effect on Health Care**
> Readings:
> • Spector, *Cultural Diversity*, Chapter 5
> • Lavelle, *America's New War on Poverty—A Reader for Action*

Week VI **Faith and Healing**
> Readings:
> • Spector, *Cultural Diversity*, Chapters 6 and 7
> • Starr, *Social Transformation*, pp. 79–144, 198–234
> Kelsey, *Healing and Christianity*
> Film: "We Believe in Niño Fidencio"

---

*For complete bibliography data on readings, see the Bibliography.
•The bullets indicate required reading.

Week VII **Health and Illness in the Hispanic Communities**
Readings:
- Thomas, *Down These Mean Streets* or *Savior, Savior, Hold My Hand*
- Lewis, *La Vida*
  Clark, *Health in the Mexican-American Culture: A Community Study*
- Spector, *Cultural Diversity*, Chapters 13 and 14

Week VIII **Health and Illness in the American Indian Communities**
Readings:
- Spector, *Cultural Diversity*, Chapter 10
- Deloria, *Custer Died for Your Sins*
  Kluckhohn, *The Navaho*
  Brown, *Bury My Heart at Wounded Knee*

Week IX **Health and Illness in the Asian/Pacific Communities**
Readings:
- Spector, *Cultural Diversity*, Chapter 11

Week X **Health and Illness in the African (Black) Community**
Readings:
- Spector, *Cultural Diversity*, Chapter 9
  Haley, *Roots*
- Grier, *Black Rage*
  Wright, *Black Boy* or *Native Son*
  Gutman, *The Black Family in Slavery and Freedom*
  Angelou, *I Know Why the Caged Bird Sings*

Week XI **Health and Illness in the European (White) Communities**
Readings:
- Spector, *Cultural Diversity*, Chapter 12
  Background information about specific groups of instructor's or student's selection.

Week XII **Institutional Barriers and Advocacy**
Readings:
- Starr, *Social Transformation*, pp. 235–449
- Spector, *Cultural Diversity*, Epilogue

Week XIII **Implications for Nursing and Health-Care Delivery**
Readings:
- Spector, *Cultural Diversity*, Epilogue

Week XIV **Evaluation and Interethnic Dinner**

Appendix

Suggested Course Activities

The study of cultural diversity comes alive the moment the student leaves the confines of the classroom and goes out into the community. One way to appreciate a given ethnoreligious community is to go into a particular community and observe firsthand what daily life is like for a member of that community. The following outline can serve as an assessment guide to the community:

Demographic data
    Total population size of entire city or town
    Breakdown by areas—residential concentrations
    Breakdown by ages
    Other breakdowns
        Education
        Occupations
        Income
    Nations of origin of residents of the location and the target neighborhood
Traditional health and illness beliefs
    Definition of health
    Definition of illness
    Overall health status
Causes of illness
    Poor eating habits
    Wrong food combinations
    Viruses, bacteria, other organisms
    Punishment from God
    The evil eye
    Hexes, spells, or envy
    Witchcraft
    Environmental changes

Exposure to drafts
Over or underwork
Grief and loss
Methods of protecting health
Methods of maintaining health
Methods of restoring health
Home remedies
Visits and use of M.D. or other health-care resources
Health-care resources, such as neighborhood health centers
Anyone else within community who looks after people, such as traditional
    healers
Child-bearing beliefs and practices
Child-rearing beliefs and practices
Rituals and beliefs surrounding death and dying

A second phase of this activity is to go on a walk through the given community. Point out the various services that are available. If possible, visit a community health-care provider, visit a church or community center within the neighborhood, visit grocery stores and pharmacies and point out differences in foods and over-the-counter remedies, and eat a meal in a neighborhood restaurant.

I have shared this experience with many groups of students, and the experience has been well received.

Appendix IV

Heritage Assessment Tool

This set of questions is to be used to describe a given client's—or your own—ethnic, cultural, and religious background. In performing a *heritage assessment* it is helpful to determine how deeply a given person identifies with his or her traditional heritage. This tool is most useful in setting the stage for assessing and understanding a person's traditional health and illness beliefs and practices and in helping to determine the community resources that will be appropriate to target for support when necessary. The greater the number of positive responses, the greater the degree to which the person may identify with his or her traditional heritage. The one exception to positive answers is the question about whether or not a person's name was changed. Background rationale for the development of this tool is found in Chapter 4.

1. Where was your mother born? _____

2. Where was your father born? _____

3. Where were your grandparents born? _____

   a. Your mother's mother? _____

   b. Your mother's father? _____

   c. Your father's mother? _____

   d. Your father's father? _____

4. How many brothers ____ and sisters ____ do you have?

5. What setting did you grow up in? Urban ____ Rural ____

6. What country did your parents grow up in?

   Father _____

   Mother _____

7. How old were you when you came to the United States? _____

8. How old were your parents when they came to the United States?

Mother _____

Father _____

9. When you were growing up, who lived with you?

_____

10. Have you maintained contact with

   a. Aunts, uncles, cousins?   (1) Yes _____ (2) No _____

   b. Brothers and sisters?   (1) Yes _____ (2) No _____

   c. Parents?   (1) Yes _____ (2) No _____

   d. Your own children?   (1) Yes _____ (2) No _____

11. Did most of your aunts, uncles, cousins live near your home?

(1) Yes ____ (2) No ____

12. Approximately how often did you visit family members who lived outside of your home?

(1) Daily ____ (2) Weekly ____ (3) Monthly ____

(4) Once a year or less ____ (5) Never ____

13. Was your original family name changed?

(1) Yes ____ (2) No ____

14. What is your religious preference?

(1) Catholic ____ (2) Jewish ____

(3) Protestant ____ Denomination ____

(4) Other ____ (5) None ____

15. Is your spouse the same religion as you?

(1) Yes ____ (2) No ____

16. Is your spouse the same ethnic background as you?

(1) Yes ____ (2) No ____

17. What kind of school did you go to?

(1) Public ____ (2) Private ____ (3) Parochial ____

18. As an adult, do you live in a neighborhood where the neighbors are the same religion and ethnic background as yourself?

(1) Yes ____ (2) No ____

19. Do you belong to a religious institution?

    (1) Yes _____ (2) No _____

20. Would you describe yourself as an active member?

    (1) Yes _____ (2) No _____

21. How often do you attend your religious institution?

    (1) More than once a week _____ (2) Weekly _____ (3) Monthly _____

    (4) Special holidays only _____ (5) Never _____

22. Do you practice your religion in your home?

    (1) Yes _____ (2) No _____ (if yes, please specify)

    (3) Praying _____ (4) Bible reading _____ (5) Diet _____

    (6) Celebrating religious holidays _____

23. Do you prepare foods special to your ethnic background?

    (1) Yes _____ (2) No _____

24. Do you participate in ethnic activities?

    (1) Yes _____ (2) No _____ (if yes, please specify)

    (3) Singing _____ (4) Holiday celebrations _____

    (5) Dancing _____ (6) Festivals _____

    (7) Costumes _____ (8) Other _____

25. Are your friends from the same religious background as you?

    (1) Yes _____ (2) No _____

26. Are your friends from the same ethnic background as you?

    (1) Yes _____ (2) No _____

27. What is your native language? _____

28. Do you speak this language?

    (1) Prefer _____ (2) Occasionally _____ (3) Rarely _____

29. Do you read your native language?

    (1) Yes _____ (2) No _____

Quick Guide for Cross-Cultural Nursing Care

PREPARING

- Understand your own cultural values and biases.
- Acquire basic knowledge of cultural values and health beliefs and practices for client groups you serve.
- Be respectful of, interested in, and understanding of other cultures without being judgmental.

ENHANCING COMMUNICATION

- Determine the level of fluency in English and arrange for an interpreter, if needed.
- Ask how the client prefers to be addressed.
- Allow the client to choose seating for comfortable personal space and eye contact.
- Avoid body language that may be offensive or misunderstood.
- Speak directly to the client, whether an interpreter is present or not.
- Choose a speech rate and style that promotes understanding and demonstrates respect for the client.
- Avoid slang, technical jargon, and complex sentences.
- Use open-ended questions or questions phrased in several ways to obtain information.
- Determine the client's reading ability before using written materials in the teaching process.

PROMOTING POSITIVE CHANGE

- Build on cultural practices, reinforcing those that are positive, and promoting change only in those that are harmful.
- Check for client understanding and acceptance of recommendations.
- *Remember*: Not all seeds of knowledge fall into a fertile environment to produce change. Of those that do, some will take years to germinate. Be patient and provide nursing in a culturally appropriate environment to promote positive health behavior.

From: (Adapted for nursing) Schilling, B. and Brannon, E. *Cross-Cultural Counseling—A Guide for Nutrition and Health Counselors.* (Alexandria, VA: United States Department of Agriculture, United States Department of Health and Human Services, Nutrition and Technical Services Division, September, 1986), p. 19. Adapted with permission.

Appendix VI

Data Resources

Countless resources are available for information regarding the health-care delivery system. The following are a small sample:

Monthly Vital Statistics Report
U.S. Department of Health and Human Services
Public Health Service
Centers for Disease Control
National Center for Health Statistics
6525 Belcrest Road
Hyattsville, MD 20782
(301) 436-8500

NCHS Advancedata
U.S. Department of Health and Human Services
Public Health Service
Centers for Disease Control
National Center for Health Statistics
3700 East-West Highway
Hyattsville, MD 20782
(301) 436-8500

The Center for Public Policy and Contemporary Issues
2301 South Gaylord Street
University of Denver
Denver, CO 80208

Committee for a National Health Program
15 Pearl Street
Cambridge, MA 02139
(617) 868-3246

Health-Pac Bulletin Subscriptions
17 Murray Street
New York, NY 10007

SCAPHA News
2516 N. Seminary
Chicago, IL 60614

National AIDS Information Clearinghouse
P.O. Box 6003
Rockville, MD 20850
1 (800) 458-5231

Appendix

NIH Office of Alternative Medicine

DIRECTORY OF ALTERNATIVE HEALTH-CARE ASSOCIATIONS

This list is not comprehensive but gives a range of professional associations grouped by type of alternative or complementary medical treatment. The categorization is not definitive; several therapies could be grouped differently. Generally, training institutions have not been included unless they provide a primary resource for information on a particular therapy.

Inclusion in this list does not constitute endorsement of any of the associations by the Office of Alternative Medicine, National Institutes of Health.

HOLISTIC HEALTH CARE

Association of Holistic Healing
Centers
109 Holly Crescent
Suite 201
Virginia Beach, VA 23451
(804) 422-9033

Alliance/Foundation for
Alternative Medicine
160 NW Widmer Place
Albany, OR 97321
(503) 926-4678

American College of Nurse-
Midwives
1522 K Street, NW
Washington, DC 20005
(202) 289-0171

American Foundation for
Alternative Healthcare,
Research and Development
25 Landfield Avenue
Monticello, NY 12701
(914) 794-8181

Source: National Institutes of Health, Office of Alternative Medicine, 1994.

American Holistic Medical
Association
4101 Lake Boone Trail
Suite 201
Raleigh, NC 27607
(919) 787-5146

American Holistic Nurses
Association
4101 Lake Boone Trail
Suite 201
Raleigh, NC 27607
(919) 787-5181

American Holistic Veterinary
Medical Association
2214 Old Emmorton Road
Bel Air, MD 21015
(410) 569-0795

American Medical Student
Association
1890 Preston White Drive
Reston, VA 22091
(703) 620-6600

American Preventive Medical
Association
459 Walker Road
Great Falls, VA 22066
(703) 759-0662

Canadian Holistic Medical
Association (CHMA/OMC)
491 Eglinton Avenue West, #407
Toronto, Ontario M5N 1A8
(416) 485-3071

Committee for Freedom of Choice
in Medicine
1180 Walnut Ave
Chula Vista, CA 92011
(800) 227-4473

Holistic Dental Association
974 N. 21st Street
Newark, OH 43055
(614) 366-3309

International Association of
Holistic Health Practitioners
3419 Thom Boulevard
Las Vegas, NV 89130
(702) 873-4542

Mankind Research Foundation
1315 Apple Ave.
Silver Spring, MD 20910
(301) 587-8686

I DIET/NUTRITION/LIFESTYLE CHANGES

American College of Nutrition
722 Robert E. Lee Drive
Wilmington, NC 28480
(919) 452-1222

American Natural Hygiene
Society
11816 Racetrack Road
Tampa, FL 33626
(813) 855-6607

International Association of
Professional Natural Hygienists
204 Stambaugh Bldg.
Youngstown, OH 44503
(216) 746-5000

Art, Music, Dance, Humor Therapy

American Association for
Therapeutic Humor
12 S. Hanley St.
St. Louis, MO 63105
(314) 863-6232

American Association of Music
Therapy
PO Box 80012
Valley Forge, PA 19484
(215) 265-4006

American Art Therapy
Association, Inc.
1202 Allanson Rd.
Mundelein, IL 60060
(708) 949-6064

American Dance Therapy
Association
2000 Century Plaza, Suite 108
Columbia, MD 21044
(410) 997-4040

Dinshah Health Society
100 Dinshah Dr.
Malaga, NJ 08328
(609) 692-4686

National Association for Music
Therapy
8455 Colesville Rd., Suite 930
Silver Spring, MD 20910
(301) 589-3300

Radiance Technique Association
International
P.O. Box 40570
St. Petersberg, FL 33743
(813) 347-3421

Trager Institute
33 Millwood
Mill Valley, CA 94941-2091
(415) 388-2688

III TRADITIONAL AND ETHNOMEDICINE

Acupuncture and Traditional Chinese Medicine

Acupuncture Research Institute
313 W. Andrix St.
Monterey Park, CA 91754
(213) 722-7353

American Association of
Acupuncture and Oriental
Medicine
4101 Lake Boone Trail, Suite 201
Raleigh, NC 27607
(919) 787-5181

American Academy of Medical
Acupuncture
5820 Wilshire Blvd., Suite 500
Los Angeles, CA 90036
(213) 937-5514

American Association of
Acupuncture and Oriental
Medicine
1400 16th St., N.W., Ste. 710
Washington, DC 20036
(202) 265-2287

American Foundation of
Traditional Chinese Medicine
1280 Columbus Ave., Ste. 302
San Francisco, CA 94133
(415) 776-0502

East–West Academy of Healing
Arts
450 Sutter, Ste. 916
San Francisco, CA 94108
(415) 788-2227

International Foundation of
Oriental Medicine
42-62 Kissena Boulevard
Flushing, NY 11355
(718) 321-8642

International Veterinary
Acupuncture Society
2140 Conestoga Rd.
Chester Springs, PA 19425
(215) 827-7245

Ayurveda

Ayurvedic Institute
11311 Menaul NE, Suite A
Albuquerque, NM 87112
(505) 291-9698

Maharishi Ayurveda Assn. of
America
PO Box 282
Fairfield, IO 52556
(515) 472-8477

Kinesiology

International College of Applied
Kinesiology
PO Box 905
Lawrence, KS 66044
(913) 542-1801

Herbalism

American Botanical Council
PO Box 201660
Austin, TX 78720
(512) 331-8868

American Herbalists Guild
PO Box 1683
Sequel, CA 95073
(408) 438-1700

American Herb Assn.
PO Box 1673
Nevada City, CA 95959
(916) 265-9552

Herb Research Foundation
1007 Pearl Street, Suite 200
Boulder, CO 80302
(303) 449-2265

Herb Society of America
9019 Kirtland Chardon Road
Mentor, OH 44060
(216) 256-0514

Homeopathy

American Institute of Homeopathy
1585 Glencoe
Denver, CO 80220
(303) 370-9164

Homeopathic Academy of
Naturopathic Physicians
14653 South Graves Road
Mulino, OR 97042
(503) 829-7326

Homeopathic Medical
Association of America
18818 Teller Ave., Suite 230
Irvine, CA 92715

International Foundation for
Homeopathy
2366 Eastlake Ave, E, #30
Seattle, WA 98102
(206) 324-8230

National Center for Homeopathy
801 N. Fairfax St., Ste. 306
Alexandria, VA 22314
(703) 548-7790

Craniosacral Therapy

Cranial Academy
3500 Depaw Boulevard
Indianapolis, IN 46268
(317) 879-0713

Upledger Institute
11211 Prosperity Farms Road
Palm Beach Gardens, FL 33410
(407) 622-4706

V   PHARMACOLOGICAL AND BIOLOGICAL TREATMENTS

Cell Therapy

ICBR North American
Information Office
PO Box 509
Florissant, MO 63032
(800) 826-5366

American Academy of Neural
Therapy
1468 South Saint Francis Drive
Santa Fe, NM 87501
(505) 988-3086

Detoxification Therapies

American Colon Therapy
Association
11739 Washington Boulevard
Los Angeles, CA 90066
(310) 390-5424

International Association of
Professional Natural Hygienists
Regency Health Resort and Spa
2000 South Ocean Drive
Hallandale, FL 33009
(305) 454-2200

Chelation

American Board of Chelation
Therapy
70 West Huron St.
Chicago, IL 60610
(312) 787-ABCT

American College of Advancement
in Medicine
23121 Verdugo Dr.
Suite 204
Laguna Hills, CA 92653
(714) 583-7666
(800) LEAD-OUT

Great Lakes Association of
Clinical Medicine, Inc.
70 West Huron Street
Chicago, IL 60610
(312) 266-7246

Rheumatoid Disease Foundation
5106 Old Harding Road
Franklin, TN 37064
(615) 646-1030

Naturopathy

American Association of
Naturopathic Physicians
2366 Eastlake Ave. E. Suite 322
Seattle, WA 98102
(206) 323-7610

American Naturopathic
Association
1377 K Street NW, Suite 852
Washington, DC 20005
(202) 682-7352

American Naturopathic Medical
Association
PO Box 96273
Las Vegas, NV 89193
(702) 897-7053

Oxygen Therapy

International Association for
Oxygen Therapy
PO Box 1360
Priest River, IA 83856
(208) 448-2504

International Bio-Oxidative
Medical Foundation
PO Box 61767
Dallas/Ft. Worth, TX 75261
(817) 481-9772

International Ozone Association
31 Strawberry Hill Avenue
Stamford, CT 06902
(203) 348-3542

VI BIOELECTROMAGNETIC APPLICATIONS

Light Therapy

American Optometric Association
(AOA)
243 N. Lindbergh Boulevard
St. Louis, MO 63141
(314) 991-4100

College of Optometrists and
Vision Development
PO Box 285
Chula Vista, CA 91912
(619) 425-6191

College of Syntonic
Optometry
1200 Robeson Street
Fall River, MA 02720
(508) 673-1251

Magnetic Field Therapy

Bio-Electro-Magnetics
Institute
2490 West Moana Lane
Reno, NV 89509
(702) 827-9099

Vision Therapy

Society for Light Treatment and
Biological Rhythms
PO Box 478
Wilsonville, OR 97070
(503) 694-2404

Optometric Extension Program
Foundation, Inc. (OEP)
2912 Daimler St.
Santa Ana, CA 92705
(714) 250-8070

American Optometric Association
243 N. Lindbergh Blvd.
St. Louis, MO 63141
(314) 991-4100

Networks: Selected Health-Related Organizations

AFRICAN (BLACK) AMERICAN

Association of Black Cardiologists
13404 S.W. 128th Street,
Suite A
Miami, FL 33186
404/724-9199

Association of Black
Psychologists
P.O. Box 55999
Washington, DC 20040-5999
202/722-0808

Association of Black Sociologists
Howard University
P.O. Box 302
Washington, DC 20059
708/957-5025

Black Congress on Health, Law and
Economics
1025 Connecticut Ave., NW,
Suite 610
Washington, DC 20036
202/659-4020

Black Psychiatrists of America
2730 Adelin St.
Oakland, CA 94607
415/465-1800

Institute on Health Care for the
Poor and Underserved
Meharry Medical College
1005 D.B. Todd Boulevard
Nashville, TN 37208
800/669-1269 or 615/327-6279

National Association for Sickle
Cell Disease
3345 Wilshire Blvd.
Suite 1106
Los Angeles, CA 90010-1880
310/216-6363

National Association of Black Social
Workers
P.O. Box 92698
Atlanta, GA 30314
313/862-6700

National Association of Blacks in Criminal Justice
P.O. Box 66271
Washington, DC 20035-6271
301/681-2365 or 713/484-4988

National Black Association for Speech, Language and Hearing
P.O. Box 50605
Washington, DC 20004-0605
202/727-2608

National Black Child Development Institute
1023 Fifteenth Street, NW
Suite 600
Washington, DC 20005
202/387-1281

National Black Nurses Association
1012 Tenth Street, NW
Washington, DC 20001
202/393-6870

National Black Women's Health Project
1237 R.D. Abernathy Boulevard, SW
Atlanta, GA 30310
800/275-2947

National Center for the Advancement of Blacks in the Health Professions (NCABHP)
P.O. Box 21121
Detroit, MI 48221
(313) 345-4480

National Council of African American Men
Academic and Professional Programs
Department of Continuing Education
University of Kansas
Lawrence, KS 66045
913/864-3284

AMERICAN INDIAN, ALEUT, AND ESKIMO

American Indian Health Care Association
1550 Larimer Street
Suite 225
Denver, CO 80202
303/607-1048

American Indian Institute
National American Indian Conference on Child Abuse and Neglect and Mental Health Issues for the Emotionally Disturbed North American Indian Child and Adolescent
College of Continuing Education
University of Oklahoma
555 Constitution Street
Norman, OK 73037-0005
405/842-6633

American Indian Rehabilitation Research and Training Center
American Indians With Disabilities Conference
P.O. Box 5630
Flagstaff, AZ 86011-5630
602/523-4791 or 602/523-1695

Annual Wellness and Native Men Conference
University of Oklahoma
Health Promotion Programs
555 E. Constitution Street
Norman, OK 74037
405/325-1790

Association on American Indian
Affairs
245 Fifth Avenue
Suite 1801
New York, NY 10016-8728
(212)689-8720

Association of American Indian
Physicians
1235 Sovereign Row, Suite C-7
Oklahoma City, OK 73108
405/946-7072

U.S. Department of Health and
Human Services
Public Health Services
Health Administration
Indian Health Service
5600 Fishers Lane
Rockville, MD 20857

National Congress of American
Indians
900 Pennsylvania Avenue, SE
Washington, DC 20003
202/546-9404

Native Fitness Training and
Certification
University of Oklahoma
Health Promotion Programs
555 E. Constitution Street
Norman, OK 74037
405/325-1790

National Indian Education
Association
1819 H Street, NW, Suite 800
Washington, DC 20006
202/835-3001

National Indian Health Board
1385 South Colorado Blvd.
Suite A-708
Denver, CO 80222
303/759-3075

National Native American AIDS
Prevention Center
6239 College Avenue, Suite 201
Oakland, CA 94618
510/658-2051

Rural Alaskan Community Action
Program (RurAl CAP)
Alaskan Child Development and
Prevention Conference
P.O. Box 200908
Anchorage, AK 99520
800/478-7227 or 907/279-2511

Society for the Advancement of
Chicanos and Native Americans in
Science (SACNAS)
University of California
Sinsheimer Lab
Santa Cruz, CA 95064
408/459-4272

ASIAN/PACIFIC ISLANDER

Asian American Health Forum
116 New Montgomery Street
Suite 531
San Francisco, CA 94105
415/541-0866

Asian Pacific Center
on Aging
1511 Third Avenue
Seattle, WA 98101
206/624-1221

Association of Asian Pacific
Community Health Organizations
(AAPCHO)
1212 Broadway, Suite 730
Oakland, CA 94612
510/272-9536

Association of Phillipine Physicians
of America
1129 20th Street, NW, Suite 400
Washington, DC 20036
202/785-3336

Asian Pacific American Heritage
Council
1129 20th Street, NW
Suite 454
Washington, DC 20036
703/356-2619

Cambodian Network Council
713 D Street, SE
Washington, DC 20003
202/546-9144

Chinese American Medical Society
281 Edgewood Ave
Teaneck, NJ 07666
201/833-1506

Filipino-American National Action
Foundation
5310 Macarthur Blvd., NW
Washington, DC 20015
202/371-8933

Hawaiian Department of Health
Office of Refugee and Immigrant
Health
Pacific Islander Health Promotion
Office
1250 Punchbowl Street
Room 257
Honolulu, HI 96813
808/586-4525

Hawaii University Program for
Development Disability
College of Education
SPED-UAP
1776 University Avenue:, UA4-6
Honolulu, HI 96822
(808)956-5009

Korean Medical Association
162 Deer Run
Watchung, NJ
908/755-5262

National Asian Pacific
American Families
Against Substance Abuse
(NAPAFASA)
420 E. Third Street, Suite 909
Los Angeles, CA 90013-1647
213/617-8277

National Asian Pacific Center on
Aging
Melbourn Tower, Suite 914
1511 Third Avenue
Seattle, WA 98101
206/624-1221

National Association for the
Education and Advancement of
Cambodian, Laotian, and
Vietnamese Americans Conference
(NAFEA)
2460 Cordova Lane
Rancho Cordova, CA 95670
916/635-6815

National Research Center
on Asian American
Mental Health
405 Hilgard Avenue
Los Angles, CA 90024-1563
213/825-6251

Organization of Chinese Americans
1001 Connecticut Avenue, NW
Suite 707
Washington, DC 20036
202/223-5500

Organization of Pan Asian
American Women
P.O. Box 39128
Washington, DC 20016
202/659-9370

Philippine Medical Society
5220 N.W. 64th Street
Kansas City, MO 64151
816/741-3969

Southeast Asian Refugee
Community Health (SEARCH)
4422 North Pershing Ave., Suite D-2
Stockton, CA 95207
209/953-8843

Thailand Health Research Institute
1168 Phaholyothin 22,
Phalholyothin Road
Ladyao, Jatujak, Bangkok 10900,
Thailand
662/939-2239

HISPANIC AMERICAN

ASPIRA
1112 16th Street, NW
Suite 2900
Washington, DC 20036
202/835-3600

Hispanic Health Council
9648 Cedar Street
Hartford, CT 06106
203/527-0856

Interamerican College of Physicians
and Surgeons
Hispanic National Medical
Association
1101 15th Street, NW, Suite 602
Washington, DC 20005
202/467-4756

Midwest Hispanic AIDS Coalition
Conference
P.O. Box 470859
Chicago, IL 60647
312/772-8195

National Coalition of Hispanic
Health and Human Services
Organizations (COSSMHO)
1501 16th Street, NW
Washington, DC 20036
202/387-5100

National Coalition of Puerto Rican
Women
5 Thomas Circle, NW
Washington, Dc 20005
202/387-4716

National Council of La Raza
810 First Street, NE,
Suite 300
Washington, DC 20002-4205
202/289-1380

National Hispanic Council on
Aging
2713 Ontario Road, NW
Washington, DC 20009
202/265-1288

National Hispanic Nurses
Association
University of South Florida MDC
Box 2212901
Bruce B. Down Blvd.
Tampa, FL 33162
813/974-2191

National Latina Health
Organization
P.O. Box 7567
Oakland, CA 94601
510/534-1362

National Puerto Rican Coalition,
Inc.
1700 K Street, NW
Suite 500
Washington, DC 20006
202/223-9315

National Puerto Rican Forum
National Association of Puerto
Rican Women
31 E. 32nd Street, 4th Floor
New York, NY 10016
212/685-2311

Society for the Advancement of
Chicanos and Native Americans in
Science (SACNAS)
University of California,
Sinsheimer Lab
Santa Cruz, CA 95064
408/459-4272

MULTI CULTURAL

American Public Health
Association
African American, Asian, Hispanic,
and Native American Caucus
1015 Fifteenth Street, NW
Washington, DC 20005
202/789-5600

Association of Minority Health
Professions Schools
Biomedical Symposium
720 Westview Drive, S.W.
Atlanta, GA 30310
404/325-1790

Children's Defense Fund
25 E Street, NW
Washington, DC 20001
202/628-8787
3/9-11
Seattle, WA

National Council for International
Health
1701 K Street, NW,
Suite 600
Washington, DC 20006
202/833-5903

National Medical
Association
1012 Tenth Street, NW
Washington, DC 20001
202/347-1895

National Migrant Resource
Program
1515 Capital of Texas Highway
South
Suite 220
Austin, TX 78746
512/328-7682

National Minority AIDS Council
(NMAC) Public Policy Conference
300 Eye Street, NE, Suite 400
Washington, DC 20002
202/544-1076

National Association of
Community Health Centers
1330 New Hampshire Avenue, NW
Suite 122
Washington, DC 20036
202/659-8008

National Minority Health
Association
P.O. Box 11876
Harrisburg, PA 17108-1876
717/763-1323

National Rural Health Association
301 E. Armour Boulevard, Suite 420
Kansas City, MO 64111
816/756-3140

National Multicultural Institute
3000 Connecticut Avenue, NW
Suite 438
Washington, DC 20008
202/483-0700

From: Jones, K.C. *Minority Health Calender* (Silver Spring, MD. International Minority Affairs Cooperative, 1995). Reprinted with permission.
Calenders that list events sponsored by these organizations may be ordered by writing or calling:
International Affairs Cooperative
P.O. Box 10072
Silver Spring, MD 20914
(301)890-0608

Index